MAGNUM OPUS

MAGNUM OPUS

THE STORY OF THE MEMORIAL ART GALLERY

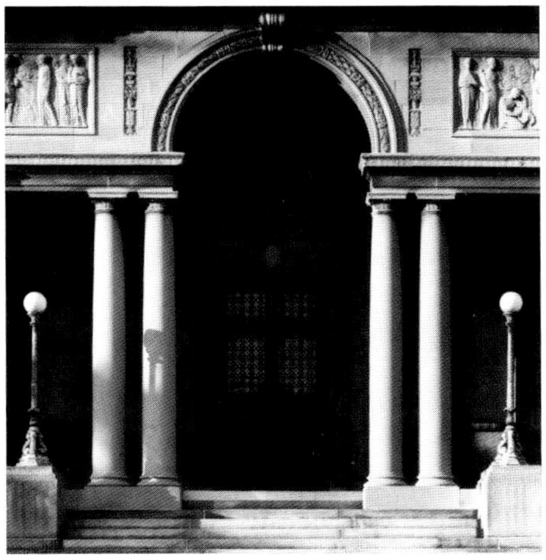

1 9 1 3 • 1 9 8 8

ELIZABETH BRAYER

MEMORIAL ART GALLERY OF THE UNIVERSITY OF ROCHESTER

Memorial Art Gallery of the University of Rochester
Rochester, New York 14607

First Edition published 1988
Printed in the United States of America

Library of Congress Cataloging-in-Publication Data

Brayer, Elizabeth.
Magnum opus.

Bibliography: p.
Includes index.
1. University of Rochester. Memorial Art Gallery.
I. Title.
N719.B73 1988 069'.970814789 88-42979
ISBN 0-918098-02-5

Designer: Bill Buckett Associates, Inc.
Managing Editor: Deborah Rothman
Editor: Thomas Fitzpatrick
Typography: Setronics Ltd., Rochester, NY
Printer: Monroe Reprographics

All photographs are from the collections of the Memorial Art Gallery or Elizabeth Brayer unless otherwise noted.

Parts of Chapter 8 of the present work appeared in a slightly different version in *Rochester Review* (Spring 1981): 14-17.

Note to the Reader:
In referring to individuals the full name was used upon first introduction, followed by surname in subsequent references. The proliferation of Watsons and Herdles, however, has led to the following usages for second references: Mrs. Watson for Emily Sibley Watson; Watson for James Sibley Watson; Sibley Watson, Hildegarde Watson, and Michael Watson for their son, daughter-in-law, and grandson; and Gertrude and Isabel for the daughters of George Herdle.

Contents

FOREWORD

Soon after man began to walk the earth, art became one of his first means of communication. Through the cave paintings he left behind, we know that earliest man used art as a means of relating both to his gods and to the natural world.

Before any form of writing was developed, drawings were used to send messages from one group to another or to pass down information to succeeding generations. But almost from the beginning, art began to be used also to decorate the habitations of primitive man.

The excavations at Pompeii and other ancient sites prove that visual art, for decoration as well as for storytelling, was important to mankind. Special too must have been the persons who could produce the art. What magicians to be able to take crude tools and paints and re-create images on blank spaces. They must have been regarded by the communities as holy.

Through the centuries, these creators felt compelled to search one another out—to meet, to learn, to teach, to demonstrate their abilities. The earliest tribes probably had their artists who could create images to soothe the gods or produce messages to be carried to other tribes. Others, in some distant time, first began to think of collecting the renderings of these gifted people.

The leaders of the early nations that grew from the nomadic tribes were likely the first collectors. Certainly by the birth of the Christian era, collections of works of art were being gathered in the Greco-Roman world. Centuries before, in Egypt and the Far East, goods and artifacts to accompany the deceased on their travels into the hereafter were placed in the tombs of the leaders.

Through the Middle Ages, art collections were concentrated in monasteries and religious institutions, and later, among kings and emperors. As civilizations advanced, commoners also began to collect for their own enjoyment and enlightenment. Written histories of early collections go back to medieval times.

In what is today the United States, as soon as the early settlers had sufficiently tamed the wilderness to allow themselves some leisure, decorative objects began to appear.

Betsy Brayer's *MAGnum Opus* is the story of the growth of collecting in Rochester and the museum that houses its results. Long proposed, this book tells of the Memorial Art Gallery and the people who dreamed its dream, brought it to birth, and nurtured it until it grew to be the fine institution we have today.

Three-quarters of a century after the Gallery's opening, we are blessed to have with us still the two daughters of the founding director and guiding light of the original museum. The Herdle sisters are a living history of the Gallery, having themselves served for seventy of the Gallery's seventy-five years. Even now, in retirement, they still serve when called upon.

This book is not only a history, but is also an entertaining narrative, packed with anecdote, of the people who fostered the growth of the Memorial Art Gallery and were themselves changed by the experience.

Betsy Brayer is one of those people. An artist and a journalist, she has been active for many years at the Gallery, as a member of the Women's Council, on the Board of Managers, and as a docent. She has lived a good share of this history and has known personally many of the people of whom she writes. Her permanent record is truly a work of love.

I have been proud to be part of that ever-increasing group of people who have served the greater Rochester community by serving the Memorial Art Gallery. It is not false humility that causes me to say that I have always received more from the Gallery than I have given.

I am pleased to be part of *MAGnum Opus* but even more pleased to be able to read about all those who filled such vital roles for the Gallery in the past but who were heretofore only names to me.

HERBERT W. VANDEN BRUL
Chairman
Board of Managers

Acknowledgments

In a sense this book began when Isabel Herdle retired as the assistant director of the Memorial Art Gallery in 1972. Colleagues and friends from every segment of the Gallery family urged her to write down its history as only she and her sister, Gertrude Herdle Moore, director emeritus, knew it. As of 1988 the Herdle sisters have accrued eighty-four years as senior staff members and half again that much, forty-two years, of continuing service to the Gallery in "retirement." And their childhoods were spent as daughters of the Gallery's first director, all making for an astonishing, first-hand, and uninterrupted knowledge of this remarkable institution from pre-dedication days to seventy-fifth anniversary.

About 1980 I became their amanuensis. Together we pored over scrapbooks, annual reports, acquisition records, correspondence, Art Committee and Board of Managers minutes, and Gallery publications. After the stories accompanying each historical event had been recorded, some thirty hours of tapes resulted. Since the Herdles have been kind enough not to interfere in the transposition of tapes to book, all flaws should be considered the author's. But the best parts belong to Gertrude and Isabel.

Recording the Gallery story did not stop there. Further interviews were held with George Angle, Marion and Thomas Hawks, Grant Holcomb, Whitney Hoyt, Carl F. W. Kaelber Jr., John Mahey, Charles Rand Penney, Bret Waller, Dr. James Sibley Watson Jr., and Anne Prior Whitcomb. Many of these people also read portions of the manuscript. Margaret Bond, Langdon Clay, Susan E. Schilling, Herbert W. Vanden Brul not only provided insight and information through interviews but read the entire draft, offering suggestions without damaging old friendships. To all I am grateful.

The staff of the Gallery under Grant Holcomb responded to my repeated cries for assistance, particularly Deborah Rothman, who acted as managing editor in guiding the manuscript through production, Marie Via, who ferreted out many of the archival photographs used, and Mark Donovan, who was involved in many aspects of design and production. Board member Margaret Stolze compiled the chronological list of the Board of Managers found in the Appendix. Langdon Clay, recently retired as director of education, returned to help choose and identify photographs, write captions, and assist with the indexing. Photographs are by James M. Via, David Henry, Richard Margolis and other Gallery photographers, past and present.

Outside Gallery walls Karl Kabelac, manuscripts librarian at the University of Rochester, alerted the author to the existence of the Rush Rhees correspondence pertaining to the Gallery, a hitherto unresearched source containing not just letters to and from Rhees about the founding of the Gallery but also primary material to and from George Herdle. Photographs of James Averell, board members, and Gallery construction came from the Department of Rare Books and Special Collections, University of Rochester Library. At the New York Historical Society, plans and correspondence about the 1926 addition were found in the McKim, Mead and White papers, quite by accident. Elizabeth Holahan, president of the Rochester Historical Society, generously loaned photographs from that collection. Barbara Mackintosh provided pictures from her personal collection.

Designer Bill Buckett is responsible for the look of the publication. Editor Tom Fitzpatrick offered revisions with infinite charity and kept the participles from dangling. G. Sheldon Brayer was a model of patience when midnight oils were burning.

Finally, without its publisher, Herb Vanden Brul, president of the Board of Managers, who envisioned the unique role a history of the Gallery involving such primary sources could play, this book would not exist. To him we are all grateful.

Elizabeth Brayer

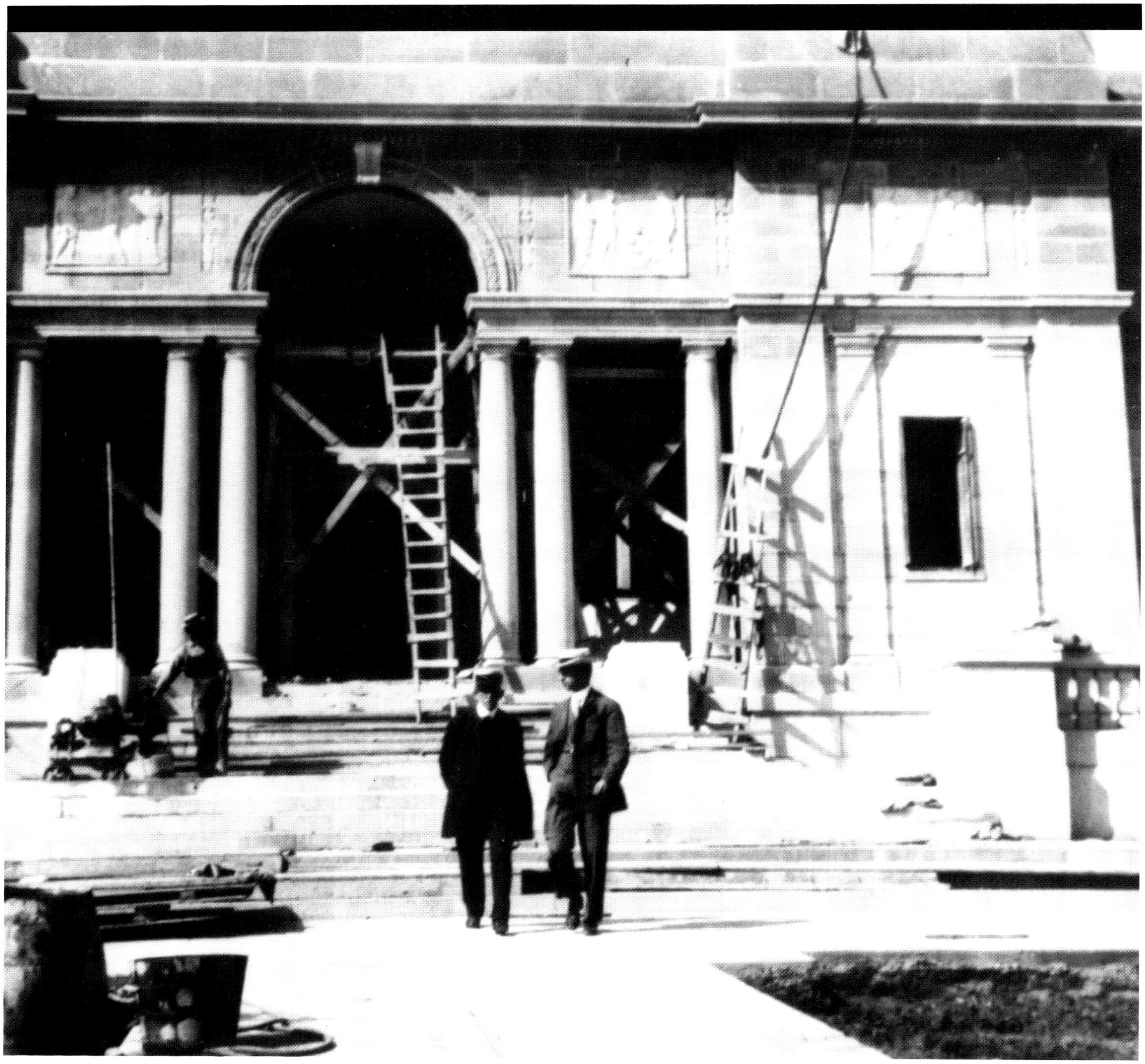

Prologue: A Gift for the People of Rochester

Announcement was made by President Rush Rhees of the University of Rochester late yesterday afternoon that the city of Rochester is to have finally an art gallery which it is expected will be completed within a year's time....

The building, for the foundations of which ground will be broken within a week, will be one of the best examples of Italian Renaissance architecture in the world and will be a copy of one which [James Averell] had seen during his travels abroad and admired greatly.

Rochester *Union* | 23 April 1912

The Memorial Art Gallery under construction, 1913. Photograph courtesy of the University of Rochester Library.

Silks rustled and formal shirts showed a spanking-white expanse as the invited guests mounted steps leading to the balustraded terrace. Passing into the deep portico, under frescoed arch, and through bronze doors, they funneled into the dim and narrow Entry. The high-ceilinged Entrance Hall with its alabaster lamps suspended from gleaming brass chains beckoned them into the expansive and skylit Hall of Casts. There the gowns and frock coats completed their dramatic processional, and found seats. It was the Wednesday afternoon of 8 October 1913, and the official beginning of the Memorial Art Gallery.

This "distinguished company of Rochester people," as the evening newspaper reported, had joined company with "guests and representatives from New York City; Worcester and Northampton in Massachusetts; Buffalo, Geneseo, and many other of our neighboring towns" to absorb with muffled and dignified exclamations the bright sights of Rochester's new temple to culture.

By four o'clock every seat was taken. Rush Rhees, president of the University of Rochester and of the Gallery's Board of Managers, rose to begin the dedication ceremonies which would culminate in an address by Robert de Forest, vice president of the Metropolitan Museum of Art.

"This day sees the realization of many dreams," Rhees began. He spoke briefly, as de Forest would after him, of the individuals and groups who had long hoped for an art building for Rochester.

"They dreamed dreams," de Forest would say, "but I doubt if they ever dreamed so beautiful a dream as Mrs. Watson has turned into reality."

Principal dreamers were the members of the Rochester Art Club. Founded in 1872 as an informal sketching club, the organization soon attracted the best local talent as well as associate members from as far away as New York City. Beginning with their first public exhibition in 1875, the members "labored earnestly," Rhees said, "but without much encouragement, to arouse the people of Rochester to the need for a suitable gallery." Instead, the club was shunted around for thirty-seven years to paint and hold exhibitions in banks, schools, and at other ad hoc sites.

Emily Sibley Watson, neighbor of the University of Rochester's Prince Street Campus, friend of Rhees, daughter of Rochester's first major art collector, a shrewd collector herself, and a long-standing friend and patron of the Rochester Art Club, had been casting about for a suitable means to memorialize her son. When Rhees suggested a community art building on the university's campus, Mrs. Watson's enthusiastic response was, he said, "in significant measure a response to the efforts of the art club." Furthermore, in September 1913, the club's president, George L. Herdle, was named acting director for the new Memorial Art Gallery and secretary of its Board of Managers.

Rhees then spoke of Emily's father, Hiram Sibley, who had given the university a library building in 1874. On the second floor of Sibley Hall the donor had hung his personal art collection, assembled during European trips made in the expectation of encircling the globe with a telegraph cable.

"It was Mr. Sibley's hope that these pictures would attract the public," Rhees said, "and that his collection might form a nucleus for a growing gallery of art. The public was not ready to make that response. Mr. Sibley soon abandoned the idea and his collection of pictures was subsequently scattered. It is interesting that Mr. Sibley's daughter, by giving the university this exquisite art gallery, is fulfilling that dream which her father cherished."

Changing his subject from Emily Watson's father to her son, Rhees continued:

"Over these galleries there hovers perpetually a spirit—as of the young man who loved life and beauty and honour—whose memory has led his mother to give this building to the cause of the spiritual culture of the whole community through the ministries of Fine Art." Rhees's words epitomized the contemporary belief that merely gazing upon beautiful paintings was so morally and spiritually uplifting that it was the duty of educators to bring art and its message to the people.

The spirit of James G. Averell permeated the building's early Renaissance facade with its carved stone wreaths in which the initials "JGA" could be discerned. Inside, as punctuation to the entrance vista, his mother had installed a statue of *Memory* by William Ordway Partridge, a leading academic sculptor. Nearby, Averell's cousins and other boyhood friends had placed a vase-shaped lamp with an eternal flame.

The main speaker of the afternoon, Robert de Forest, would within the month succeed the late J. Pierpont Morgan as president of the Metropolitan. In October 1913 the Metropolitan was riding high, having just received, in Rhees's words, "that magnificent Altman bequest." Scion of an old New York family and son-in-law of the Metropolitan's first president, de Forest would remain its president until his death in 1931 and with his wife would give its fabulous American Wing. (The de Forests were well acquainted with Rochester's Sibleys and Watsons through social engagements in New York and Paris.) As president of the American Federation of Arts, de Forest was eminently qual-

1

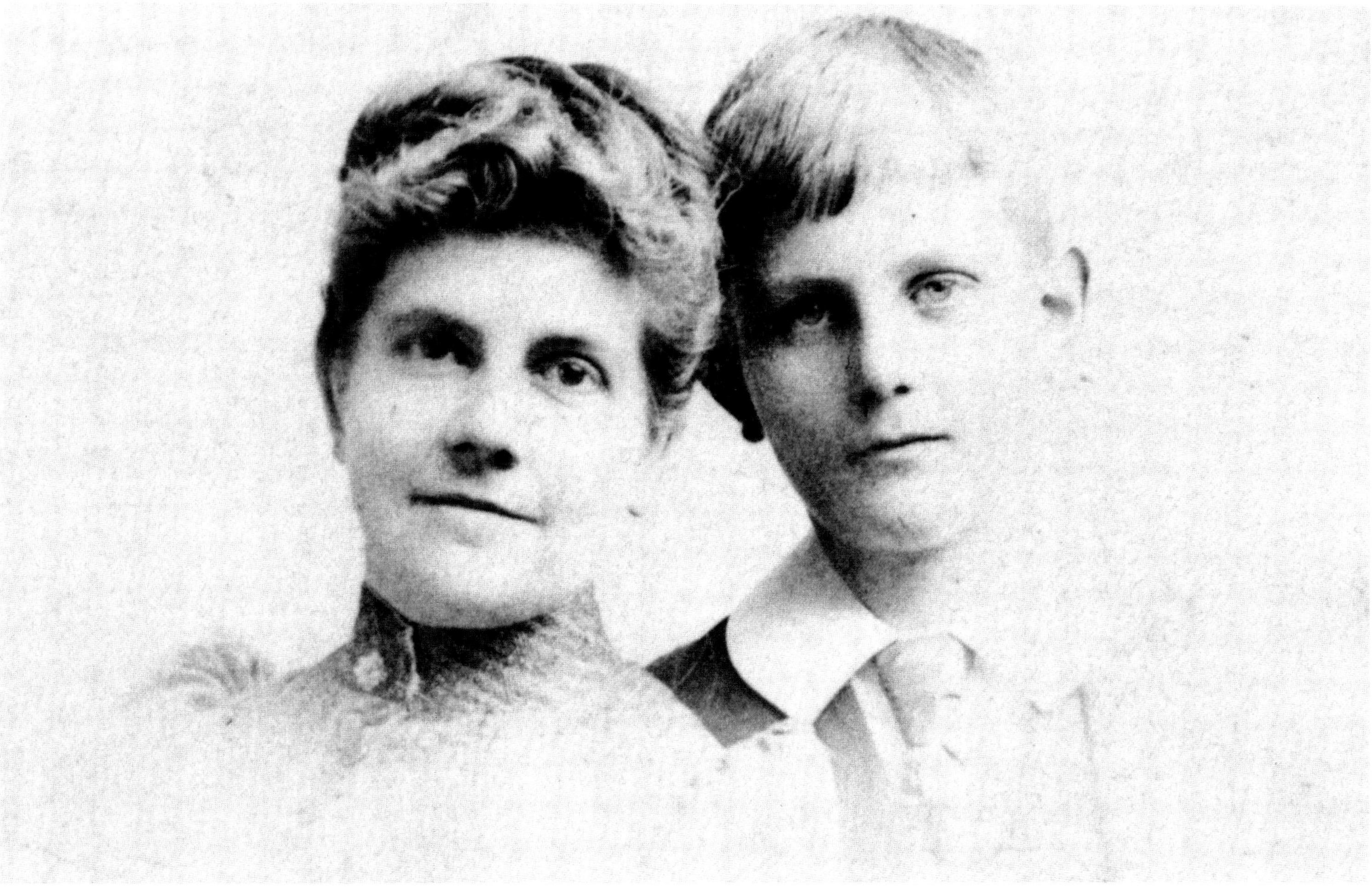

1 *Emily Sibley Averell (Watson) and her son, James George Averell, ca. 1885. Photograph courtesy of the University of Rochester Library.*

ified to speak on the philosophy and state of American art museums in 1913 or, as he put it, "the honourable birthright of the gallery which we dedicate today."

"The very presence of this gallery," de Forest said, "would have created the need which it is intended to supply. But it must be a greater satisfaction for Mrs. Watson to know that...she has realized aspirations and fulfilled hopes which date back to a generation that has passed away."

The Memorial Art Gallery was the fifty-first American art museum to open during a period of escalating construction in the field. Of the seventy-nine American institutions then exhibiting art, only ten had been organized before 1870. And of those seventy-nine, nearly half were "organically connected with educational institutions"—colleges, universities, or libraries. What de Forest did not note was the Memorial Art Gallery's dual function as both university museum and community art center. The Gallery was unusual in that the donor was providing only a building—without collection or endowment. Her expectation was that art-minded citizens would become paying members of the new Gallery, making it "truly their own." In this way, she hoped, the cause of art would prosper, rather than, as in the case of her father's frustrated attempt, wither and die from lack of community involvement.

European museums, de Forest continued in his dedicatory address, had been "assembled through the ambitions and plunderings of royal or near-royal personages for the purposes of display, gratifications of personal taste, or expressions of national, even imperial grandeur." In contrast, American museums evolved for "educational, altruistic, and even moralistic reasons," the speaker maintained.

"What king ever thought of educating people or even giving pleasure outside of his court surroundings when he assembled the treasures of art which we now see in the great picture galleries? It has remained for the present generation to realize the relation between art galleries and education and to bring them into their proper relation to the school and university."

That relation needed objects as well as courses on aesthetics: "Only the actual sight of things beautiful enables us to recognize...[and] create that which is beautiful," de Forest said.

The founders of the Memorial Art Gallery did view its purpose as primarily educational. Within the decade a contemporary art magazine would praise the Gallery for its "tendency toward aesthetic decentralization" and note editorially that it "strongly supported the movement that the

2

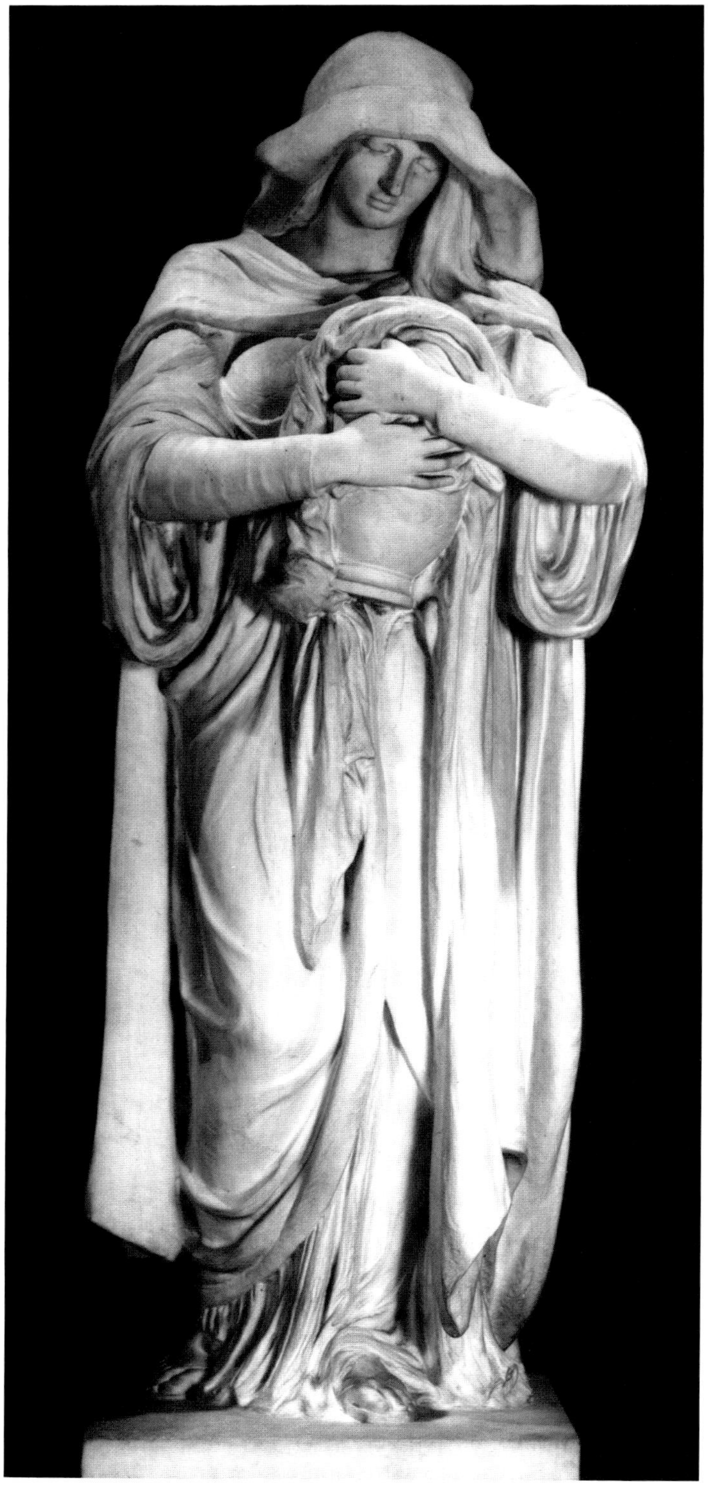

Gallery helps to advance: the publicity of art rather than its confinement by the accumulations of permanent collections.... The system of loan exhibitions extends to a greater number of persons the benefits and advantages of modern art than would permanent collections." As Rhees told an inquiring artist, "Very frankly, we have no funds for the purchase of pictures."

De Forest spoke of growing realizations "that the fine arts of painting and sculpture, represented almost exclusively in art galleries of the past, are not the only arts, but only part of the whole." The *Kleine Kunste* (minor arts) and the industrial arts which "minister pleasure not only in aesthetic enjoyment but through utility" were welcome too. Whether they be pictures or spoons, statues or doorknobs—they all had their place, he said. He cited museums "of the present generation" on both sides of the Atlantic that were beginning to "elevate the useful and industrial arts to their proper place in the art galleries of the people."

That the Gallery had touched a need in the general public became obvious during its first five days of existence. Mrs. Watson had sent out 748 invitations to the dedication. By the following Sunday, an additional thousand visitors had thronged to the first exhibition. Rhees observed that they were precisely the kind of people whom it was a delight to see there—"a number of artisans with children as well as people of more generally recognized interest in art."

Questions of elitism versus democracy and the governmental view of the arts worried de Forest. "You may argue," he said, "that the educational necessity for galleries is universally recognized and the encouragement of art collections is a matter of acknowledged national concern. This is not so.... New York State taxes bequests to museums because they are classed, with the dime museums of the Bowery, as places of amusement.... A great many of our public men still have to be convinced that art is not merely the luxury of the rich, but an essential factor in the education of every American, old or young, rich or poor."

Such was the world into which the Memorial Art Gallery was born.

Two individuals were conspicuously absent from the podium. Emily Sibley Watson chose not to speak; later she would make a practice of attending only the private viewings, and not the public openings at the Gallery. Hers was not a public role. Her presence would be felt through frequent, unannounced Gallery visits, as chair of the powerful art committee, and in her ubiquitous persona as lady of the manor.

3

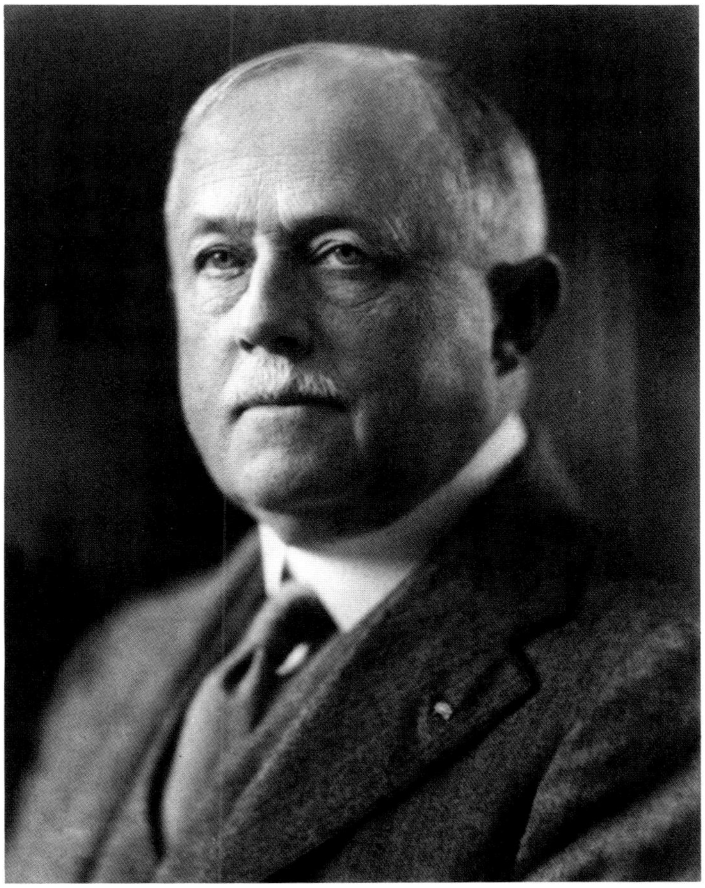

2 *William Ordway Partridge (American 1861–1930), Memory, 1914, Marble, 82½ x 26¾ x 29⅝ in. Gift of Emily Sibley Watson. 13.2*

3 *Rush Rhees, 1917. Photograph courtesy of the University of Rochester Library.*

4

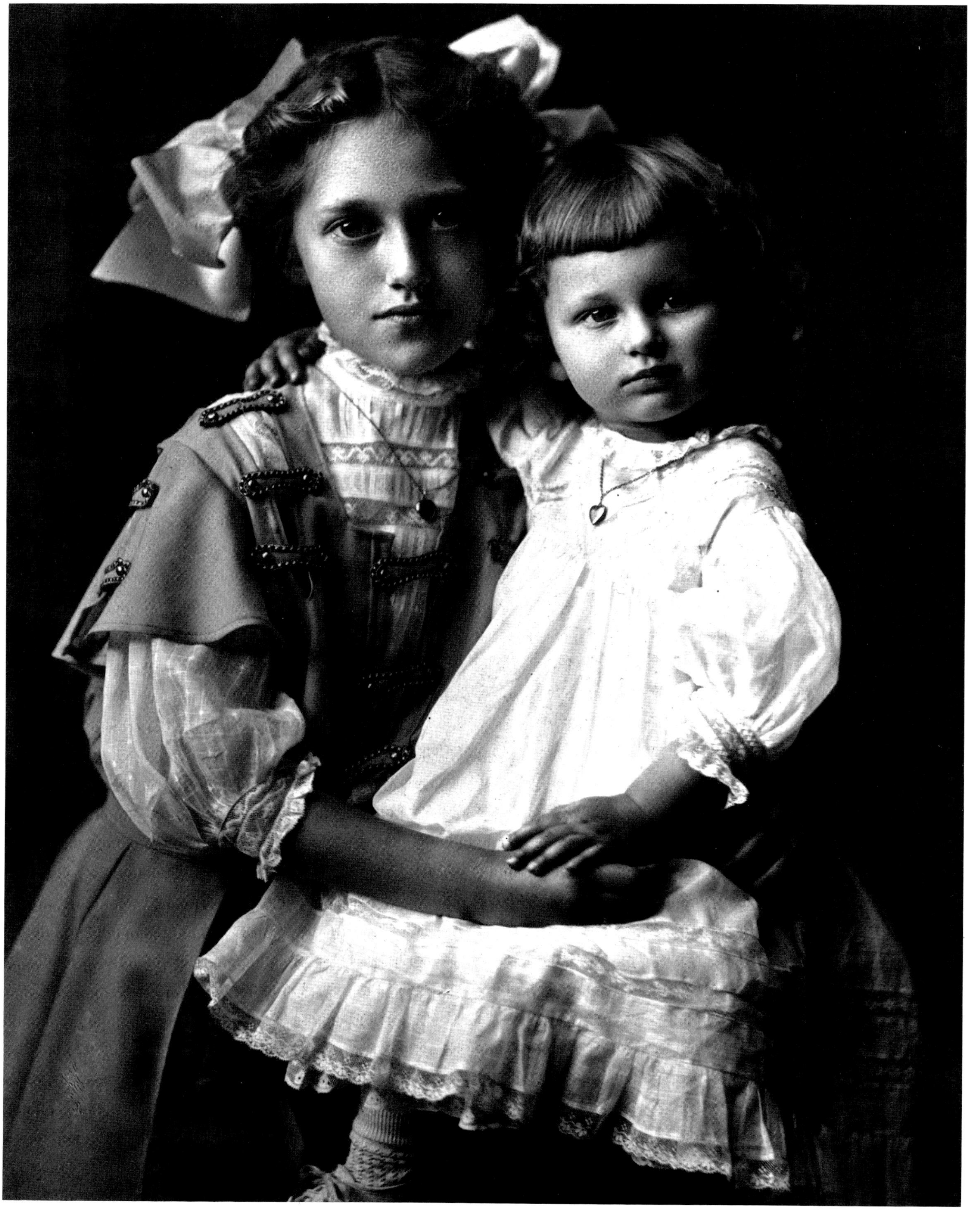

Neither did George Herdle speak, although he was a member of the board in three capacities: as representative of the art club, as secretary, and as acting art director. Herdle had as yet no voice in policy making; nor had he been consulted in the planning and construction of the building. Indeed, unknown to Herdle, Rhees as a search committee of one was combing the universities and museums for "two or three young men who have taken work in fine arts at Harvard and have had some experience in one of the large museums" from which to choose the permanent director. Rhees's inquiries, however, were leading to a dead end. Of the candidates suggested, all were either happy in their present positions, rated as "something of a dilettante," or known to "cause friction" among their peers. It would be several more months, however, before Rhees finally abandoned his search for an academically trained director and the board named Herdle the permanent art director.

Meanwhile, the inaugural exhibition, scheduled to open at eight o'clock that evening, had been selected and hung by Herdle, who had also prepared a "concise history of the art club" for use by the afternoon speakers. Herdle's solid local standing was based not only on his role as a painter and president of the Rochester Art Club since 1902, but also on his work as a member of the executive board of the "Department of Fine Arts" of the Rochester Exposition at Exposition Park, where a new art building had recently opened. His reputation, however, was for assembling lively, sometimes *avant-garde*, and often controversial loan exhibitions for the art club. A scant week before the dedication Rhees had told a colleague that he was happy to have been "able to persuade Mr. Herdle to accept the position of Acting Director, which makes it possible to give him not only our thanks but some compensation for his labor."

Foreshadowing monumental roles yet to come, the acting director's elder daughter, Gertrude Herdle, a student at East High School, was among the audience that October afternoon. His younger daughter, Isabel, was not—too little and squirmy, her parents had decided. Besides, she had a bad case of poison ivy.

As ceremonies concluded, a commotion from the back of the Hall of Casts was heard. Prancing and snake-dancing their way around the plaster icons of antiquity came the high-spirited university football team garbed in uniforms of dandelion yellow, to add their own uproarious show of approval to this addition to the campus.

It had been a full afternoon.

5

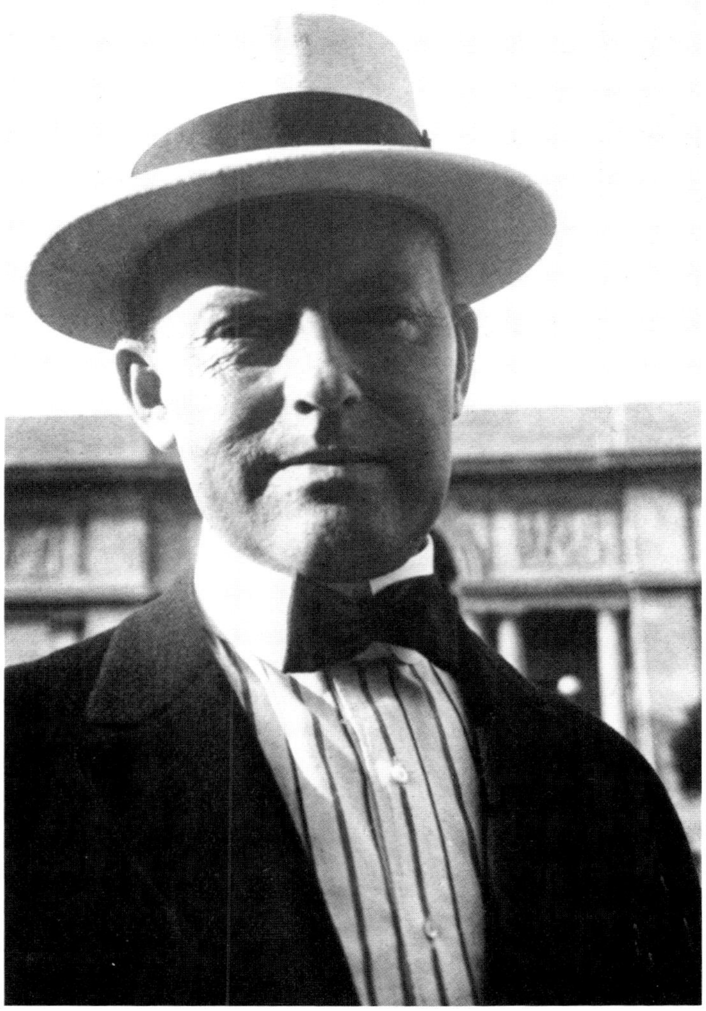

4 *Gertrude and Isabel Herdle, shortly before the opening of the Memorial Art Gallery. Photograph courtesy of the Herdle family.*

5 *George Leonard Herdle, ca. 1913. Photograph courtesy of the Herdle family.*

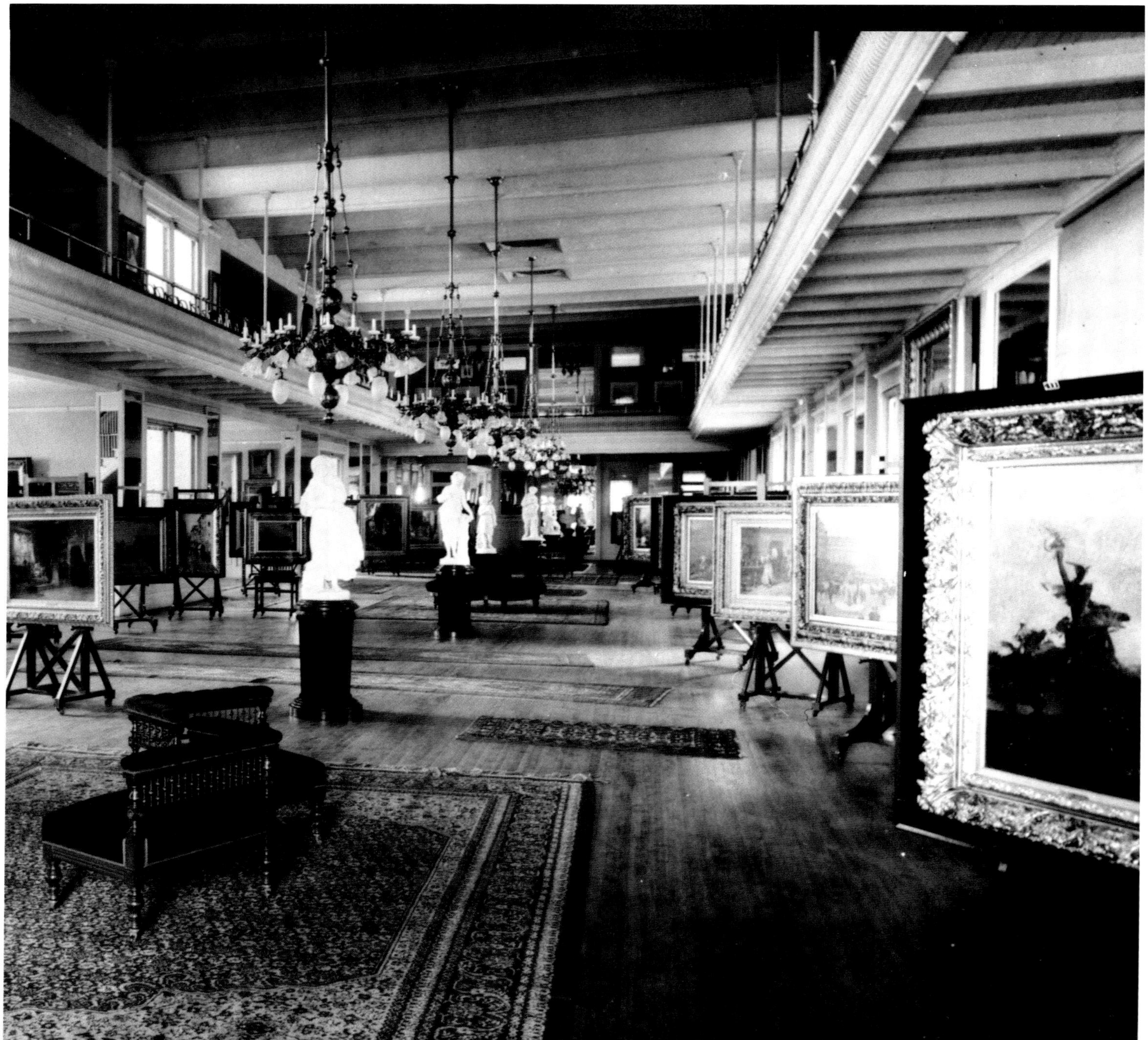

1

The first artists to visit Rochester were curious travelers en route to Niagara who stopped off to see the romantic loveliness of the Genesee falls.

Rochester City Historian | Blake McKelvey, 1955

Manifestations of taste and liberality in reference to the Fine Arts are increasing in Rochester in ration commensurate to the prosperity of the citizens.

Sketches of Rochester | Henry O'Reilly, 1838

Powers Art Gallery, 1880s. Photograph courtesy of Craig Smith.

George Leonard Herdle never wanted to be anything but a painter. Instead, he became the founding director of a major art museum. Rush Rhees combed academia for the right person, only to find him in the man hired to select and hang the inaugural exhibition. How was this painter able to launch this historically important institution?

Born in Rochester in 1868, Herdle worked for a short time as a commercial artist, but devotion to his own art made him willing to forego that regular stipend. His wife, Elizabeth Bachman, encouraged him to return to painting, and the family, which included their two daughters, made do on the barter of Herdle's paintings for goods and services. Oriental rugs were acquired by the exchange of a painting or two. So was the care of the children's teeth and tonsils.

In 1899 Herdle went to Europe with his wife and infant daughter, Gertrude. He spent the next two years studying and painting in Paris, Amsterdam, and Düsseldorf. With fellow Rochesterian Charles Gruppe, he painted in the fishing village of Katwijkaan Zee. Back home, he worked as a freelance artist in the impressionist tradition and taught at the Rochester Athenaeum and Mechanics Institute. Nationally, he exhibited his landscapes at the Corcoran Gallery of Art in Washington, D.C., the Pennsylvania Academy of Fine Arts in Philadelphia, the National Academy of Design in New York, and the New York Watercolor Society.

Avocationally, Herdle was a member of the Alembic Club, informally called the "Basement Brains"—a group of journalists, editors, and friends who met Saturday nights in the basement of the Nathaniel Rochester House after the Monday edition of the *Post Express* had been put to bed. Many an editorial, it was said, emerged from that basement. Contact with these wordsmiths may have honed Herdle's own writing skills; his newspaper reviews and catalog entries evidence a literate style as well as a knowledge of the cosmopolitan art world. For example:

At a time when men were painting anemic, emasculated transcripts of nature, or rather studio recollections of the great world outside, George Inness had the courage to break away from traditions to set out on a path he blazed for himself and to stand on his own theories, evolved after serious thought, analysis, and experimenting.

In 1902 Herdle became president of the Rochester Art Club, a position he held until his death. The club's custom was to invite established New York artists—Thomas Moran, J. Francis Murphy, James Hart, or John Henry Twachtman—to become associate members and exhibit with local artists. Herdle was the adventuresome leader, picking radicals of the period—the experimental work of Arthur Dove or the

1

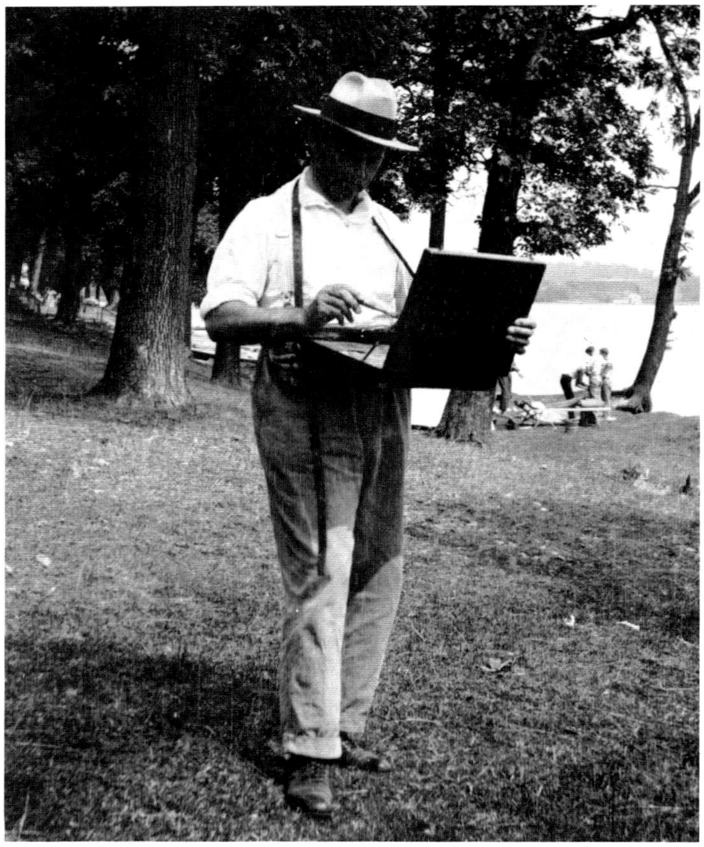

1 *George Herdle in his role as painter. Photograph courtesy of the Herdle family.*

2 *Rochester Art Club outing. Photograph courtesy of Barbara Mackintosh.*

2

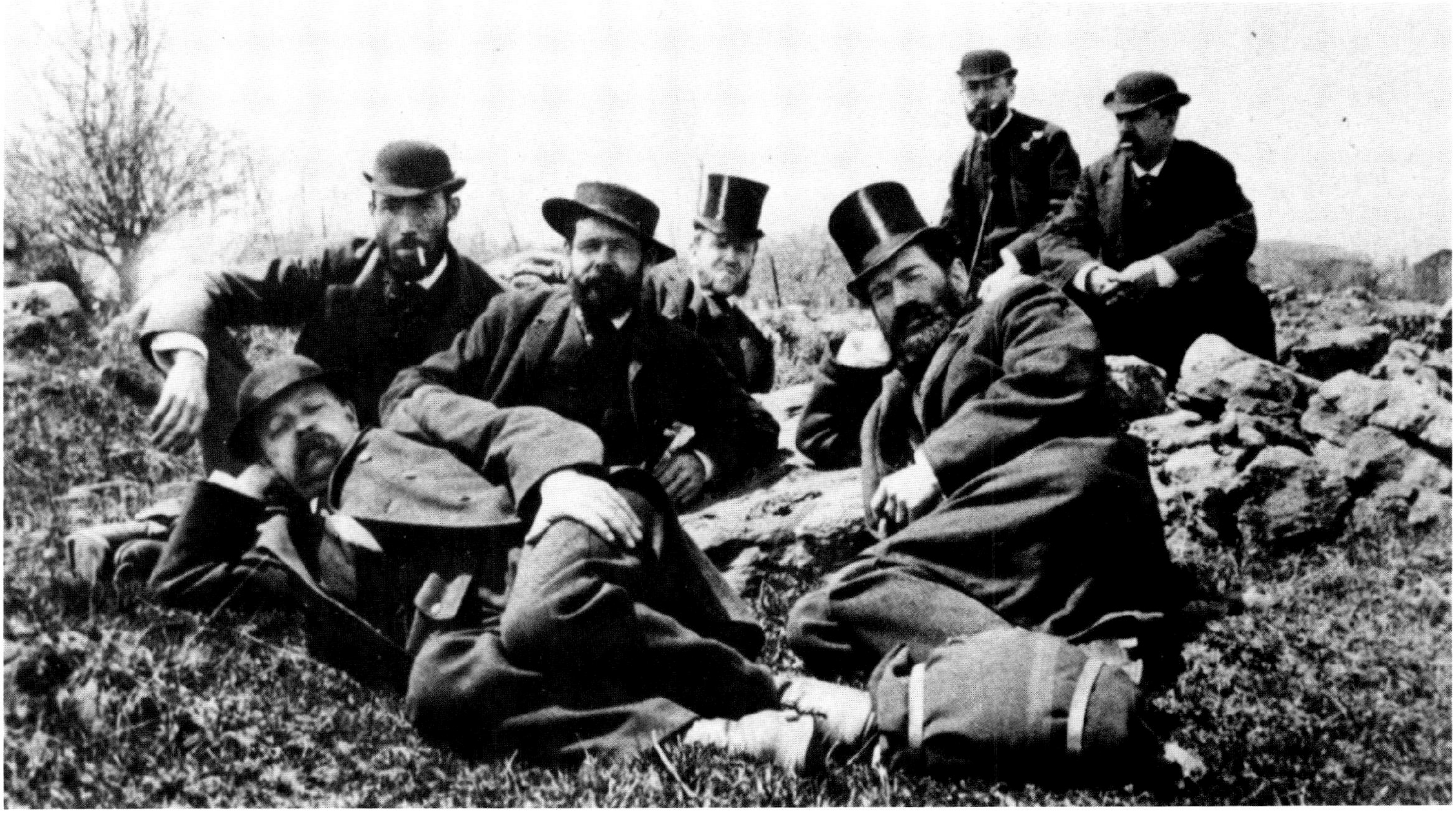

cubist art of Marcel Duchamp—to the bafflement of the citizenry.

———

The prestige of European art, even if only through oil copies or mezzotints, diverted attention from local artists, who were not invited to exhibit in galleries showing European works. And so the search for a permanent exhibition hall preoccupied the Rochester Art Club, long after it was founded informally in 1872 for sketch outings, held its first exhibition in rented quarters in 1875, and was officially incorporated in 1882.

Club members, many of whom made their living from commercial work, met for mutual criticism, employed models (never nude when female members were present), and took on a few pupils for instruction. Informal sketching excursions to Keuka Lake resulted in exhibitions at East High School and later at Edgerton Park.

Certain Rochester collectors such as Emily Sibley Watson, George Eastman, Jesse Lindsay, Hannah Gould, and Margaret Woodbury Strong did buy Rochester Art Club works in generous quantity. Among once-shiny names whose reputations have since faded (but may be due for rediscovery) is the Reverend James Hogarth Dennis, the club's first president and an Episcopal priest who earlier trained at the National Academy of Design. Another is M. Louise Stowell, transplanted New Yorker and influential teacher, who was in great demand as an exhibitor herself at leading museum shows. Ada Howe Kent studied with Abbott Thayer and James McNeill Whistler and was a member of the New York Watercolor Club. The Canadian Horatio Walker moved on to New York in 1885, continuing to garner gold medals at major national expositions.

Maud Humphrey's successful commercial illustrations graced women's magazines, baby food labels, and the genteel nursery books of a bygone era. The "Maud Humphrey baby" was once as famous as Maud's own baby, Humphrey Bogart, would become. Her improbable and immaculate "Little Rosebuds" (as the subject of one of the five children's books she illustrated between 1888 and 1898 was called) do not drool nor throw their spinach. Among her wide-eyed models were little Marie Adelaide Devine and Marie Adelaide's siblings, Louise Devine and Adrian Devine, future benefactors of the Gallery. Even after Maud married Dr. Belmont DeForest Bogart and moved to New York, she continued to exhibit her watercolors annually with the Rochester Art Club late into the 1920s.

Harvey Ellis, perhaps the club's most gifted member, drew upon his architectural training to give structure and discipline to his mixed-media paintings while his interest in mysticism, medievalism, the arts and crafts movement, and *Japonisme* gave his paintings their unmistakable aura. President of the club in 1884, his influence on students and other Rochester artists was powerful even after he left the city (about 1885), and worked as an often anonymous designer and renderer for various midwestern architectural firms.

Local artists were beginning to study abroad. The first, Guernsey Mitchell, returned in 1880 with a clay maquette of the famous bronze statue *Mercury* by Giovanni da Bologna (ca. 1574), now in the Bargello Museum in Florence. His sister, Mrs. William Kimball, liked the figure so much that she persuaded her husband to have a giant copper-plate copy of *Mercury* mounted atop the smokestack of his new tobacco factory. This sleek creature still presides as the familiar and beloved symbol of the Rochester skyline. Mitchell, who would be a charter member of the Gallery board, also commenced work on a commanding statue of Martin Brewer Anderson to adorn the university's Prince Street Campus (and move with the women students to the River Campus in 1955).

Mitchell's studio, along with Herdle's, was housed in the skylit mansard of the Rochester Savings Bank building. (Earlier, Herdle had his studio in the Reynolds Arcade and would later move it into the Cutler Building, a coincidence of art, architecture, and names that would not reach fruition until 1987 when Cutler Union became part of the Gallery complex.)

Herdle became the transitional figure in the Rochester Art Club. Able to tap the early enthusiasm, which darted in many directions at once, he transformed it into that more formalized structure, the Memorial Art Gallery.

Interest in art in the Genesee Country predated both George Herdle and the art club. The ninety-three foot main cataract of the Genesee River, tumbling over the same limestone ledge as Niagara Falls and almost as spectacular to record, was the main attraction for the first European artists to pass through the lands of the Senecas in central and western New York. Captain Thomas Davies arrived in the Genesee Country to sketch the falls in about 1755, followed in 1797 by the painter Count Beaujolais with his brother, later King Louis Philippe of France.

Next came itinerant French naturalists, then self-taught Americans, sketchbooks in hand. The first traveling art exhibit arrived in Rochesterville via the new Erie Canal in 1823. Few of the itinerant portrait limners stayed long,

3

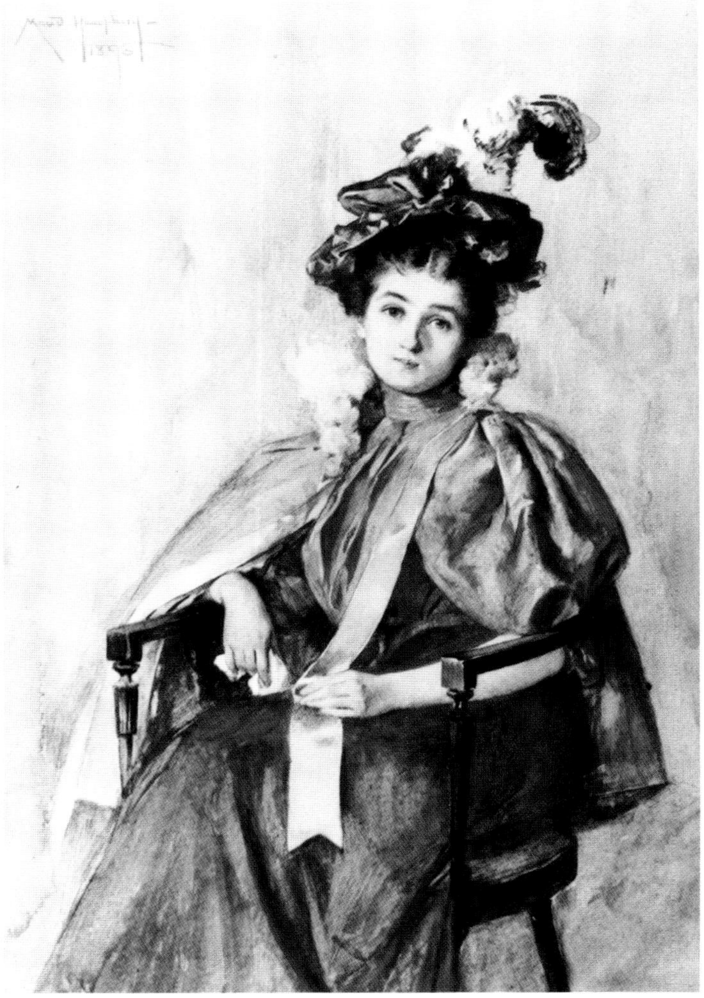

3 *Portrait, 1895, possibly of Marie Adelaide Devine, by Maud Humphrey.*

4 *The statue of Mercury, by Guernsey Mitchell, adorned the Kimball Tobacco Factory. The drawing by Ralph H. Avery, Creative Workshop instructor, was submitted to the Gallery's Picturesque Rochester Competition in 1929. Photograph courtesy of the Rochester Historical Society.*

but they helped to make the Clinton House, kept by J.L.D. Mathies, himself "an eccentric genius who occasionally seized the palette," Rochester's first art center. Mathies's portrait of the Indian Chief, *Red Jacket*, "arrested the traveller's attention on entering the parlour of that hotel," but Mathies's attempt in the 1820s to establish the first commercial gallery of art in Rochester proved premature.

By 1834, Grove Gilbert had made the newly chartered city his home, going on to become the favorite portrait painter of Rochester families. "In 1885, the year of Mr. Gilbert's death at nearly 90 years of age," wrote Emma E. Lampert, art club secretary, "were gathered together and exhibited 233 of his paintings. We know this was not an entire list."

Daguerrean studios, dioramas, and stereopticon shows became standard attractions in the Reynolds Arcade during the 1840s. The Arcade, Rochester's "crystal palace," first shopping mall, and agora for sidewalk philosophers, housed the Athenaeum— a library that would later combine with Mechanics Institute and still later become the Rochester Institute of Technology—as well as a few skylit studios for artists.

4

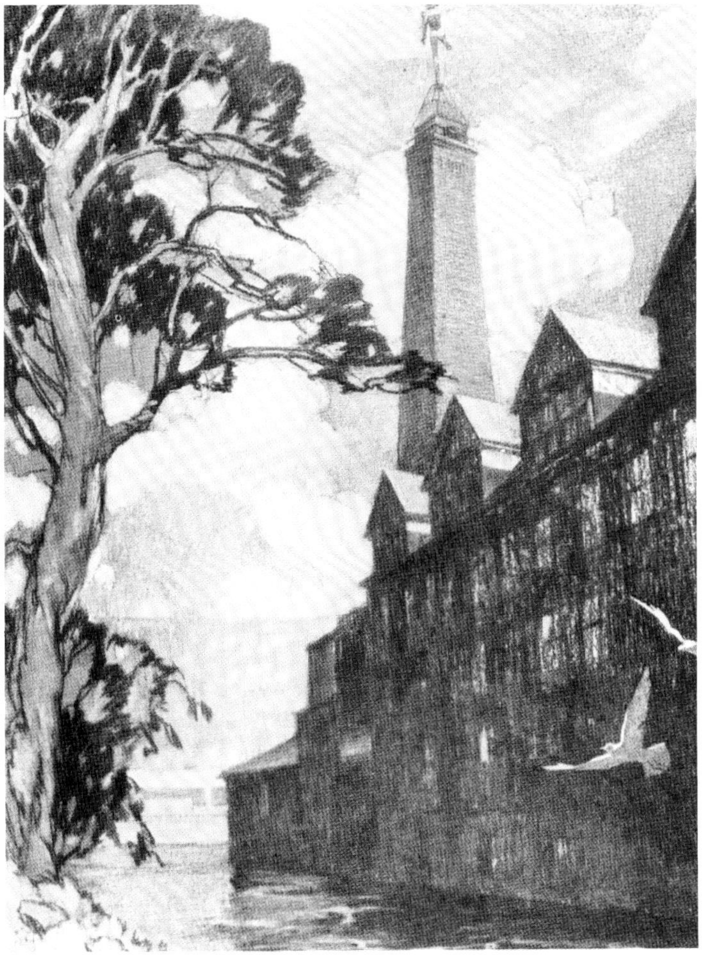

Interest in art quickened after mid-century.

Rochester women were instructed in figure and flower painting, the latter particularly useful in view of the constant demand among Rochester nurserymen for colored illustrations and the rise of the city's printing industry to become the center of color lithography in the world. Representing the infant craft of photography, the New York State Daguerrean Association met in Rochester. Lectures on fine art were given at Corinthian Hall. Sons of wealthy families embarked on study trips of European galleries. A few prominent citizens took the Grand Tour, bringing back modest collections of paintings and prints as the only European originals in Rochester; most citizens, even the most learned or affluent, were familiar only with engravings of the old masters.

Even before combining with the Athenaeum, the Mechanics Institute had been engaged in collecting, exhibiting, and teaching art, particularly "applications of fine art in industry." Founded in 1885 as a night school in a donated classroom, the Institute taught drawing—both mechanical and freehand—for teachers, architects, and children. Later china painting, oil painting, and watercolor instruction were added. Completion of the Eastman Building in 1901 and the Bevier Building in 1903 gave the Institute a host of new classrooms and studios where many of the new generation of Rochester artists, George Herdle included, would study and later teach.

The University of Rochester, a small Baptist college for men founded in 1850 in the United States Hotel on West Main Street, was among the first such institutions in the country to give special attention to the history of art. President Martin Brewer Anderson, "of commanding presence and thundering voice," lectured from 1872 to 1886 on the history of painting, sculpture, architecture, engraving, and etching. Open to the public, the lectures attracted much local attention and continued after the university moved in 1861 to Azariah Boody's donated cow pastures on the outskirts of town. (Here the Memorial Art Gallery would rise, on a campus that took its name from Boody's favorite horse, Prince.) In donating his pastures, Boody had stipulated that should the land ever be used for noneducational purposes, it would revert back to Boody or his heirs. This requirement was later removed in a quit-claim deed.

Anderson exerted a mighty formative influence during his long tenure, 1853-1890, but the art lectures did not continue under his successor, David Jayne Hill, 1890-1896, or during the years of administrative interregnum that beset the university until its third president, Rush Rhees, arrived in 1900.

Rhees had strong convictions about the relationship of town to gown, of academic art to the community. In his inaugural address he voiced them: "One reason why the formal recognition of the study of art seems so desirable to me is that the college might in this way begin a ministry to the community which would grow into one of great value." Four years later, in 1904, the wily Rhees had campus architects Heins and LaFarge of New York draw up a master plan for the university which included music and art buildings. Even Rhees conceded that the realization of these goals might be "sometime in the future." For the music building he would wait fifteen years; for the art building, nine.

In 1874 the Academy of Art organized, leasing an old theater on State Street for exhibits. That same year Hiram Sibley, president of Western Union, imported fifty-four paintings from Europe as Rochester's first major collection. He placed them on exhibition at the Academy and later on the second floor of Sibley Hall, which he had built as a library for the university. The public showed little interest in Sibley's paintings, however; the educational experiment was abandoned and the paintings were dispersed. One legacy of that collection did survive: *Interior of a Mosque* (1870s), by Jean-Léon Gérôme, passed to Sibley's grandson, F. Harper Sibley, and then into the Gallery collection.

Two later, even larger, private collections left the city as well—those belonging to William S. Kimball, the tobacco magnate who commissioned *Mercury*, and the other to Charles A. Green, nurseryman, whose collection of American paintings had been assembled by Herdle from New York galleries and studios.

These events were overshadowed when Daniel Powers's new gallery opened in 1875 in three spacious and sumptuous parlors on the fifth floor of the Powers Block, a prominent structure built at the city's important Four Corners as a monument to its owner. For the inaugural exhibition of the Powers Art Gallery, the owner himself went to Europe to choose sixteen watercolors and 121 oil paintings; many were copies of old masters but Powers also owned a Delacroix, a Courbet, and dozens of Barbizon paintings. By 1877 Powers had added three more parlors, an orchestrion, and a stereopticon machine. Huge receptions accompanied each new feature, attracting hundreds of viewers and dwarfing all competition. The Powers Gallery absorbed much of the Sibley collection and continued to extend its parlors into the triple mansard roofs which the owner had added to the Powers Block. By 1884 no fewer than thirty rooms, including a Rotunda and Grand Salon measuring thirty by ninety feet, were devoted to art. The Powers catalog listed 996 paintings and seventeen items of statuary. "Believing that a precious gem should have a beautiful setting," the Powers brochure noted, "his gallery is not a plain, somber, bare-floored tunnel or series of dismal chambers, but a suite of richly and artistically ornamented and luxurious parlors."

When Daniel Powers died in 1897, his gallery died with him. He had already closed the three floors of art galleries to protest their being taxed at the same rate as the commercial floors. Despite a public outcry over losing the paintings, the municipal tax laws remained hostile to a municipal art gallery. After Daniel's death the Powers family sold the thousand-plus items at auction in New York. Rochester was poised to revert to a cultural backwater.

Two final attempts to harness the ephemeral enthusiasm of artists and their supporters underscore the winning combination that Rhees, Herdle, and Mrs. Watson would

5

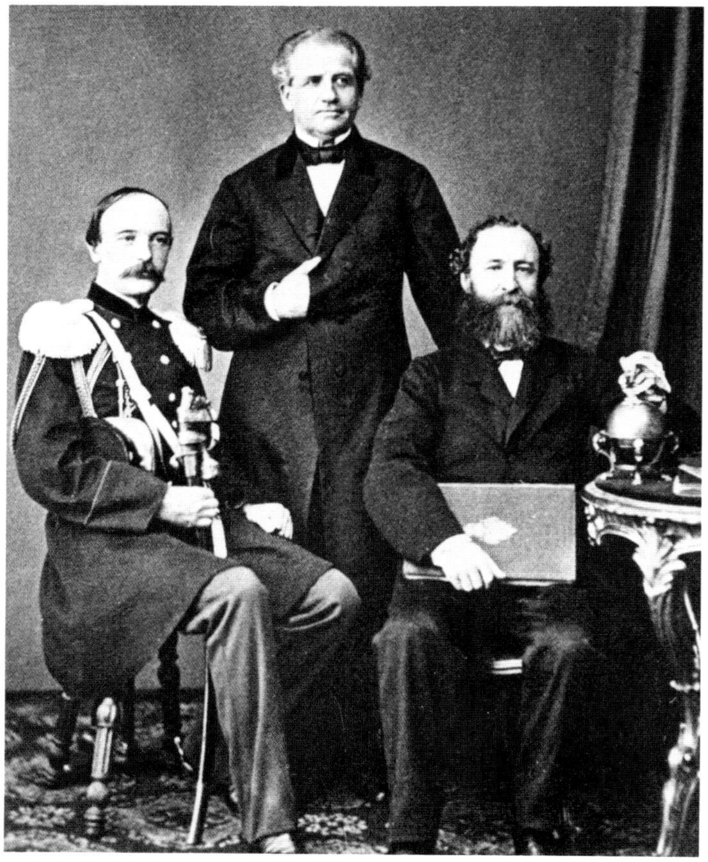

6

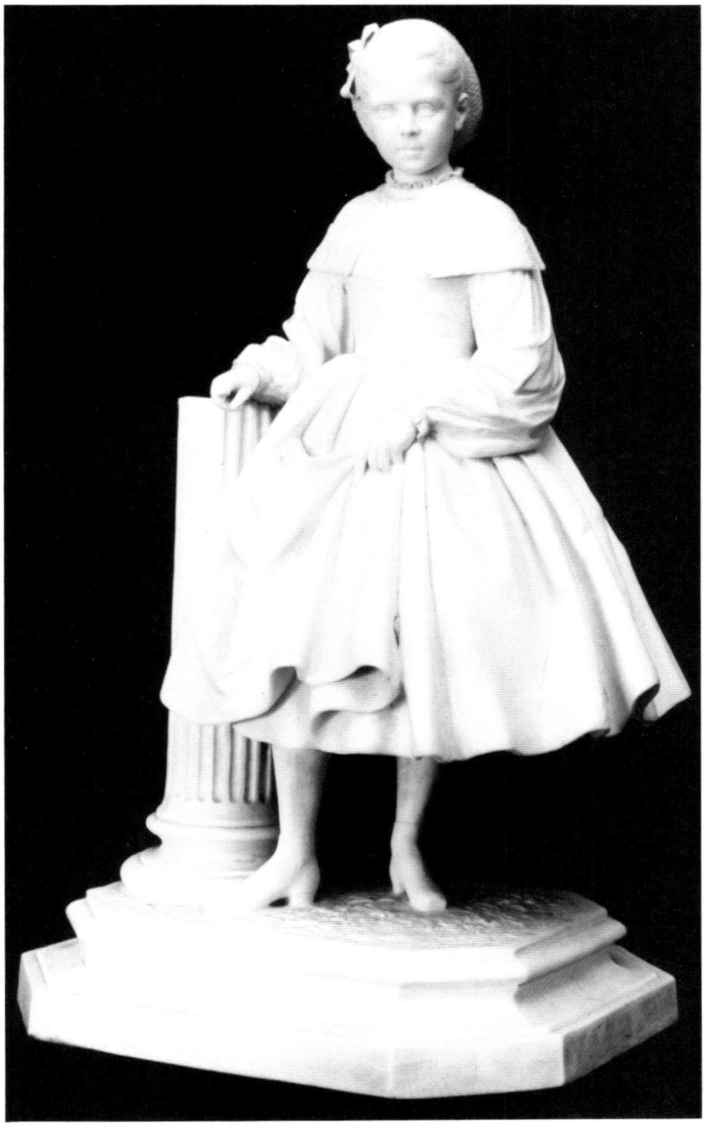

5 *Hiram Sibley in Russia, 1864. Photograph courtesy of the University of Rochester Library.*

6 *Bisque statuette of Emily Sibley, ca. 1865. Collection of the Rochester Historical Society. Photograph courtesy of the Rochester Historical Society.*

later be. The Rochester Art League, organized in 1910 for "the advancement of art," had as its vice-president the prominent architect Claude Bragdon and Herdle as its treasurer; Ada Howe Kent and James B. Arnold, Bragdon's sometime partner, "represented the professional artists." Exhibitions were held and a salesroom maintained on the Mechanics Institute campus, but the League disbanded completely with the opening of the Gallery.

In 1911, when the first Rochester Industrial Exposition was held at Edgerton Park, the Rochester Art Club was invited to hold its twenty-eighth annual exhibition there. So successful was the show that in 1912 a new building with a special gallery devoted solely to art opened at this annual exposition of the county's farm produce and industries. Again Herdle organized the exhibitions there and again the opening of the Gallery stole the thunder. The era of makeshift headquarters for local exhibitions was passing.

For the Rochester Art Club exhibition of 1908, Herdle had included twelve paintings by French Impressionists, with an eye to exposing the Rochester public to new directions in art. (Although Impressionism was hardly new in larger metropolitan centers, it was not generally known or collected in Rochester. And this was five years before the landmark Armory show in New York City.) Seven of the paintings were by Monet, the rest by Sisley, Renoir, and Pissarro. To these, Herdle added another Monet, *Waterloo Bridge*, owned by Emily Sibley Watson. Durand-Ruel, the New York dealer supplying the bulk of the paintings, agreed that only the transportation costs need be paid; Herdle reasoned that by tacking an extra nickel onto the usual twenty-five-cent admission fee, these funds could easily be raised.

People stayed away in droves. Those who came, left clucking in bewilderment. Reporters and critics attacked the "wild" paintings in four of the city's five newspapers. The exception was A. W. Moore, member of the Rochester Art Club and editorial writer for the *Democrat and Chronicle*, who inferred that the lack of response revealed "Rochester's cultural blight." Moore concluded that "every man, woman, and child should be dragged by the hair to see this great exhibition."

The transportation costs remained outstanding until Herdle paid them out of personal funds. When Mrs. Watson heard about this, she wrote to the club, covered all the costs, and asked to be notified of further worthwhile exhibitions organized by the organization. This early encounter led to Mrs. Watson's assessment of Herdle as a knowledgeable judge of modern art and someone who stood up for his principles. Herdle was able to pull off his career transition and launch a new cultural institution partly because he had the respect, support and assistance of a powerful ally. If Emily Sibley Watson was the "angel" who rescued Herdle and the art club exhibition of 1908, she would be a one-woman seraphim to the founding of the Gallery.

7

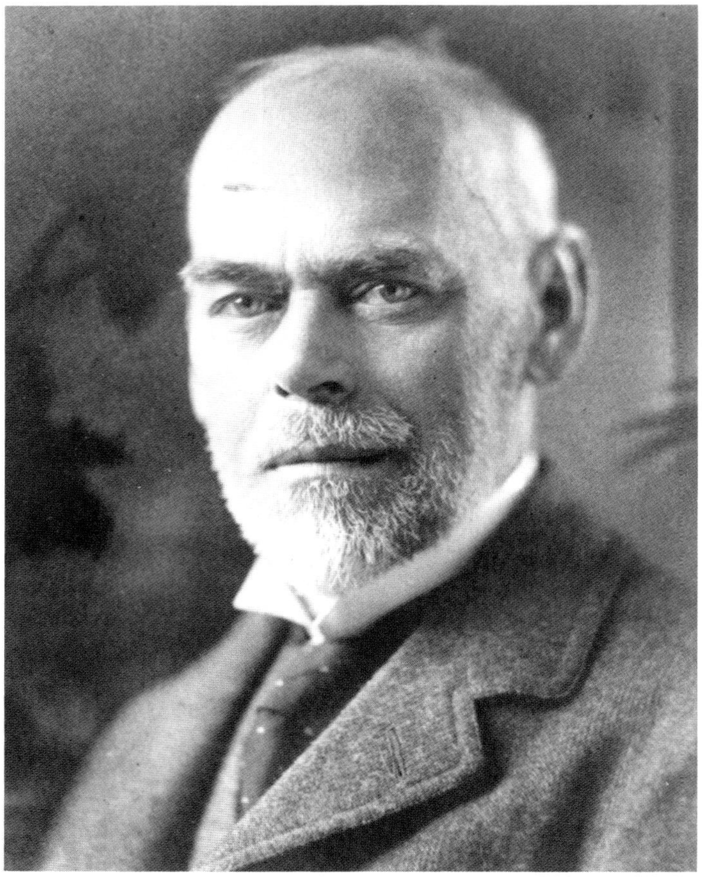

Emily Sibley, born in 1855, was educated in Rochester and Europe. When Hiram Sibley went to Russia in 1864 to spend a long winter negotiating with Czar Alexander II and his minions for the rights to lay a telegraph line across Russian Alaska, the Bering Straits, and Siberia to Europe, he took his wife and two younger children as far as Berlin. Undoubtedly, the trio whiled away the hours in art galleries there and possibly selected the paintings Sibley would bring back to Rochester. Emily and her brother, Hiram Watson Sibley, attended boarding schools in Heidelberg. In Paris a ten-inch bisque statuette was made of the ten-year-old girl by a sculptor who had photographed her from every angle and then used mathematical instruments to transfer contours and measurements into three dimensions.

Back in Rochester, Emily continued to lead a sheltered, aristocratic existence. The men around her—her father, her brother, her adoring second husband, even her doctor—tried to act as buffer against any harsh experience. To them she was a privileged person who must be spared any disturbance. After the birth of her last child, James Sibley Watson Jr., she was confined to a wheelchair for six months. Seasonal excursions to New York produced an impeccably groomed and beautifully dressed Emily—typically in white or grey. The impression prevailed that she could scarcely lift a fork—so tiny were her hands—let alone accomplish any more formidable task. Her feet were equally small in handmade shoes. Yet she was sufficiently athletic to play on the city croquet team.

Photographs of Emily reveal a petite woman with large dark eyes, romantic but sad. No one could shield her from the harsh experiences of watching her first child, Louise, age seven, die from diphtheria in 1884 or from hearing the "bad news," recorded in her diary of the same year, that Isaac Averell, whom she had married in 1876, had gone to Denver and was not coming home to her and their six-year-old son, James George Averell. The divorce that followed, unusual for its time and Emily's social stratum, was handled with great discretion.

Her marriage to James Sibley Watson represented not only a love match but an alliance of Western Union families—their fathers had been business partners.

Mrs. Watson became a discriminating collector and patron of the arts, acquiring works through New York galleries and encouraging young artists through her afternoon salons and the purchases of their works. At first her collection had a period flavor—she had her Bouguereaus, Theodore Rousseaus, and Corots—but then at an unfashionably early date she bought not one but two Monets. In 1908 she and Sibley Watson Jr., age fourteen, visited a Picabia exhibit at Alfred Stieglitz's *avant garde* Gallery 291. She bought works by Picasso and Matisse, not because they were "in"—which they certainly were not then —but because she liked them.

Mrs. Watson's cultural and civic interests were wide-ranging. With her mother-in-law she worked to equip and enlarge the Homeopathic (now Genesee) Hospital so that the Sibleys and the Watsons would have a suitable hospital near their homes. She was a pillar of the Philharmonic, held Tuesday musicales in her home, and with George Eastman, fostered the education of the gifted child violinist, David Hochstein. When World War I raged in Europe, Hochstein, then age twenty-five, enlisted. After the Stradivarius violin which Eastman had purchased for his use was destroyed in an automobile accident, Hochstein despaired of continuing his music and applied for active duty in France. Less than thirty days before the Armistice was signed, Second Lieutenant Hochstein was killed by an exploding enemy shell during the Battle of the Argonne. Emily Watson, who had previously lost two children, now lost her prodigy. She purchased the Hochstein family home and made it into the David Hochstein Memorial Music School so that other gifted yet needy children might study music.

James George Averell—"J. G." to intimates—was a handsome youth, an athlete who crewed, rode to the hounds, played golf and polo, and engaged in the competitive family squash matches in the courts behind Hiram Sibley's East Avenue home. Idealistic, sheltered, and sensitive, J.G. was his mother's companion and confidant until her remarriage in 1891. He graduated from Harvard in 1899, having studied architecture. During a postgraduate year in Italy, he came across and sketched the Tempio Malatestiano at Rimini, a Gothic church renovated in 1450 by Leon Battista Alberti with a monumental triple-arched entrance facade and arcaded recesses along the side walls. In April of 1904, Averell entered the office of Herbert Hale in Boston. In November of 1904, Averell, age twenty-six, died from cholera.

James Sibley Watson was the son of Don Alonzo Watson, Hiram Sibley's partner in Western Union. The partners bestowed each other's surname upon their sons as middle names, an occurrence which, particularly after Hiram Watson Sibley's sister, Emily, married James Sibley Watson, continues to confuse. (The fact that brothers-in-law Jim and Hiram looked like brothers down to their white goatees did not help.) Younger by six years than his wife, whom he had loved since childhood, James Watson was a tall man whose physical dimensions changed not a whit during his adult lifetime. Twice each year his favorite tweeds arrived automatically from his London tailor; after his death at ninety-one, box after unopened box from Saville Row were found among his possessions.

At seventeen James enrolled in but did not attend the University of Rochester, class of 1881, and soon followed the call of the gold rush to Wyoming and Nevada. Returning, he again studied at home and took his exams for a bachelor of science degree with the class of 1888. Watson went to work in a bank, where, he always contended, the

8

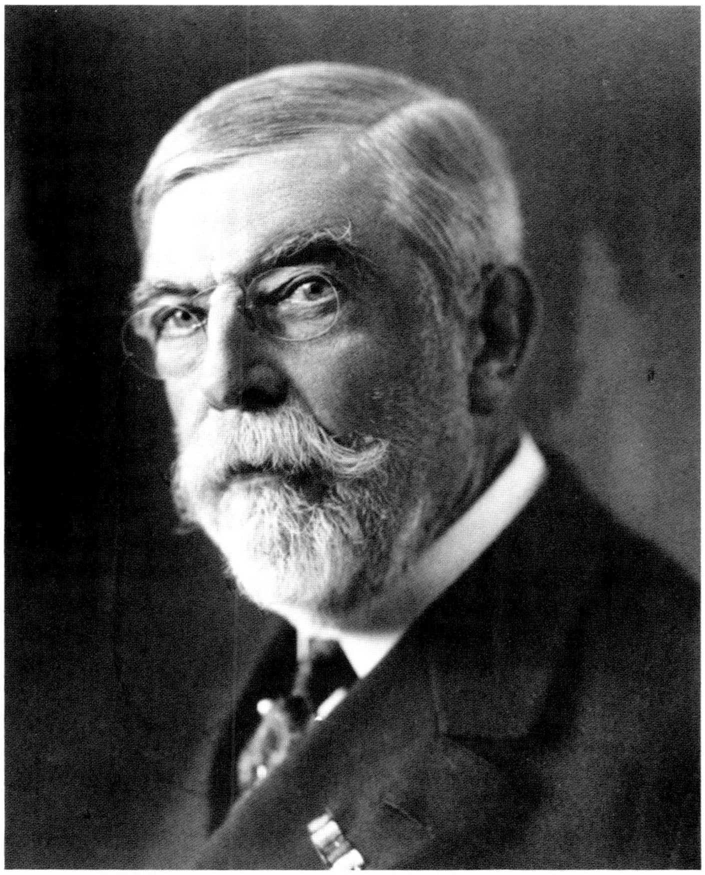

7 *James Sibley Watson, 1917. Photograph courtesy of the University of Rochester Library.*

8 *Hiram Watson Sibley, 1917. Photograph courtesy of the University of Rochester Library.*

9

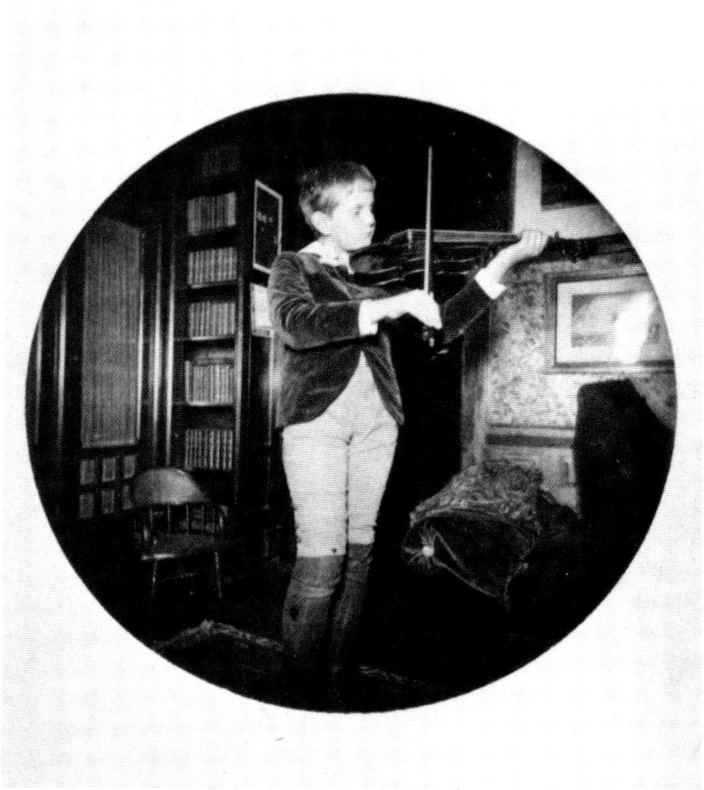

9 *"J. G." Averell as a violin student, ca. 1885. Photograph courtesy of the University of Rochester Library.*

10 *Plan of the University of Rochester Campus, 1905, proposed by Rush Rhees, contained a "Site for Art Museum" approximately where Cutler Union was later built. Annual Report of the President of the University of Rochester, 1905–1906.*

constant handling of paper and gold (said to kill germs) saved him from the dread smallpox. A founder of the Security Trust Company in 1892, he was named bank president in 1911 and chairman in 1940. He unabashedly listed his profession as "Capitalist," but was "Uncle Jim" to his employees. People set their watches by his ancient electric automobile ("The first and last one in Rochester," he said) as he drove around the corner to the Genesee Valley Club every afternoon at four and home again at six. A taciturn man who mumbled rather than spoke, he was a charter member of the Genesee Valley Club, the Genesee Valley Hunt, and the Country Club of Rochester.

There was a gentle side to this prospector, rancher, athlete, horseman, photographer, capitalist, and "last of the Argonauts." He grew to share his wife's interests in music and art and once recited Virgil's *Georgics* to Gertrude Herdle on the golf course in Florida.

(The reserved and bookish Dr. James Sibley Watson Jr. told this writer that he always felt that his glamorous and gregarious half-brother, J. G. Averell, was more the son his own father, James Sibley Watson, wanted, than was he, Sibley, with his quieter scientific and cultural pursuits. Perhaps that bond motivated Watson Sr.'s own interest in the Gallery.)

Watson paid for half of the 1926 Fountain Court addition to the Gallery and became fascinated by Chinese bronzes and ceramics and the bright colors of medieval stained glass. Amenable to suggestions that he and his wife celebrate Christmas with a gift to the Gallery, his chief question each year became, "Is it my turn or Emmy's?"

With the dawn of a new century, Rush Rhees, age forty, ordained Baptist minister and professor of New Testament interpretation, was inducted as the university's third president. The faculty numbered seventeen, the student body consisted of 157 day students, the physical plant of three mortgaged buildings plus Sibley Hall with its meager library of 35,000 volumes. Among small colleges, and even in its own city, the university (a courtesy title) enjoyed no great prestige. But, unbeknownst to all, one of the great academic executives of the twentieth century had just come on board.

In 1902 Rhees called Elizabeth Denio to the faculty to teach the history of art. Denio had taught at Wellesley College and would train docents for the Panama Pacific Exposition in San Francisco in 1915. Rhees then began drawing up an ambitious master plan for campus expansion which included a sizable art museum—envisioned where Cutler

Union would rise. By the time Rhees retired in 1935, he had far exceeded the 1906 plan by building not one but two undergraduate campuses plus an art museum, medical center, and music school. "Short in stature, long in impact," Herdle's daughters would say.

Although initially overlooking Herdle, Rhees was discerning enough to recognize that an academic degree was not everything. Always formal, yet unfailingly kind, the president brought daily reports of Gallery business and happenings to the Herdle home during the director's last two years of failing health.

The director's salary, once Herdle had outdistanced his competitors for the job, hovered around $2,000 a year. This was not commensurate with his image or professional status in the community. However, that never stopped Herdle from going to the Gallery on a Sunday afternoon in his Prince Albert coat, striped trousers, and Oxford vest, because *that* was the way an art museum director dressed.

The director's duties included choosing and mounting monthly loan exhibitions, writing catalogs and newspaper articles, and lecturing to assembled groups of adults or children. He served on the art committee, executive committee, and board in his three capacities and chaired the membership committee. He composed individualized letters to each new Gallery member he or another board

10

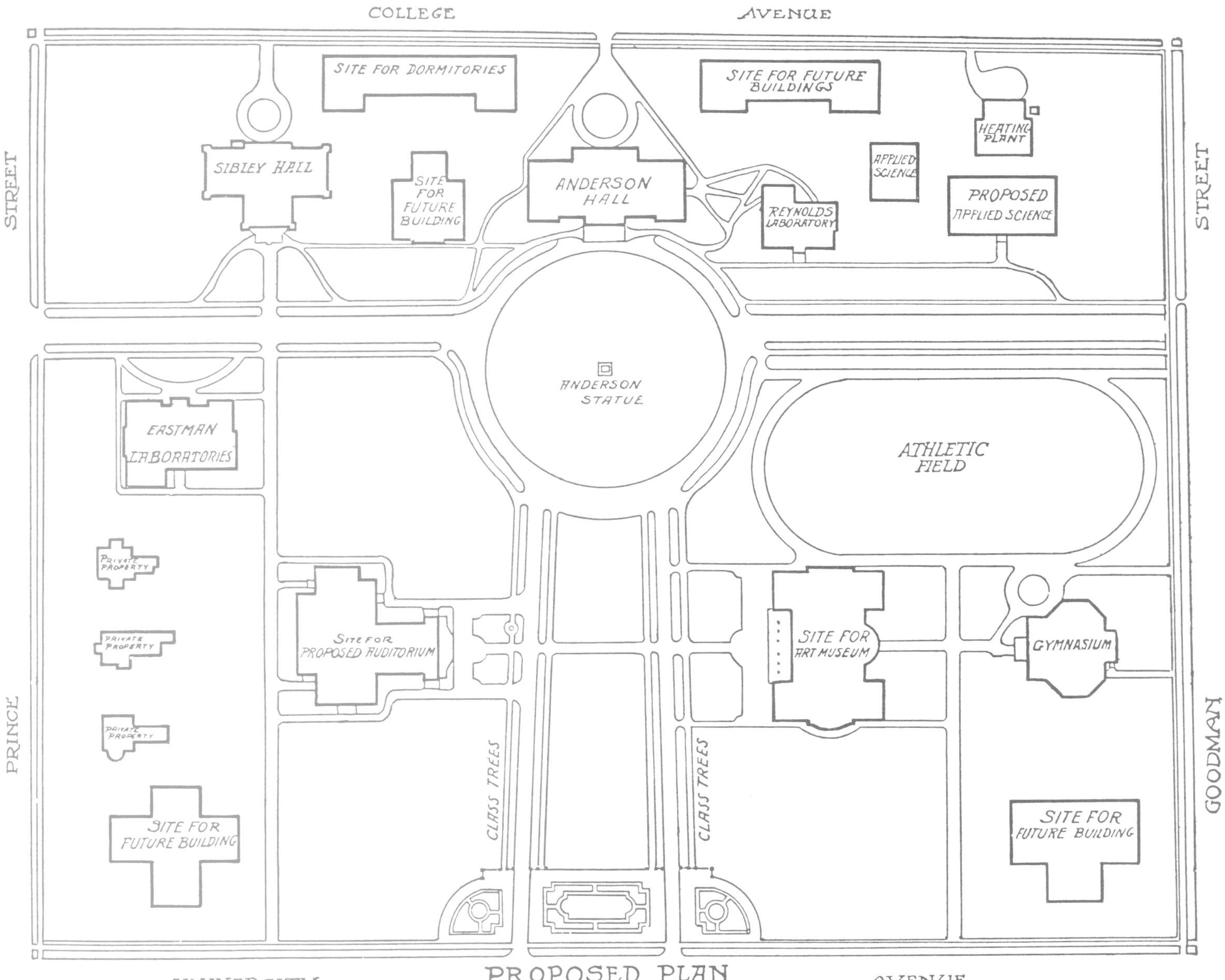

PROPOSED PLAN OF THE CAMPUS.

member could entice to join. The duties extended to non-artistic areas: early minutes record authorization to purchase six fire extinguishers, a vacuum cleaning system, a sliding curtain to obstruct the view of the packing room, and half-bleached cotton sheeting to stretch across the ground glass skylights in summer.

Herdle prepared the budget, submitted annual reports, recorded gifts with date and provenance, filed correspondence, kept records and archives, and when the art committee rejected a gift, "negotiated an exchange for a more representative work."

Besides the director, the Gallery's original staff numbered four: Herdle's secretary, Dorothy Carson, who applied to Rhees for the position from her post as registrar at Wells College in Aurora; the librarian, Miss Barbour; the receptionist, Mrs. A. W. Moore, wife of the artist and supportive journalist; and the superintendent, Ray Pike, George Herdle's mandated choice. ("Yes I will be your director," Herdle told Rhees, "if you will hire Mr. Pike too.") Mr. Pike's salary was $1,100 a year. Miss Barbour was paid $600, and Mrs. Moore the same—both a princely $.25 an hour.

Mr. Pike's duties included sweeping the Gallery clean, opening it each morning, unpacking and repacking the monthly exhibits, framing works of art, and in later years soothing a young Gertrude Herdle's jitters with automobile rides before her lectures. "Mister" Pike, as he was always called, established such packing and framing standards and was held in such high esteem that colleagues continually pressed him to head the superintendents' division of the American Association of Museums. A shy person, he always declined. His thoughtfulness and general knowledge became legendary: he knew each Gallery member by name including which ones might need a chair. The friendly feeling that pervaded early Gallery years was due in large part, Isabel Herdle says, to its superintendent.

On 30 October 1912 a letter went out from Rush Rhees:

You have kindly consented to serve as one of the managers of the Memorial Art Gallery, which Mrs. Watson is building upon the Campus. A meeting of these managers will be held Friday noon, November the first, at 12 o'clock, in the office of Mr. Hiram W. Sibley, 100 Sibley Block, Main Street East.

The purpose of the meeting is to take such preliminary steps as may seem wise and necessary for the permanent organization of

11

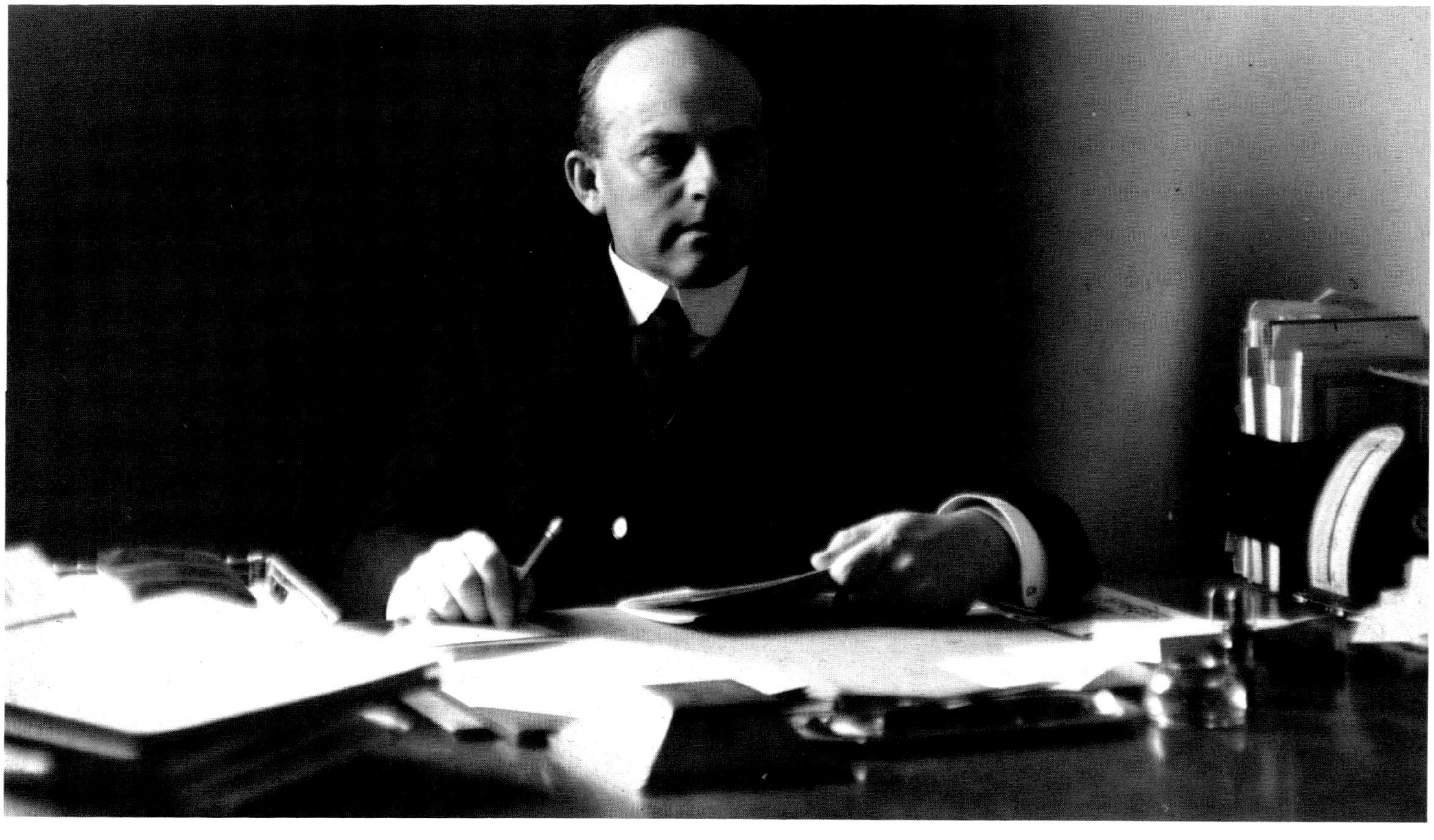

12

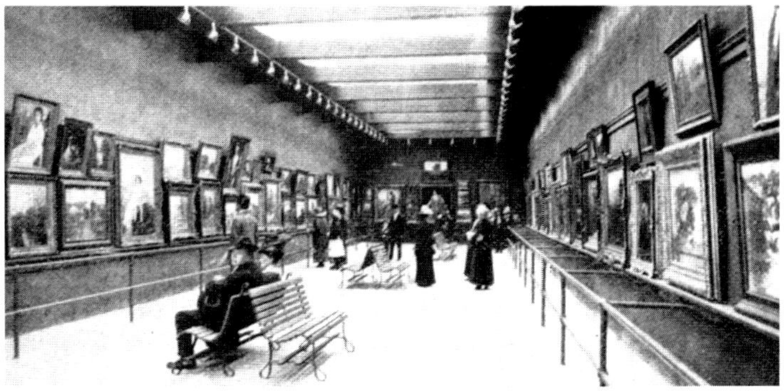

13

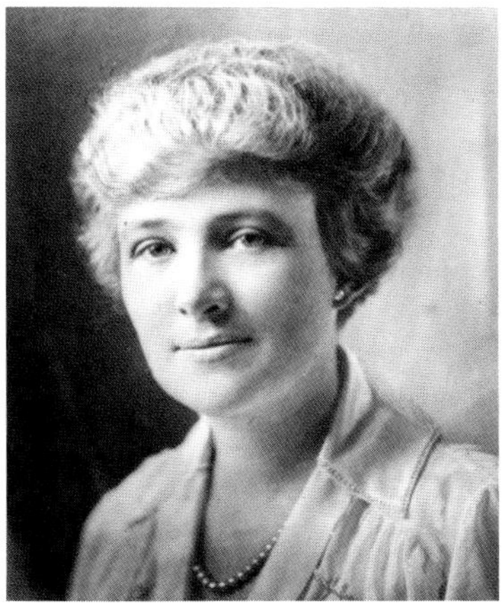

11 *George Herdle in his role as museum director. Photograph courtesy of the Herdle family.*

12 *The fine arts gallery on the Rochester Exposition grounds was headed by George Herdle from 1912 to 1922.*

13 *Mrs. George D. B. Bonbright, 1917. Photograph courtesy of the University of Rochester Library.*

the Board of Managers and the adoption of rules and by-laws to govern its actions.

It is sincerely hoped that you will be able to be present at the place and hour named.

By the time the bylaws were drawn in April 1913, the Board of Managers had become the Board of Directors, "to comply with the terms of Mrs. Watson's gift." Then in 1923 a newspaper noted that John J. Inglis had succeeded George Herdle as Gallery "director" (Rochester Art Club representative) and in the ensuing confusion people wondered what had happened to Gertrude Herdle (who, of course, had actually succeeded her father as administrative head of the Gallery). It took eight years to resolve the untidiness but in 1931 the board again became the Board of Managers and has remained so ever since.

The first board, appointed for life terms, was heavily peppered with Watsons and Sibleys, their relatives, and friends. Perhaps by accident it was half male, half female. Mrs. Watson's name headed the list but without title (although she chaired the powerful art committee). Rush Rhees was president; James Sibley Watson, vice president; George Herdle, secretary; Joseph Alling, chairman of the university trustees, treasurer; and Julius M. Wile, secretary of the Security Trust Company, bursar. Theoretically the officers were "elected annually from among the directors"; in practice they changed only through death or retirement. Board meetings were held on the second Thursday of February, April, June, October, and December. Herdle was the administrative head of the Gallery but a board member only because he was the representative of the Rochester Art Club.

Board members included Mrs. Watson's brother, whose establishment of the Sibley Music Library made him a cultural leader in his own right. Hiram Watson Sibley's collection of musical manuscripts and books, begun in 1904, deposited in Sibley Hall and later the Eastman School of Music, would grow into the largest collegiate music collection in the country and one of the foremost music research libraries in the world. Hiram's ivory collection would pass to his daughter Ruth Gade, his armor to his daughter Urling Iselin, and father Hiram's painting by Gérôme to son Harper and then to the Gallery.

Besides designing the Gallery's first logo and bookplate, Claude Bragdon was supervising architect for the building and secretary pro tem before Herdle's appointment. Fresh from his most important commission—the New York Central Station in Rochester, designed in 1910—he was at the height of his prestige as an architect. Yet most of his jobs were small domestic ones, including Ruth Sibley's bedroom and the interiors of the Watson yacht. Bragdon would leave architecture and move to New York in 1923, returning often to lecture at the Gallery. He would remain widely regarded in Rochester, a cult figure almost, as architect, lecturer, author, stage designer, mystic, and raconteur of great charm.

Sculptor Guernsey Mitchell and Charles Mulford Robinson were other non-family appointments. Robinson's selection was based on his national reputation as originator and proselytizer of the "City Beautiful" movement; indeed, he coined the term. Witty and prolific, Robinson wrote more than 100 articles and books on Rochester history before abandoning journalism for city planning. His plans for Detroit, Denver, Omaha, Los Angeles, Cedar Rapids, Oakland, Fort Wayne, Raleigh, Binghamton, and Columbus led Bragdon to call him the "first American to make the 'Science of Cities' a life work."

The nascent cultural institutions of Rochester were midwifed by several leading families. Eastman was the major patron of music; Mrs. Watson played the secondary role here in persuading Eastman to subsidize David Hochstein's career. In art, Mrs. Watson held the central public role with her gift of the Gallery, with Eastman serving as board member.

Eastman's dramatic arrival at Gallery board meetings in fur coat and hat created the same lasting impression on a young Gertrude Herdle as it did on Eastman's British employees when a nervous tremor spread that the "man from the North Pole" was on board. Eastman amassed the only significant old master painting collection in Rochester and an even larger collection of American, Dutch, and Barbizon landscapes. Of the sixty-odd paintings and prints Eastman bequeathed to the university, most would eventually be placed at the Gallery.

The sons of John Jacob Bausch, who with Henry Lomb had started the optical business bearing their names, staked out different philanthropic territories. Edward Bausch built a new home for the Rochester Museum of Arts and Sciences. William Bausch started the first dental clinic in the country and interested Eastman in fostering dental care for children on an international scale. William Drescher, a Bausch son-in-law and Gallery board member, would head the Gallery's first city wide membership drive in 1926.

The Gallery charter required board membership for the president of the university, the president of the Rochester Art Club, and the superintendent of the Department of

14

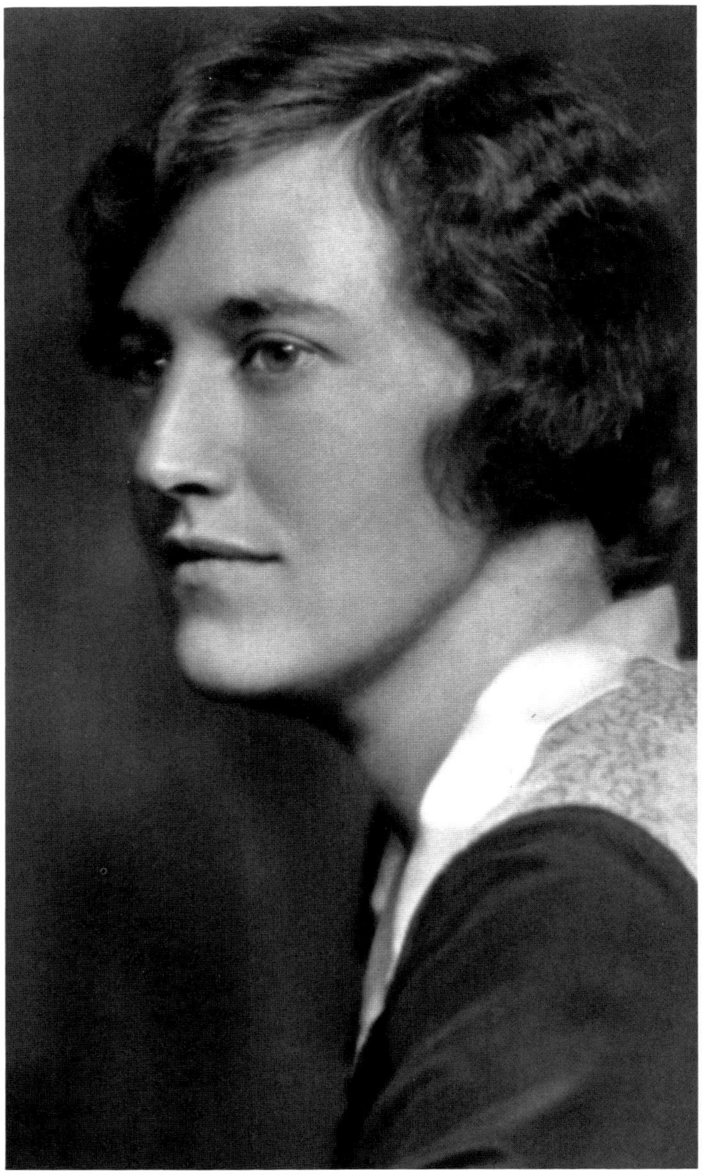

14 *Gertrude Herdle became her father's assistant upon her graduation from the University of Rochester in 1918. Photograph courtesy of the Herdle family.*

Applied and Fine Arts at the Mechanics Institute. Frank von der Lancken was the first representative from the institute. Generally, institute members represented a conservative point of view, favoring the acquisition and exhibition of narrative works of art, a view consistent with the mission of teaching commercial art, illustration, and architectural rendering.

Among women board members, Elizabeth Averell, niece of Isaac Averell and cousin of J. G. Averell, and later Mrs. Rogerson, was an interior decorator, listing George Eastman among her clients. Beth Averell was a free spirit who bounced around the country, solicited her share of charter members for the Gallery, and was a member of George Herdle's "Special Exhibition Committee." As such, she "has been empowered to consult with you," Herdle told a New York dealer. Since Averell was in New York part of the time anyway, first with the Carroll Gallery and then with Arden Studios, it stretched the Gallery's meager budget for her to act as Herdle's agent in contacting galleries or artists invited to show in the Inaugural Exhibition. Averell also "did" the walls of the Hall of Casts, the largest and most prominent room in the new Gallery. She covered them with canvas above a dado, then stippled and antiqued the canvas in gold and green paint, the fashionable effect of which Herdle was kind enough or politic enough to praise in his annual report.

Mrs. George D. B. Bonbright was an art lover and friend of Mrs. Watson. Elizabeth (Mrs. Granger A.) Hollister was James Watson's sister. Edwina (Mrs. Henry) Danforth was the first woman president of the Rochester Board of Education and a founding regent of Mount Vernon, George Washington's home. At the time of the 1913 inaugural she was living in Washington, D. C. with her Congressman husband. The Grace Curtice of the 1912 board became Mrs. Jesse Lindsay by the time of the Gallery opening. Mrs. William R. Taylor, a Prince Street neighbor of Mrs. Watson, was the wife of the prominent minister of Brick Presbyterian Church.

Marie Atkinson (Mrs. Ernest R.) Willard was the daughter of Mrs. Watson's sister, Louise Sibley Atkinson. Mrs. Willard's second husband was the editor of the *Post-Express*. Since childhood, and through two marriages, she had lived in "Woodside," an 1830s house that became home to the Rochester Historical Society upon her death. Charlotte Whitney (later Mrs. Atkinson Allen), Walter Cassebeer, and Helen Ellwanger all became lifetime board members within the first five years of the Gallery's existence.

Although the board was dominated by the first families of Rochester, the Gallery was acquiring a "first family" of its own.

The Great War first brought Gertrude Herdle the few steps from classroom to director's office. During the spring of 1918 Dorothy Carson, secretary to the director, resigned to distribute powdered milk to Belgian babies. Despite a notable absence of typing skills, the director's daughter filled in. Educated at Concord School No. 18 and East High School, Gertrude was officially named Miss Carson's successor on the day she graduated from the University of Rochester: 13 June 1918.

By the next year Gertrude had instituted "biweekly picture-story hours for children under 14." They "began last year rather fitfully," the scrapbook of 1920 records, "with 20 or 25 children who gathered around the story-teller and handled the various art objects. Soon the group grew so large that more intimate treatment proved impracticable. In today's Gallery a story illustrated by lantern slides is given in the Gallery Lecture Room to a group that averages 80 to 120.

"Many a child who attends Gallery picture-story hours will one day think his or her appreciation of art is a natural gift. But if memory harks back to the lecture room underneath the Gallery where so many art treasures are housed, it will be remembered that underneath the careful sugar coating of well-chosen words was expert instruction in art appreciation such as many adults have never been privileged to enjoy," the scrapbook prophesied.

It would be the first of an almost endless skein of innovations from the two talented and energetic daughters of George Herdle.

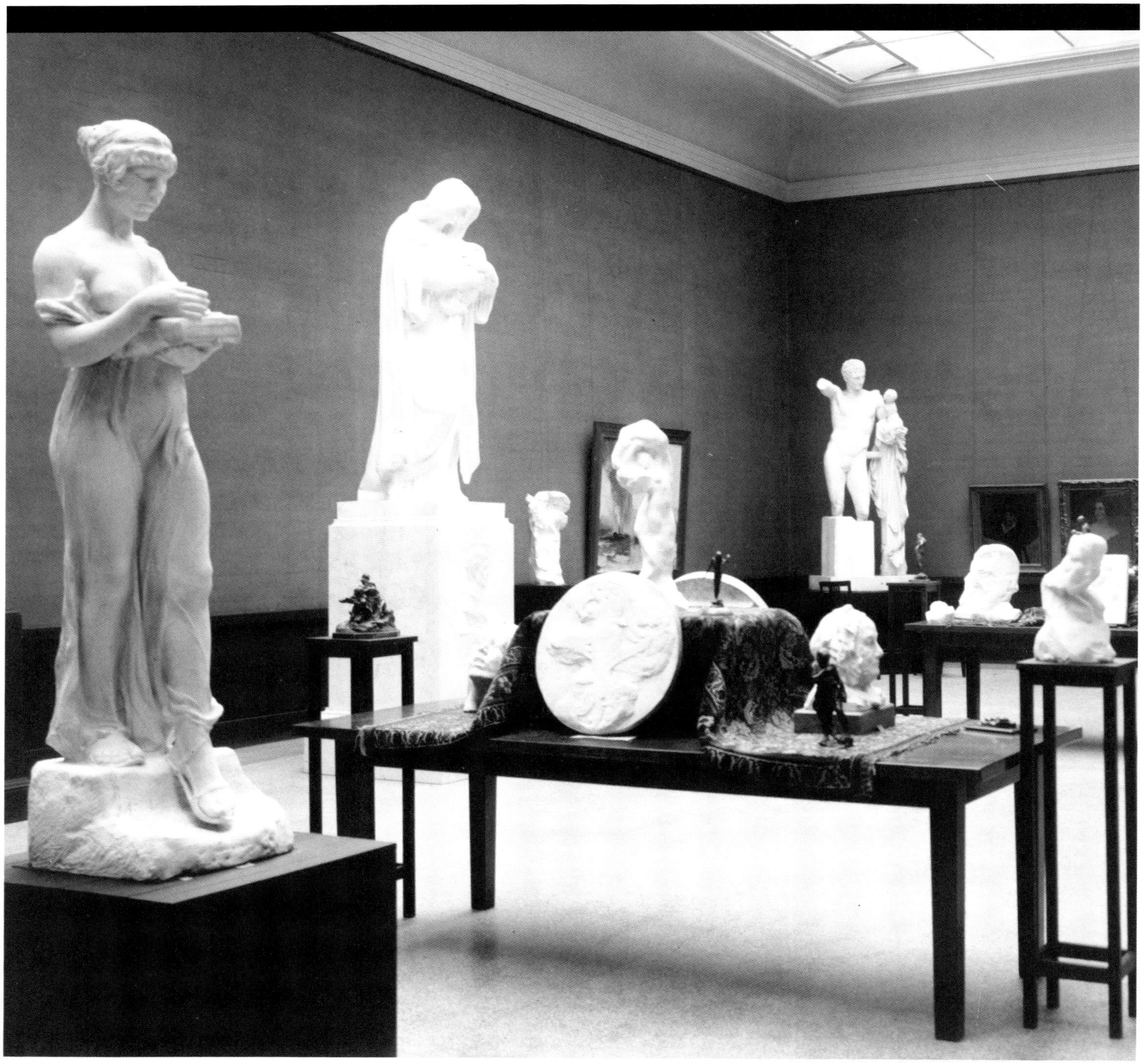

2: Treasures from Denuded Walls

2

> Your generosity in denuding your walls for the summer of their highly prized treasures and permitting them to be shown for the edification and enjoyment of the public is most gratefully appreciated.

George Herdle | 1914.

The Hall of Casts, ca. 1914, included the hooded marble figure of Memory.

Those Rochester citizens who lent their treasures during the summer exhibition of 1914 contributed to what George Herdle called "the most notable" of any yet held at the Gallery, "providing tangible evidence that catholicity and high standards of taste govern the picture lovers of Rochester."

From Rochester walls for this and subsequent summer loan exhibitions came works that covered the spectrum from Corot to Van Dyck, from Gainsborough to Turner. Among those George Eastman lent, paintings by Hals, Rembrandt, Reynolds, Romney, and Van Dyck were eventually left to the university upon Eastman's death, and again hang on Gallery walls. Two Monets, on loan from Emily Watson, have since returned too, one as her gift, the other from her son. The paintings were arranged "by the harmony in tones, one to another" and hung in a single horizonal line "to avoid the danger of overcrowding" rather than grouping them, one above the other, as had been done for the Inaugural Exhibition.

In the beginning there was scarcely any collection and no endowment to acquire one. To fill the walls the director was expected to mount monthly loan exhibitions. Rush Rhees described the Gallery as "small... devoted exclusively to pictures and casts... prints and photographs. We do not contemplate the development of a museum in the large sense of the term," he said in 1914, "as illustrated in the Metropolitan of New York or the Museum of Fine Arts in Boston." However, the Herdles—both father and daughters—always had in mind a more comprehensive collection. Indeed, even before Rhees wrote those words, Herdle had accepted a piece of antique lace from a donor, thus insuring that the collection would encompass more than pictures and casts, prints and photographs.

Before leading Rochesterians had "denuded" their walls for the sake of the summer showing, Herdle had launched the Inaugural Exhibition the previous October. He assembled 145 paintings, "valued at half-a-million dollars," Rhees wrote proudly. Two were by Europeans and the rest by contemporary Americans. Most were for sale, with prices ranging from $1,200 for watercolors by George Bellows or Winslow Homer to a high of $15,000 for a painting by George Inness Jr. The Gallery took a 10 percent commission on sales. From the Inaugural Exhibition Rochesterians purchased paintings for their own walls while a few—Watsons and Sibleys mostly—bought for Gallery walls, donating their purchases. When the exhibition closed on 29 October, 5,715 people had seen it.

One hundred artists selected by Herdle were invited to participate. "From living artists we have had a gratifying response," Rhees told Robert de Forest. The director wanted "deceased masters" too, listing Inness, Wyant, Fuller, Twachtman, Martin, and La Farge in a request for loans from New York dealers William Macbeth and M. Knoedler & Co. Beth Averell collected the New York City loans, including paintings owned by F. B. Pratt of Brooklyn and several other private collectors. (She also planted a news report about the new Gallery through "a friend" at the *New York Times.*) Rhees contacted city and college museums, arranging for loans from Cincinnati, St. Louis, and Smith College. The Smith paintings happened to be on loan during August 1913 to the Albright Gallery in Buffalo, where the aggressively enterprising Cornelia Bentley Sage held forth as pioneer woman director and promoter. Sage sent canvasses by Whistler, Thayer, and Tarbell back to Smith via the Rochester Inaugural Exhibition along with her missives to Rhees and Herdle, which invariably ended "Devotedly your friend,...." Upon receiving the invitation "to the opening of your beautiful new Gallery," she assured Rhees that "I shall be there with great joy."

In addition to the above, Bellows, Chase, Davies, Hassam, Henri, Hunt, Homer, Luks, and Sloan were represented, along with other painters whose reputations have since faded. Three watercolors by the late Harvey Ellis, given by the Rochester Art Club; a sketch by the late Robert MacCameron; and a small but fine collection of etchings and engravings that James Averell had gathered and his mother gave to the Gallery, were all on display downstairs in the Print Room. The new library, also downstairs, showed its collection of books on architecture, the gift of former architect James G. Cutler.

Gifts from the inaugural exhibition began the permanent collection. *Morning Star* by Eugene Bracht and *The First Snow* by Horatio Walker were purchased and given by Mrs. Watson. Ruth Sibley Gade presented *Morning on the River* by Jonas Lie, in memory of her cousin, James Averell; Hiram W. Sibley gave *On the River Annisquam* by William L. Picknell; and Mrs. Ernest Willard chose *Waiting* by John Lavery, one of the European artists. James Sibley Watson, Elizabeth Watson Hollister, and an anonymous donor added three more works.

The entire permanent collection was hung in the small southeastern gallery (where now the collection of Ancient Art hangs), leaving the Hall of Casts and the other two side galleries free for casts and changing exhibitions. Gradually the collection grew. In 1916 Mrs. Watson presented *The White*

1

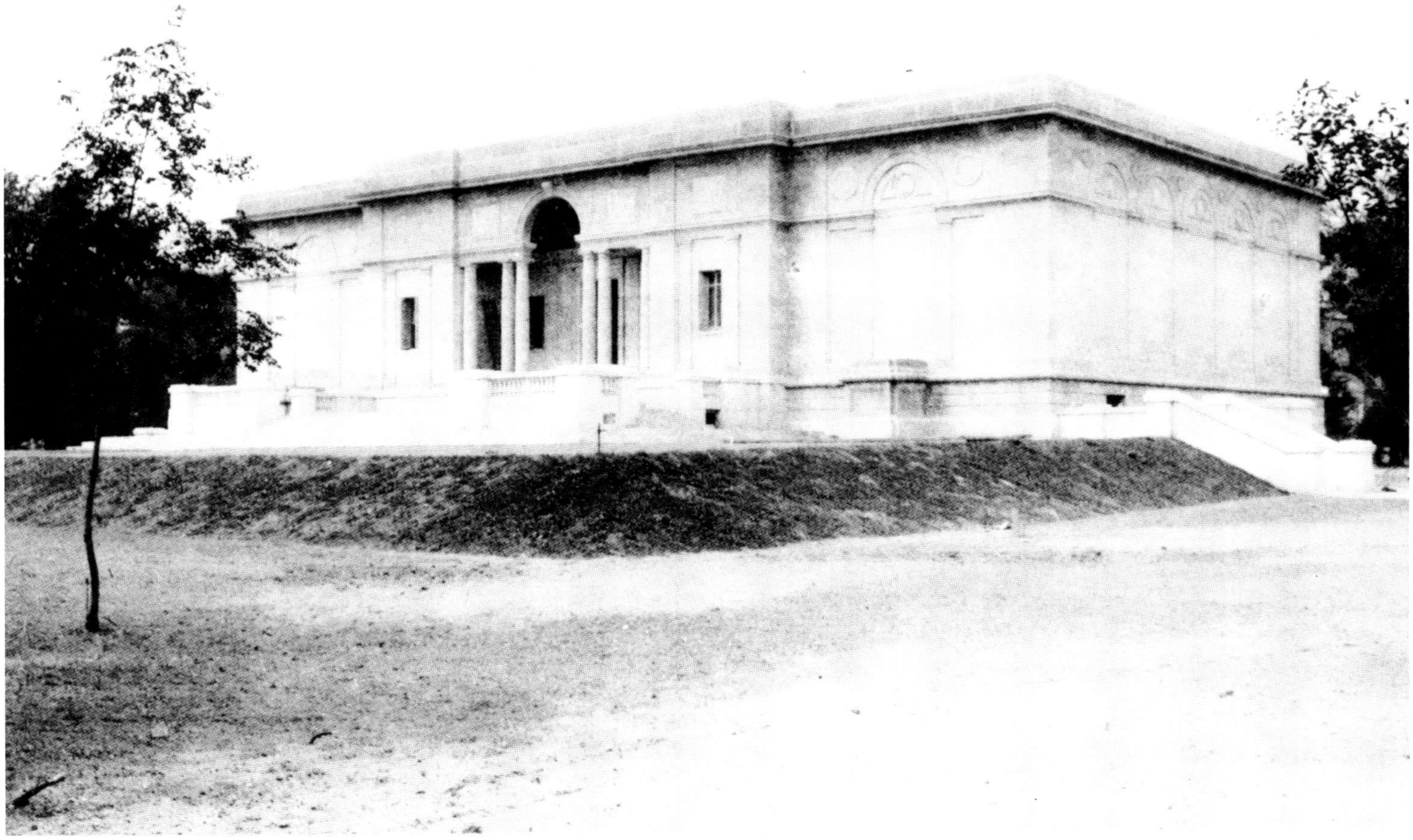

1 *The Gallery, pristine upon a greensward, during the directorship of George Herdle, 1913–1922.*

Bridge by John Twachtman. That year too nine European canvasses of the seventeenth to nineteenth centuries, including portraits by Sir Henry Raeburn and Sir Joshua Reynolds, were placed on a "permanent" loan from the Mayo Gallery in Boston until they were recalled and sold years later.

No sooner was the Inaugural Exhibition down than Herdle was mounting the next one—paintings of French interiors by Walter Gay of Paris and a retrospective of the work of Robert Lee MacCameron. MacCameron had spent his boyhood as a lumberjack, then studied art in Paris with Whistler and Gérôme. He won prizes in the Paris Salon, and eventually was awarded the Legion of Honor. Having achieved sudden fame at age forty (1907), he was dead by forty-five. Marriage to a Rochesterian brought MacCameron many Rochester portrait commissions including one to paint Eastman's mother, a portrait that hung for years in the Eastman School of Music.

By 10 December of the Gallery's first year it was time for the director to write and publish the next catalog and hang the next show—twenty-two murals and nine drawings portraying "the romance and poetry of American engineering" by Fred Dana Marsh plus the works of Albert Steiner of the Munich School whose "most distinguishing characteristic is a vital rendering of mood." This show came down 2 January, and four days later oils and watercolors by the late George Inness plus works by Alexander Wyant and Aston Knight went on display.

On went the busy art season. Works by four contemporary Americans in February were followed by the thirty-first annual Rochester Art Club Exhibition in March. Five paintings by Herdle himself were lent to the latter by Hannah Durand (Mrs. Samuel) Gould, whose friendship with Herdle would result two decades later in the largest endowment for acquisitions in Gallery history. Mrs. Watson lent her Herdle painting as well. In April works by Jonas Lie were featured, and in May "European masters"—including Fantin-Latour and Joaquin Sorolla Y Bastida, whose *Oxen on the Beach* Mrs. Watson purchased for the Gallery. In June, and for two summers thereafter, the loan exhibition from Rochester's denuded walls was hung. Except for the park band's playing on Gallery grounds, July and August were hiatus months in which to get ready for the next season.

It is not surprising that George Herdle had little time to paint.

Among other early exhibitions of note, Eastman Kodak's introduction of a two-color process sparked a pho-

2

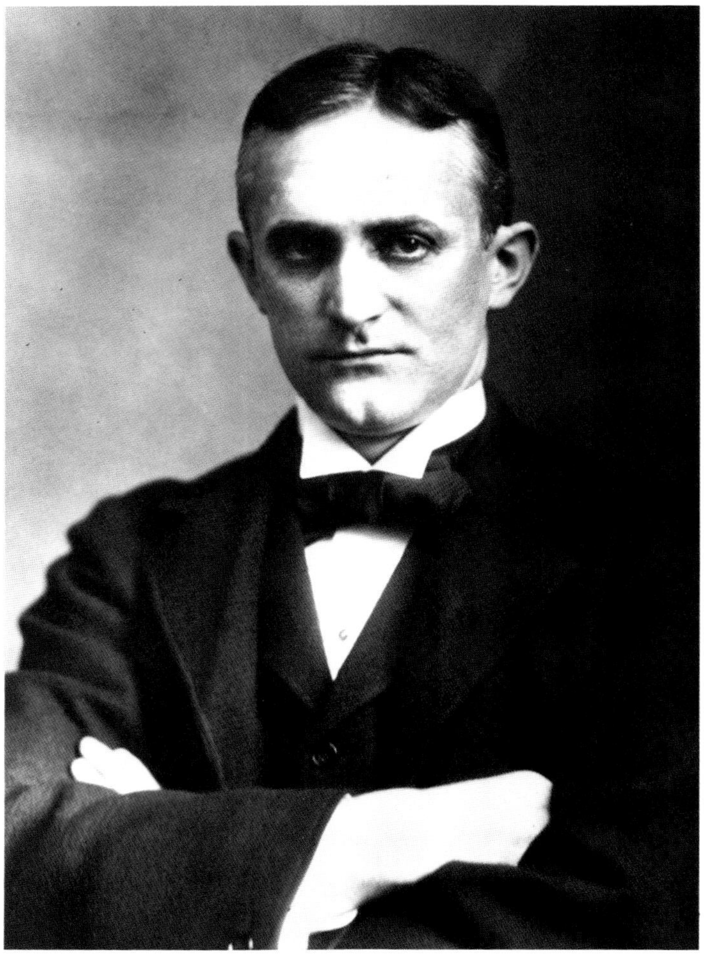

2 *George Eastman in 1900. Photograph courtesy of the Eastman Kodak Company. (The Eastman Kodak Company's new color process was introduced at the Gallery in 1914.)*

tography show. The world premiere of the new Kodachrome color plates—not to be confused with the color film of the same name introduced in 1935—took place at the Gallery on Halloween of 1914. This unveiling of "the first samples of this great advance in the art of photography," as Eastman himself described the Kodachromes, had been hastily arranged a month earlier. Meanwhile, a world war was breaking out, and photographic dyes from Germany were under embargo. Eastman wrote:

I showed the samples yesterday [24 September 1914] to Mr. Herdle, Managing Director of the Memorial Art Gallery, and arranged with him to give an exhibition November 1.... We only have enough of the red dye to last three or four more days and may be held up on that account. In the meantime we have about twenty specimens of very great beauty.... Mr. Herdle was very enthusiastic and said he believed that when people became accustomed to these pictures they would not have black and white. He said it seemed to him the same as with oil paintings, that after a man had bought one good one he would not be satisfied with poor ones.

A "few grammes of the Komplementar Rot D" dye were smuggled through Sweden and soon thirty-two Kodachrome portraits, mostly of women and children bearing the familiar names of Sibley, Rhees, Adler, Lindsay, Dryden, and so on, were up on the Gallery walls. A special private viewing for a select nineteen Kodak men and their families on Saturday afternoon was followed by the public opening on Sunday when 2,800 people crowded into the minuscule Gallery to see eight-by-ten glass positives mounted in shadow boxes, and illuminated from behind. In the auditorium, C. E. Kenneth Mees, head of Eastman Kodak's new Research Laboratory, lectured on "this new two-color process, placed before the public for the first time." Herdle called the process "the latest achievement in one of the most important practical arts, an art, the artistic possibilities of which are daily gaining wider recognition."

Downstairs in the Print Room, 188 black-and-white photographs of Italian architecture, sculpture, and paintings taken some years earlier by James G. Averell were shown.

Eastman had advised how to hang the Kodachrome show: "When these pictures are set up for exhibition see that they have plenty of separation and that they are sorted as to color so as not to detract from one another."

"Do not call them colored photographs," Eastman admonished. "They are quite a different thing—*color* photographs." The whole show, he told Herdle, was "splendid." In appreciation, Eastman gave the Gallery its first purchase fund which Herdle used to buy ***Coast of Cornwall near St. Ives*** from the 1915 "Exhibition of Paintings by Paul Dougherty."

G. Hamner Croughton, art critic, examined the Kodachromes "minutely with a small magnifying glass held in the eye as a watchmaker does" and wrote about their "beauty, correctness of color, tone values, absolute lack of grain... and the curious stereoscopic effect attained. For all the world it looked as if we were gazing directly and closely into the brilliantly lit faces of the subjects." After the Rochester exhibition a selection of fifteen Kodachromes was shown at the Royal Photographic Society, London. Others went to the Panama Pacific Exposition in San Francisco, to a smaller exposition in San Diego, and to the New York State Photographers Convention, held in Rochester in 1915. The color process, good for portraits but poor for landscapes, and so complex only a professional could manipulate it, was rarely used thereafter.

Later, at a Museum Directors Association meeting, Herdle was roundly criticized for exhibiting a strictly commercial process. He countered by arguing that photography could be as interpretive, expressive, and creative a process as any other medium. The assessment stands: the 200 or so Kodachrome portraits of Eastman's family, friends, and business colleagues, mostly made by the Rochester photographer J. E. Mock and now at the International Museum of Photography at George Eastman House, are remarkable for their artistic merit even though technically the fledgling two-color process did not reproduce color as well as three-color photography does.

The Kodachrome show warmed Eastman's acquaintance with Herdle to the point that he dropped the director little notes on artistic matters from time to time. Eastman's two chief hostesses for his many social affairs—Josephine Haskins Dickman of London, Boston, and New York, and Mary Durand Mulligan of Rochester—both made early gifts of paintings to the Gallery. Once Eastman sent Herdle a copy of Alfred Stieglitz's ***Camera Notes*** that contained a letter of complaint about the kind of art Stieglitz was showing in his Gallery 291. Circled for Herdle's attention, the letter said in part: "So many strange things have occurred in art.... It is the tearing down of the old faith... without substituting anything in its place.... The utter disregard of form, or beauty as I understand it, the stupidity in the arrangement of composition lines, are all things my art notions rebel at." Eastman noted that this description "contains such a good estimate of the freak artists of the Cubist stripe that I thought it would appeal to you."

For years after 1915 most Rochesterians would agree with this view of modern art held by the city's largest

3

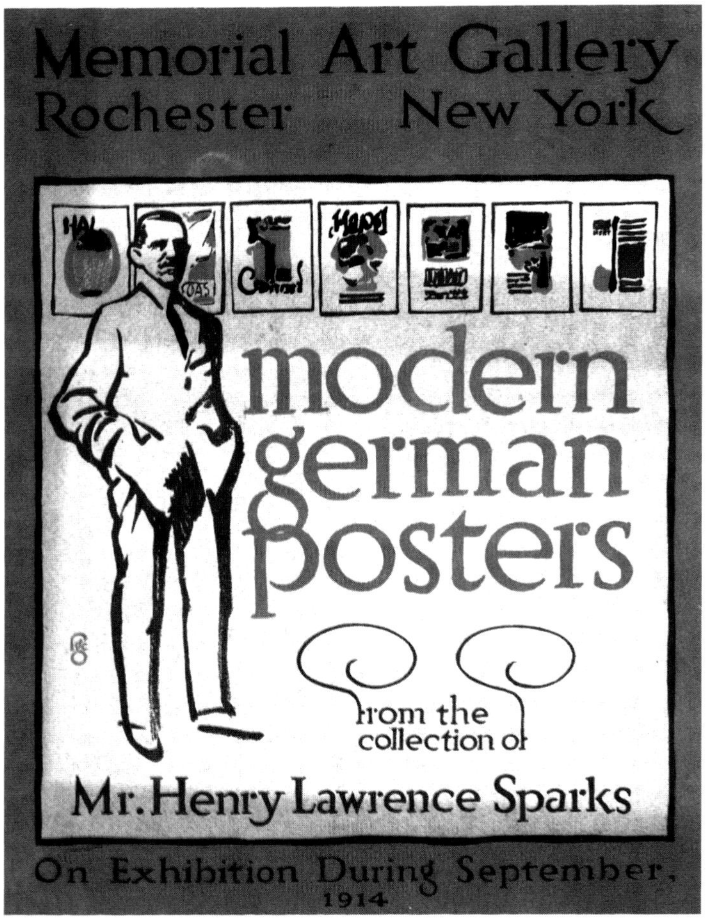

3 *An exhibition of German posters was coincidentally on display when World War I began.*

4 *The Gallery's entrance corridor, ca. 1920s.*

employer; indeed as late as 1944 the same howls of protest were heard concerning a cubist painting that won the Jurors Award in the Finger Lakes Exhibition. Herdle, who had a different assessment of "the freak artists of the Cubist stripe," wisely kept his own counsel.

More controversy came Herdle's way that second season when an exhibition of contemporary European advertising posters was mounted (among them works by Toulouse-Lautrec). What, purists wondered this time, was advertising material doing in the hallowed halls? "Herdle responded," board minutes record, "by reminding his critics that Rochester is a world center of color lithography," and therefore the exhibition "is of great local benefit."

The viewing public and art critics were just recovering from this assault to their tastes and complacency when Herdle imported some works of the modernist stripe (some of them cubist) featuring American artists Charles Sheeler, Charles Demuth, Man Ray, Walt Kuhn, William Glackens, and Arthur B. Davies. A lone voice of support for these works came in an editorial in the ***Post Express*** by Ernest Willard, husband of Mrs. Watson's niece, who pleaded with people to "look at them freshly, and try to put yourselves in the same mood as the artists."

In September of 1915 Herdle mounted another exhibition from local sources—this time of oriental carpets. Carpets were probably the most collected art form in the city, particularly among those families of German descent living along East Avenue from whom most of the rugs were borrowed. Thus the director continued to broaden the field of what could be exhibited beyond that of the fashionable "gazing galleries" of the time.

(Gazing galleries were a period concept: one gazed at inspirational or narrative paintings and came away better for the experience. The fact that the Gallery was called a "gallery" rather than a "museum" indicates that Mrs. Watson was initially somewhat influenced by the concept. Her willingness to have the Gallery's horizons broadened, however, indicates her own discernment.)

Of the 134 Persian, Caucasian, Turkoman, and Turkish carpets, prayer rugs, and mats on display, twenty-one were lent by Mrs. William Ellwanger, whose husband wrote the catalog. The 1915 exhibition was the first of three on carpets: a second one was held in 1925 and a third in 1975 when some of the same carpets returned yet again. Meanwhile, since 1916 when the first donations were made, the Gallery had garnered a small but impressive collection of its own; in 1978 its collection of forty-nine rugs was appraised "in excess

4

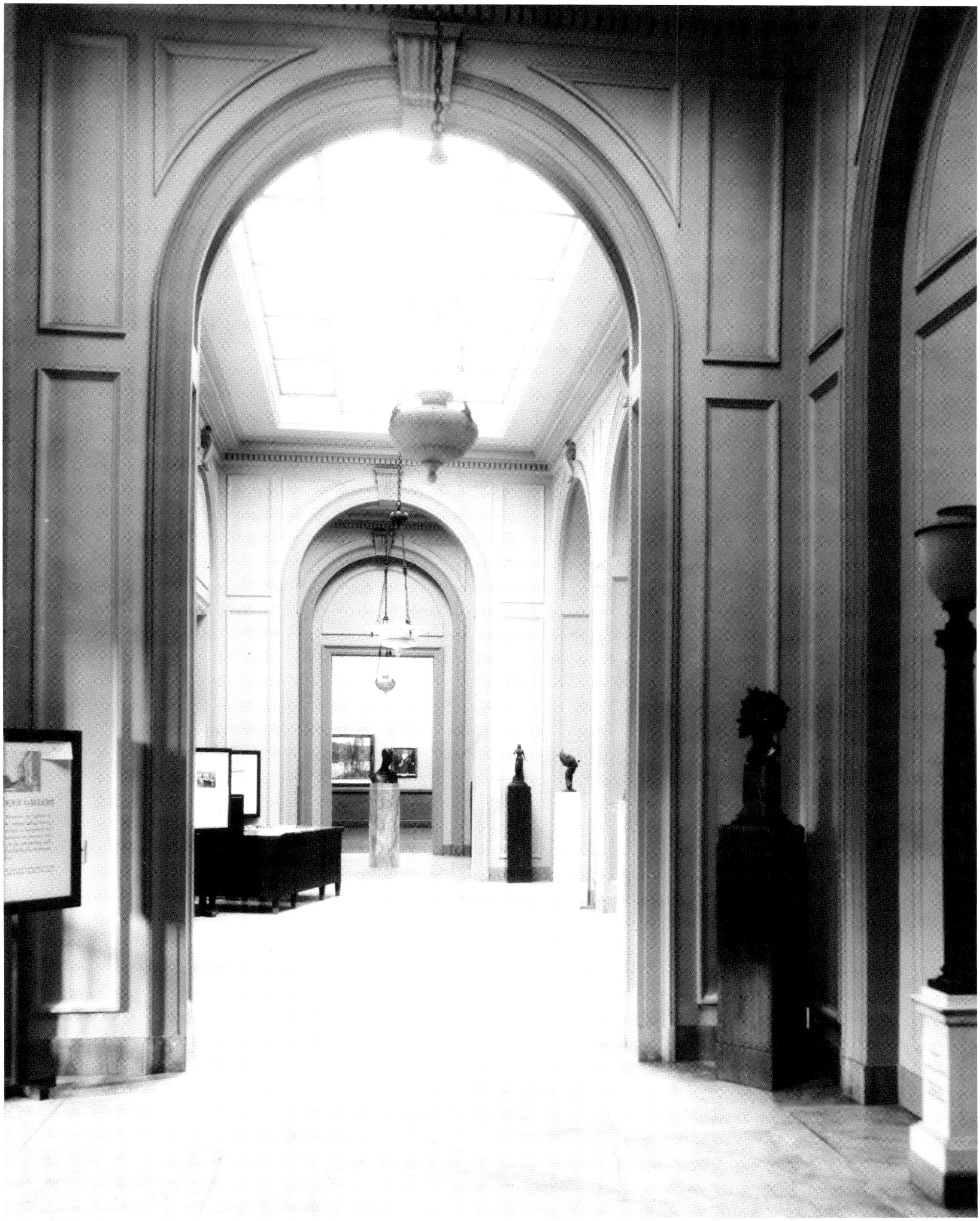

of $100,000" and called "certainly the finest collection of Oriental rugs in this area" by the appraiser.

Other exhibitions of the George Herdle era—some typical of their time, some progressive for their era—included: the romantic travelogue paintings of India by Colin Campbell Cooper and his Rochester-born wife, Emma Lampert Cooper; local architectural drawings; five American women artists; and the sculpture of Gertrude Vanderbilt Whitney. Herdle sought out the paintings of the American giants of his generation—Childe Hassam, Arthur G. Dove, and Robert Henri—as well as period furniture from the Hayden Company; and the potpourri summer exhibition of 1919 that featured everyone from Renoir to Frank von der Lancken.

Among the Henri portraits was one of Emma Goldman, the well-known (some said notorious) anarchist, pacifist, and crusader for sweat shop reforms—who was also the aunt of David Hochstein, Emily Watson's protégé.

New art forms were pondered. In 1917 a committee formed to investigate the introduction of motion picture shows in art galleries. Cleveland and Toledo museums had movie equipment, remarked its chairman, Claude Bragdon. "Lunch is served while victrolas play," he reported, marking perhaps the first yearning for a Gallery restaurant. The investigations were soon "indefinitely tabled," however.

People were beginning to hear about the pioneering art education at the Gallery. In 1920 Herdle was invited to speak to a New York State teacher's convention on "The Educational Work of an Inland-City Museum."

During most of the Herdle years, the Gallery was open from 10 o'clock to 4:30 Tuesday through Saturday in winter and 10 to 5 in summer, as well as 1:30 to 4 on Sundays. It was closed Mondays. Admission was free on Sundays and twenty-five cents for nonmembers the rest of the week. Later, Wednesday became a free day to accommodate school groups. Attendance from the Inaugural Exhibition of October 1913 to the first annual meeting in April 1914 was recorded as 39,218, of which 32,694 came on free days. Herdle's tenure saw attendance hover at about 40,000 a year, except during the 1918-1919 season when it broke 50,000, thanks to the Luxembourg Exhibition. About ten exhibitions were held each year.

The Gallery's precarious financial situation was explained succinctly by Rhees when he wrote to prospective members:

The maintenance of such an art gallery is costly. The city of Buffalo appropriates $25,000 a year to the Albright Art Gallery. Syracuse gives $10,000 a year to its Museum of Fine Arts. We have to rely on the readiness of public spirited citizens to make our Gallery fully useful to the Community.

For the Memorial Art Gallery, membership support always assumed a critical function. In 1913 there were five classes of membership. Eighteen individuals opted to become Supporting Members at $250, forty-eight Sustaining Members at $100 to $250, seventy Contributing Members at $25 to $100, ninety-seven Annual Members at $10 to $25, and forty-one Associates (artists, school teachers, architects, and craftsmen actively practicing their professions) for $5. The number of original memberships—276 including the two "honoraries": John Gade, architect, and William Ordway Partridge, sculptor of *Memory*—was not large, but the degree of personal commitment in a community with the population of 230,000 was.

In 1938 Gertrude Herdle (by then she was Mrs. Moore, having married in 1932) compared the original names of members to the current list and found "a most remarkable record of sustained interest."

Looking back at the membership rolls from her vantage point of 1988, Gertrude said, "When you have only that number of members, you can be much more certain of continuing re-enrollment. These are people with convictions, personal connections. It's an unfair comparison, but when you expand into the highways to get your members in, you get much less dedicated people. Once we got much beyond 600 members [with the 1926 expansion] the turnover rate increased dramatically."

That the turnover was minute in early years can be gleaned from the 1919 Annual Report: "Membership has lost four by death and there have been two declinations. On the other hand, eight new members joined the Gallery within the past year."

The outbreak of World War I brought changes to the Gallery. In September 1914, three months after the assassination of Archduke Francis Ferdinand and one month after Germany declared war on Russia and France, invaded Belgium, and drew Great Britain into the war, the Memorial Art Gallery opened an exhibition of "Modern German Posters." It was too early for partisan reactions to the war in far-off Europe and the exhibit of handsome graphics was allowed to stand or fall on its artistic merits. Herdle wrote the introduction to the catalog of the poster show before war broke out and anticipated reactions of a different kind by noting: "It may be that the criticism will be made that too many of the German posters are not sufficiently serious but have been conceived and executed in too light and flippant a spirit."

After the United States declared war on Germany in 1917, many Rochester stores and industries closed Mondays to conserve heat and light. Herdle was able to convince the civic authorities and the Gallery board that it was in the public interest for the Gallery to remain open on "workless and heatless" Mondays, giving people a place to go, not only to keep warm, but also to be entertained and perhaps enlightened. Herdle welcomed the visitors with talks about art.

Exhibitions took on a patriotic aura. "War Work in Lithography" brought one artist, Joseph Pennell, to the Gallery to lecture on "The Wonder of Warwork." While in Rochester, Pennell joined local artists and Colin Campbell Cooper in depicting the Main Street Bridge with its crowded shops obscuring the river in as picturesque a manner as the Ponte Vecchio in Florence.

As a result of the war and the Panama-Pacific International Exposition of 1915, two outstanding international exhibitions were scheduled which ordinarily would have gone only to much larger museums. The Persian Exhibition during the summer of 1917 encapsulated an extraordinary selection of Persian glass, miniatures, carvings, textiles, embroideries, rugs, potteries, and illuminated manuscripts from the "buried cities of Persia," dating from the tenth to the eighteenth centuries. The relatively low cost of insurance and transportation in those days made bringing these treasures to Rochester feasible.

Organized by the French government from the collections of the Luxembourg Museum, the Luxembourg Exhibition, also from the Panama-Pacific Exposition, was sitting in crates in New York City, ready go back to France. (The Luxembourg Museum is the Louvre's waiting room: a French artist must have been dead for ten years before his work can hang in the Louvre.) Then suddenly French authorities decided to circulate the works to American museums rather than jeopardize them by a trans-Atlantic trip through German-infested waters. The directors of the Brooklyn Museum and the Art Institute of Chicago, both friends of Herdle, were charged with circulating the paintings. The paintings were then loaded onto trucks in Brooklyn, all ready to go again, when the United States government placed an embargo on nonessential domestic shipments over a certain weight. Herdle suggested the paintings could be shipped unframed, but French authorities declined and the works were unloaded. It was 1919 before the embargo was lifted and the paintings arrived in Rochester.

They were worth the wait. Seven Cézannes, mostly from the artist's late *L'Estaque* series, were included, along with paintings by Degas, Delacroix, Gauguin, Pissarro, Boudin, Fantin-Latour, Sisley, and Toulouse-Lautrec. These along with Monet's *Rouen Cathedral* series and Manet's large balcony scene made it "the most impressive exhibition of masterpieces ever to come to the Memorial Art Gallery," Herdle wrote. Some damage was sustained to a painting by Puvis de Chavannes, and there was pressure, to which Herdle did not yield, to take down, or cover up, a painting of a nude. Despite these minor altercations, Herdle's assessment holds today. Works that today would travel, if at all, to only the largest museums were installed in what is now called the Renaissance Room and the smaller galleries east and west of it.

The Luxembourg Exhibition was a milestone in educational as well as aesthetic terms. By 1916 schoolchildren were coming to the Gallery in fairly large numbers. Isabel Herdle remembers being brought with her class at No. 15 School and hearing her father, garbed in Prince Albert coat, hold forth on the current exhibition.

But behind the scenes, heated discussions brewed regarding the place of those noisy little creatures in the hushed halls of art. Some board members argued that weekdays should be reserved for adult members. Others, led by Mrs. Watson, were eager that students come at any time. "There are none too small or too young," she maintained. "These are the members of tomorrow." Herdle viewed the whole matter as dramatizing conflicting views of just what a museum is *for*: the classic dilemma of the private quality of the museum experience versus the mandates of education and social action. He saw an opportunity with the Luxembourg Exhibition that could be seized only if a large attendance was guaranteed. With Mrs. Watson's support, he decided to take a stand. Three school groups scheduled daily could secure that attendance through what Herdle called "the first organized effort to bring children of the higher grades to the Gallery." Assisting the director in handling the increased crowds, Elizabeth Denio and Frank von der Lancken became perhaps the first "docents" in Gallery history.

From then on, children were welcome at all times, and special "members only" days disappeared.

One artist who saw the horror as well as the patriotism of war lent his paintings for an exhibition in December 1919. George Bellows, former newspaper artist, had painted a war series and two of these paintings, *The Murder of Edith Cavell*, now in the Springfield Museum, and *The Return of the Useless*, a graphic portrayal of maimed, deranged, and dispossessed persons transported in animal box cars, elicited a stormy protest. In letters to the Gallery board, to the university trustees, and to Rhees personally, James G. Cutler (who had just come on the Gallery board following the death of Charles Mulford Robinson) demanded that either the two pictures be removed or Herdle be asked to resign. Rhees responded by asking Herdle for an assessment of Bellows's artistic significance.

"He's one of the foremost artists of his generation," said Herdle. Rhees then assured Herdle that the university would stand behind the director's decision to keep the paintings on display, thus establishing the director's authority in matters of artistic decision.

A 1920 exhibition of British war paintings featuring the works of Augustus John, Muirhead Bone, and John Nash was expected to draw crowds similar to those of the Luxembourg Exhibition. "This was the first attempt," the catalog stated, "of British artists working in unison to put on the record some aspects and activities called forth by the Great War and the Ideals by which those activities are inspired." Apparently people had had enough of wars and their "ideals." Attendance was poor.

As it turned out, the most important exhibition of 1920 was "The Evolution of Printing," organized locally by Elmer Adler—clothier, aesthete, specialist in the history of fine printing, and, upon the death of Guernsey Mitchell in 1920, a Gallery board member. Adler drew from his own collection and other local sources. Beginning with Egyptian hieroglyphics, Babylonian clay tablets, ancient Jewish phylacteries, Coptic manuscripts, Papal Bulls, breviaries, Hebrew parchments, and Koran manuscripts, the exhibition moved into incunabula (books printed before 1500), sixteenth century printing ("the golden age"), and on to the decline of fine printing in the seventeenth and eighteenth centuries. The final section featured early American printing, nineteenth century machine printing, and "Early Rochester in Print." The catalog was written by John Rothwell Slater, professor of English at the university; for decades it continued to be requested by sister museums.

Adler performed other invaluable services. Not only did he print catalogs of the highest quality, he saved every catalog, invitation, and annual report, binding them together in volumes that today form the most complete record of those early days in the Gallery's possession.

"**G**eorge Leonard Herdle died yesterday," the ***Post Express*** reported on 30 September 1922, "after two years of progressive weakness and suffering sustained through the fatal disease he had borne for five years. He was the exemplification of what a man may do toward shaping his own career and cutting a very deep niche for himself.... From his schoolboy days until the hour he was struck down, he was a student of art.... In his early years he spent his evenings drawing. His only normal training was during the two years' stay in France and Holland.... As a painter he exhibited at the National Academy of Design and at the Corcoran Gallery.

"He led in the development of a high artistic consciousness in this city and out of his efforts the Memorial Art Gallery grew," Herdle's friend and Alembic Club colleague Ernest Willard wrote. "He installed loan exhibitions of selected local, privately owned artworks augmented by pieces from New York galleries.

"For 20 years he was president of the Rochester Art Club and managed the art collections of the Rochester Exposition at Exposition Park. He started the Homelands Exhibitions and installed exhibitions in the Chamber of Commerce. He made the Gallery popular not only with art connoisseurs and artists but with the general public and the city's children through his numerous newspaper articles and popular Gallery talks....

"He made people see that art is always in the making."

At the Gallery a memorial exhibition of the paintings of George Herdle was mounted.

5

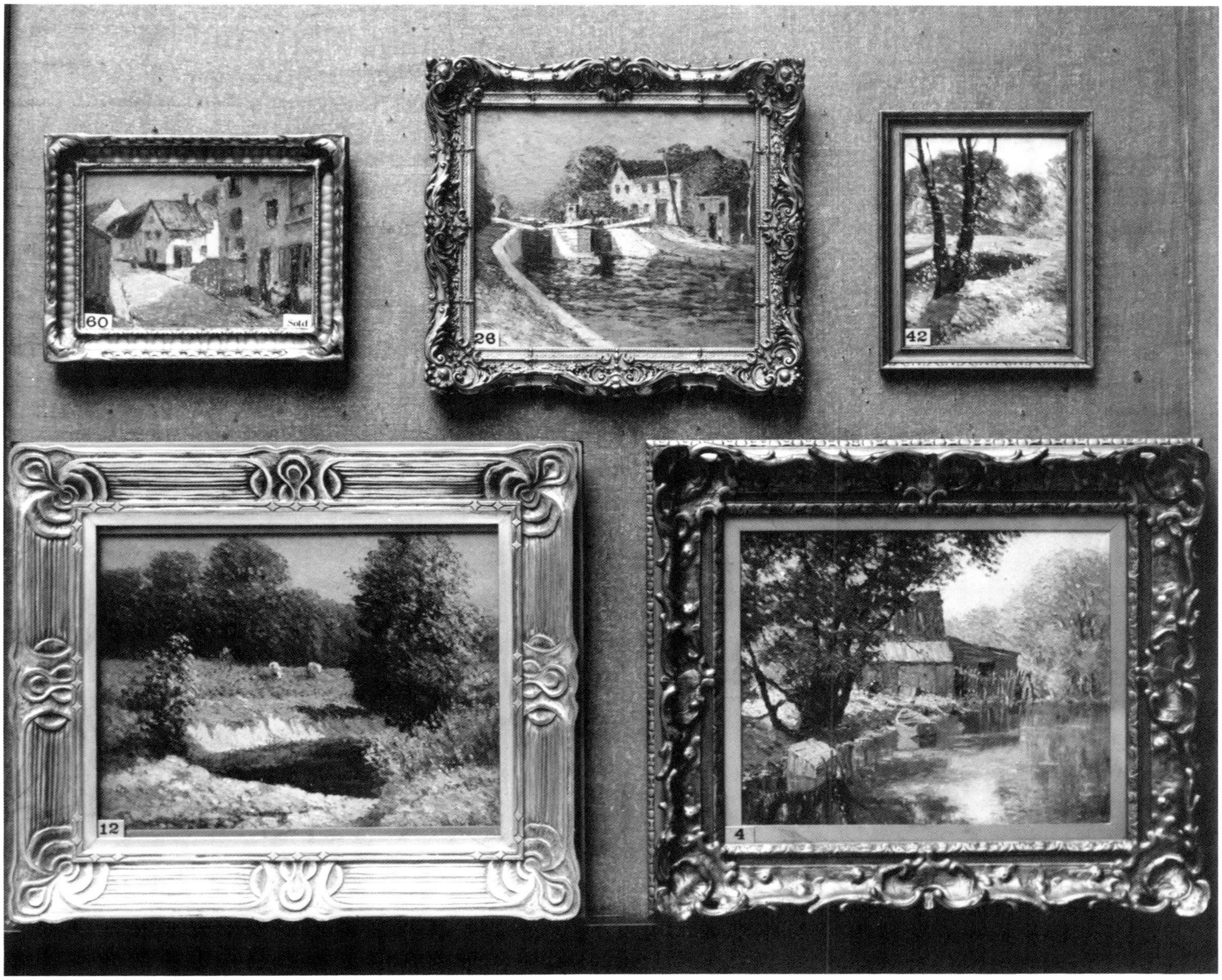

5 *Memorial exhibition of the paintings of George L. Herdle, 1922. Photograph courtesy of the Herdle family.*

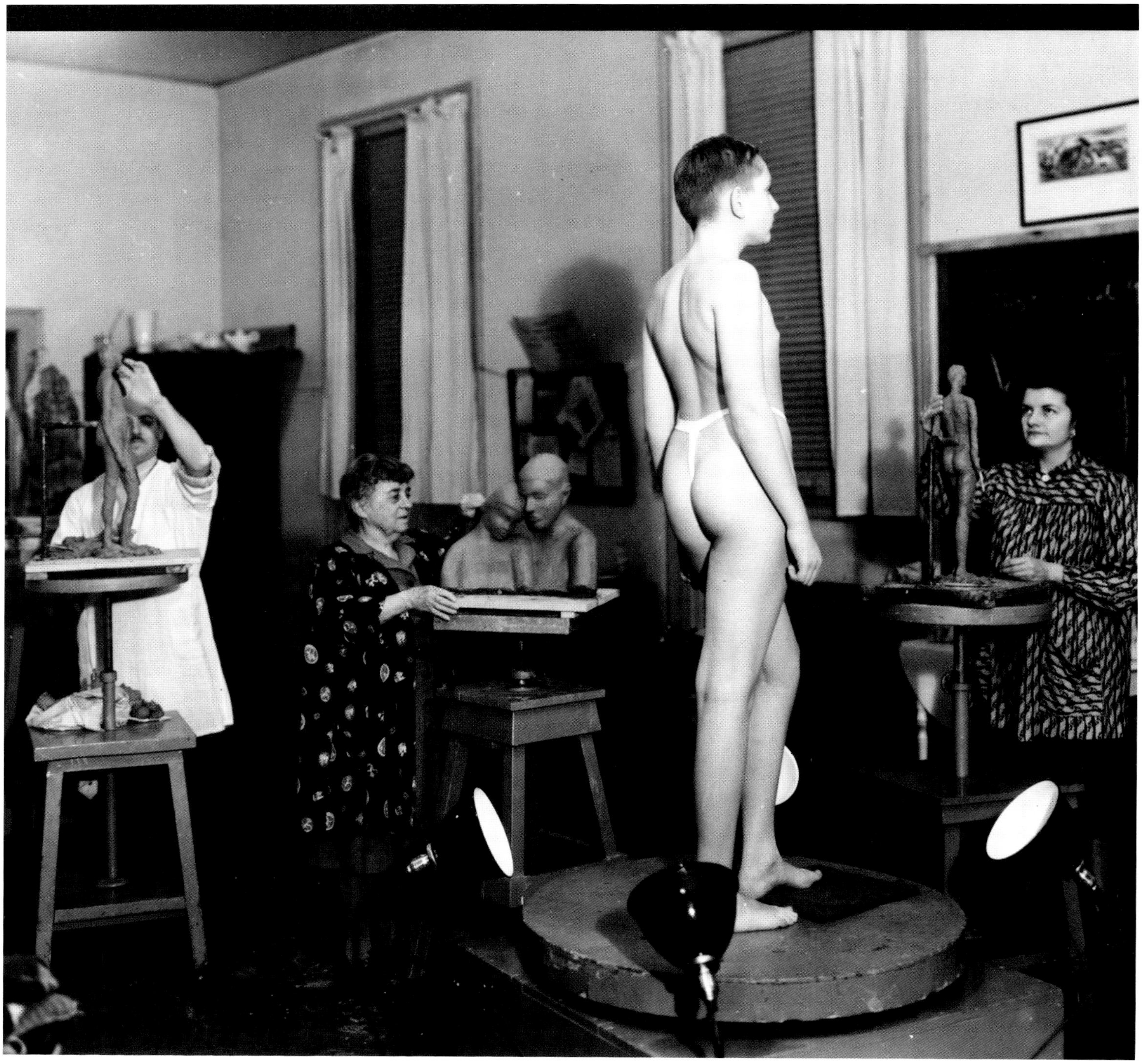

3

The primitive stage of painting is...drawing with a disregard for color. In the second stage color, the scientific analysis of light, is added. The third stage, expressionism, is when the artist studies his own subjective sensations to objects and expresses them as he pleases....This last stage began about 1874 when photography attained perfection in the art of exact scientific representation....

It then became incumbent upon the artist to present rather than represent, hence came the philosophical element in modern art which produced so many isms. These [are often ridiculed, but should be treated with a sympathetic attempt to understand. They] are experiments in one of the most spectacular ages since the cave man drawings....

Gertrude Herdle | From a talk in the 1920s

Creative Workshop Sculpture class, William Ehrich, instructor, 1942.

In 1922 Gertrude Herdle was named acting director to succeed her father. She was twenty-five years old. A few months later, the position was made permanent, and she held the directorship of the Gallery for the next forty years. Somewhat uncomfortable with her youthful appearance, when it came time for her official portrait photograph, she purchased a pair of pince-nez Oxford glasses on a black velvet ribbon to make herself look older.

When elected to the American Association of Museum Directors in 1923, she was that august body's youngest member. Along with Cornelia Sage, director of the Albright Art Gallery, and Juliana Force, director of the Whitney Museum of American Art, she was one of three women directors in the country.

Her four years of on-the-job training as education assistant to her father, a training she lived day and night at the Gallery and at home, had been supplemented by sessions with directors and curators of art museums in Toledo, Cleveland, and Chicago. She spent her vacations working under the tutelage of George W. Stevens, Toledo's director, making special trips at other times for typical events. Informally (since there were no formal programs) she was introduced to department after department—receiving hands-on experience in accessioning, recording, education, and management. For many years the Gallery's systems would be based on Toledo's. Although Gertrude felt some lack of formal schooling in museum studies, few directors of her era had such post graduate training. Of those who did, most went abroad to spend a year's apprenticeship in the various departments at the Victoria and Albert or Kaiser Friedrich museums. In 1921 Gertrude did take a three-month trip to Europe to visit and study galleries in France and Italy.

Gertrude's great interest was programs for school-age children, which she instituted almost immediately after joining the staff in 1918.

Like her father before her, Gertrude at first tripled as director, head of education, and publicity person. Saturday morning story hours, begun earlier when she was her father's assistant, were bringing increasing numbers of children and their mothers to the Gallery. When the hour for interpretation of a work of art through a beguiling story was over, no one wanted to leave. Soon the teacher (Gertrude) was handing out paper and crayons so that children and adults could incorporate a studio-art experience. "Through the doing of art," she says now, "the Gallery's three most important roles—collecting, publishing, and giving understanding of art—were interpreted." From these modest beginnings came the whole studio art program, the Creative

1

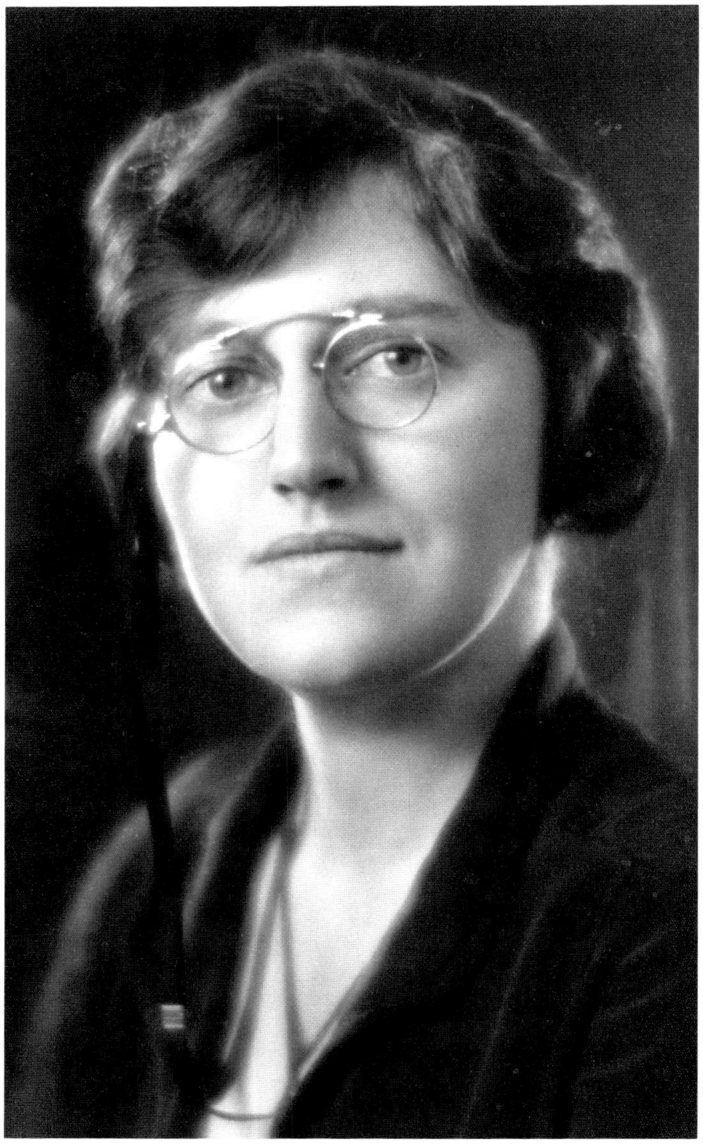

1 *Gertrude Herdle, the new director, 1922. Photograph courtesy of the Herdle family.*

Workshop. "It all came about so informally," she recalls, "it probably isn't even in Gallery records."

"Picture Story Hours they are called," she wrote in 1928, after a Children's Museum had been added in the ground floor of the Gallery for such activities, "but they may be moving pictures, stories illustrated by lantern slides, drawing contests, or puppet plays, after which the children are taught to make puppets for themselves. As often as possible the Story Hour is applied to a current exhibition on the main floor."

The crowds of little people grew so large that a second storyteller, Fern Wall, was added. "A Little Woodcarver's Christmas," "Pilgrimages in Early England," "The Festival of Roses" (from a French tapestry), and "Jason and the Golden Fleece" were some of the topics of the story hour, scheduled for three in the afternoon and illustrated with lantern slides. For "The Princess Is a Mummy: The Three Oldest Things in Egypt," the storyteller impersonated an Egyptian princess and borrowed 4,500-year-old mummy wrappings from the Rochester Theological Seminary, a Baptist seminary near the Gallery.

Lecturers and loan materials such as reproductions and lantern slides began to go out to elementary and junior high schools throughout the city.

The proximity of East High School "offers a constant opportunity for special cooperation," noted *The Bulletin*. This bimonthly magazine, which was both scholarly and chatty, and liberally illustrated besides, was first published by the Gallery in October of 1928.

The class with the highest standing at Washington Junior High School was "offered the privilege of visiting the art gallery in reward for its work." The B. Forman Co. provided the bus. When "children from a distant school cannot afford their own car fare, an East Avenue bus is sent for them and delivers them to the Gallery," said the magazine. At first, friends of the Gallery contributed the bus fare. Later the Joseph Simon Fund paid for this service.

Sixty children from the School for Crippled Children, as many more from the Open Air School and Hillside Home, and several hundred from grammar and junior high schools came during a week of extension activities. Gallery talks with slides "visualized the study of history and geography," *The Bulletin* said.

Adults were drawn to the Gallery not only to see the current exhibition but by a variety of programs: Thursday evening lectures, informal talks on Sundays, the Archeological Society, which had met at the Gallery since 1914, or special lectures by Claude Bragdon and Frank Lloyd Wright. Robert MacLean of the University of Rochester classics department spoke on the discovery of the Tomb of King Tutankhamen as that drama unfolded.

The Gallery staff did not shy away from the controversial. Reviewer Thurston V. Darling called the show of Aubrey Beardsley drawings in December 1924 "just over the borderline of balance... good, clean dirt and pregnant with a keen satire." An art museum was "no place for censorship," Darling declared, "unless it eliminates poorly done work. It should not extend to subject matter. It should be uninterested in the morality of pictures."

The public's attitude toward the Gallery as it moved into its second decade was favorable. Typical was the response of *The Reflector*, house organ for Bausch and Lomb:

The Gallery, set on its formal terraces among the spacious greens on the university campus, enshrines the heart of artistic Rochester. From the children who flood it for the free picture story hours to the groups of employees from the neighboring industries who wander in for a half hour of peace and beauty at noontime, range all ages and kinds of art lovers.... In fact, many are not art lovers at all—until their third or fourth visits.

In a talk before the Women's City Club on 8 March 1925, Gertrude compared Gallery visitors to the creatures of Aesop's Fables.

The mollusk enters wearing its bones on the outside, considering itself apart from the world. It makes up its mind and retires behind its bones: "I know nothing about art but I know what I like."

The tortoise, a steadier class trudging close to the ground, is unable to lift its head and find beauty. The tortoise is always looking for story interest and constantly calling pictures "sweet, adorable, cunning."

The hare leaps along, full of ecstatic responses, dealing in superlatives, "loving" everything on Gallery walls.

The clam maintains a mud line below which it never sinks and above which it never rises. "I have never seen a purple cow and I never mean to see one," says the clam.

But the frog is the aristocrat of Gallery-goers, possessor of a backbone of knowledge, sensitivity and imagination. His adaptability makes him at home on land or water, able to leap through the air in keeping up with the rapid strides of art.

It is not the Gallery's purpose to teach art criticism but to make people critics, *making them appreciate that tolerance is the state of mind in which to approach an exhibition. Nor should an art museum be a sepulchre vault for the hoarding of art treasures of a by-gone day... but should take an active part in the community life of the present, furnishing education in art and inspiration for present-day artists.*

On 15 June 1925 at the university graduation exercises, Gertrude R. Herdle received "an unusual honor," the *Rochester Herald* reported, for her "expansion of activities of the Gallery, the bringing of widely-sought exhibitions to this city and tremendous increases in attendance."

"It is with peculiar pleasure," Rush Rhees said as he bestowed the mantle on the first woman so honored by the university, "that we seize the opportunity today to give public expression to our appreciation of the work you have done... taking and carrying on to usefulness an appreciation of the fine arts begun by your honourable father.... For your intelligence, your sympathetic understanding, the intelligent endeavors to widen the educational services of the Gallery, I am pleased to confer upon you the honorary degree of master of arts."

Almost from the beginning, Gallery periodicals have served an important function for the museum. *The Bulletin* was discontinued in 1933, a victim of the Great Depression, and the scholarly periodical *Porticus* was started in 1978. *Gallery Notes*, begun in 1929 as a series of short, breezy articles of topical interest contained within *The Bulletin*, achieved a life of its own in 1935 as a monthly (except during World War II when it had to be published every two months). *Gallery Notes* has undergone many changes from magazine to newspaper format and back again to a slick-paper format not unlike that of the 1928 *Bulletin*. It continues today as *the* vital line of communications from Gallery to members (and once again is published every other month).

As for lectures, "Sundays at Four," begun in the 1920s, has been reincarnated as "Tuesdays at 5:30" in the 1980s. The predominant makeup of the audience may have shifted from families to young, urban, professional singles, but the hunger for understanding of specific works in the Gallery collection, many the same now as then, has not changed.

The titles of lectures in the 1920s sound surprisingly current: "How do you look at a painting? A sculpture? Judge architecture?" So too does the exhibition in April 1922 of seventy-seven women artists, members of the National Association of Women Painters and Sculptors.

Membership income was expected to support acquisitions, exhibitions, heat and light, and so forth. It was soon evident that the permanent collection would have to wait in favor of changing exhibitions that took the pulse of art around the country.

Even so, by 1926 the collection (not including the study collection) numbered 318 items: 126 paintings, 46 prints, 26 sculptures, and 139 objects classified as minor arts. "Minor arts," a now-discredited term, included tapestries, Carthaginian antiquities, Egyptian glass, Indian baskets, lace, and peasant embroideries. Seventy-one donors provided this nucleus. During its first thirteen years, the Gallery had held 125 special exhibitions.

Significant membership expansion came in 1926. With the goal of increasing membership from 489 to 1,750, 200 volunteers worked a five-day campaign. Each day at noon they reported in. The Women's Division, headed by Helen Ellwanger, reported the greatest increase, with Mrs. Stuart Symington's team second. Campaign chairman William Drescher spearheaded a drive for corporate members—"virgin territory in those days," Gertrude says. There was also an English Division and an Italian Division as workers zeroed in on each area of the city. The largest single gift, $10,000, came from Mrs. Granger A. Hollister, earmarked for the art library.

The director was now adding staff and delegating functions she previously initiated and performed herself. In 1923 she hired a secretary. Longevity being a hallmark of Gallery employment, Jessie A. Vaughn retired in 1954 "after 31 years of devoted service," and Janet Otis took her place as secretary to the directors (Gertrude and Isabel) and then archivist until 1983. Following the addition of the Fountain Court in 1926, the Gallery staff numbered fifteen.

Mabel Trathen Wright, director of museum education and publicity secretary, became one of the first commentators on art to take to the airwaves in the 1920s through the new medium of radio. Newspapers published her script so listeners could follow along. Keeping up with the march of technical progress, in the 1950s the Gallery staff conducted a weekly television program called "Art in Your Life." Little lectures by a harried and overworked staff ("I remember finishing the text of mine in a taxicab on the way to he station, already five minutes late," says Gertrude) were followed by a segment on "Hands at Work," featuring artists working in various media.

Blanca Will (1881-1977), a Smith College and Mechanics Institute graduate who had traveled extensively and taught at her Maine studio, became the director of art instruction in the 1920s and an instructor of sculpture in the Creative Workshop. She won prizes for her sculpture including the coveted Lillian Fairchild Award in 1930. Will was a wonderful teacher, particularly of students in their early

2

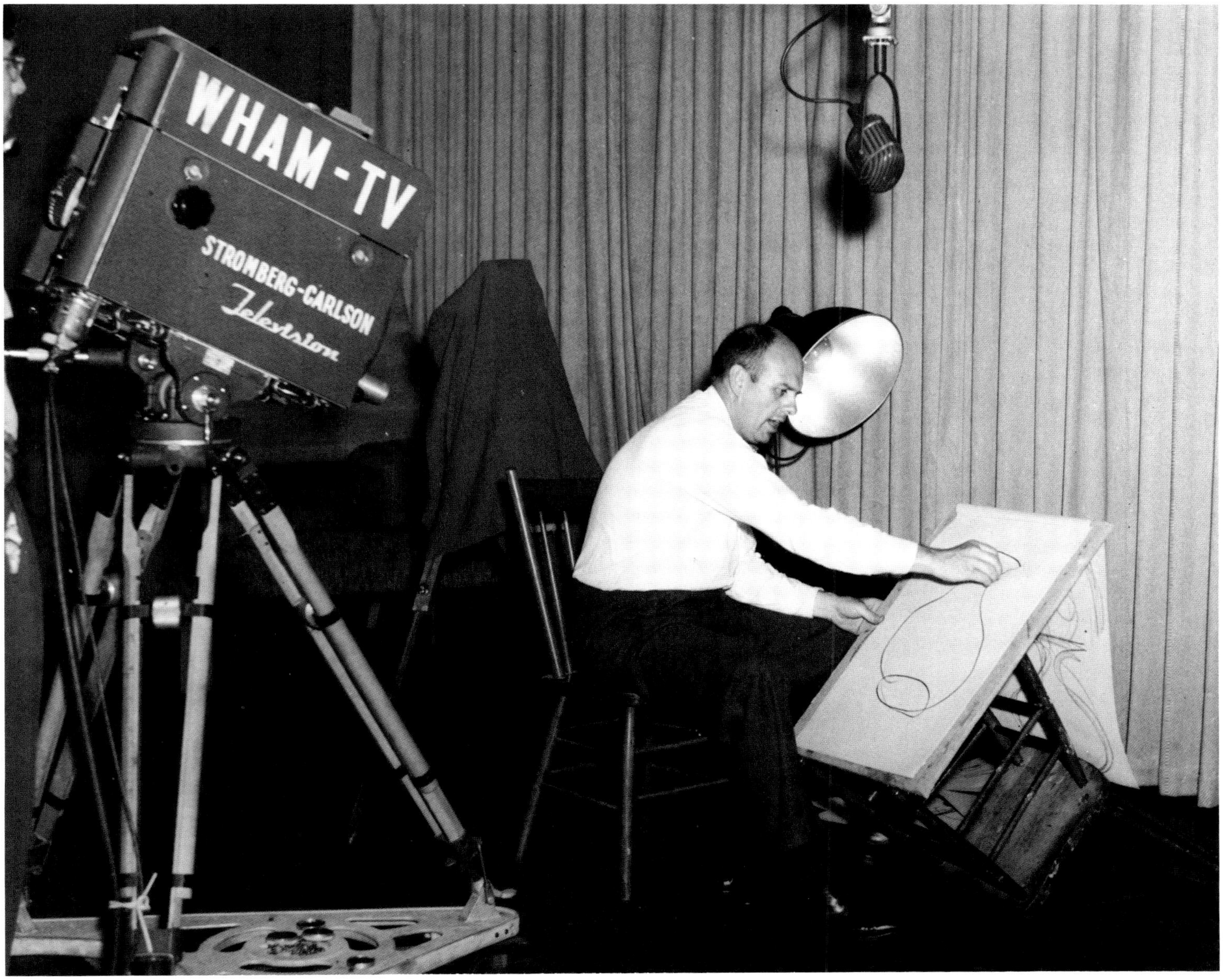

2 *John Menihan, Creative Workshop instructor, sketches on television.*

teens for whom she conceived a highly successful and long-lived art fellowship.

In October 1928 Sally Kitchen, a painter with a lively personality, was engaged for a special education project in connection with Wednesday Children's Museum Hours, Saturday Afternoon Picture-Story Hours, and Sunday Sketching Hours. This expansion was made possible by two gifts—one from Gertrude's university class of 1918 which devoted its Tenth Year Gift to "this significant effort in public art education."

"**I** shall have to have a luncheon for you so that people will know I approve of the match," said Emily Sibley Watson when informed in 1932 of Gertrude's intention of becoming Mrs. Moore. The wedding took place, again at Mrs. Watson's behest, in the Fountain Court. It was just in time: two Miss Herdles would have been too confusing and a second one was about to appear on the Gallery scene.

That year Isabel C. Herdle joined the staff, and a new era of professionalism came on board with her. A graduate of the University of Rochester (Phi Beta Kappa in history, art history as a major still not being available), Isabel represented the more formal preparation available a decade after her sister's schooling: the fellowship from Harvard, graduate work at the Fogg Museum, the University of London, the Technical High School in Stockholm, and a stint at the de Young Museum in San Francisco. In all innocence she had enrolled in a master's program at the Fogg Museum having previously taken only two art courses: a general survey and medieval art. "No wonder I had to study until three in the morning," she says now. "I didn't know what they were talking about."

For forty years Isabel served first as assistant director, (1932-1956), then as associate director, (1956-1962) in charge of exhibitions, programs, and collections, and finally as assistant director for curatorial services (1962-1972). As chief curator too, her wonderful exhibition-display abilities enriched the Gallery. With a dedication rare except in religious circles, the partnership of the Herdle sisters has continued to benefit the Gallery long beyond the official retirement dates of both.

When Gertrude took a six-month leave in 1935, Isabel carried on for them both, lecturing on "Medieval Roads for the Modern Traveler" and "Great Gothic Cathedrals of France"; circulating and installing group exhibits for towns and villages, women's groups, and educational societies; and writing articles about art for the Sunday *Democrat and Chronicle*. Isabel's first Gallery exhibition in 1932 had centered on

3

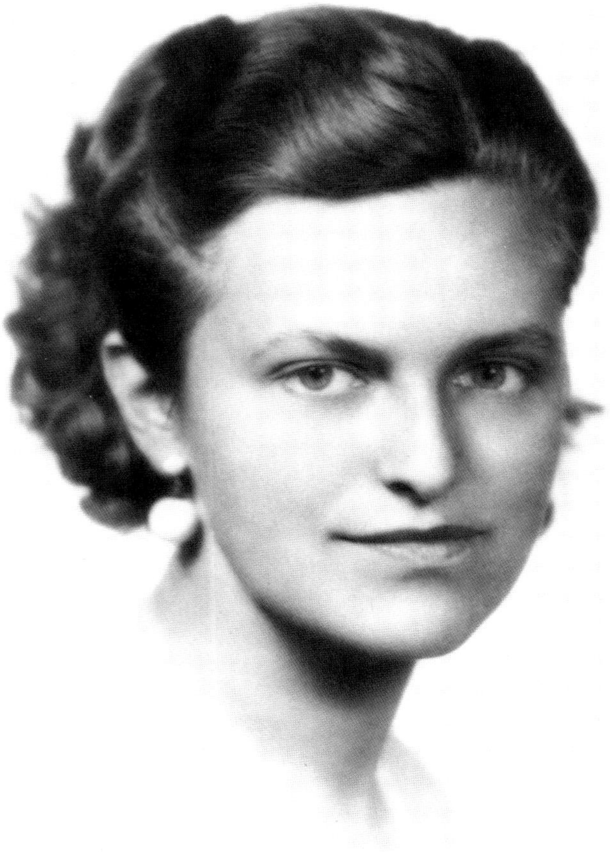

3 *Isabel Herdle joined the staff as assistant director in 1932. Photograph courtesy of the Herdle family.*

4 *Creative Workshop sketching class, 1920s.*

4

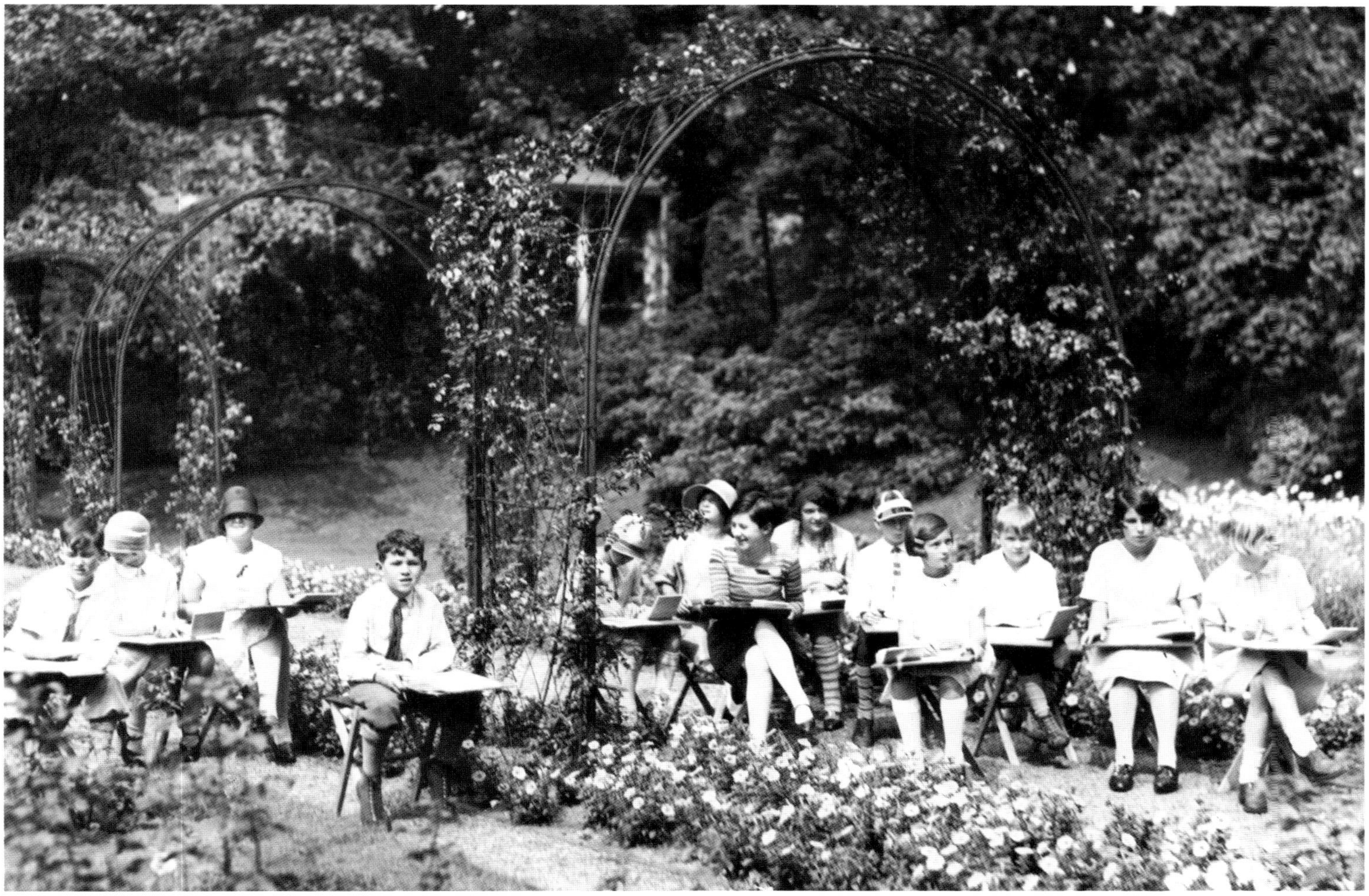

developing the Madonna theme through five centuries, the twelfth through seventeenth. Mrs. Watson underwrote the expenses so that Isabel could go to New York to obtain help and loan materials from Joseph Brummer, an important dealer in medieval art. The encounter solidified an enduring friendship, as breezy Isabel sailed into the Brummer Gallery to announce, "I've come to find Virgins in New York City," and the sophisticated dealer exploded in gales of laughter.

In recruiting artists to teach at the Creative Workshop, Gertrude and Isabel looked for two characteristics: those who were tops in their fields and also had teaching experience through which they related well to both adults and children.

William Ehrich (1897-1960) emigrated from Königsberg, Germany, in 1929 to teach sculpture at the Art Institute in Buffalo where he directed the Federal Art Project until 1938. From 1939 until 1960 he taught sculpture and ceramics in the Creative Workshop and sculpture at the University of Rochester. Sweet and shy, exuding a childlike warmth, Bill Ehrich created in his pupils, who called him "Teacher," a deep devotion. "How is Teacher?" Jocelyn Macy Sloan, a star pupil, asked for many decades as if she had never had another teacher. When the alabaster light fixture which guarded the old main entrance was taken down, Ehrich carved numerous fish, fowl, and fauna from the curved alabaster and presented them to staff members. On a more serious level, his wood sculpture was indicative of the transition from German Expressionist sculptor Ernst Barlach to the modernists. After his death Ehrich was succeeded at the university by Archibald Miller.

Fritz Trautman (1882-1971) had studied engineering, landscape architecture, and city planning before coming to Rochester as an associate of Claude Bragdon. After Bragdon left for New York, Trautman stayed on to teach at Mechanics Institute until 1938 and in the Creative Workshop, 1938 to 1971, where he was a popular and influential instructor. His special strength grew out of his color theories. Trautman's *Galaxy*, painted in 1942 as a thesis of form in space, was accompanied by a volume of explanatory material. Purchased through the Gould Fund in 1956, it became one of the all-time popular paintings of the collection; indeed, a walk-through *Galaxy* would be installed in the new Children's Room of the 1987 enlargement of the Gallery. No one would have been more surprised by this turn of events than Fritz Trautman.

Like Bragdon, Trautman was intensely interested in color theories, the supernatural, and the occult. He loved to test people by handing them dozens of colored circles, asking them to name their ten favorites. Much to his subjects' dismay, he was usually able to analyze their personalities frighteningly well. An interesting cook, Trautman presented guests at his farmhouse near Honeoye Lake with brain food one day and emotional food the next, depending on his readings of nature that day. While his selections may have fed the brain and emotions, they were not always palatable. "You were wise," Isabel says, "to carry a sandwich."

Ralph Avery (1906-1976) from Savannah, Georgia, graduated from Mechanics Institute in 1928 and went on to a distinguished career as a watercolor painter and illustrator, producing several covers for *Reader's Digest*. He garnered many awards including the Lillian Fairchild Award in 1954 and a Marion Stratton Gould Purchase Award from the Finger Lakes Exhibition in 1948. Avery taught an evening class in watercolor at the Creative Workshop and served on the Board of Managers in his capacity as president of the Rochester Art Club, from 1935 to 1938. But his greatest contributions to his adopted city were his haunting and poetic steel-grey watercolors of Rochester, especially those of the old Third Ward (where he lived) on a rainy or snowy night.

John Menihan, a native Rochesterian who had studied at the University of Pennsylvania, taught drawing and painting at the university and at the Creative Workshop from 1946 to 1965. Although he works in a variety of media, Menihan is perhaps best known for his numerous portraits and the many polyester and glass murals in Rochester's public buildings. He won the Lillian Fairchild Award in 1940 and Purchase Awards in 1946 and 1947. A retrospective exhibition of his prints was held at the Gallery during the summer of 1988.

Edna Weeks Smith was the first to teach handicapped children both at the Gallery, where they came in wheelchairs for ceramics classes and at School No. 5 which she visited each week. She also worked with senior citizens at the Rochester Friendly Home.

From the 1930s to the early 1950s Julia de Gogorza, a sculptor who had trained at the Rhode Island School of Design, taught in the workshop. With a special gift for stimulating children and a wonderful feeling for design and color, she was able to work effectively with a variety of youngsters—even the so-called "difficult." She taught classes at the Lewis Street Settlement House and the early classes for the blind that Gertrude started at the Gallery in the late 1930s.

———

The faithfulness of the maintenance staff over the years has been a Gallery hallmark. The early 1950s saw the retirement of Ray Pike, who had been George Herdle's very first appointment to the staff. Forty years of service for "Mister" Pike was not enough. After retiring, he returned daily to his old haunts, sat for hours in the Fountain Court and watched the passing parade. He who had located so many chairs for weary visitors over the years, finally was the object of courtesy himself. As he grew more and more feeble, his old friends would bring him a chair.

With the increased space of the 1926 addition, Mr. Pike, superintendent of building and grounds, had acquired an assistant, William Hondorf. Hondorf in turn trained his nephew, Bob Young, who started in the 1930s, left for the duration of World War II, and then returned to the Gallery, retiring in 1978. Young in turn trained his successor, Stanley Brew.

Young was an excellent carpenter who also became

5

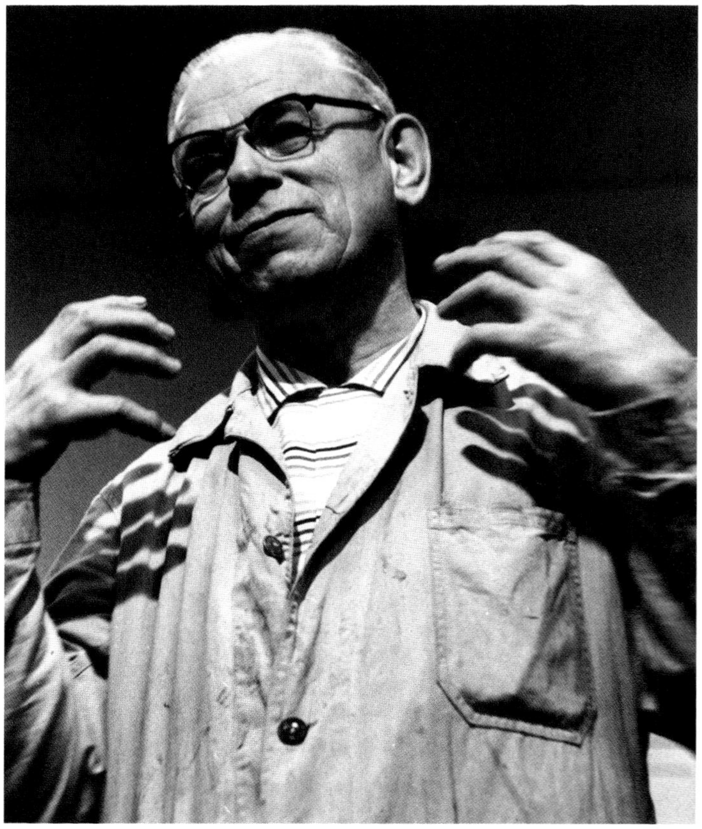

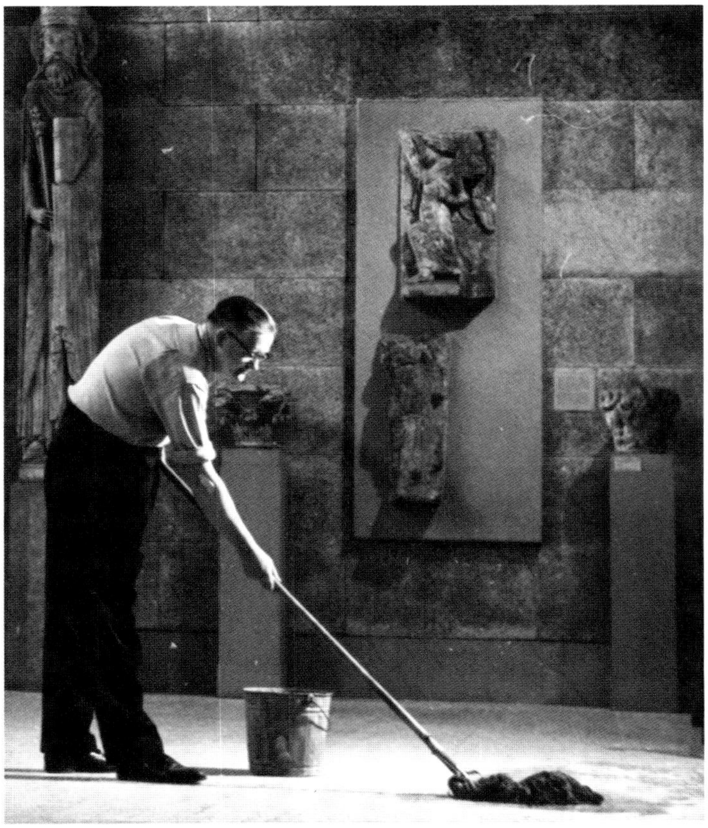

5 *William Ehrich, Creative Workshop instructor of ceramics and sculpture.*

6 *Maintenance staff member Lloyd Diehl worked long hours.*

noted for back-room imitations of the directors (usually with a mop of yarn on his head to simulate authenticity). "I wish I could see the one he does of me hanging an exhibition," Gertrude says. "I understand he has me down pat when he mimics me saying, 'What percentage have we still to do?' or 'What do *you* think should come first?' "

Young was Isabel's "helper" too. When she would ask if a painting appeared to be hanging straight, he would answer: "I don't know, Miss Herdle, it looks a little high in the middle."

Another "shady story" Gertrude tells involves the time Young heard her say that she wished a certain tired old cast would disappear. Lo and behold, the cast was never seen again.

Like the rest of the staff the maintenance people did double duty. After helping Mr. Pike clean the Gallery in the morning, Mr. Dunnigan of the maintenance staff put on his best suit and took up his stand as a guard. In that role he reveled in instructing visitors to watch the eyes of the portraits follow them around the room. "He had people marching back and forth all day long," Isabel observes, "telling them exactly which floorboard produced the best results."

Through the years Mr. Pike (no one, not even George or Gertrude Herdle, called him "Ray") was assisted by other colorful figures. Joe Keegan, janitor, whose Irish brogue no one could fathom, had the job of opening the boiler valves to let in the heat each morning. When there was trouble with the heat, Keegan would crouch to speak to the Little People who lived in the valves, and soon the Gallery would become warm again.

Sam van Wuyckhuyse appeared to be a shy, taciturn, Dutch carpenter—the perfect old-school craftsman who made impeccable traveling boxes for the paintings. Then at one Christmas party Sam startled the staff and assembled guests by tossing into the air with great expertise the delicate plates that Mrs. Charles Babcock had just given the Gallery for "private view teas." Sam later admitted that he had been an accomplished vaudeville juggler. His early career on the stage extended to shortened versions of *Uncle Tom's Cabin*, where he and his brothers knelt by Little Eva's bedside, wafting her to heaven on the wings of their rousing rendition of "Nearer My God to Thee." After such a career the Gallery must have seemed like tame stuff to Sam.

In 1937 Susan Eisenhart, a graduate of Mount Holyoke College (Phi Beta Kappa) with graduate work in fine arts at the Fogg Museum, Harvard, met Gertrude in New York to interview for the position of director of education. Forty

7

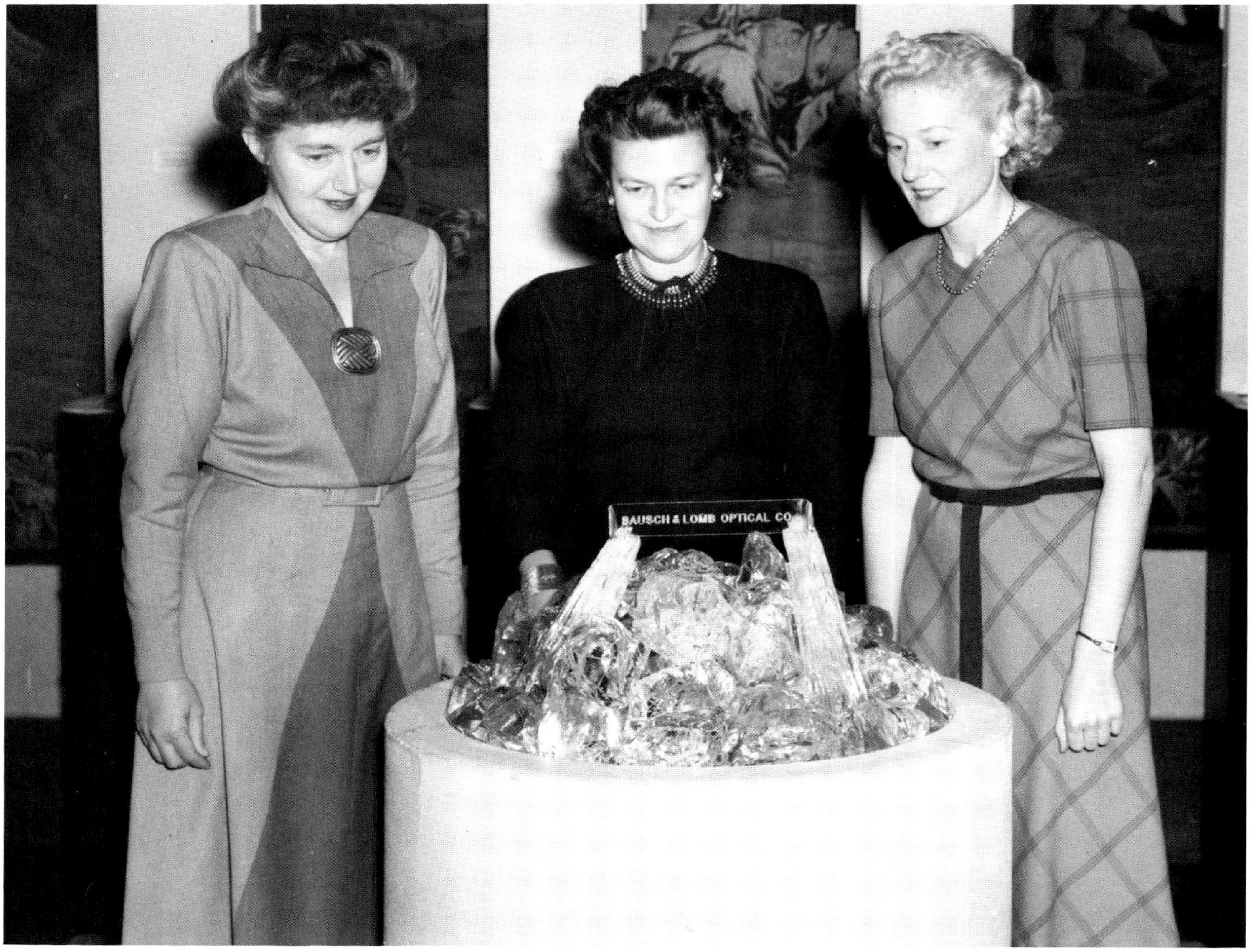

years later, in 1977, she retired from the staff but not from active duty; 1988 found her still lecturing, contributing as research curator emeritus, and as active member of the Art Committee. Looking back to when the staff was one-quarter the size it is in 1988 she was amazed "at all the things we did because there was no one else to do them." In the early days she functioned as Education Department head, director of school programs, researcher, lecturer, librarian, writer, and tour guide.

Charged with "revitalizing" the public schools' interest in the Gallery—the school program had not changed much since 1917—Eisenhart worked with teachers to devise tours relating to the schools' social studies curriculum, concentrating on grades four through eight. During World War II, when busing to the Gallery stopped, Eisenhart and an assistant, Jean Milligan, began giving lectures and slide talks in area high schools. Material from Gallery storage formed exhibits in high school display cases. Colorful Guatemalan textiles and artifacts, Peruvian costumes, Javanese batiks and puppets, transported by Eisenhart and her Women's Council volunteers, brightened school corridors and provided instruction in other cultures.

In the late 1940s Eisenhart developed an adult study series that met biweekly, from October to May, in a university classroom. The seminar theme centered on the art of a particular country; on that created around a certain historical figure such as Hadrian, Alexander, or Charlemagne; or on what art was being made at a specific date, such as 1066 or 1776. The seminars had a steady following for many years, evolving into the popular Spotlight Series.

When, in 1949, Miss Eisenhart became Mrs. Bernard Schilling, she chose to continue at the Gallery on a part-time basis. She continued to lecture and to research, compile, contribute to, or write the Gallery's catalogs. These included the first Erie Canal catalog in 1953, the Gallery *Handbook* to the collections of 1961 (with Langdon Clay), *Traditional Art of Nigeria* in 1964, the booklet published in conjunction with the Medieval Faire in 1974, and portions of the *Treasures from Rochester* catalog of 1975. After retiring, she edited or co-edited six annual issues of *Porticus* beginning with its inception in 1978, setting the scholarly quality and tone of that publication.

When the docent program was systematically organized in the early 1960s, Schilling helped with the ongoing training of each new group until her retirement in 1978. Beyond education and programming, her intellectual interest in the collection led her to research many of its objects through contacts with visiting scholars. One such correspondence yielded new information on the provenance of an Egyptian relief acquired in 1942 and vaguely identified as "New Kingdom." Erhart Graefe, a German scholar with access to nineteenth century publications and drawings of German excavations in Egypt, was able to positively identify the relief as dating from the fourteenth century B.C. tomb in Saqqâra belonging to Maya, chief architect for King Haremhab, successor to the now famous King Tut.

Vacation trips found Schilling visiting experts on their home turf and stalking the British Museum in search of objects and research material which would relate to the Gallery collection. Such hours of unpaid scholarly work on the part of senior staff members were vital to the Gallery. It could not pay extra for these tasks, but needed them performed to remain a credible institution.

University of Rochester and Eastman School of Music graduate Thomas Tibbs volunteered at the Gallery for special jobs in the 1940s and was subsequently hired as an all-around and quite valuable administrative assistant. Filling in where needed most, Tibbs lectured, wrote publications, curated children's shows and reported on them at American Association of Museums conferences, and helped to install the first international jewelry exhibition, held at the Gallery. When Schilling went part-time, Tibbs filled in by assuming some of her duties. From Rochester, Tibbs went on to become director of museums in Huntington, West Virginia and Des Moines, and of the Museum of Contemporary Crafts in New York. As of 1988 Tibbs was teaching the history of art and pursuing his music near San Diego.

After Tibbs left, the search for a full-time director of education ended with the hiring of Langdon F. Clay. In 1948 he had graduated from Harvard with a degree in Fine Arts

8

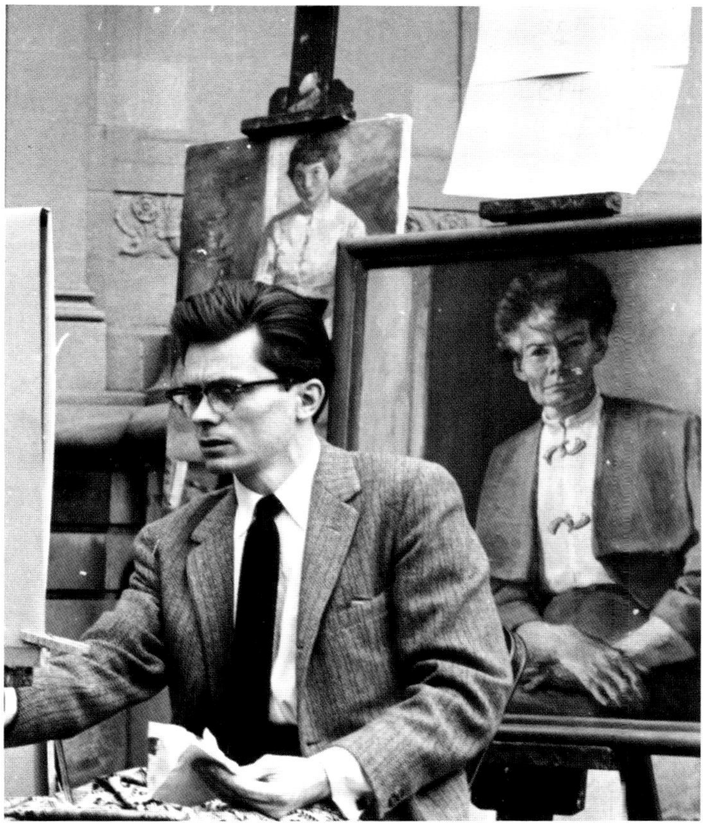

7 *Gertrude H. Moore, Isabel C. Herdle, and Susan E. Schilling at a Bausch and Lomb exhibit.*

8 *Portrait of Edna Weeks Smith, Creative Workshop instructor, by Joseph O'Leary.*

9

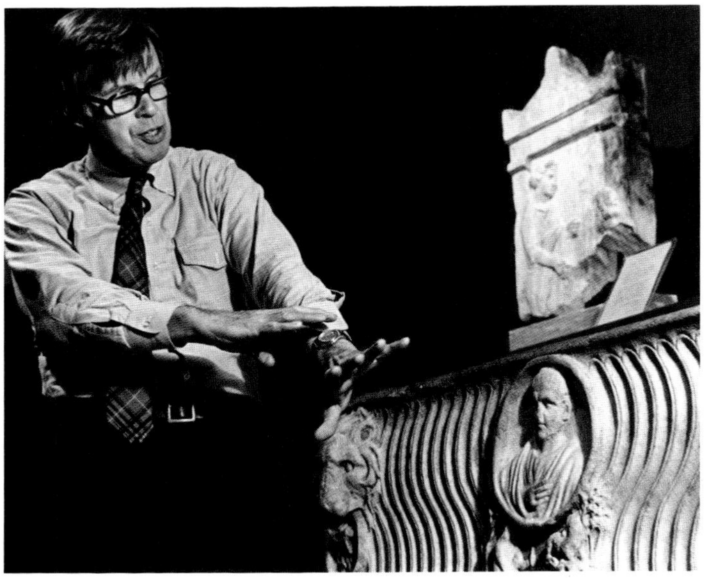

(originally a member of the class of '46, he spent three years in the army before completing his degree in an accelerated course). He did a term at a textile school to please his family (but not himself) and then enrolled as a graduate student in the New York University Institute of Fine Arts. Following a half-year in the Netherlands, Germany, and Italy, and a term at the Sorbonne in Paris, Clay returned to NYU, graduating in 1952. That summer Gertrude and Isabel were in New York interviewing for the new director of education and finding the applicants from large metropolitan museums "disappointing" (they all seemed most concerned with how many junkets to Europe the Gallery would sponsor). So the Herdles selected Clay, who asked instead what programs the Gallery planned for Rochester's ethnic groups.

For his part Clay recalls meeting "a couple of sweet ladies. You just wanted to hug them, yet they asked the most cogent questions, such as 'Why do you want to work in a museum as opposed to a university?'" Lang and Ellen Clay came to Rochester with two children and put down roots; their family grew to include six children, and an indeterminate number of dogs and horses.

Under Clay the education staff worked round-the-clock with school groups as well as church, ethnic, and women's groups.

Security, Clay recalls, was not a major concern in those halcyon days before the great art heists. It meant one staff member and one guard locking the front gate and securing the Gallery after an evening or Sunday program by looking under the seats of the auditorium and calling through the restrooms for dilatory visitors. Clay doubled as transporter of art works. Today, professional couriers with vans and sophisticated crating equipment are employed by the Gallery. In those days, Clay and Bob Young would bump around the landscape in a station wagon, or whatever vehicle was available, picking up priceless works of art. There were times too, with Sue (Eisenhart) Schilling on sabbatical, Gertrude and Isabel on vacation, when Clay was running the Gallery with one secretary.

Such informality did not, however, preclude serious, scholarly, groundbreaking exhibitions. "In Focus, a Look at Realism in Art," for example, was curated by the Gallery staff and introduced Pop Art to Rochester audiences in the early 1960s before it became a national phenomenon. A show of Nigerian Art in 1964 was prompted by the connection between the university's School of Medicine and Dentistry and the newly established medical school of the University of Lagos. Rochester physicians had brought back Nigerian sculpture and artifacts that were augmented by loans from museums and New York dealers.

In 1945 Emily Sibley Watson died at age ninety. Felled by a stroke several years earlier, Mrs. Watson was generally confined to the second floor of her Prince Street home. From that post she could watch the comings and goings on the street below which led to the nearby Gallery and university. Not just friends but also World War II servicemen on their way to the Main Street armory daily exchanged waves with that small, white-haired, still smiling countenance in the upstairs window.

The museum Mrs. Watson had so much to do with founding and nurturing would have to make do without her as it moved into the post-war years.

0

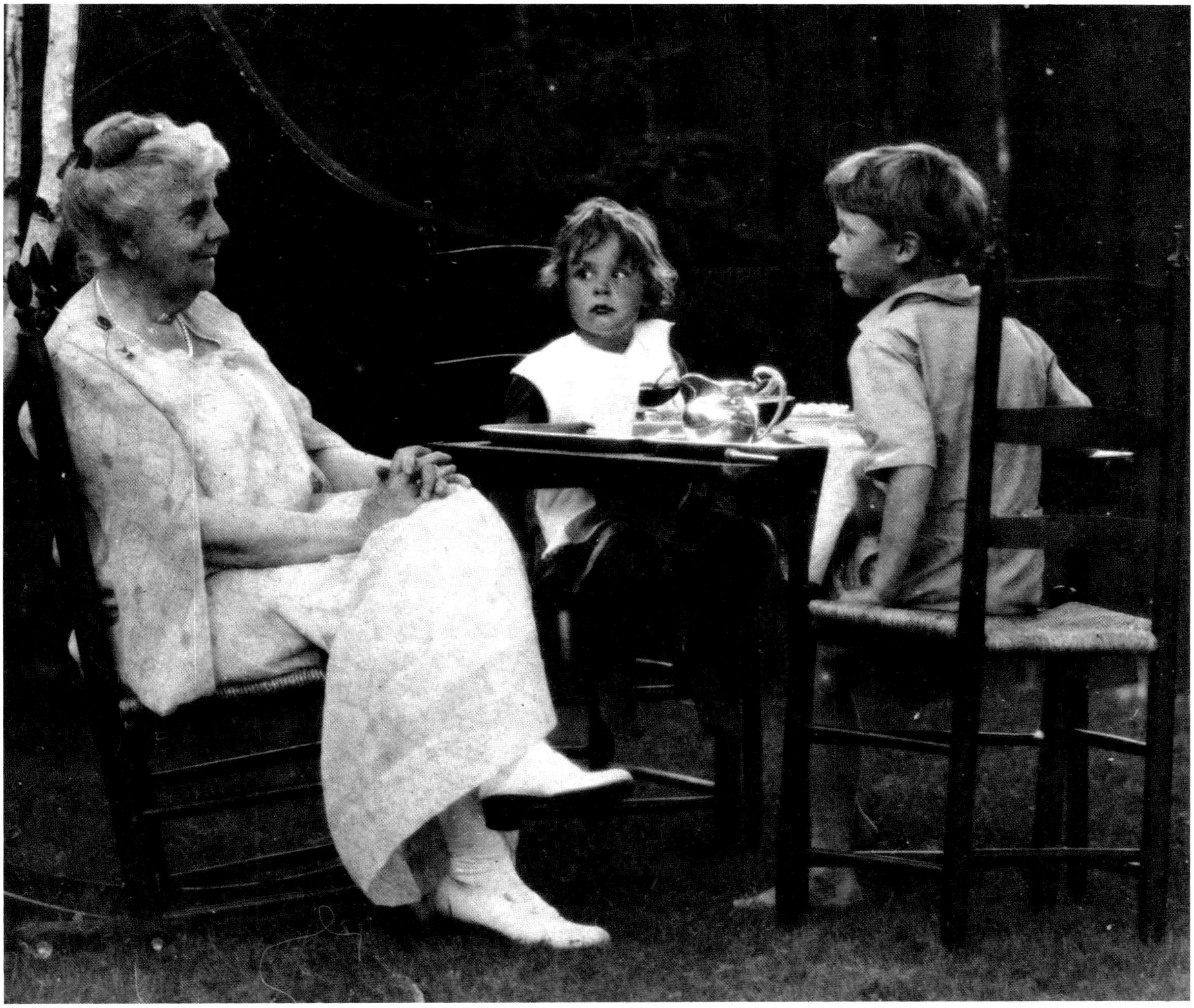

9 *Langdon Clay discusses Roman sarcophagus.*

0 *Emily Sibley Watson and her grandchildren. Photograph courtesy of the Herdle family.*

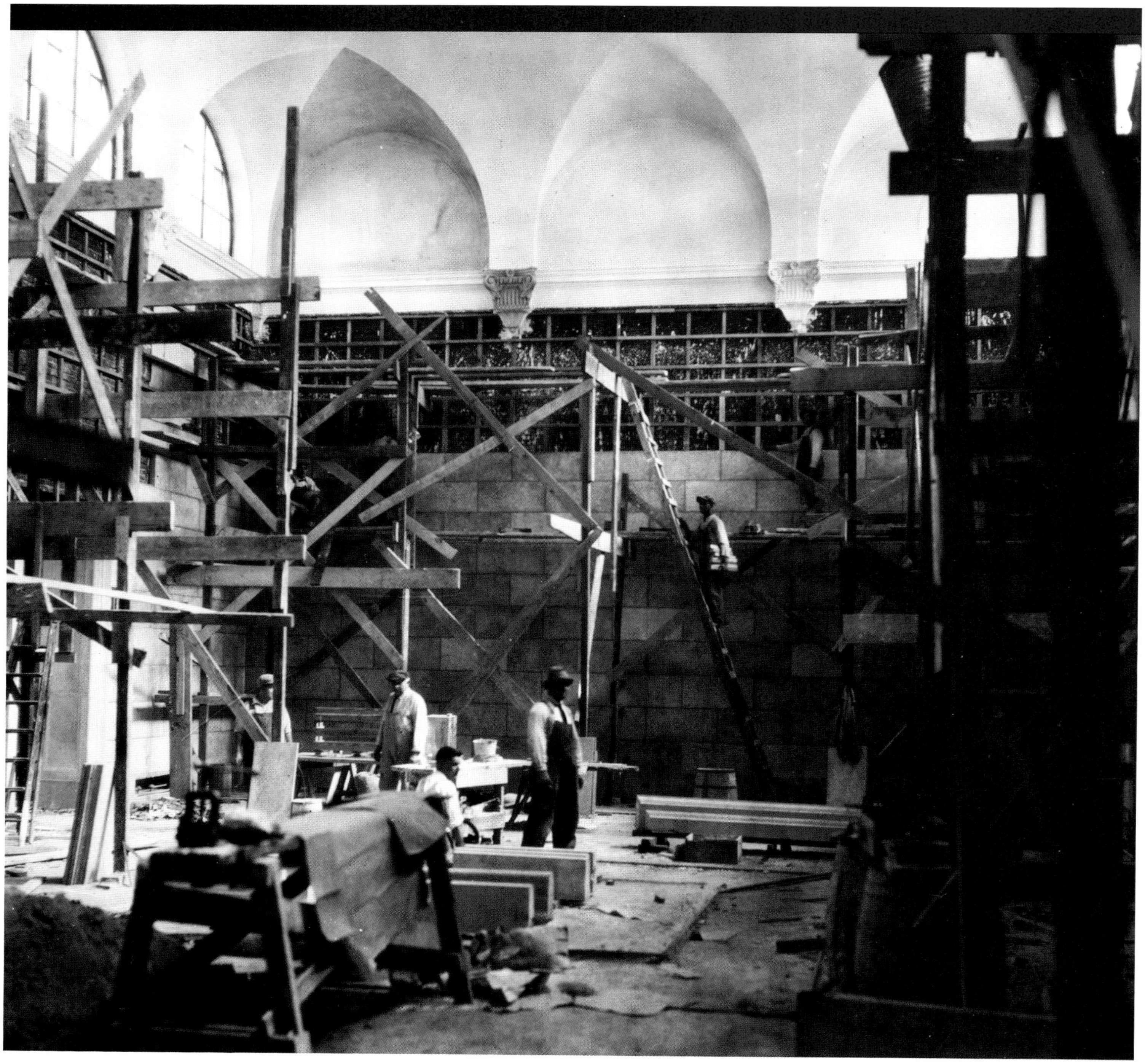

4

In general style the building will resemble the J. Pierpont Morgan Library in New York City and more nearly like, in general character and details, the Chapel of the Malatestas at Rimini. The arcades that will form the sides of the building will be patterned after the south arcade of the Malatesta Mausoleum.

Rochester Times | 23 April 1912

If you alter the measures and proportions of the pilasters, all that music will fall into discord.

Leon Battista Alberti | (1404-1482)

The Zenitherm wall goes up in the new Fountain Court, ca. 1925.

1

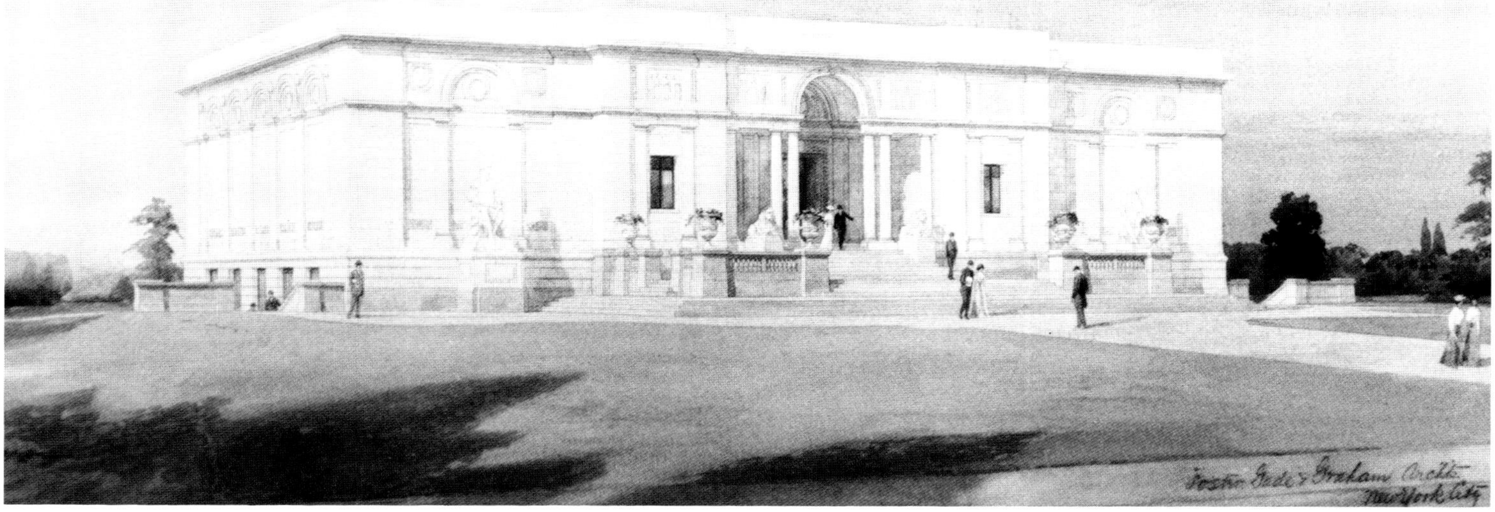

1 *Brigden (for Foster, Gade and Graham, ca. 1912), Rendering of Original Memorial Art Gallery, gouache on paper mounted on cardboard. Gift of Northrup, Kaelber and Kopf. 80.60*

The Renaissance jewel box that rose on the choicest corner of the university campus presupposed an audience with classical educations and interests. The deep Palladian entrance of the central bay was the strongest feature of the building, and, flanked by bays with shallow reveals, does indeed resemble the facade of the Morgan Library, built in 1906 on Madison Avenue in New York City. The Morgan Library was built of rusticated stone without mortar and capped by a dome, however, while the Gallery was faced with smooth, Indiana Blue limestone and topped by skylights. The Morgan had the look of an urban strongbox, the Gallery of a precious jewel box set high on a terraced greensward.

The architects were Foster and Gade of New York City who were also inspired by a building in Rimini, Italy, by the Early Renaissance architect, Leon Battista Alberti—a structure that J. G. Averell had also admired.

In 1450 Alberti transformed the Gothic church of San Francesco, Rimini, into a memorial honoring the local tyrant of the time, who bore the prepossessing name of Sigismondo Pandolfo Malatesta. Alberti designed a marble shell to encase the old building, with the front freely based on a Roman triumphal arch (symbolizing the triumph over death). The side walls of the transformed church are pierced by arched recesses for the sarcophagi of scholars and poets whose bones Sigismondo had pilfered in Greece. Subsequently called the Tempio Malatestiano, it was sketched by Averell (including its bas-reliefs) during a visit to Rimini in 1900. The Gallery's Palladian entrance echoes the three recessed arches of the Tempio's facade. The blind arcades flanking the 1913 building are derived from the arcaded recesses on the flanks of the 1450 building.

The ornamental stringcourse (carved stone border) across the bottom of the Gallery arcades consists of intertwined wreaths of roses containing lamps of memory and the initials "JGA"—ultimately derived from the carved stone wreaths at Rimini honoring Sigismondo and his mistress, Isotta, whose symbol was the rose.

Above the portico four stone relief panels, designed and executed by Donnilly and Ricci of New York, recount symbolic tales of Painting, Sculpture, Architecture, and Music. In the first panel, the painter stands in the light of Inspiration facing three figures holding hands to represent the unification of Glory, Love, and Poetry—a classical ideal toward which Renaissance painters strove.

Ancient, Renaissance, and Modern Sculpture are represented in the next panel by the Sphinx, Michelangelo, and Rodin's *Thinker*. One figure holds a branch of laurel, another looks back to ancient sculpture for guidance, while an aged figure contemplates the skull of Mortality (or perhaps Anatomy) and holds the book of Knowledge.

In the third panel the architect stands before a church. Figures of a mother and child suggest domestic Architecture. Three other figures symbolize Decoration, Sculpture, and Archaeology.

The fourth narrative panel symbolizes Music by depicting Apollo, god of poetry and music, playing his lyre for Greek maidens to sing and dance.

Four carved medallions represent the big four of Renaissance art and architecture: Raphael, Michelangelo, Leonardo, and Bramante.

The panels were not complete by the time the contractor, Adam Friedrich, wanted them, so one Peter Rosack had to finish them in place, a newspaper of the time said. Rosack had another deadline. He was due to start work on the facade of the Grand Central Terminal in New York. When an April blizzard complicated Rosack's in situ work on the Gallery, a large and enthusiastic crowd gathered to cheer him on as he rushed to finish.

Danish muralist Frode Rambush frescoed the portico ceiling with the signs of the zodiac surrounding a blazing gold sun. Rambush's method—applying gold leaf, then watercolor and finally a glaze—was one that had recently been rediscovered, the newspaper said, and this was its first use in this country. (It worked well: in 1988 the fresco appears just as fresh and new as on the day it was completed.) Above the doors are a carved logo of the Palladian entrance, and the letters "MAG" between Inspiration kneeling before the lamp of Memory, and Wisdom, with her scroll, genuflecting before an owl.

Globe lamps atop bronze lions stand at the head of the granite steps. Flanking the portico are pedestals designed to receive statuary. Renderings show them occupied, but they never were. When James G. Cutler "offered casts [for the Hall of Casts] of the two Medici figures by Michelangelo, it was decided [by the 1913 board] to decline both because the design of the building calls for the erection of similar figures on the facade." Some things are best left undone.

The Renaissance jewel box was one of the most photographed buildings in the city. "The Gallery is the frequently used background of most of the automobile agencies in town," notes the caption on a newspaper advertisement for "Early model of the horseless carriage Olds Mobile."

Construction of the new 14,000-square-foot pantheon of culture took fourteen months following the June 1912 ground-breaking. The service, library, and lecture-hall entrances were tucked behind the terraces on the level of the entrance doors of the rest of the campus. Emily Sibley Watson paid for a sidewalk to go from the main steps of the Gallery, through a new gate in the iron fence surrounding the campus, onto University Avenue where trolleys now made a special stop. "Take the University Ave. streetcar (four tickets for 25 cents) or walk (free) to the Memorial Art Gallery," a newspaper instructed. "Take the whole family."

John Gade, partner in charge of the project and the businessman of the firm, was married to Mrs. Watson's niece, Ruth Sibley. In 1912 Gade had just finished converting the 1880 Italianate villa of the late Hiram Sibley on East Avenue into a Neo-Georgian mansion for the Western Union magnate's grandson, F. Harper Sibley, and his bride, Georgianna Farr. The firm would also design a home for Mr. Atkinson Allen and his wife Charlotte (nee Whitney) and a university dormitory, Catharine Strong Hall (now the Visual Studies Workshop), for Henry A. Strong, president of the Eastman Kodak Company. In addition Foster and Gade would collaborate with Claude Bragdon on the Rochester Chamber of Commerce building of 1915 and become the new campus architects for the university on the strength of the Gallery commission.

Claude Bragdon was the local supervising architect for the Gallery building, but there is little in the detailing of the 1913 building that would indicate Bragdon's hand. Indeed when Bragdon and Gade got together again on the design for the Chamber of Commerce, Bragdon fumed in retrospect that "Gade saw me as a tame cat on the art gallery."

At Rimini, Alberti had designed a Renaissance facade to encase an already existing Gothic church. The Gallery's Renaissance shell "had little relation to use or space," Gertrude Herdle Moore says. "What they did, I think, was to draw up a beautiful facade and then just divide up the interior arbitrarily." The director's office was a virtual broom closet behind the cloak room. The exhibition galleries were on the second level and there was neither ramp nor elevator for delivery one floor up from the street. Large art objects had to be wrestled up several tiers of either indoor marble or outdoor granite steps.

The central and largest room was the Hall of Casts—a designation that would remain on architectural plans until 1968. Focally placed against the rear wall, immediately visible to the visitor, stood *Memory*, surrounded by full-size plaster reproductions of the *Victory of Samothrace*, *Hermes of Praxiteles*, *Venus of Melos*, and *Victory of Paeonis*, all on mahogany pedestals. A Parthenon frieze was mounted on the wall. "The treatment of the walls is unusual," George Herdle noted, not without reason. "A foundation of canvas, thoroughly covered with green paint, was then treated with a gold lacquer, on which a clouded color was put. The effect is one of quiet richness and great depth and softness, on which pictures show to great advantage. All these interior decorations were made by the Carroll Art Galleries of New York" (to which board member Beth Averell was then attached). The textured and stippled canvas covered diagonally mounted tongue-and-groove wood strips above a dado of fine Keene cement and slate baseboards. The Watsons had wanted walls that were beautiful in themselves but it soon became evident that the cement showed every kick mark and the canvas every nail hole. The floors of the side galleries were oak strips (replaced by parquet in 1968), with terrazzo for the Hall of Casts.

Expansive skylights were the latest innovation in museum construction, providing a living light particularly nice for sculpture—or, in this case, casts and one sculpture, *Memory*. But problems were multitudinous. Flexible linen louvers—which Mr. Pike adjusted with a long pole—were installed to cut the glare, but intense heat and light consumed them within five years. Artificial lights shining through the louvers at night cast strange, strong shadows, while pinpoints of light stabbed the viewer in the eye. After the louvers were discarded (about 1930), the skylights were whitewashed so that summer storms would wash off just enough paint for proper lighting during the long gray winter. This makeshift operation worked reasonably well for the next twenty years. In the 1950s the skylights were covered (although leakage continued) and a primitive system of dropped strip lighting installed.

The copper roof led its own life too, expanding and contracting with temperature changes. When it expanded, the glass in the skylights cracked; when the roof contracted, it leaked to the accompaniment of great banging noises—particularly eerie at exhibition openings on cold, rainy nights.

Mrs. Watson's donation of $200,000 to the original building, plus another $150,000, her half of the 1926 addition, was precisely the share of her estate Averell would have inherited had he lived.

"Workmen in Overalls and Young Intelligentsia Create Demand for Larger Memorial Art Gallery" the 1924 headline blared. "During the noon hour dozens of workmen from factories along University Avenue come to the Gallery in overalls to spend part of their lunch time in study of the

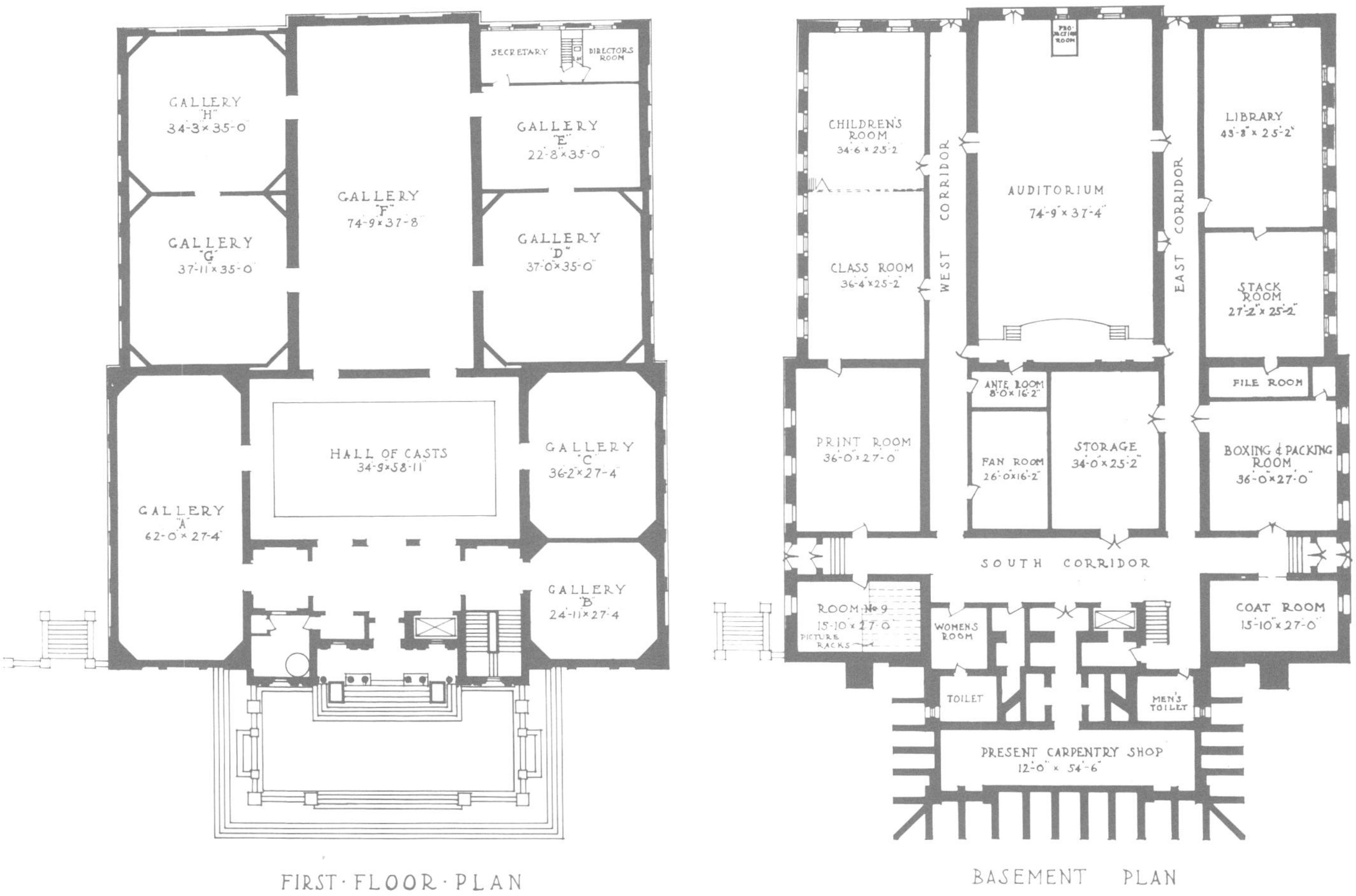

2 *Plans of main and ground floors, 1926–1968.*

exhibitions," the article continued. "Their attitude toward art is one of reverence.... Spirited discussions regarding the merits of the paintings are carried on."

As early as January 1922, less than ten years after the Gallery opened, there was agitation for more space. "Only the high cost of building is holding up...twelve more galleries [being built] in the rear or as two wings at either side." The galleries were to be used as "permanent space for industrial arts...lack of which has seriously hindered the appeal of the Gallery to the public." This rationale, which included the hope of "increasing the membership to 1000 from the present 300," sounds more like George Herdle than the Watsons. Herdle's untimely death cut short plans for the permanent exhibition of industrial arts.

As designed and constructed, the rear wall of the 1913 building was a temporary brick one, allowing for future expansion to the north. Not only was more exhibition, storage, and office space needed but an area for creative classes was desirable. Attendance reached new heights of 43,943 visits in 1924, 5,000 more than in 1923.

In 1924 the university began a campaign to raise funds for a new men's campus along the Genesee south of the city. But the Gallery's needs on the old Prince Street campus where the women would remain would not be forgotten. The James Sibley Watsons pledged $100,000 for an addition.

A new architect had to be found. By this time John Gade had given up architecture for Wall Street; later he became military attaché to the consulate in Brussels. Gade recommended Lawrence Grant White of McKim, Mead & White, who had earlier designed the Eastman Theatre and School of Music. White was the son of the fabled Stanford White, the country's most famous architect, partly by virtue of his being the victim of the most sensational murder of the early part of the century.

Cousin to Antoinette Granger of Canandaigua, who would later be an important Gallery donor, Larry White moved in the same social and Geneseo hunt circles as the Watsons. Like his father, White loved to borrow from the architectural vocabulary of the past and rummage the dealers for just the right antique decorative touch for his classical interiors. As "one of the last architects trained in the Beaux Arts classical manner," Gertrude recalls, "he could sketch a cornice or a capital from memory." In his letters White eschewed the first person pronoun, preferring instead the editorial "we," or better still, the third person: "When Mr. White was last in Rochester," White would write, "there was some discussion regarding the quality of glass in the skylights."

3,4

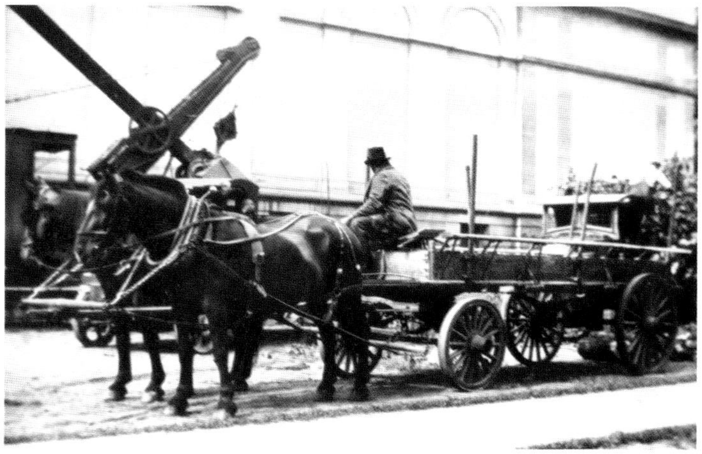

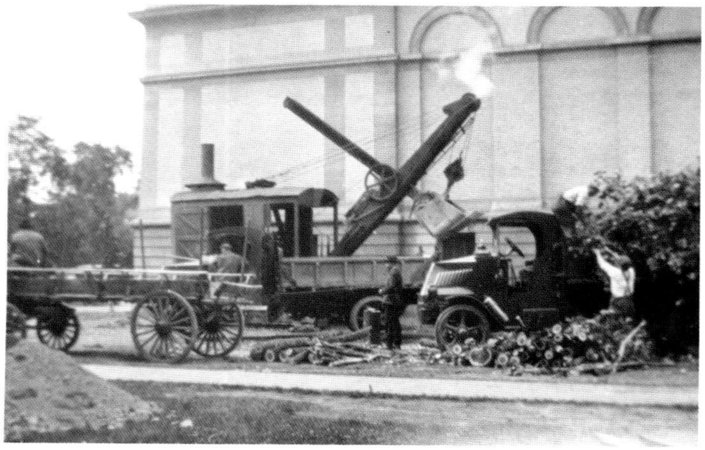

3,4 *Horses were still used for construction work in 1925.*

5 *McKim, Mead and White elevation for the 1926 addition as built.*

5

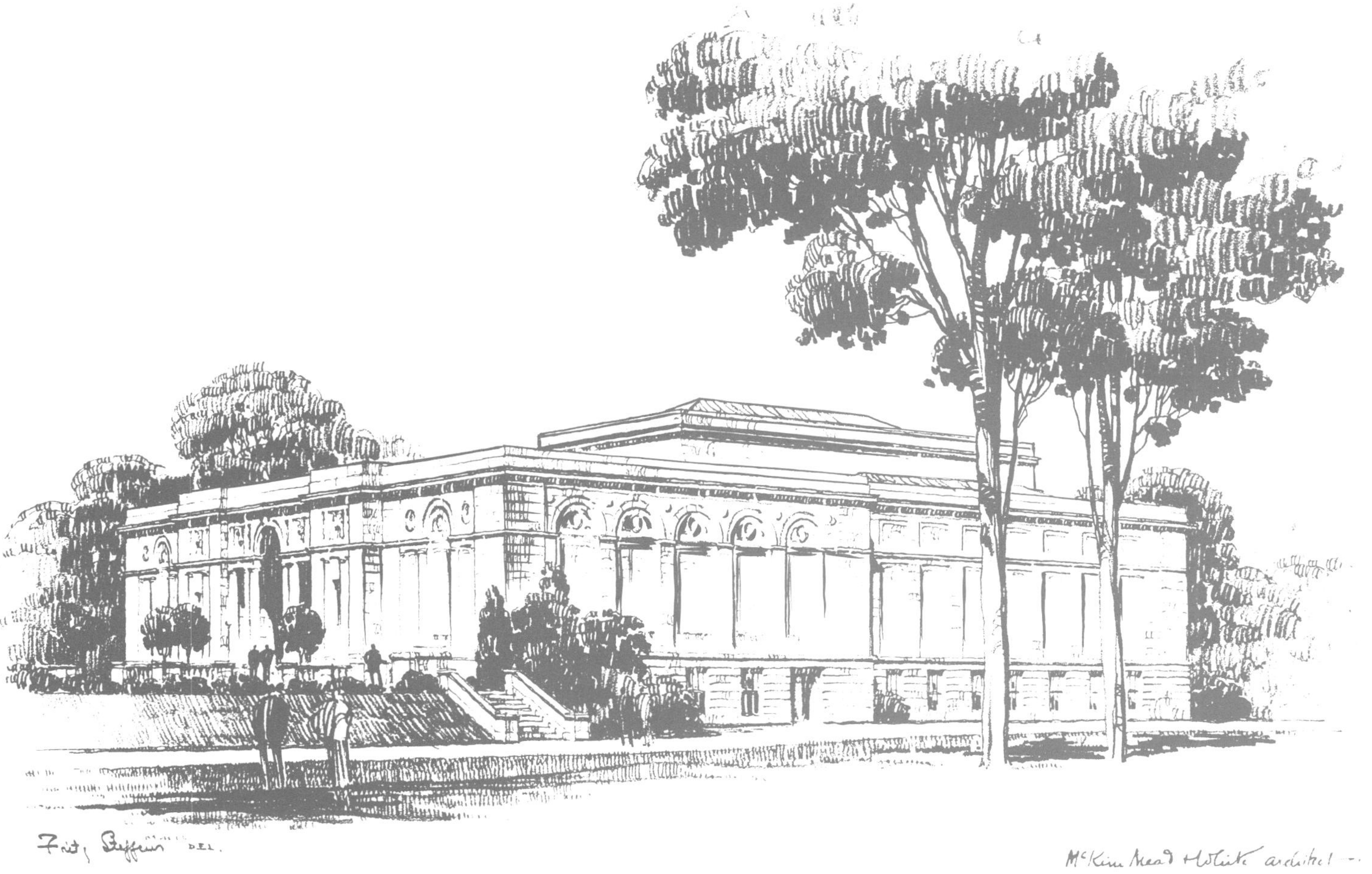

The contractor, A.W. Hopeman & Sons, was simultaneously engaged in the construction of the university's River Campus and within a few years would be building the Gallery's nearest neighbor, Cutler Union.

At 8:15 on the morning of 25 June 1925, spade attacked ground and for the next year and a half, the Gallery remained in the throes of construction. By July the *Democrat and Chronicle* could report that "the din of big steam shovels digging up the campus is vying with the University of Rochester summer lectures."

By September reporters noted that "as students within college halls listen intently to catch bits of their professors' lectures above the noise from outside, the two large dredging machines are gobbling up the campus green in large mouthfuls."

And by November:

Towering above the skylight roof... among the trees of the campus... a derrick is piling up the walls of the beautiful addition.... Those who have watched the momentous activities... taking place behind the rear wall of the present gallery... at last see the completion of the new skyline as the cornice was finally placed this week.

After the plodding slowness of the work on the constructions and foundations, the three new walls... have seemed to rise as if by magic this past month, setting their limestone faces north and east and west toward the larger future which lies immediately within and beyond them...

With its new rear wall 74 feet beyond its old one, the Gallery is more than doubling its floor and wall space [15,500 square feet was added] without impairing the beautiful completeness and faultless proportions of the first unit. The Gallery remains one of the most exquisite architectural possessions of the city. From University Avenue, only the higher roof of the central portion of the new section will be visible and there will be no lateral extension to destroy the scale and line of the beautiful front wall.... The side walls of the addition will not repeat the blind arcades of the present walls, but extend back in a series of temporary recessed panels. [The temporary panels are still there.] When the third part has been built, all the walls will be finished to match the original.

On his own, apparently, White had drawn up plans for a third section, which the Watsons postponed, and by the time of the next addition in the 1960s, requirements had

6

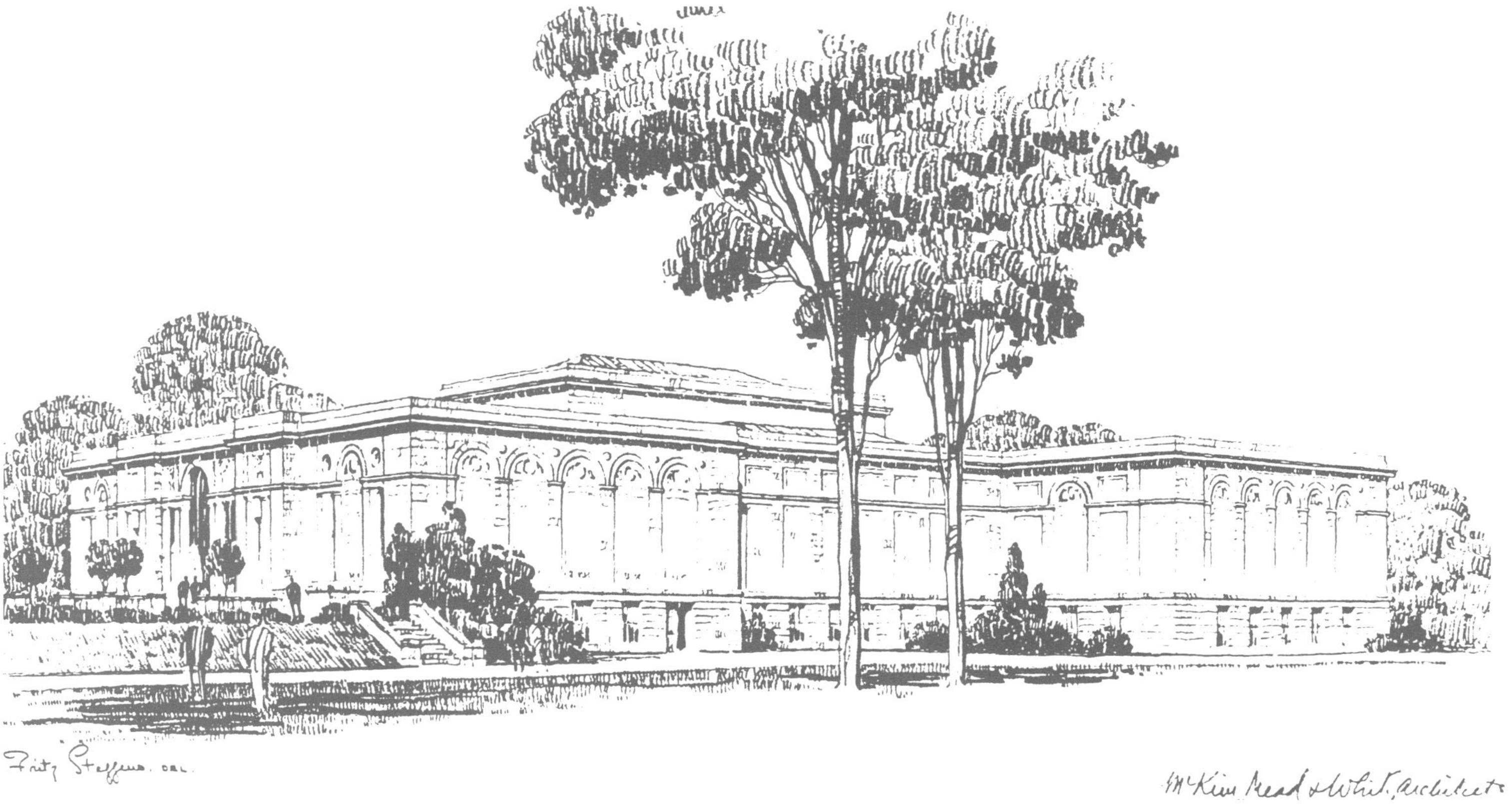

changed and some of the land to the north had been sold.

The central feature of the 1926 addition was a large, finely proportioned and detailed basilica-type court with clerestory windows flanked by two pairs of side galleries, bringing the total of side galleries tó seven. White had planned a "circulating corridor" between the central court and galleries, but as we shall see, met up with the indomitable director. New staff offices were placed in the northeast corner. The floors were travertine marble and the walls Zenitherm, an acoustical compositional material that looks like stone (but burns like wood). White had used Zenitherm for the interior of the Eastman Theatre.

No museum people had been consulted for the 1913 building, but Gertrude was determined to have a say in the 1926 addition. She was surprisingly successful.

In late 1924 White submitted plans to the Watsons and Gade for a two-stage Gallery addition. When the third (but never built) section was complete, the Gallery would be three times its original size. The immediate addition, a central court with side galleries, was first drawn by White as long and narrow (until at Mr. Watson's behest, it was made more nearly square). The next and final addition was to mirror the original building with an added apse, semicircular in plan, to the north. Inside this apse a semicircular auditorium was planned for the main floor and a library for the ground floor. The Watsons opted to build only the first addition but to face its north wall not with limestone but with brick (as in the north wall of the original building) in anticipation of a second addition.

White further designed a circulating corridor between the court and side galleries which would have provided "200 feet of wall surface for prints and watercolors," as he told Gertrude. "Moreover, if we look ahead to the future addition, the corridors will be most desirable for circulation to the auditorium and the new wings. Even at present, as you yourself point out, a much better access to the offices is provided."

But the director was adamant. The most important thing, in her estimation, was "the length of visits gained," that is, how long people spent in the galleries looking at the art. "My dear Mr. White," Gertrude wrote,

Dr. Rhees and I have had a change of mind which I fear will be rather disastrous to the present plans.... Instead of having the four small galleries open into the two corridors which flank the central court, we wish them to communicate with one another and open directly into the court. The corridors will thus be eliminated.... The court becomes the central place of passage.... The connecting galleries will also be a means of access.... Roughly sketched, this is our idea, on the enclosed plan. It leaves the central court as it was, and adds the width of the corridor to the four galleries... a much better use of our finest and largest gallery.... I am not convinced the corridors are necessary to the access to the gallery of the future.... As for wall-space gained, I agree with you arithmetically, but feel that the eighty feet of running wall-space in the galleries is worth a great deal more than the two hundred feet of corridor wall.... The position of the doors we leave a question. To allow the very desirable length of visits through the galleries, I suppose that they should be in alignment....

With great reluctance, White abandoned his circulation corridors, one of his favorite notions.

Gertrude, with Rhees's backing, shortened the auditorium (now to be placed directly beneath the new central court along with a library and children's museum) and changed the recessed platform therein so that projection apparatus could be used with art lectures. "Such means of illustration are so usual as to be nearly essential," Rhees explained to White. Four marble pilasters (instead of the marbleized cement originally planned) framed the stage. White specified the doors of the auditorium and throughout to be natural oak, with wainscoting and door trims a soft gray-green. The painting and gilding of the stage and the Fountain Court ceiling (light blue with gold leaf) was entrusted to Ezra Winter—the artist whose talents graced White's other Rochester commissions such as the Eastman Theater and the Franklin Street branch of the Rochester Savings Bank.

Gertrude designed the library layout in consultation with Rhees and worried continually about "seepage into the elevator pit in this low-lying campus." Seepage, particularly through the front terrace into the carpenter shop, would be a perennial problem.

The freight elevator installed to the west of the building could theoretically lift packing cases from the basement floor to the tail boards of trucks, thus eliminating carrying heavy objects up stairs. But the elevator never worked very well.

Revised estimates raised the building cost to $350,000, but the Watsons cheerfully tripled their pledge.

Gertrude meanwhile was courting a potential donor and on 15 December 1925 told White that "I have at last secured the definite promise of a fountain for the Children's Museum from Mrs. Samuel Gould of Rochester, who is to present it as a memorial for her daughter [Marion Stratton Gould, whose name was later memorialized in the Gallery's largest acquisition fund]. She has stipulated the sum of $500.... That, of course, cuts off the possibility of securing the beautiful Janet Scudder 'Frog Boy,' which is our first favorite [and which White was also pushing]. I should hesi-

7

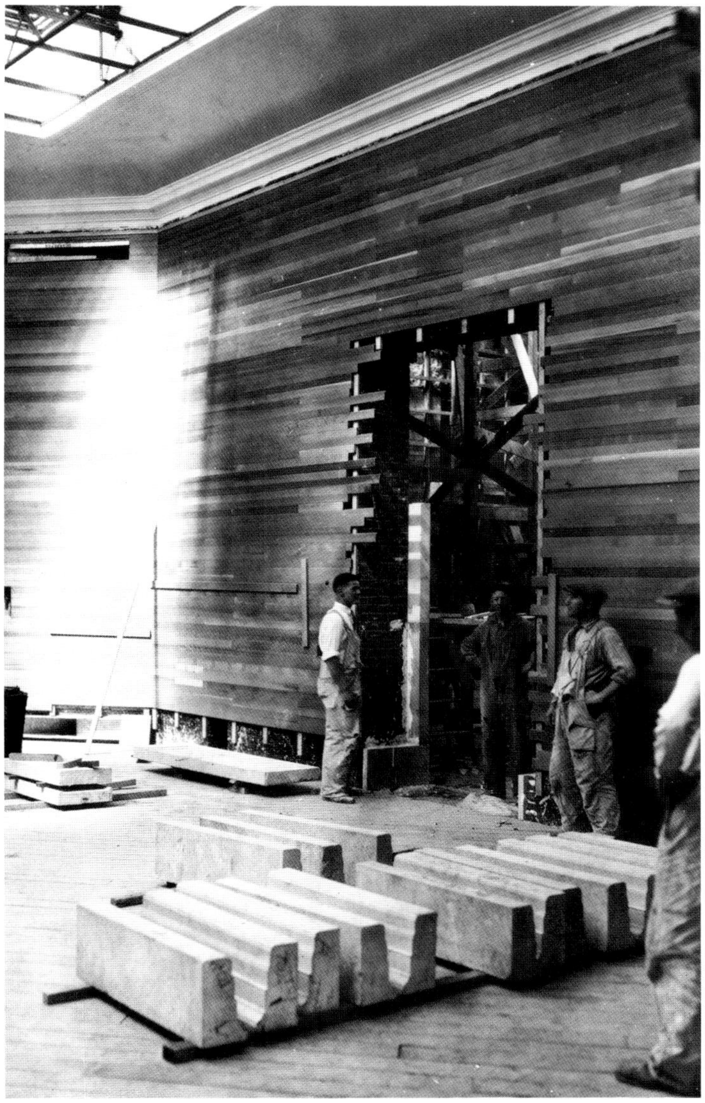

6 *McKim, Mead and White proposal for later addition.*

7 *The Gallery off the Fountain Court, under construction, ca. 1925.*

8

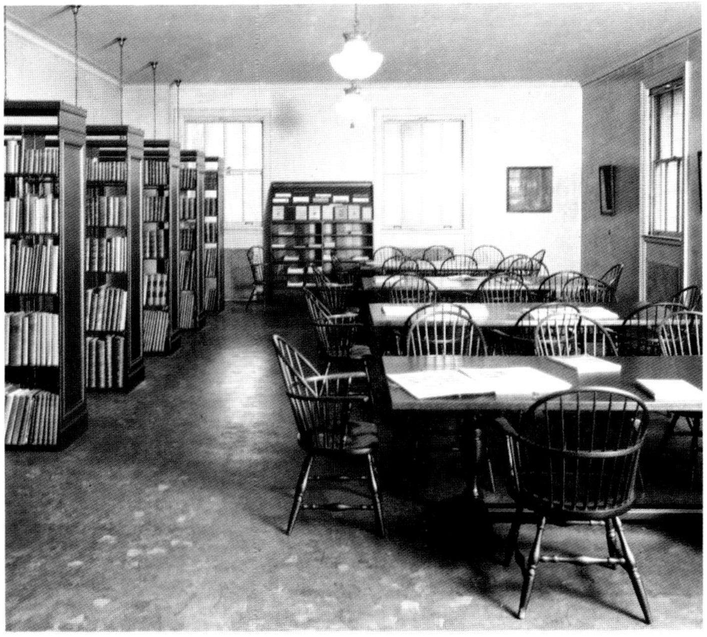

8 *The library as built, 1926.*

9 *Library layout, as sketched by Gertrude Herdle, 1926. Collection of the New York Historical Society.*

tate cabling her an offer of $500." Instead, Gertrude showed Mrs. Gould photographs of sculptures in the $225 to $250 range and the donor immediately decided that she would want something "nicer."

White then went to see "Miss Scudder, who says that she is so anxious for her figure to be in your Museum that she will let you have it for $500, on condition that you won't tell anybody she sold it at that price." To which Gertrude had to respond by telegram:

DONOR OF FOUNTAIN JUST INCREASED GIFT 500 TO 1200 WATSONS THEREFORE PREFER VERROCCHIO IN CHILDRENS MUSEUM AND ADULT SUBJECT FOR UPSTAIRS COURT REGRET INABILITY TO ACCEPT MISS SCUDDERS GENEROUS OFFER MRS WATSON DOES NOT WISH TWO CHILD SUBJECTS.

"I have just received the enclosed telegram," White wrote Scudder, "greatly to my disgust. I do not want the Verrocchio Boy in the Children's Room, and I do want it in the central hall; but as Mrs. Watson is paying for the whole museum, and is in Florida, I am afraid her decision is irrevocable." To Gertrude, White wrote: "We have just seen Mr. Lachaise, the sculptor who made the bust of Mr. Sibley Watson in your museum. It occurred to us that as Mrs. Watson knows him and admires his work, she might care to have him make a fountain figure for the large gallery...."

Gertrude *was* interested. "I hope that you stated the maximum price, however. The Watson family has done so much for him [Gaston Lachaise] in the way of public presentation and actual financial aid that I had hoped we might use that consideration in getting a special commission from him."

Mrs. Gould, caught up in the excitement of the project, raised her ante to $2,000 and offered to donate the fountain. Gertrude and Mrs. Watson felt that "as a permanent and decorative feature it would add greatly to the beauty of the room and be compatible with anything that might be on view." The director seized the opportunity of all that plumbing talk to suggest that a lavatory be installed next to her office.

Lachaise built a small scale model for White (who worked up a drawing of the longitudinal section with figure drawn to scale) and sent a plaster cast of it to Mrs. Watson. "Although I admire his work," White said, "I was not favorably impressed with this example of it. Moreover, he expects $4,000 for the figure in gilded bronze. This would raise the total cost of figure and fountain to about $6,000 which I should think would be more than Mrs. Gould would be willing to give."

It was. "The general choice," Gertrude's cable stated, was "a copy of the fountain in the Palazzo Vecchio,

9

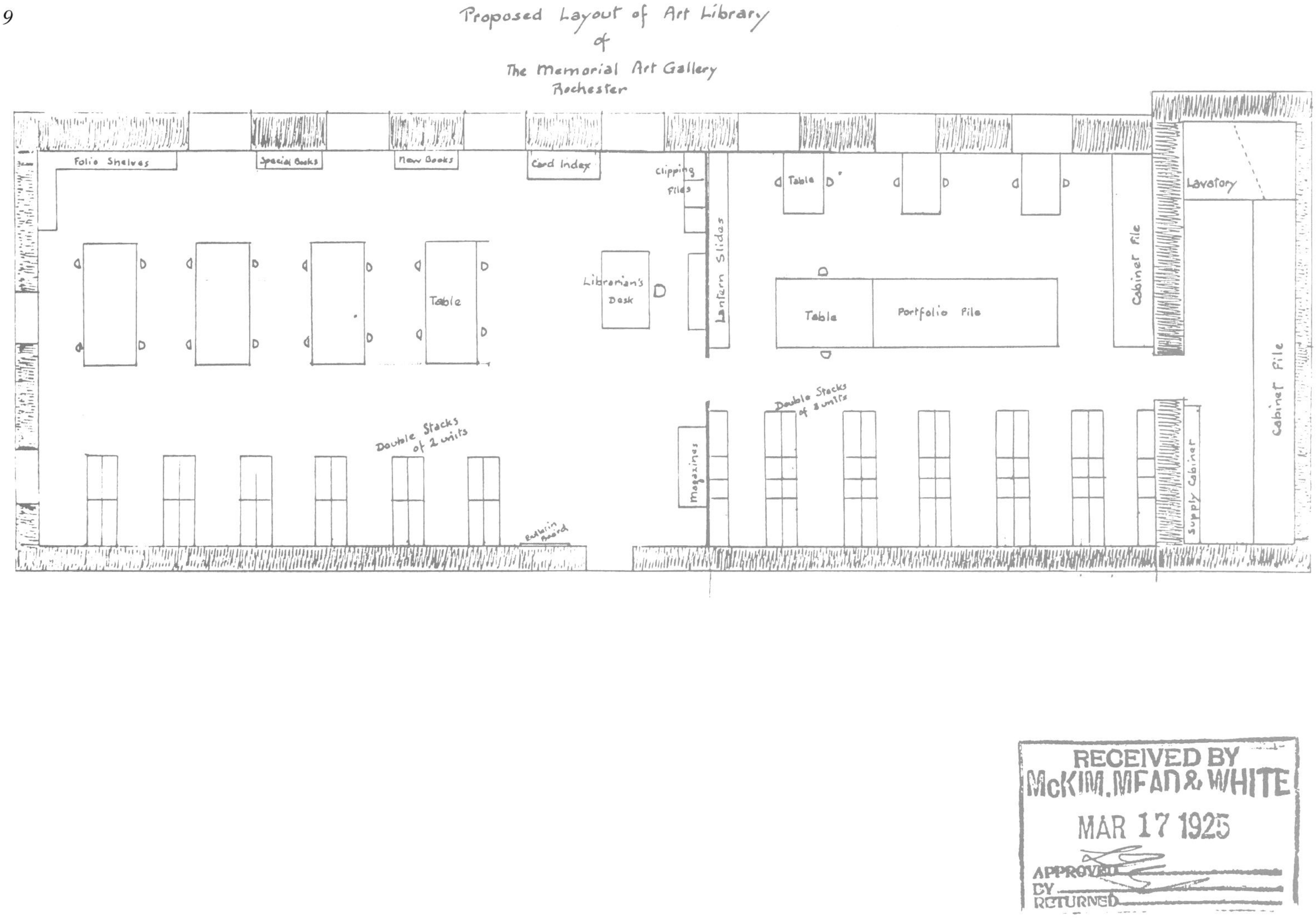

Florence."

"The strikingly low figure of $850 [for the fountain figure, duty-free for a public institution] is a startling example of the great variation between work done here and abroad," White wrote. "It would seem that there would be enough money left over for Mrs. Gould to give the four Verona [marble] columns as well."

There was and she did—as part of this first gift in memory of her daughter.

On the heels of the corridor discussion came the wall-covering debate. Watson still wanted those beautiful walls, now favoring a Fortuny silk damask from Venice, Italy, in a beautiful buff and blue-green. Gertrude thought something more neutral like monk's cloth would set paintings off to better advantage. (Besides, small panels of Fortuny could always be used to set off a sculpture, she argued.) A compromise was reached: the galleries to the west of the Fountain Court would be rendered in silk damask and to the east in monk's cloth. Within five years the bank president had capitulated to the young director and all side galleries were done in monk's cloth (although that damask remained underneath it until the 1968 renovation).

Meanwhile the walls of the Fountain Court were blank and bare. Tapestries, the same that had warmed medieval castle walls, could relieve the starkness of the Zenitherm, the Watsons and White decided. Gertrude contacted Arden Studios, Janet Scudder, Grand Central Galleries, and P. W. French & Co., all of New York, for loans of tapestries for the Grand Opening with the hope of interesting donors in purchasing them. (Museums relied upon French & Co., a major firm specializing in antique tapestries and furniture, for loan shows as well as acquisitions; Fogg Museum professors sent students such as Isabel Herdle there for instruction.) But then White decided to scour the market himself and in April 1926 found

. . . a Flemish tapestry, woven in Brussels about 1580, of a wood-

land hunting scene with Seigneurs on horse and afoot in pursuit of game. In the middle distance is a chateau and in the border Diana, goddess of the hunt with flowers, fruit and grotesques... 16′8″ x 9′8″... worth $6000 or $7000 but only asking $4500....

The price became $3,500 when the tapestry was found to be from the collection of White's famous father. White then arranged for Watson to buy the woodland hunting scene, the first purchase in his tapestry-buying spree. Two years later, in 1928, Watson purchased the two major Franco-Flemish Gothic tapestries, *Arithmetic and Astronomy* and *Judgement of Emperor Otto III*, as well as the French *Millefleurs* (c. 1500), all of which still hang in the Fountain Court. The director experienced a wave of panic when the bill arrived for *Arithmetic and Astronomy*, the most expensive object to enter the permanent collection thus far, until the bank president handed her his check for $70,000 without a word.

Gertrude had second thoughts about any wall covering when she saw the hunting tapestry. "The scaffold has been removed from the north wall of the Fountain Court," she wrote White in June 1926, "and reveals such a beautiful surface of Zenitherm that we dislike the thought of covering it even with a tapestry. The room is now showing more than a promise of what it will be, and we are all delighted with it." All Rochester would be delighted with the Fountain Court for years to come; many people still call it the most beautiful room in town.

As would be the case following all Gallery additions to the physical plant, attendance increased noticeably the first year after a renewed Gallery was in operation. In 1926 it reached 61,000 as against a former high of 51,000.

———

Elsewhere on the Prince Street Campus, another building was hatching that would eventually join the complex known as the Memorial Art Gallery: Cutler Union, the house the mail chute built.

According to Bragdon, James Goold Cutler was "Rochester's leading architect" in the 1880s. Early in Cutler's career a client had requested some means of getting mail from the ninth to the ground floor; in response, Cutler designed and patented the mail chute found in most public buildings. It made him a millionaire, allowing him to give up architecture and move on to several distinguished terms as mayor of Rochester.

Early in the century the ubiquitous Cutler, among his many roles a University trustee and staunch advocate of higher education for women, had sat next to Rhees at a

10

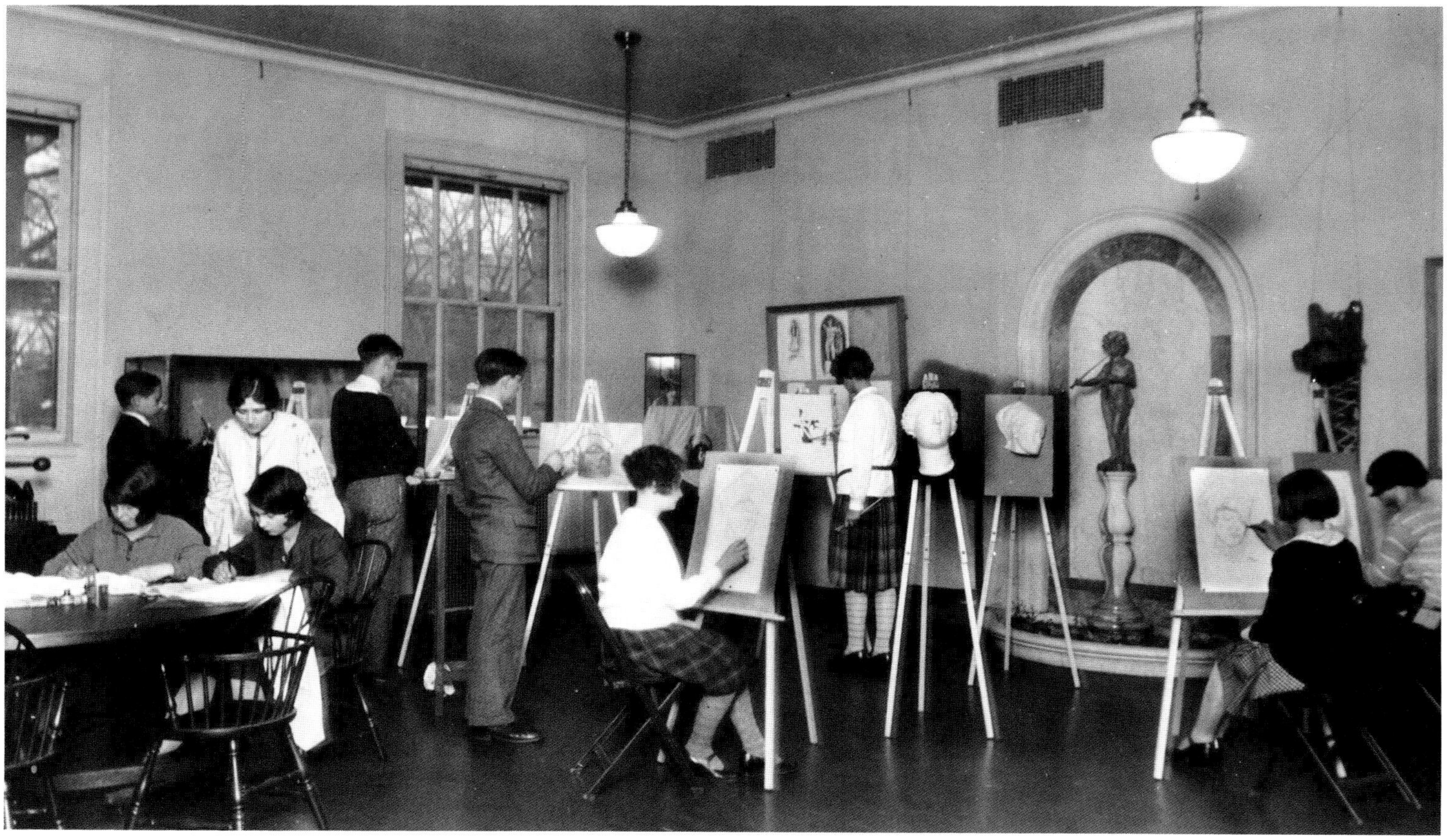

banquet in the old Alumni Gym on Prince Street. "I should like to see some day on this campus a noble building, with a fine tower...," Cutler told Rhees. "After I am gone, and Mrs. Cutler has gone, you may find some provision for realizing such a desire."

In 1927, as the male students were preparing to leave for the River Campus, the trustees voted to use Cutler's sizable bequest to build a women's student union—considerably larger than the men's new Todd Union—with a "noble clock tower" at Prince Street. During heated discussions as to whether the River Campus should be "Colonial" or "Collegiate Gothic" in style, Cutler had come down so hard on the side of the latter, that it was decided to make the new student union a magnificent example of Collegiate French-Gothic architecture. The style and material—"shot-sawn" Indiana limestone—were "acceptable to Mrs. Watson... as harmonizing with the Art Gallery."

When it opened in September of 1933, Cutler Union was heralded as "the most attractive and completely equipped student union in America." Architecturally it was considered the rival of Yale's Harkness Memorial complex as a watershed for the Collegiate Gothic style.

A watershed in other respects too, Cutler Union represented the climax of Rhees's remarkable thirty-five-year building program which included twelve new structures for the Prince Street Campus as well as a whole new River Campus, Medical Center, and the Eastman School of Music. Cutler Union may have been the last building for Charles Platt, university consulting architect who died in 1933, and the last designed during the lifetime of Edwin Gordon, university architect. And it was a culminating achievement for Philipp Merz, principal detailer of the Eastman Theatre and School of Music in downtown Rochester and the River Campus.

From Merz's fertile imagination and facile purple crayon on brown wrapping paper (he was color blind, as his renderings showed) came the university seal with its motto "Meliora," as well as the imposing tower of the River Campus's Rush Rhees Library. The latter was said to have been a copy of a Franco-Prussian War monument in Merz's native Bavaria, which evidently also served as model for all the lions, griffins, Valkyries, and Germanic printers' marks that adorn the library, inside and out. Cutler Union's soaring tower with commanding clock face, double chimney, dedication plaque, carved lettering by the west doors, banisters and balustrades, and the painted ceiling of Cutler Hall—are all evidence of Merz on a romp through his own version of the French Gothic.

11

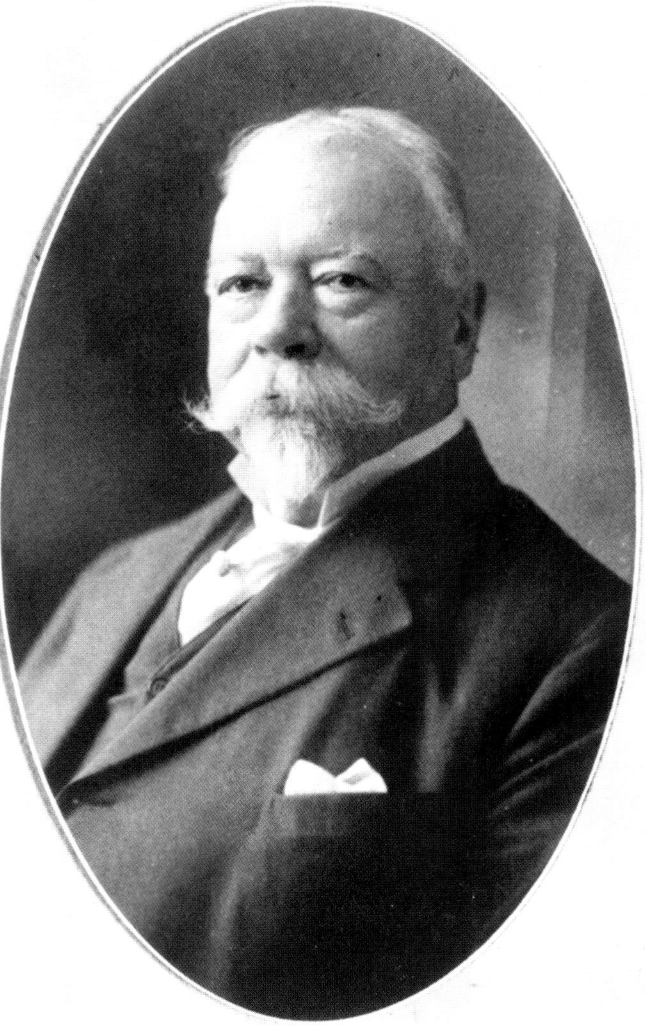

10 *Drawing class in the Children's Museum, 1927.*

11 *James Goold Cutler, 1917. Photograph courtesy of the University of Rochester Library.*

12

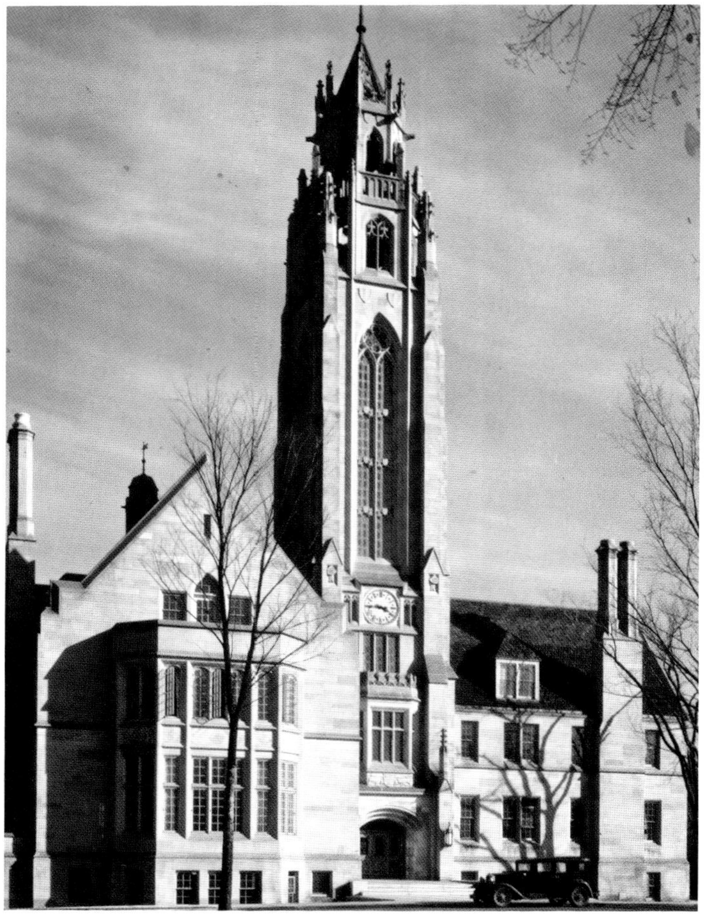

12 *Cutler Union in the 1930's*

13 *Cutler Union under construction, 25 October 1932.*

"On the first floor of Cutler Union a certain social refinement will prevail," said the *Tower Times*, newspaper of the College for Women, the offices of which were on the second floor along with the Sketch Club, the alumnae secretary, and the YWCA (presided over by Mrs. Harper Sibley as "religious advisor").

"While the organization rooms are simple and businesslike and the lounges downstairs suggest eighteenth century elegance, the YWCA room is modern with smooth wood surfaces, soft and unusual colors, and the straight and simple lines of the new design," the *Times* went on. The YWCA room would later become the Howard Hanson Chapel after the women moved to the River Campus in 1955 and the Eastman School of Music received Cutler Union in exchange for $650,000 of its endowment funds.

"The greatest part of the basement is given over to the cafeteria and dining rooms. Long windows, practically all above ground, will allow plenty of light and ventilation," the *Times* of 1930 continued. In 1966 the same rooms would make wonderful Creative Workshop studios as designed by Langdon Clay.

The basement cafeteria served as the restaurant for the neighborhood, a kind of Algonquin Hotel for the university and Gallery staffs, and any coffee house philosophers who should happen to walk in. After 1966 the dumbwaiter would serve as kiln flue for ceramics classes. In 1987, when Cutler Union became part of the Gallery complex, a public restaurant opened on its balustraded terrace, adjacent to a plant-filled sculpture court. The wrought iron of the staircases in Cutler Union was designed and fabricated by Samuel Yellin, as were the University Avenue gates, which now lead to the 1987 entrance.

Yellin (1885-1940) was a blacksmith who achieved master status forging armor in his native Poland before emigrating to Philadelphia. Working prolifically from 1910 until his death, Yellin employed 200 blacksmiths for the largest wrought-iron commission ever awarded, the Federal Reserve Bank in New York. Widely acclaimed during his working career, Yellin was the first craftsman in America to be honored with a medal from the American Institute of Architects in recognition of his work.

Another Philadelphia metalsmith grew up surrounded by Yellin's commissions. When the second metalsmith

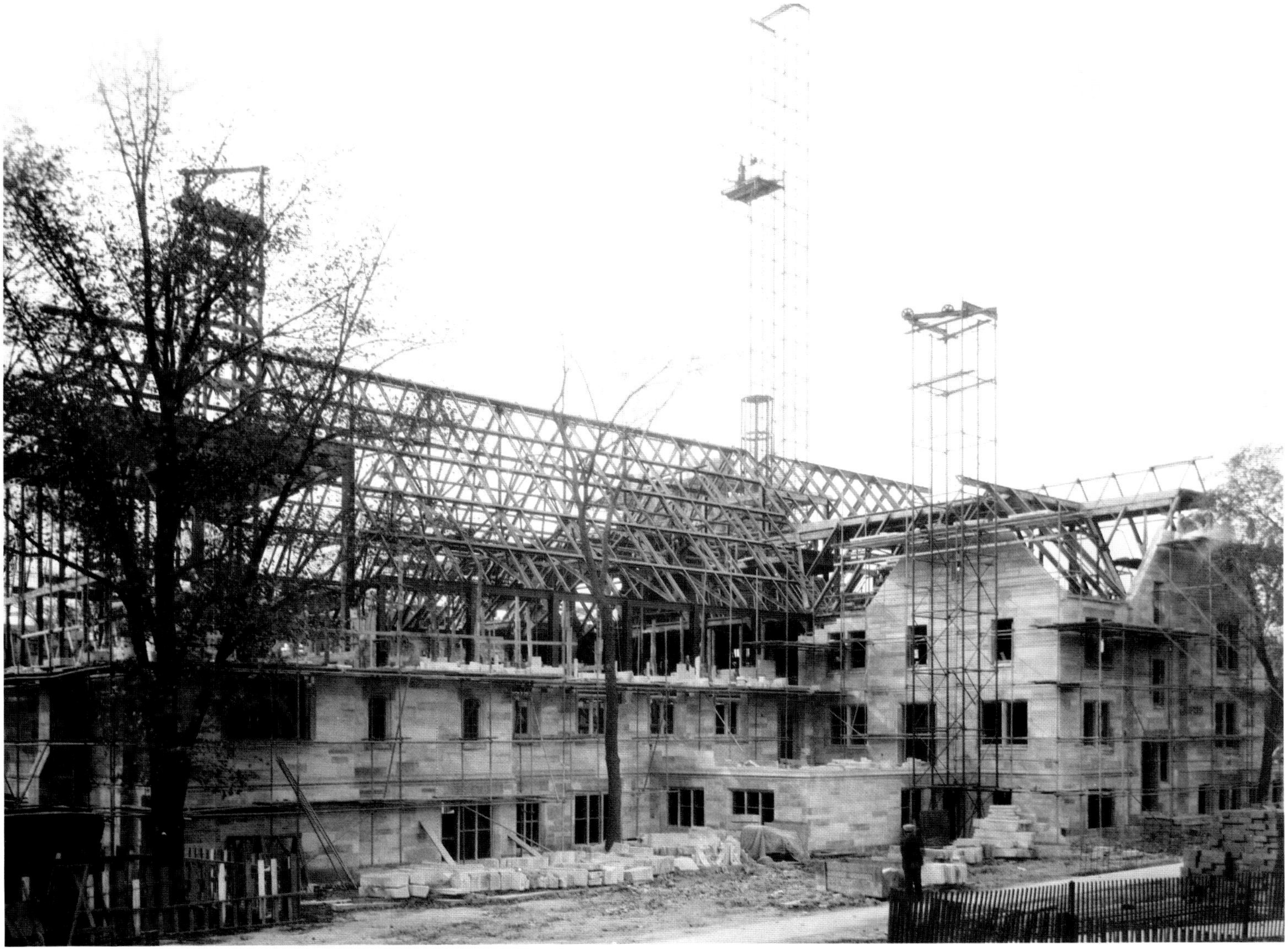

moved to Rochester he immediately recognized his idol's work in the decorative grillwork in the conservatory of the George Eastman House. It is fitting that a major sculpture by that second metalsmith, Albert Paley, now stands just yards from Samuel Yellin's beautiful gates, which once again serve as grand portals of entry to the Memorial Art Gallery.

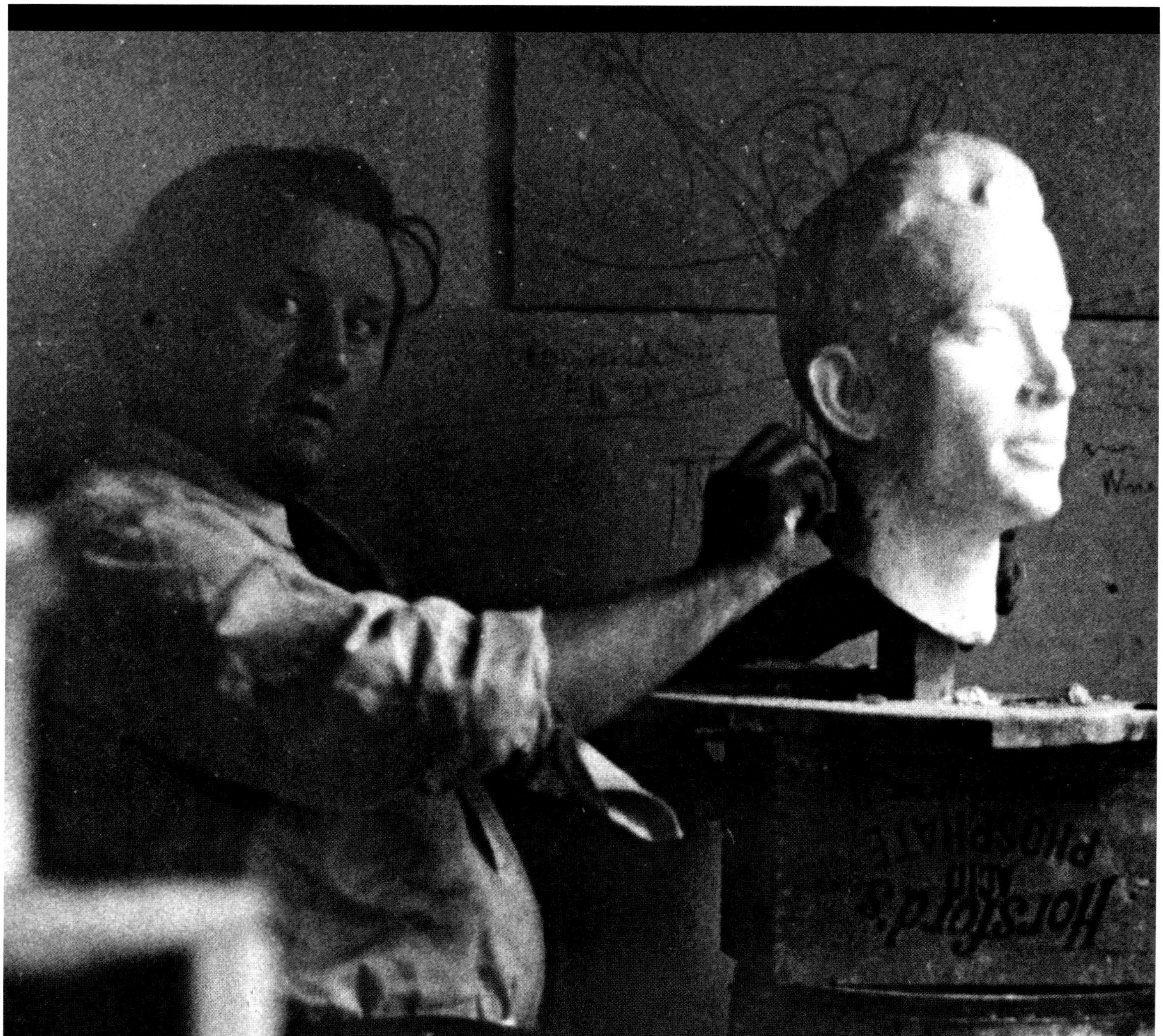
Horsford's
ACID
PHOSPHATE

5: Collecting with a Purpose

5

The permanent collection is the best balanced of any art museum in the state outside of metropolitan New York City.

Art Tours & Detours in New York State | S. Lane Faison Jr., 1964

The collection was formed from the beginning to be "an instrument of art instruction."

Gertrude Herdle Moore, Isabel C. Herdle | 1961

Gaston Lachaise working on the portrait head of James Sibley Watson Jr.

"A fine piece of rare old lace was given by Mrs. Keddie Fletcher of London," the first annual report of October 1914 ended. Bearing the acquisition number 13.1, that lappet of Burano lace began the permanent collection, insuring that it would encompass more than just contemporary painting. Without endowment or a preformed donor collection, the acquisition of "masterpieces" was impossible. The liaison with the university favored developing along general historical rather than specialized lines. The emphasis on a solid teaching collection is expressed in the founding purpose of the Gallery as "an instrument of art instruction."

That by 1964 the collection was "the best balanced" in the state after such encyclopedic giants as the Metropolitan and Brooklyn museums, as Faison's epigraph beginning this chapter indicates, is testimony to astute collecting. George Herdle was convinced that no period or type of art was unsuitable for an art museum to collect, and his philosophy prevailed.

For educational reasons nineteenth century museums "procured casts in plaster of the most beautiful pieces of ancient sculpture in the Louvre," Robert de Forest had noted at the opening ceremonies, and "the seed they planted nourished through many years by other efforts, seemingly abortive, finally blossomed" into the art museums of the twentieth century. Casts served the same function that copies of European paintings in the Powers Art Gallery had: to educate, entertain, visually excite, and heighten the aesthetic sensitivity of a population which had little chance of ever seeing the originals.

By 1914 the collection had twelve oils, seven watercolors, ten casts, one sculpture, *Memory*, and one decorative object (the lace). By the director's Annual Report of 1915-1916, twenty-one oils, eight watercolors, six drawings, six casts, one sculpture and three laces were listed, plus 1,519 books, 1,556 lantern slides, 4,156 photographs, and 4,000 photographic reproductions in the study collection. The collection languished for twenty-five years, with educational material outstripping original art, until an endowment for acquisitions became operative. Then a more organized effort began, and by 1988 the permanent collection of original works of art consisted of almost 10,000 objects.

About 4,500 or almost half of the 1988 works are on paper: prints, drawings, and watercolors. The watercolor collection began in October 1913 with three paintings by Harvey Ellis—one the gift of Erickson Perkins and two presented by Ellis's Art Club colleagues. That year also saw the start of the print collection—with a small, choice selection of post-Renaissance etchings and copper engravings (includ-

1

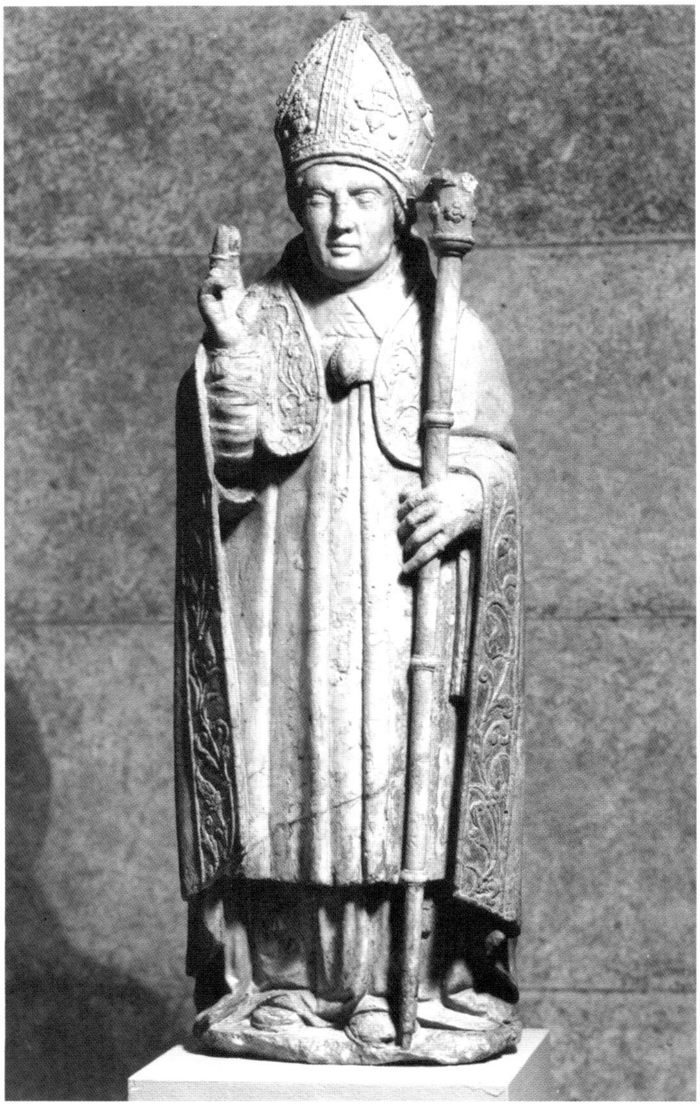

[redacted]

1 *French, region of Amiens, fourteenth century, A Bishop, limestone with traces of polychrome, h. 39½ in. Gift of George J. Demotte, 23.9*

2 *The Sculpture Hall (formerly the Hall of Casts) in 1955 included Memory and the cast of the Parthenon frieze as well as cases for ancient and ethnic art designed by Tage Frid of the Rochester Institute of Technology.*

2

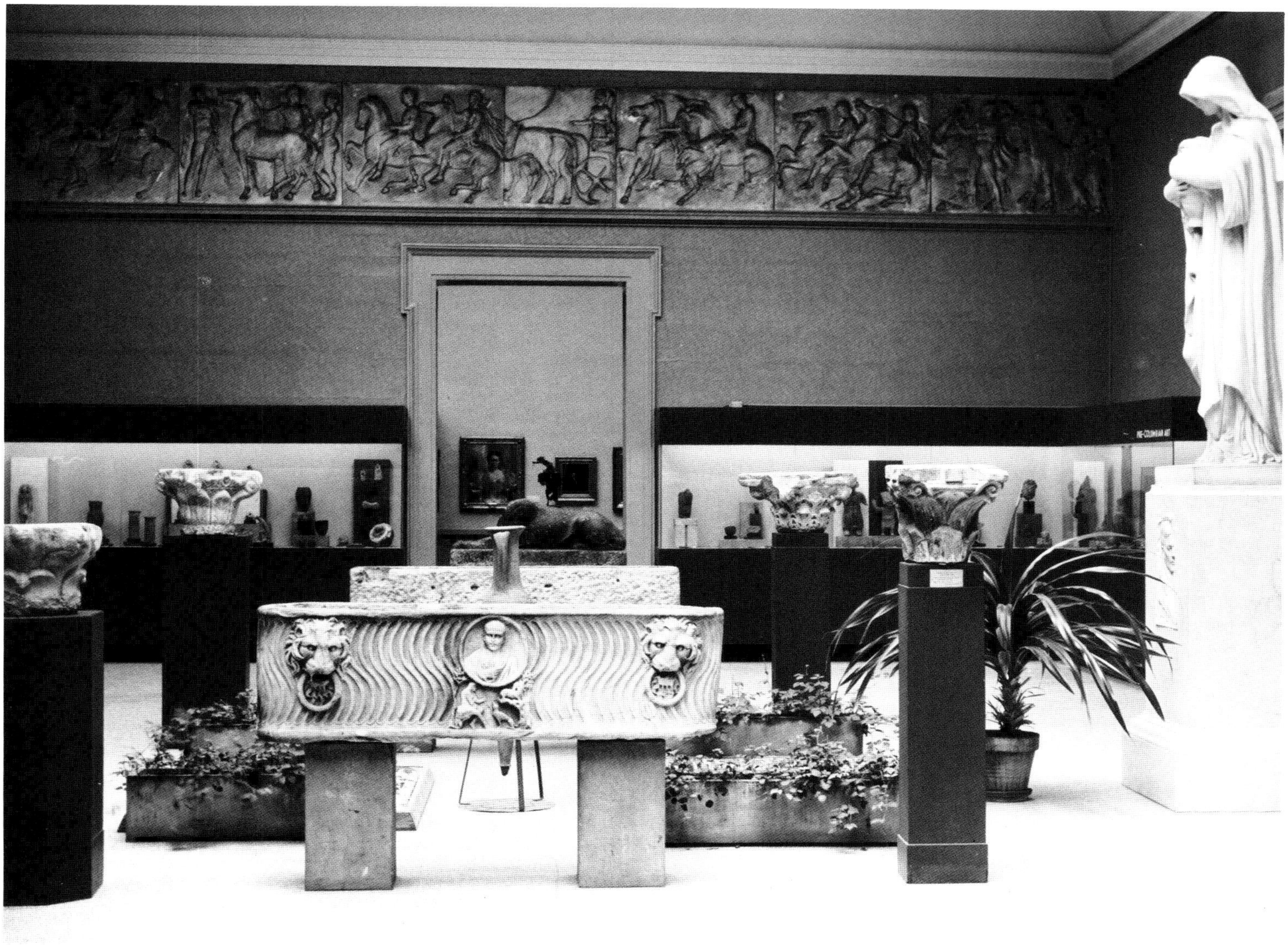

ing some by Dürer) formed by J. G. Averell. It was enlarged in 1924 by English, French, Dutch, and German prints, including some by William Sharp and Lucas Cranach, from the estate of Martin Brewer Anderson.

Herdle's interests were evident from the very beginning. Nine of the thirty-one works of art acquired in 1913 were American paintings.

During the many years the Gallery went without endowment, "you not only had to persuade people to give," Gertrude Moore says, "you had to get them to give what you wanted and needed." "Individual possession almost invariably precedes public gift," de Forest had counseled. He did not advise, however, what to do about gifts one does not wish to accept, a perennial problem that had also begun in 1913 when Rush Rhees wrote Cornelia Bentley Sage a week before the dedication:

We have an offer of a donation of a picture from Mr. Harrington Fitzgerald, Art Editor and Proprietor of the Philadelphia Item. *I have told him that his generous proposal would be submitted to our Art Committee.... We are conscious of the fact that art galleries have to look gift horses in the mouth. I am therefore interested in Mr. Fitzgerald's statement that the Albright Art Gallery has one of his pictures. What can you tell me about it?*

The question was less acute when the Rochester Art Club offered paintings it had collected for the public museum it had long labored to achieve. George Herdle presumably passed on those works himself.

When the Art Committee said "No," the director became the messenger of bad news, sometimes persuading an artist or donor to exchange a work for a more appropriate one. "The Gallery is unable to accept many objects offered as gifts," Herdle would explain in softening the blow, "because they do not belong in an art gallery" or "because

3

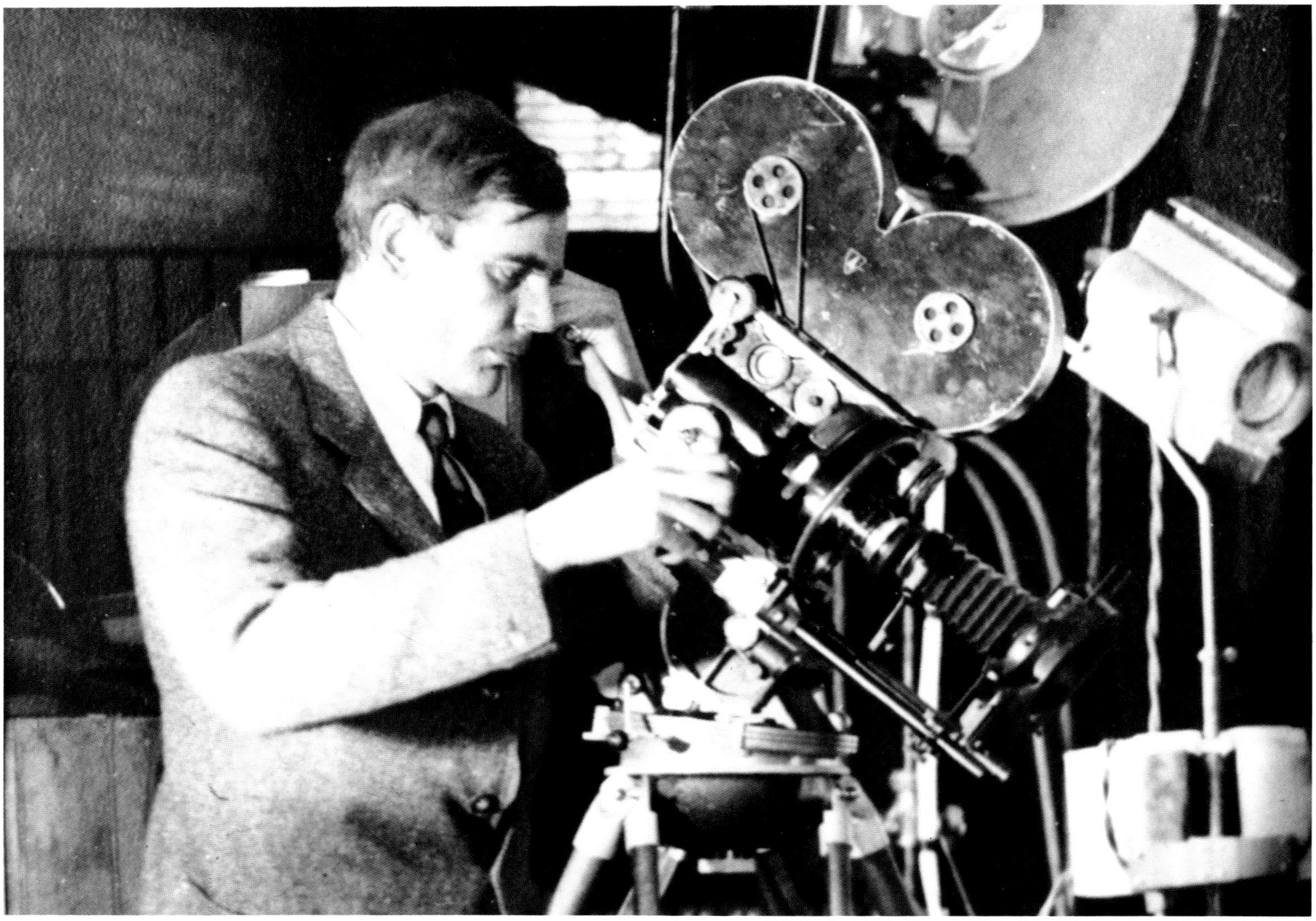

3 *James Sibley Watson Jr. filming in his Prince Street studio.*

while they are representative they are not up to museum standards.... Your offer is very much appreciated."

By 1926 seventy-one donors had contributed to the permanent collection.

The right connections helped. Gertrude Herdle had been director for only a few months when George Demotte, dealer in French medieval sculpture through a Paris museum and salesroom with a New York branch, began making goodwill gifts to selected museums. Since the Gallery specialized in pictorial art, it was not included in the list. Enlisting Rhees's help, the new director "brought to [Demotte's] attention the place the Gallery was trying to fill in Rochester" and was invited to New York. Allowed to choose from among six sculptures, she selected a forty-inch, fourteenth century, Picardy School figure of a bishop, reputedly from a church in Amiens, in limestone with traces of polychrome. Following removal from its original site, the work had been part of the famous "Madame X" collection brought to this country many years previous and thereafter passed to Demotte. Elated by this unexpected beginning of the medieval sculpture collection, Gertrude telegraphed the vacationing Rhees who, unaccustomed to urgent telegrams, feared that something dreadful had happened.

At the Gallery the *Bishop* was "placed on a black pedestal and behind it, a strip of red brocade."

Gertrude planted the seed with the Watsons that the best way to celebrate Christmas was by gifts to the Gallery. Emily Watson's first gift was a *Madonna and Child* painting by Joachim de Patiner, which she purchased from the Christmas exhibit of 1922. It was just a study piece, but it began the trend, and this woman who had lost two children prematurely would shortly select three more Madonna subjects as gifts for the Gallery.

On being informed that it was his wife's turn to underwrite the small Matisse painting, *Girl with a Tricorne*, which arrived late in 1924, James Watson mumbled, "Well, never mind," and promptly signed her name to the check. He could do such things: he was the president of the bank.

Matisse had personally selected *Girl with a Tricorne* for the show at the Fearon Galleries in New York. "This figure painting seems to us superior to the rest," *Art News* opined, "superior in fact to anything else in the exhibition." Emily Watson thought so too; she purchased the Matisse painting—as she had done earlier with Picasso's *Flowers in a Blue Vase*—not to make a statement or be in vogue but simply because she liked it. A *New York Times* critic wrote of "passing over the human type in the other paintings...one arrives at a recent version of a little girl...with something of the elegance of Spain in her long features.... A picture warm and mellow." The *New York Evening Post* writer latched on to "the skirt which professes to be a pinkish apricot color...[but] in reality has every hue known and many unknown to the ordinary eye." *Art News* noted Matisse's growing reputation as a colorist but maintained he also "often has his tongue in his cheek" and concluded by predicting that "the heresy of today becomes the dogma of tomorrow." Yet there is little that 1988 eyes would consider heretical about *Girl with a Tricorne*, so far have the boundaries of "art" been pushed.

While his mother was purchasing her Monets, Matisses, and Picassos, Dr. James Sibley Watson Jr. presented John Marin's *Three Master*, a typical Marin watercolor, as his first gift to the Gallery in 1925. (The local press was unimpressed, giving more prominence to a work by Inness.) In the 1920s, Sibley Watson, graduate of Harvard and New York University Medical School, was making his mark as an innovative filmmaker and copublisher of *The Dial* magazine. He and Scofield Thayer had revived this foremost literary magazine as a means of publishing the best artistic talents in the country, both literary and visual. In 1924 selections were exhibited at the Gallery from the *Dial Portfolio of Living Art*— works by Picasso, Matisse, Maillol, Signac, Laurencin, Bonnard, Demuth, Marin, Chagall, Vlaminck, Lachaise, and Archipenko. Because the *Dial* collection was purchased by Thayer and not Sibley Watson, it eventually went to other museums and not the Gallery.

During Thanksgiving week of 1926 invitations went out for a musicale in the Gallery auditorium at which Mr. and Mrs. Watson Sr. presented their daughter-in-law, Hildegarde, who sang to the accompaniment of harpsichord and piano. Born in Boston, Hildegarde Lasell had studied art and languages in Florence. She and Sibley Watson were married in 1916 and henceforth she would act in her husband's films, sing, paint, fish, and write. She was also an expert on wildflowers, a photographer, and an active preservationist.

In the 1920s the Sibley Watsons moved from New York into a family-owned home on Sibley Place next to "Woodside," home of Sibley Watson's cousin, Marie Atkinson Willard. Beginning in 1940 it would house the Rochester Historical Society. From then until her death, Hildegarde was the director of Woodside, a house museum which she filled with dioramas of mannequins in period costume. She also became active on the art committee at the Gallery as a sign that a new generation was taking hold there.

In Rochester the scientific facet of Sibley Watson's personality would emerge. As radiologist and researcher he

4

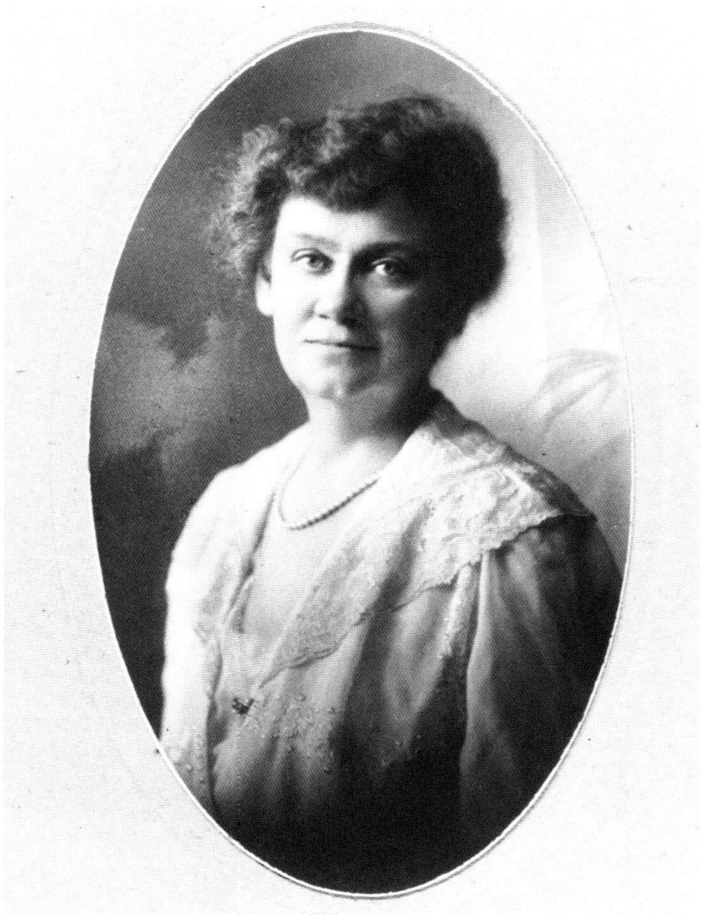

pioneered in optical printers and developed a camera with Dr. Harry Segal that took the first color pictures of the inside of the stomach through a gastroscope. In the 1950s Sibley Watson and Sidney Weinberg designed an improved "cine-fluorographic" (X-ray motion picture) camera. But Sibley Watson also found time to translate French poetry and fly his own plane.

In the late 1920s Sibley Watson and Melville Weber experimented with motion pictures, their equipment sharing the senior Watsons' spacious Edwardian carriage house with the famed "electric." Three of the Watson-Weber short and silent films—*The Fall of the House of Usher, Lot in Sodom,* and *The Dinner Party* (unfinished)—featured the acting talents of Hildegarde Watson, musician Alec Wilder, architect Herbert Stern, and a group of Eastman School students recruited by Wilder to play a crowd of Sodomites in the biblical film. As philanthropist and friend of the arts, Sibley Watson was the epitome of reticence. More than 150 works of art (including a signficant selection of sculpture by Gaston Lachaise) given to the Gallery by him and his family would be labeled "Gift of a Friend of the Gallery." That way, he mumbled with a twinkle (a family trait), he received credit for the gifts from everyone who wished to remain anonymous.

A 1926 exhibition of Irish and Spanish portraits by Robert Henri yielded *Tom Cafferty* for the collection, a gift of Elizabeth Watson Hollister. Of ten lively studies that Henri had done of Irish boys and girls during a stay in County Mayo, *Tom Cafferty* was the favorite of Rochester critics and Gallery-goers. "An alert little person, poised for mischief, with his two hands in his pockets and his hat set aslant," the newspaper reported. "The sprightly modeling of his face...the light in his eyes...the simple shaping of his nose...is done with remarkable simplicity of brush stroke.... There is decision in every brush stroke...[and] organized elimination of the unnecessary."

Hollister, whose $10,000 fund got the library off to a running start, also gave a Renaissance tapestry representing *A Trellised Garden with Animals* in 1931, which enlarged upon the three medieval tapestries given by her brother. Typical of its time in its preoccupation with perspective, *A Trellised Garden* also complemented the Sculpture Hall (formerly Hall of Casts) in which it hung.

"The Hollister tapestry," Gertrude wrote in *The Bulletin* of June-July 1931, "dominates the entire foyer from the point of entrance, assuming an architectural relationship to the building itself, for its period is similarly that of the Early Renaissance, and its formal pattern of classic columns

4 *Elizabeth Watson (Mrs. Granger A.) Hollister, 1917. Photograph by J. Ernest Mock, courtesy of the University of Rochester.*

5 *Man Ray (American, 1890-1976), Hildegarde Lasell Watson, platinum print 9¹⁵/₁₆ x 8 in. Gift of the estate of Helen C. Ellwanger, 82.46*

5

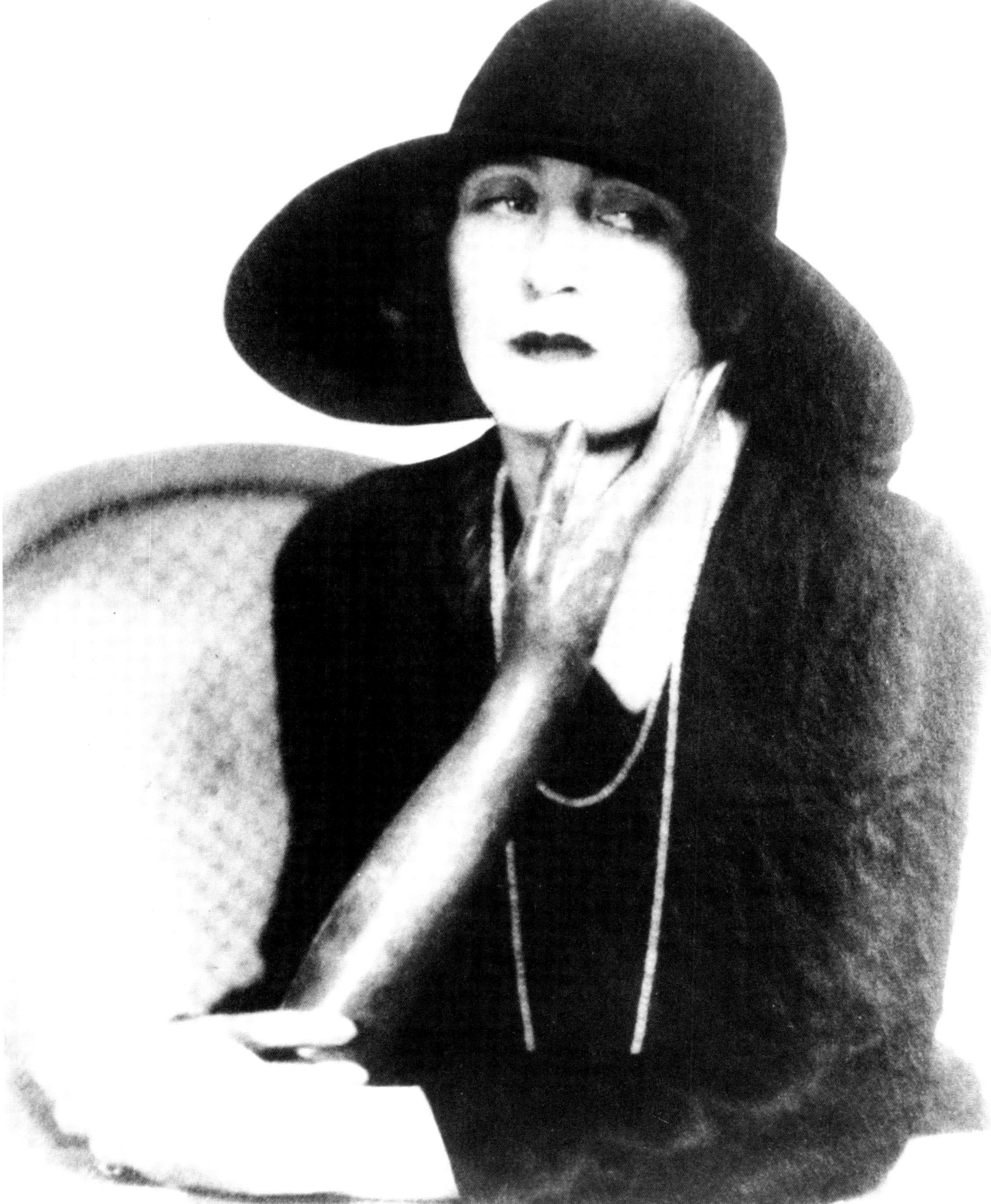

strongly architectonic. The repeated verticals of the shafts enhance the dignity of the interior [of the Gallery, while] the abundant foliation which adorns [the columns in the tapestry] brings a gracious decorative relief."

Because of its stylistic similarity to a tapestry in the Austrian State Collection and the almost certainty that it was drawn by the same cartoonist, the intriguing possibility exists that the Hollister tapestry may have been commissioned by Philip II of Spain. The monogram of famed Brussels tapissier Wilhelm de Pannemaker, court weaver to Charles V and Philip II, is incorporated into the selvage.

Medieval art was the major field of study for both Herdle sisters, resulting in a collection rich in fine examples of Romanesque and Gothic art, and to a lesser extent, early Christian and Byzantine works. Medieval sculpture (in wood, ivory, and stone), stained glass, illuminated manuscripts, tapestries, enamels, furniture, and metalwork—all were purchased at a time when such works were still affordable. Among small museums, few have as impressive medieval collections as the Gallery.

The Watsons also developed an abiding interest in medieval art. Entranced by the bright colors of stained glass, Watson gave the medallion and lancet windows, brilliant examples of their kind. He selected the medieval tapestries, and perhaps most important, he and the Herdles interested his wife in medieval art. A French Gothic *Madonna and Child, School of the Ile-de-France*, almost five-feet tall, in lime-

6

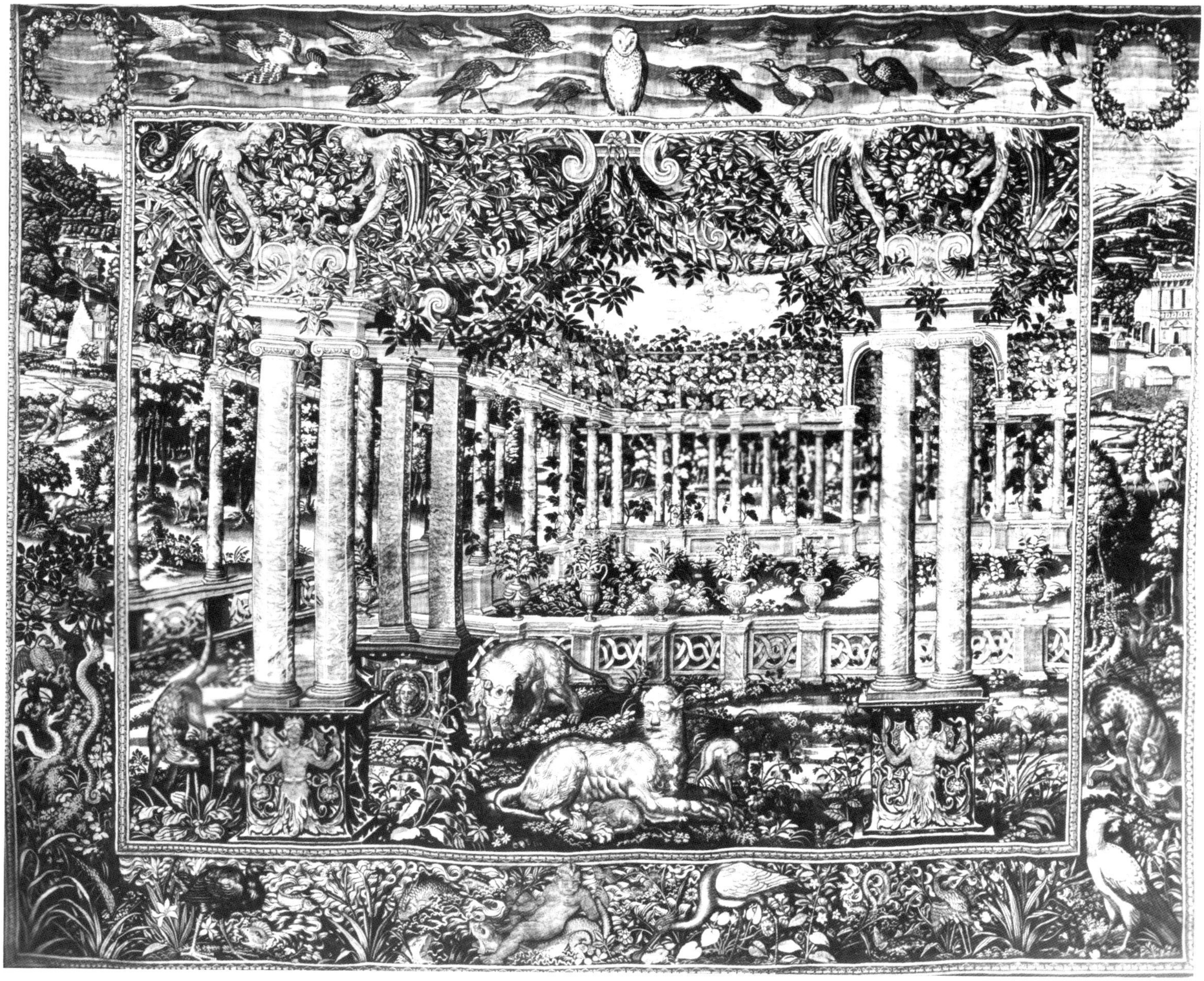

stone with traces of polychrome, was purchased by Mrs. Watson in 1928, marking the most significant medieval sculpture to date.

It is not surprising that Emily Watson would be drawn to this particular crowned rendition of the Queen of Heaven. A petite and swaying figure, she holds a medieval babe with undersized head and modest Greek tunic—no roly-poly nude Renaissance cherub he—on her left hip and the stem of a lost nosegay (probably a lily) in her other tiny hand. In describing the Madonna for the *Bulletin*, Gertrude observed that "minute delicacy of treatment is to be noted in the carving of the hands and features," and among other "benign and tender qualities... the child holds a bird signifying the soul of man."

In 1931 Mrs. Watson gave two Renaissance Madonnas, the terra-cotta style of Ghiberti being the first important Renaissance sculpture to come to the Gallery. This was the way new areas of the collection were started.

When Watson became intrigued by Chinese art and bought Tang tomb figures of a camel and a horse, a Chou ceremonial bronze vessel, and a Siamese head of a Buddha, all in the early 1930s, the Asian collection began.

Occasionally purchase funds were acquired. In 1925 Dr. Charles A. Dewey donated $20,000 for general purposes including "a portion for works of art." Physician and scholar, Dewey was a friend of Herdle, one of the "basement brains" of the Alembic Club, and a bachelor "who loved art always." He had "a regular trysting day" each Sunday at the Gallery with Gertrude to walk through the collection. The first and only significant purchase made in 1930 from the Dewey Fund was *Houses and Trees* by Maurice de Vlaminck. After 1935, with the purchase of only two paintings, the Dewey Fund, at the university treasurer's behest, was used strictly for operating expenses. In the 1980s the fund again began to be used for acquisitions.

Mr. and Mrs. George H. Clark (he was a second-generation Kodak executive) gave money for art in 1929. With the Clarks' gift in hand and the hunch that "the time to get in on Baroque art, then out of favor and hard to find at dealer galleries, was at hand," Gertrude went to the New York branch of the London-based Durlacher Gallery and invested in *St. Stephen* by Domenico Feti.

A monetary gift in 1930 from Mrs. Charles H. Babcock led to the acquisition of the Degas pastel of *The Dancers*— for what would be an absolute steal today. "A person of high intellect," Edith Holden Babcock came from an old New York family. Although she married a prosperous coal dealer and bank president from Rochester and lived out her life in

7

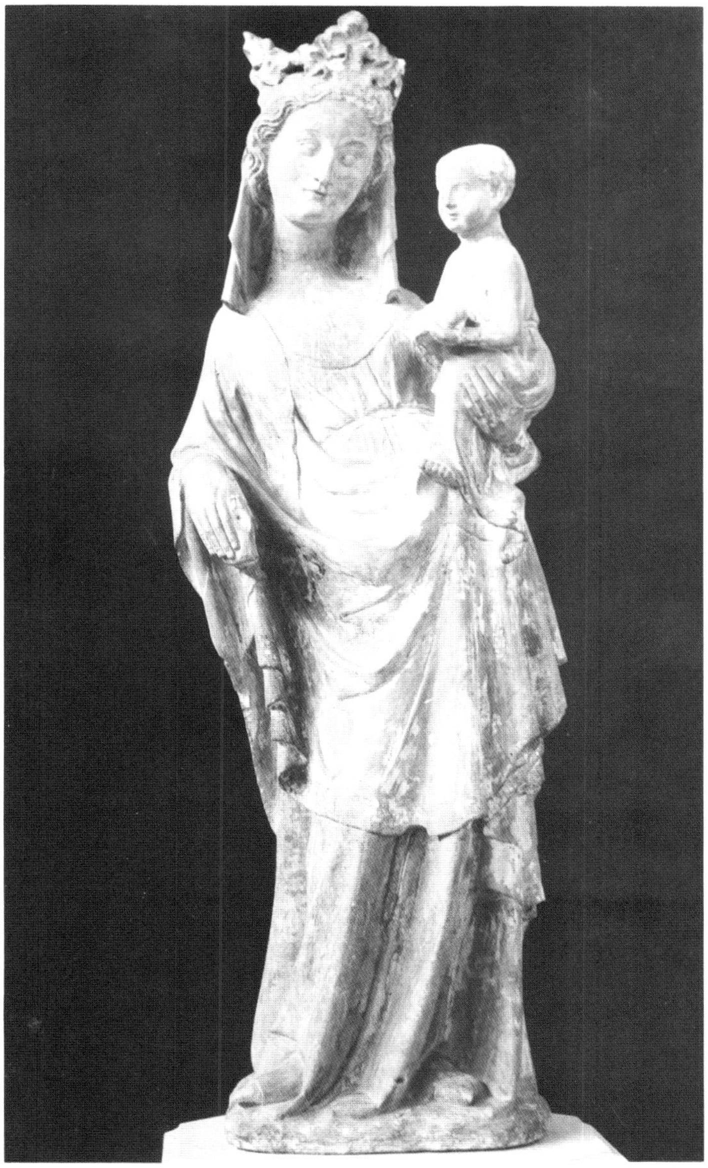

6 *Flemish tapestry, Trellised Garden with Animals, wool with silk, 12 x 15 ft. Wilhelm de Pannemaker, tapissier (active in Brussels 1548-1561). Gift of Mrs. Granger A. Hollister, 31.15*

7 *School of Ile-de-France, fourteenth century, Virgin and Child. Limestone with traces of polychrome, h. 53½ in. Gift of Mrs. James Sibley Watson, 28.466*

8

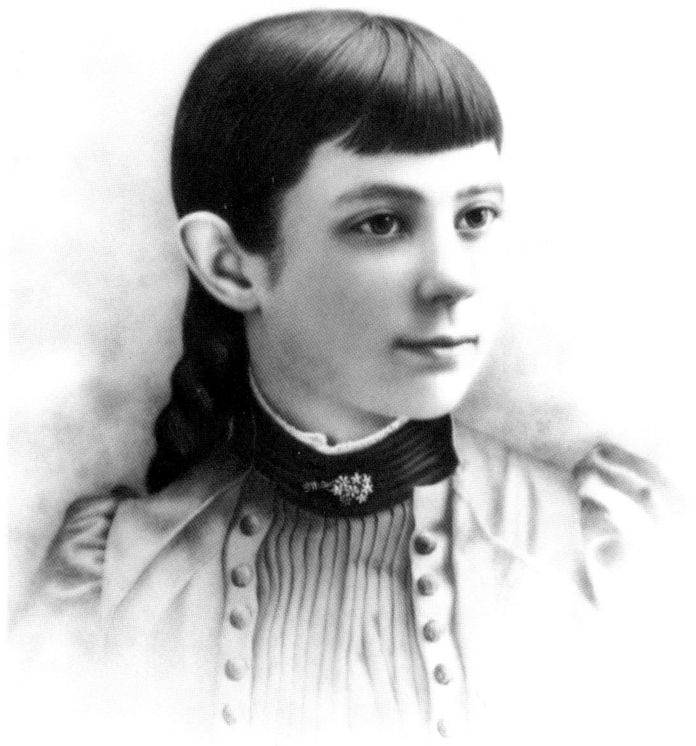

8 *Unknown (American, nineteenth century), Marion Stratton Gould, (1877-1890), hand-colored photograph on opaque glass, 13¼ x 19¼ in. Bequest of Mrs. Samuel Gould, 35.47*

9 *Hannah Durand Gould. Photograph courtesy of Barbara Mackintosh.*

the Third Ward and off East Avenue, essentially she remained a New Yorker, somewhat removed from, yet respected by, the citizens of her adopted city. Three unrestricted gifts of $15,000 each made during her life and a $30,000 bequest were complemented by twenty years of volunteer service to the Gallery. Outside Gallery walls she was chairman of the Rochester School for the Deaf and the Rochester Red Cross, and gave liberally to the Eastman School of Music.

Tall and statuesque, Babcock (1859-1947) loved art, avidly collecting American tonalists for her own home—which was left to the university and used from the late 1940s to the early 1980s as the residence for its presidents. She had a first-rate collection of English and Whistler prints which are now at the Gallery. She furnished the kitchen off the Fountain Court for use during Member Teas and brewed the tea herself using Queen Victoria's favorite recipe. She presented the Gallery with 200 silver spoons, tea cups, and plates, which, unbeknownst to Babcock, at least once were juggled by ex-vaudevillian Sam van Wuyckhuyse. But mostly she liked to come to the Gallery and "Stand and Talk." Although Mr. Pike would slip up to offer a chair she would always refuse it and go on standing and talking.

Babcock's gifts had no strings attached—"a most intelligent way," Gertrude says. She never asked to participate in the choosing. Indeed she did not even see her purchases until they had passed the art committee and were ready for installation. Some of the Gallery's finest works came in this way: *St. Mary Magdalen*, a French Gothic sculpture in stone from the thirteenth century; the Tang Dynasty stone *Kwanyin* (Gertrude's favorite work in the whole collection); and of course, *The Dancers*.

The Dancers crossed the Atlantic in apparent pursuit of Gertrude until she surrendered to their charms and bought Degas's pastel of them. With Babcock's unrestricted gift in her purse the director stopped at the Durand-Ruel Gallery in New York and saw *The Dancers* there. Captivated she was, but with three months in Europe still ahead of her, not ready to commit. Arriving at Durand-Ruel's Paris branch, she found that *The Dancers*, "looking better than ever," had gotten there first. So back across the Atlantic and to Rochester they all went.

While the primary source for art has been individual works from individual donors, other sources have been important too. Private collections, either formed around a theme or a period, or just an amalgam of miscellaneous objects, came by gift or bequest. Some works came through

9

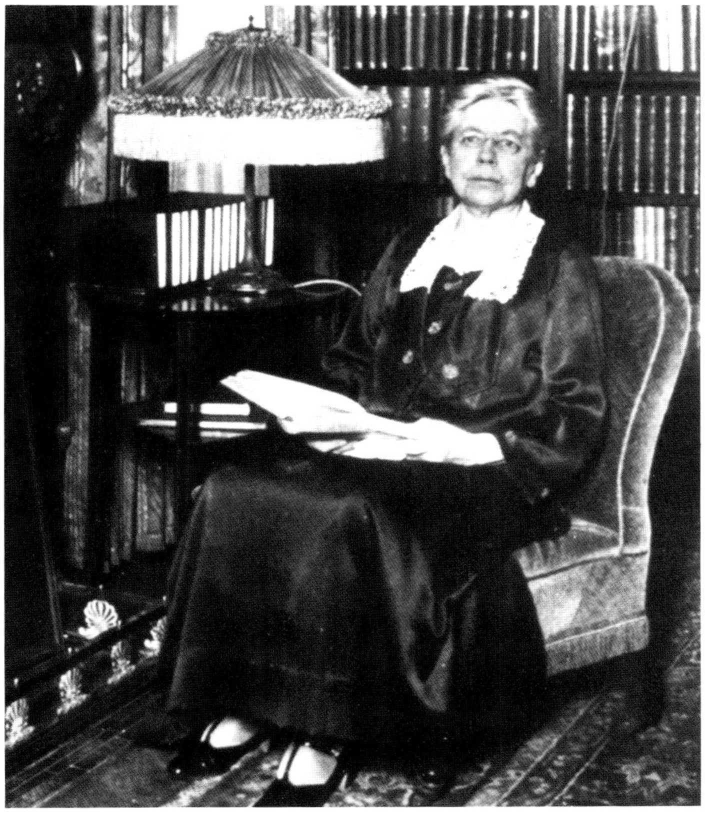

the university. In 1920, for instance, the university contributed funds to Count Byron Khun de Prorok's expedition to the site of Carthage, resulting in forty-two archeological objects entering the collection.

In 1928 the Herbert Ocumpaugh Collection of 498 items comprising Egyptian and Eastern Mediterranean antiquities was given to the university and deposited at the Gallery. The oldest artifacts now in the Gallery collection—prehistoric pottery and clay figures dating from 6000 B.C.—came from Ocumpaugh's cache. For years objects from these two sources (Ocumpaugh and de Prorok) constituted the classical department's collection of antiquities.

One of the most intriguing Ocumpaugh objects is the predynastic *Steatopagus* figure with vulture head, baby in a backpack, and an extended rear. Seeing handbook pictures, scholars have detoured to Rochester, and depending on which expert was last in town, the *Steatopagus* is either "up" or "down," on view or in storage, a rare find or a marvelous fabrication.

Ocumpaugh was a Rochester businessman and real estate investor known as "the King of Clinton Avenue," an inventor and holder of fifty-three patents who had founded the Pullman Sash and Balance Company in 1886. He never visited Egypt or the Near East but formed a lifelong fascination with these exotic lands through visits to the Metropolitan Museum of Art. Through his twenty-five years of collecting objects to augment his study of Egyptian, Greek, and Roman art, Ocumpaugh's advisors included the redoubtable Herbert Winlock—archaeologist, Egyptologist, and director of the Metropolitan, 1932-1939. Wishing to insure that his gift would remain both "alive" and a teaching collection, Ocumpaugh made a deal with Robert MacLean, head of the university's classical department, 1922-1964. In exchange for the collection, MacLean guaranteed a $200 to $500 appropriation from the university each year for twenty-five years to buy more objects. As it worked out, fourteen such objects, including the mosaic floor panel *Head of Tethys* from Antioch, were actually purchased.

Other donor-formed collections included Louis Jewel's Javanese krises (daggers), originally consigned to the Education Department as a study collection. As the value of several of these objects increased, they were upgraded to the permanent collection. Another collection that turned out more valuable than originally suspected was Loristan L. Stone's Turkish and Near Eastern textiles. Still another that rose in value was the Jesse Lindsay collection of fore-edge books. (Both the Stone and Lindsay families were charter members of the Gallery.) Fifteen more of these English books with watercolor paintings on the fore-edge were given to the Gallery in 1952 by Mr. and Mrs. Richard Ford.

English and Continental silver of the seventeenth to nineteenth centuries, given by Mr. and Mrs. Ernest L. Woodward through the university, forms the backbone of the silver collection. Delftware of the same period came in 1929 from Mr. and Mrs. John Oothout. European laces and textiles, Japanese sword guards, Northwest Indian totems, Egyptian and Palestinian textiles, and English and French engravings were among other donor-formed collections that came in the 1920s. Similar lists could be drawn up for succeeding decades.

The early Javanese batiks that Benjamin Forman presented in 1937 were assembled not as a private collection but in response to the Gallery staff's parting words, "Think of us," as the Rochester merchant embarked on one of his many travels through southeast Asia. The batiks were selected with the aid of the director of a Balinese museum.

Bequests were an important source. A miscellaneous assortment of family accumulations—paintings, glass, ceramics, sculpture, including the bust of *Francis Granger* by Hiram Powers—came from Antoinette Pierson Granger of Canandaigua in 1930. Many of the objects were loaned back to the Granger Homestead when that opened as a museum. Edward Bausch bequeathed German paintings; Ida Lynch,

American engravings and etchings; Mrs. Ernest Willard, American paintings; and Mrs. Granger Hollister, English hunting prints.

Beginning with the painting purchased for the Gallery by a group of his friends from the George L. Herdle Memorial Exhibition in 1922, group subscriptions have added works of art to the collection. Friends of Jonas Lie purchased his painting, *Evening*, for the collection. In 1927 friends of Kathleen McEnery purchased and presented her painting entitled *Mood*. More recently, the Priscilla Parker Memorial Print was given annually by a group of her students.

Kathleen McEnery (1885-1971) is one Rochester artist with strong Gallery ties whose star has risen in recent years. In 1988 her work is prominently featured in the new National Museum of Women in the Arts in Washington, D. C.

Born in Great Barrington, Massachusetts, schooled in Paris and at the Pratt Institute, McEnery studied with Robert Henri. She came to Rochester in 1914 as the bride of Francis E. Cunningham and was said to have exerted thereafter considerable influence on the coloring, if not the styling, of the Cunningham cars that her husband's family manufactured.

Her kind of professional training was a rarity in its day, particularly for a woman. The fact that she had exhibited two paintings of nudes in the scandalous Armory Show of 1913 horrified much of Rochester society. A woman of high spirits and strong opinions, she served on the Gallery's art committee and Board of Managers from 1927 until her death. Highly influential in the Rochester art world, she was also active in the women's suffrage movement, the founding of both the Harley School and the Corner Club, and delighted in controversial world issues.

McEnery's *Fallen Puppet* was a gift to the Gallery from Charlotte Whitney Allen in 1964; *Puppets* was given by Mrs. Joseph F. Taylor in 1969. In 1984 McEnery's children, Peter Cunningham, Joan Cunningham Williams, and Michael McEnery Cunningham, presented the Gallery with the full-length portraits of *Woman with Ermine Collar* and *Colette*. In 1988 *Woman with Ermine Collar* is prominently displayed as part of the American collection.

In 1925 an immensely popular exhibition of the sculpture of Ivan Mestrovic led to the organizing of 108 subscribers to purchase three of his works. An Art Patron's Purchase Award (later called the Juror's Award) was begun to secure a work from that annual survey of local art, the Finger Lakes Exhibition. One so purchased in the 1940s was Douglas

10

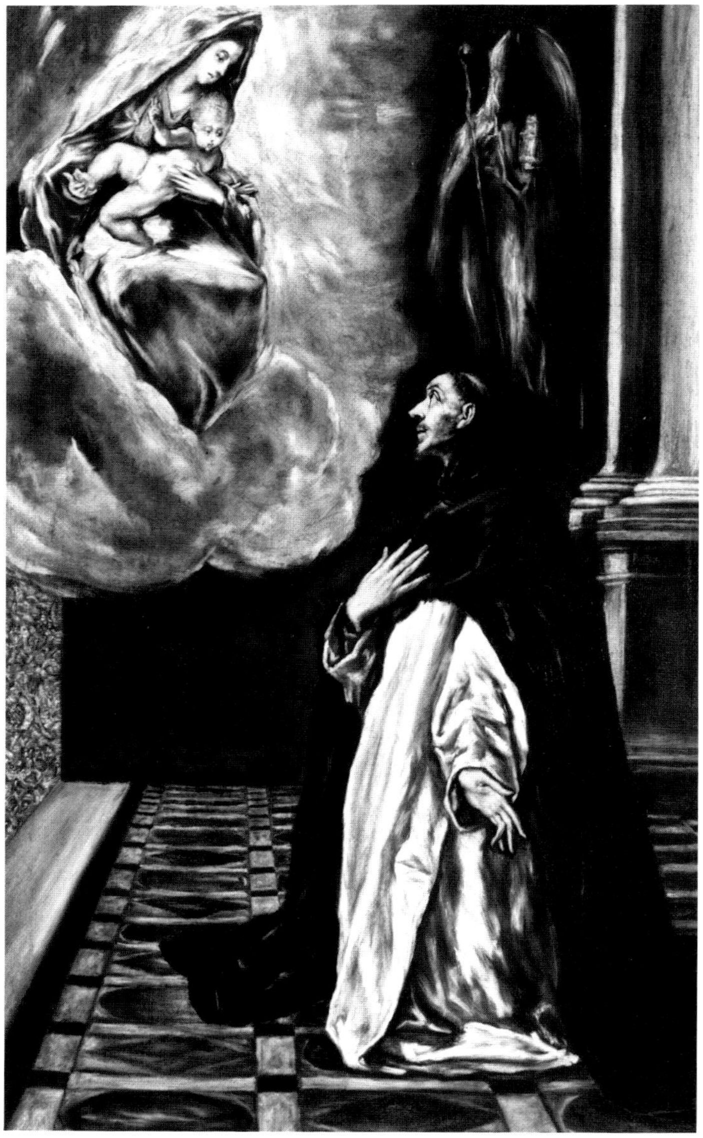

10 *Domenikos Theotokopoulos, called El Greco (Spanish 1541-1614), The Apparition of St. Hyacinth to the Virgin, oil on canvas, 38½ x 23½ in. Marion Stratton Gould Fund, 38.28*

11 *Benjamin Pyne (English), Caudle Cup: "Saltby Plate," 1710, gold, 4¼ in. Gift of Mrs. Edith Woodward, 54.13*

Gorsline's *Barroom Scene*. And the Women's Council has regularly purchased a print through its Artists-in-the-Kitchen fund-raising events.

Some acquisitions arrived most unexpectedly. In 1937, for example, an illustrated lecture by Gertrude on the English School of Nottingham was attended by Mrs. Walter G. Oakman and Mrs. James Hammond MacVeagh. Listening in the wings was their chauffeur. The trio got to talking on the way home, and the chauffeur suggested that the "thing" being used as a doorstop in the garage looked a great deal like one of Gertrude's slides. Sure enough, a short time later the ladies brought forth a fifteenth century alabaster relief, once probably the center panel from an altarpiece. Authenticated, the doorstop has since then been displayed in the Fountain Court under the label, *Trinity, School of Nottingham.*

The American Impressionist painter, Childe Hassam, was a friend of George Herdle, and while Hassam always refused a loan show at the Gallery (Rochester was too small for the sales he wanted, he told Gertrude), after his death his widow gave the Gallery some thirty of his lithographs.

That most sensible plan for acquisitions, the Marion Stratton Gould Fund, was the bequest of Hannah Durand (Mrs. Samuel) Gould. Friend of George Herdle and collector of his paintings, Hannah Gould was a member of the Board of Managers in her later years, 1924-1930. In 1920 she had given the Gallery a carbon photograph of Amiens Cathedral, apparently her first gift. Marion Stratton Gould was only thirteen when she died on Christmas Day of 1890. In 1925 her mother presented four Verona marble columns and a marble fountain for the new addition, complete with a reproduction of Verrocchio's *Putto with Dolphin* as a memorial to Marion, "whose love of beauty in the arts in her short life was given this noble commemoration." Hence the name of that central gallery thereafter: "The Fountain Court." In 1929 Hannah Gould gave a sixteenth-century Tuscan credenza in memory of Marion.

Little is known of the dark-haired, dark-eyed Marion except that she was a precocious "student of music and art." Marion's paternal uncle was Thomas Ridgeway Gould, sculptor, whose life-sized work *The West Wind* stood for years in the Powers Hotel before entering the Gallery collection, gift of the estate of Isaac Gordon. (The toe of *West Wind* is worn smooth: lawyers passing through the hotel on their way to court rubbed it for good luck.)

Marion's father, Samuel Gould, ran a nursery and seed business and was the Democratic party supervisor of Brighton—a predominately Republican suburb. He died in

11

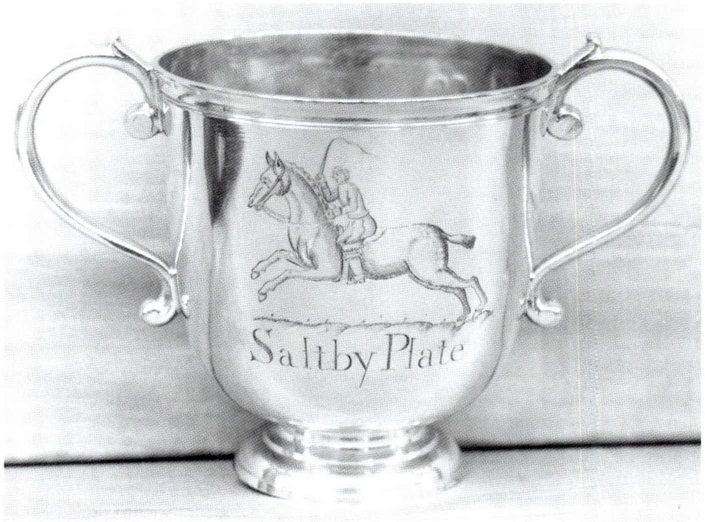

1905 at the age of seventy-seven. In the 1890s Hannah Gould was neighbor to and close friend of Maria Kilbourn Eastman, George Eastman's mother.

As still another memorial to her daughter, Hannah Gould's will of 1930 stipulated that her sister, Jane Durand, have life use of the income from a bequest which reverted to the Gallery upon Durand's death in 1938. And so in its twenty-fifth year the Gallery received its first (and still most significant) endowment for acquisitions: the Marion Stratton Gould Fund, originally worth about $365,000 and in 1988, about ten times that.

A loan exhibition, "Precursors of Modern Art," commemorated the Gallery's twenty-fifth anniversary in 1938. Exhibited were 300 paintings by "the forerunners of modern art who were tradition makers and breakers," Isabel wrote in *Gallery Notes*. Included were El Greco, Constable, Delacroix, Corot, Millet, Courbet, Daumier, Manet, Monet, Degas, Renoir, Pissarro, and Cézanne, "in evolutionary sequence." From this surfeit of riches came the first purchase from the Gould Fund: *The Apparition of the Virgin to St. Hyacinth* by El Greco.

"That painting should never leave," said Mrs. Carl Wilson, Gallery supporter and pillar of the community. She marshalled further support—not difficult since the consensus to buy the El Greco was practically unanimous—and the Gallery had its first acquisition from endowment funds.

The El Greco quickly became a hit beyond its Rochester environs. In 1939 it was featured at the New York's World Fair, and on the cover of *Art News*, and it was named by that magazine as the most significant old master painting acquired by an American museum that year.

With the substantial unrestricted endowment of the

12

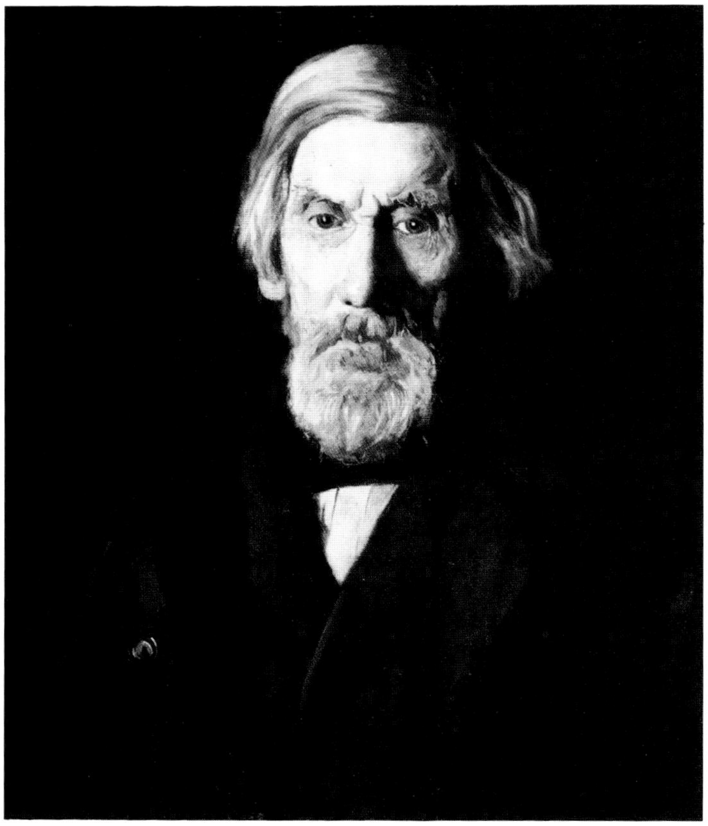

12 *Thomas Eakins (American 1844-1916), Portrait of William H. Macdowell, ca. 1904, oil on canvas, 24 x 20 in. Marion Stratton Gould Fund, 41.26*

13 *Attributed to John James Audubon (American 1785-1851), Portrait of Colonel Nathaniel Rochester, oil on canvas, 30 x 25 in. Presented by Thomas J. Watson to the University of Rochester for the Memorial Art Gallery, 34.1*

Gould Fund the director could better shape the collection. For the first time an accession plan was drawn up in collaboration with university professors Carl Hersey and Sterling Callisen, and revised and refined over the years. As of 1987, 804 items had been purchased with $1,892,466 from the Gould Fund.

In addition to the El Greco, another Gallery painting was featured at the 1939 World's Fair: the *Portrait of Colonel Nathaniel Rochester* attributed to John James Audubon. This exquisite painting, believed to be a likeness of the city's founding father, had long been in the Burlinghan Collection on loan to the Philadelphia Museum. Gertrude learned by telephone of a Sunday afternoon in 1934 that the portrait was about to be auctioned and that Mrs. Chester Dale, a native Rochesterian with a larger pocketbook than the Gallery's, had persuaded Mr. Dale to buy the painting for an exhibition she was planning. The resourceful Gertrude contacted Thomas J. Watson (1874-1956), Upstate New Yorker and president of the International Business Machines (IBM) Corporation. The upshot was that in exchange for allowing Mrs. Dale to borrow the portrait for her exhibition (which eventually fell through) or whenever she chose, the Dales agreed not to bid on the Audubon portrait. Watson then became the successful bidder and presented the *Portrait of Colonel Nathaniel Rochester* to the Gallery.

Early in her career Gertrude had what seemed a golden opportunity to purchase a work by America's premier nineteenth century portrait painter, Thomas Eakins. Museum directors meeting in Philadelphia were invited by Susan Macdowell Eakins, a fine painter in her own right, to visit her late husband's studio but at the last minute the visit was cancelled. Upon the death of Mrs. Eakins in 1938, the portrait of her father, one of at least five that her husband had painted and the only one she had kept herself, came on the market. In 1941 the Gallery purchased it with the Gould Fund from the Robert C. Vose Galleries, Boston.

The incisive and haunting portrait of *William H. Macdowell*, believed by most scholars to have been painted about 1904, making it the last and therefore summarizing one of this model, was, according to Fiske Kimball, director of the Philadelphia Museum, Eakins's own favorite portrait of his father-in-law. The Rembrandtesque *Macdowell*, a man whose hero was Tom Paine, faces his audience with a brooding, introspective stare. Like Rembrandt, Eakins loved to paint the elderly: the marks of age and experience that youth conceals and age reveals, the deepening crater around an eye, the skin stretching tightly across the skull, the cheeks sinking

13

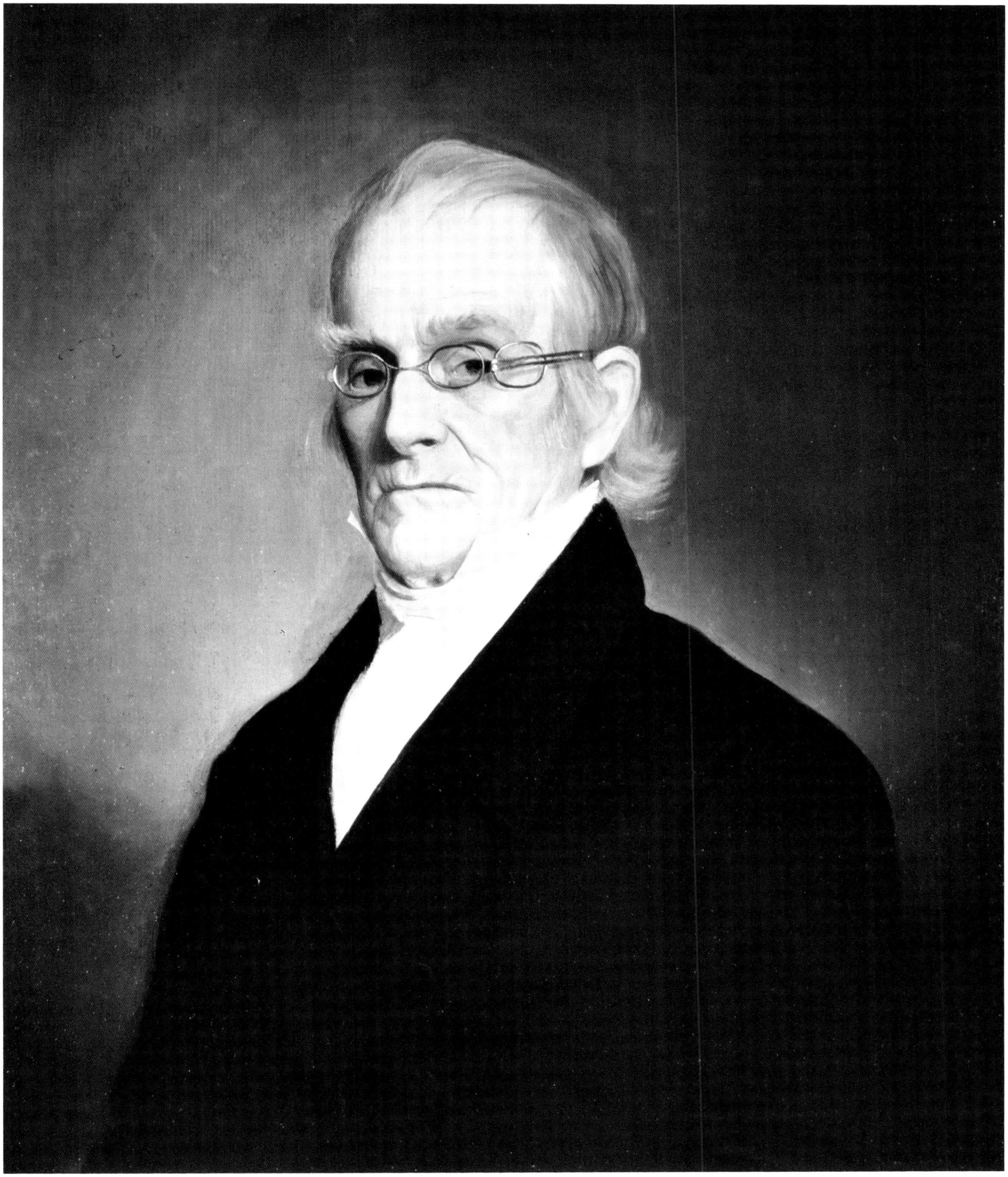

in shadow, the nose grown more formidable.

Not surprisingly, the Eakins portrait is often on tour, including a visit to Russia in 1988. Earlier, on a State Department tour to ambassadors' residences, the painting narrowly escaped serious injury when, in Munich, some damage was sustained to the background, but fortunately not the face, of William H. Macdowell.

R. T. Miller Jr. of Scottsville, New York, a tall and colorful figure garbed in all but the coldest weather in white suit and Panama hat, became one of the Gallery's serendipitous angels. Although he lived until 1958, he was the quintessential Edwardian figure. "I was never bowed to by many other people," Gertrude recalls.

A furniture exhibition at the Gallery in 1932 piqued Miller's interest. "The House of 1834," celebrating the Rochester centennial in 1934, cemented his attention. Visiting it anonymously, he contacted university officials who alerted Mrs. Moore that an exciting project might be in the offing. Impressed by the history of the Genesee region, Miller proposed installing permanent period rooms throughout the Gallery. That was not possible, Gertrude said, and introduced Miller to Mrs. Thomas Spencer and Helen Rochester Rogers of the new Landmark Society, then beginning to furnish the Campbell-Whittlesey House. Miller was skeptical. He wanted his gifts attached to a proven institution. In the end, twenty-three pieces of furniture went to the Campbell-Whittlesey house with ownership and the right to borrow them back vested in the Gallery.

The important by-product was that Romanta Tillotson Miller Jr. (1867-1958), who had adopted R. T. as his official name while keeping the Jr. out of deference to the father whose name he had reduced to initials, became convinced of the Gallery's potential as an educational institution.

Miller had graduated from Oberlin College in 1891, worked as a newspaper reporter, and attended Harvard Law School where he found Charles Eliot Norton's course in art appreciation "worth more than any half dozen other graduate courses at Harvard." He never practiced law. Instead he founded in Boston the American School, a correspondence school "for the purpose of giving practical home study for wage-earners." In 1902 he moved the school to Chicago, where for five years it was associated with the Armour Institute before Miller reestablished it independently. To facilitate its operation, he published technical encyclopedias, correspondence school books—many of which he prepared himself—and periodicals. As his enterprises prospered he set up generous loan funds for talented individuals and by the time he retired in 1937 and returned to his Scottsville birthplace, he had determined to disperse his modest fortune while he lived, making sure none of it went into bricks and mortar. He haunted art museums, developing a discriminating taste of his own that he never fully trusted. Oberlin's museum became the major target of his largess with the Memorial Art Gallery a close second. So far as is known he never bought a single work of art for himself.

During his working years Miller lived in a hotel. The major self-indulgent act of his life was the purchase of a ranch in New Mexico in 1907 which he operated as the second dude ranch in the country. He loved horses and once he and his brothers followed the trails through Cévennes as described by Robert Louis Stevenson in *Travels with a Donkey*. In retirement he wintered in a tiny Florida apartment where he cooked his own meals, and summered in Scottsville with his three sisters in a shabby old Victorian farmhouse. When Gertrude and Isabel were invited to tea, the Miller sisters appeared, one after the other, each with a tray of cookies baked for the occasion. In 1974, in memory of one of those sisters, a nephew, Robert C. Miller, gave the Gallery the ancestral portraits of Elijah Talcott and Ruth Tillotson Miller, attributed to the itinerant American folk artist Noah North.

Visiting the Gallery became a regular if unannounced habit for R. T. Miller Jr. He would simply arrive at the door, Panama hat in hand, and ask to be shown around. As he prepared to leave, his parting words were invariably the same: "I'm going home now and scrape the bottom of the barrel." A few days later a check for five, ten, or even twenty-five thousand dollars would arrive, accompanied by the single stipulation that the money be spent within a year on objects of "an educational nature." On his next surprise visit Miller would casually ask to see the result of his latest gift. He refused to participate in the selection of the works of art and his reactions were typically diffident and non-judgmental. The one exception was Winslow Homer's *Artist's Studio in an Afternoon Fog*. "At first he didn't respond," Isabel recalls, "but he grew to love it and then was warmly receptive."

During the two decades that Miller was making his educational contributions it was still possible to buy works of quality for relatively modest sums. Ninety-nine objects in the 1961 handbook were purchased through the Miller fund which totalled $100,000 during his lifetime, plus a $25,000 bequest in 1958. Gagini, Degas, and Rodin sculptures, medieval ivories, enamels, a sarcophagus, the baptismal font, and the "Doubting Thomas" capital were all purchased

14

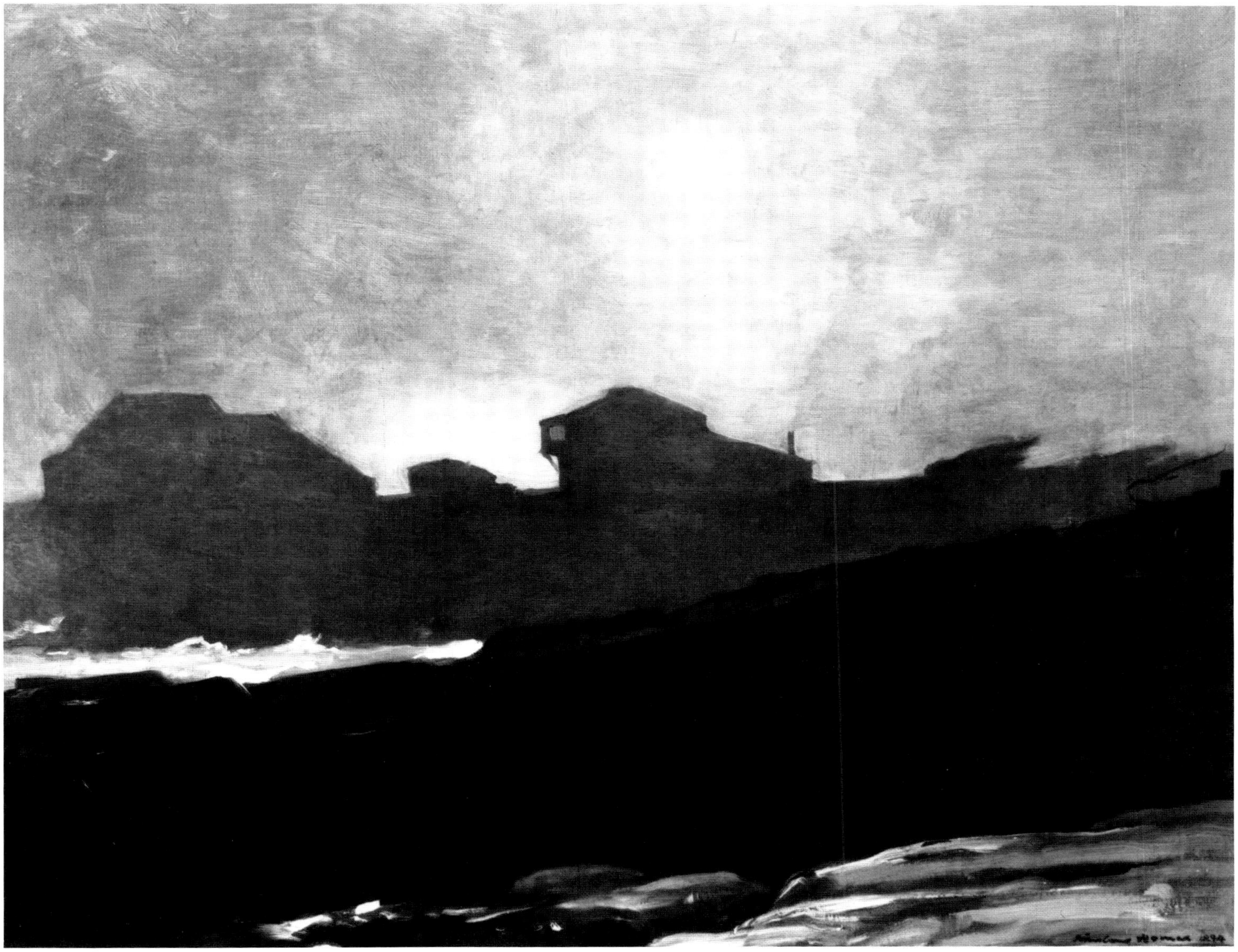

14 *Winslow Homer (American 1836-1910), Artist's Studio in an Afternoon Fog, 1894, oil on canvas. 24 x 30 in. R. T. Miller Fund, 41.32*

with the Miller largess. So were Persian reliefs, bronzes, and bowls; illuminated manuscripts; Indian sculptures; Chinese tomb figures; Chou Dynasty vessels; Wei Dynasty figures; the seated Kwanyin of the Sung Dynasty; pre-Columbian figures, textiles, vessels, and masks; Polynesian and African artifacts; Greek, Etruscan, and Roman kraters and sculptures; and Egyptian sculptures and reliefs.

Donor-formed collections that came to the Gallery, often through the university, added significantly to the permanent collection. Two major ones, besides the Ocumpaugh Collection, were the George Eastman Collection and the Buswell-Hochstetter bequest.

The largest bequest of works of art in Gallery history began to take shape in 1932 when Eastman left his mansion and its contents to the university. The sixty-odd Old Master, British, Dutch, American, and French Barbizon School paintings that once hung in his home form the nucleus of these areas of the collection today.

Eastman began collecting in the 1890s. His first purchases were watercolors by the Rochester artist Charles Gruppe in 1891, followed by salon paintings he acquired during business and bicycling trips through Europe. Once his mansion was completed in 1905 he began collecting in earnest, primarily through New York dealers Carmen Messmore of Knoedlers and the William Macbeth Gallery. His small "art committee" (his words) included Frank Babbott, a highly schooled and cultured childhood friend (Eastman was a seventh-grade dropout) who had a fine oriental collection, access to the best collections in the country, and was president of the Brooklyn Museum. Another member was Joseph Thacher Clarke of Boston and London, who trained as an architect and art historian but practiced as the Eastman Kodak Company's patent expert for Europe. A third was Josephine Dickman, widow of his London manager, who visited the Havemeyer, Frick, and Widener collections with Eastman.

His final choices reflected his idiosyncratic love of cool, aloof British portraits, bucolic landscapes usually featuring cows browsing in pastures, and cozy domestic scenes. He wouldn't buy a work until he had lived with it for a while, and somehow he persuaded dealers to leave paintings with him for years while he made up his mind. Unfortunately for the Gallery, he returned or rejected some gems, Homer's *Gulf Stream* and works by Vermeer, J. M. W. Turner, and Goya among them. Sir Henry Raeburn's *Portrait of General Hay MacDowell* once was returned to its dealer, only to be recalled when Eastman found he sorely missed it.

His collection drew scholars to Rochester. Wilhelm Bode, director of the Kaiser Friedrich Museum in Berlin and premier Rembrandt expert of the day, came to examine *A Young Man in an Armchair with Clasped Hands and a Gold Chain*.

> ... *Thank you for permission to look at your pictures and the fine and comfortable house. I was glad to see again the Rembrandt which I knew so well when it was in the coll. of my friend A. Beit and when it was in Berlin in our Museum to be cleaned. It is of course a very vigorous and sympathetic picture of his [Rembrandt's] very best time, full of life and masterly painted. The price you paid for it [$112,000] was certainly a modest one compared with the prices paid lately for Rembrandt's pictures of the same time. The Mill has been sold at 100,000 pounds [$500,000 in 1911].... As Oscar Beit had 3 other Rembrandts and no good place for this one, he gave it away after... I telegraphed him that it was worth about 25,000 L St. [$125,000]. Now it is worth certainly more. Believe me....*

Mr. Henschel of Knoedlers later told Gertrude that this particular Rembrandt portrait reminded Eastman of an underexposed photograph. Although given three years to make up his mind, Eastman surprised Knoedlers by sending his check immediately. Still, he was concerned about "the darkness of the hands." In response Bode suggested that the painting be placed "on an easel exposing it in a strong light whenever you are away from home as...that keeps it from getting too dark and is a good thing for the paint"—hardly a measure curators would endorse today.

A friendship between retiring university president Alan

15

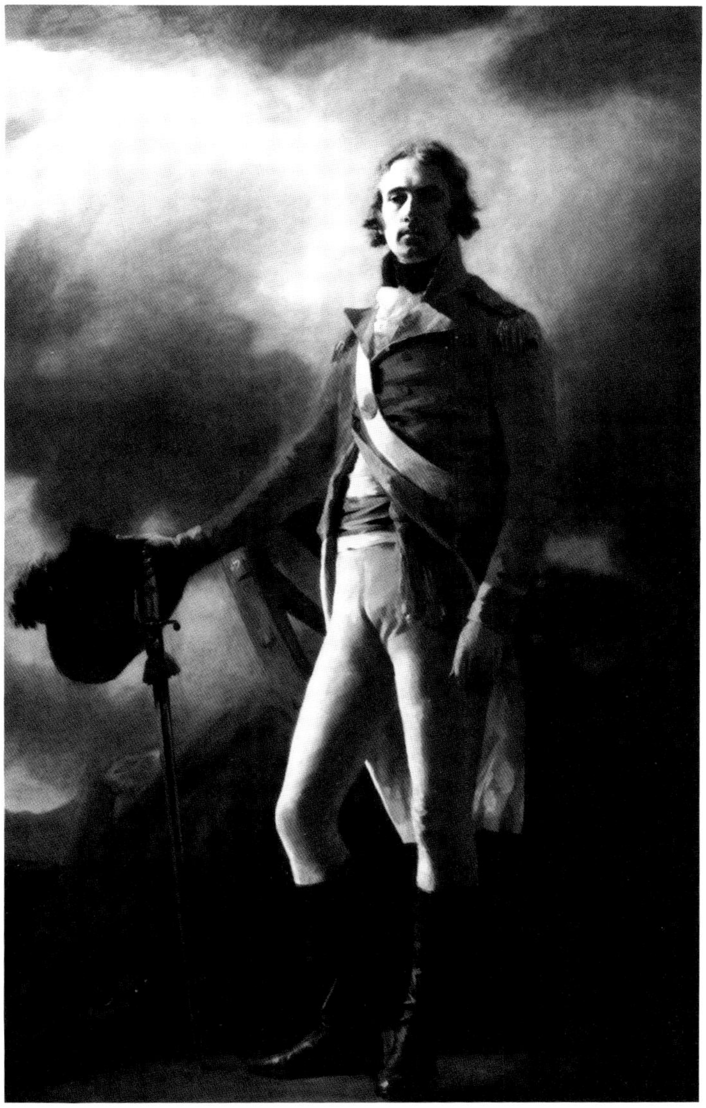

15 *Sir Henry Raeburn (English, 1756-1823), Portrait of General Hay MacDowell, 1805, oil on canvas, 93 x 58 in. George Eastman Collection of the University of Rochester, 68.102*

Valentine and former Senator William Benton of Connecticut, then chairman of the *Encyclopaedia Brittanica*, led to the purchase in 1950 of a significant core collection of American modernist works from the first half of the twentieth century. The fourteen artists thus acquired include some of Alfred Stieglitz's favorites from his Gallery 291—O'Keeffe, Marin, and Dove—as well as other seminal figures of the period.

Regionalist Thomas Hart Benton's *Boomtown* has become the most borrowed work in Gallery history. Ralston Crawford's suspenseful hard-edge *Whitestone Bridge* is well-known to art critics, while *Chinese Restaurant*, by John Sloan, joined an earlier Sloan acquisition of 1942, *Election Night in Herald Square*. The Sloans, along with *Cabby* by George Luks, were now added to the Henri to represent the group known as The Eight, also derisively called the Ash Can School for their choice of subject matter. (Shinn, Lawson, Prendergast, Davies, and Glackens are the rest of The Eight, now all represented in the Gallery collection.)

Canandaigua-born Arthur Dove first painted what he called "etractions," the same year as Kandinsky's first abstractions, and his haunting *Cars in a Sleet Storm* is one of these. *The Wanderer*, a 1943 work by the German-born George Grosz whose satire mellowed somewhat after he came to these shores in 1937, and *Discourse*, by the Russian-born Max Weber who switched from Cubism to scenes reminiscent of his ghetto childhood, are works by latter-day immigrants.

John Marin's watercolor with tilting planes, *Marin Island—Small Point, Maine*, (1931); WPA artist William Gropper's courtroom drama, *The Opposition*; Stuart Davis's immensely popular, jazzy, and colorful *Landscape with Garage Lights*; and Georgia O'Keeffe's typical *Jawbone and Fungus*, with its strange, grayed palette and simplified forms, joined works by Robert Gwathmey, Walt Kuhn, and Karl Zerbe to complete this remarkable collection.

Among the works in the *Encyclopaedia Brittanica* collection available for purchase was an Edward Hopper. "It wasn't typical," the art committee decided. But the hope of owning a typical (and affordable) one has never been abandoned.

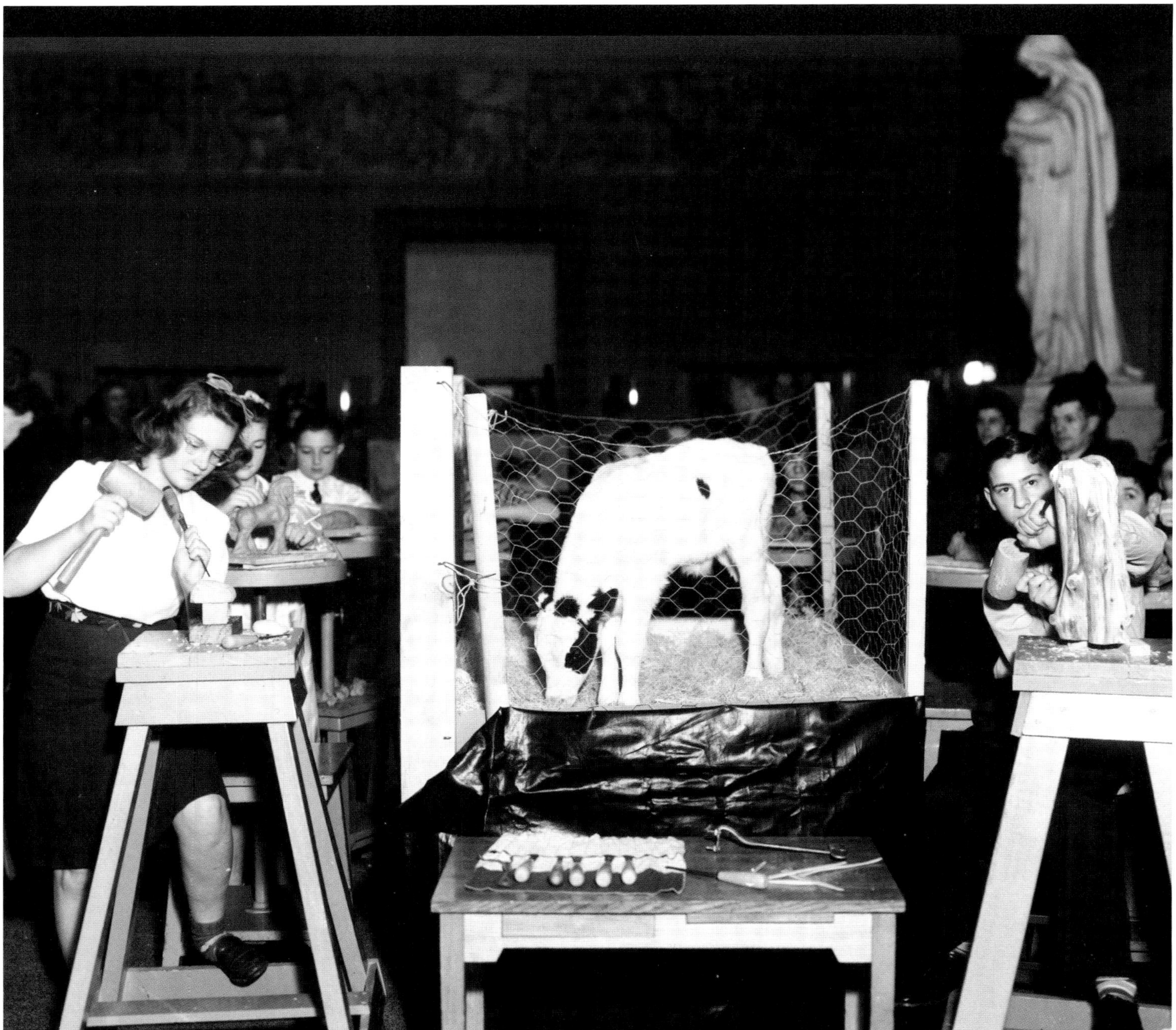

6

Said Art Gallery shall be a department of the University and shall be maintained for the benefit of the University and of the citizens of the City of Rochester....

Said building and its contents, including works of art, shall be the property of the University. Endowments shall be the property of the University, but shall be kept as a separate fund by it....

The entire management and administration hereby is committed to a Board of Directors and their successors. The Board of Directors shall have the sole right to accept, reject, sell, exchange, or dispose of any works of arts....

The first four members represent the donor, the University of Rochester, the Rochester Art Club, and the art department of the Mechanics Institute....

Agreement between the University of Rochester and Emily Sibley Watson | 26 June 1912

Sculpture class with mystery animal under the watchful eye of Memory at the Christmas Open House, 1942.

Is it a university art museum or a community art center? As a city art museum owned by a university, the Memorial Art Gallery's face turns almost entirely toward the community.

Emily Sibley Watson gave the Gallery to the university in trust for the people of Rochester, a building without collection or endowment, owned by a university and situated on its campus. "It is the only art gallery in America," an early publication asserted, "which has no endowment nor municipal support but lives entirely by means of its members." Because the director had to go to the community for operating funds, programs became geared to that community rather than to academic needs and interests.

In a sense the university president was the necessary catalyst to the creation of the Gallery. Rush Rhees wanted an art museum to augment university courses in imitation of the arrangement his father-in-law, L. Clark Seelye, enjoyed as president of Smith College. Rhees might have found a different building donor from Mrs. Watson. The Rochester Art Club, being without funds, was powerless to do anything but agitate for a building. Rhees became the linchpin of the operation.

Because of his lengthy dual roles as university president, 1900-1935, and Gallery president, 1913-1938, Rhees exerted a power and influence on Gallery affairs that no other single figure has managed.

When Loyal Durand, nephew of Hannah Gould, protested undue influence on the part of George Herdle in persuading his aunt to leave her estate to the Gallery, Rhees pacified the nephew by giving him a painting that had hung in the Gould home and a cash settlement from the Marion Stratton Gould Fund. When Ellen Dryden, niece of George Eastman, asked for paintings from her uncle's estate, Rhees gave her four of the sixty-two that Eastman had willed to the university—including a Corot landscape and a Reynolds self-portrait.

"It is natural to ask," Rhees wrote in his Annual Report of 1927, " 'If the Gallery was given to the university, why doesn't the university take care of it?' The answer is that the Gallery was placed on the university campus but not given to the university. The university was glad to set apart the choicest part of its campus for the Gallery. A legal document [of 1912] shows that the university has no jurisdiction over the Gallery."

The terms of the 1912 agreement were renegotiated after Alan Valentine became the university president in 1935. The legal name became "Memorial Art Gallery of the University of Rochester," and certain fiscal matters growing out of the "rights of ownership vested in the University" were tightened. For example, "permanent funds and endowments" would henceforth be "carried as an undivided part of the general consolidated fund of the University...computed at the average rate of return which the University earns upon its general consolidated fund...."

By the time of the 1936 agreement, the Board of Directors was again the Board of Managers and was beginning to be seen as the principal means of bridging the gap between town and gown. New bylaws specified that thirty-six members were to be elected to the board from the community at large. (The then-current members—Emily Watson, James S. Watson, James Sibley Watson Jr., Rush Rhees, Elizabeth Watson Hollister, Walter S. Cassebeer, Kathleen McEnery Cunningham, Thomas Spencer, Charlotte Whitney Allen, Elmer Adler, Lawrence Grant White, Helen Ellwanger, and Marie Atkinson Willard—would retain life memberships.) New members were to be (and still are) nominated by a committee of six, composed of three members (one its chairman) specified by the Gallery president and three members specified by the university. Certified by the Gallery Board of Managers and elected by the university Board of Trustees, members would serve three-year rotating terms. To insure that new blood would always be forthcoming, not more than eight out of the twelve elected each year could succeed themselves in any year.

Cementing this stronger bond to the university through bylaws based on the 1936 agreement, the chairman of the university Board of Trustees, the chancellor (when there is one), the president, the treasurer, the dean of the College of Arts and Science, and the chairman of the Department of Fine Arts of the university—plus, since 1952, the president of the Women's Council of the Gallery—became *ex officio* members of the Board of Managers. At the same time the directive that the building donor, the Rochester Art Club, and Mechanics Institute be represented in perpetuity on the board was dropped.

Myths about the relationship abound. The most prevalent has been that as a well endowed university, the University of Rochester provides all or most of the Gallery's operating funds, a myth that can hamper raising money in the community. While the amount of university support has risen steadily to $377,500 in 1988, it stabilized in recent years at about 16 percent of the yearly operating budget and manifests itself primarily as insurance on the building and permanent collection, as security, and as grounds maintenance. The remaining 84 percent must be raised from the community, obtained from government sources, or realized as income on endowment.

1

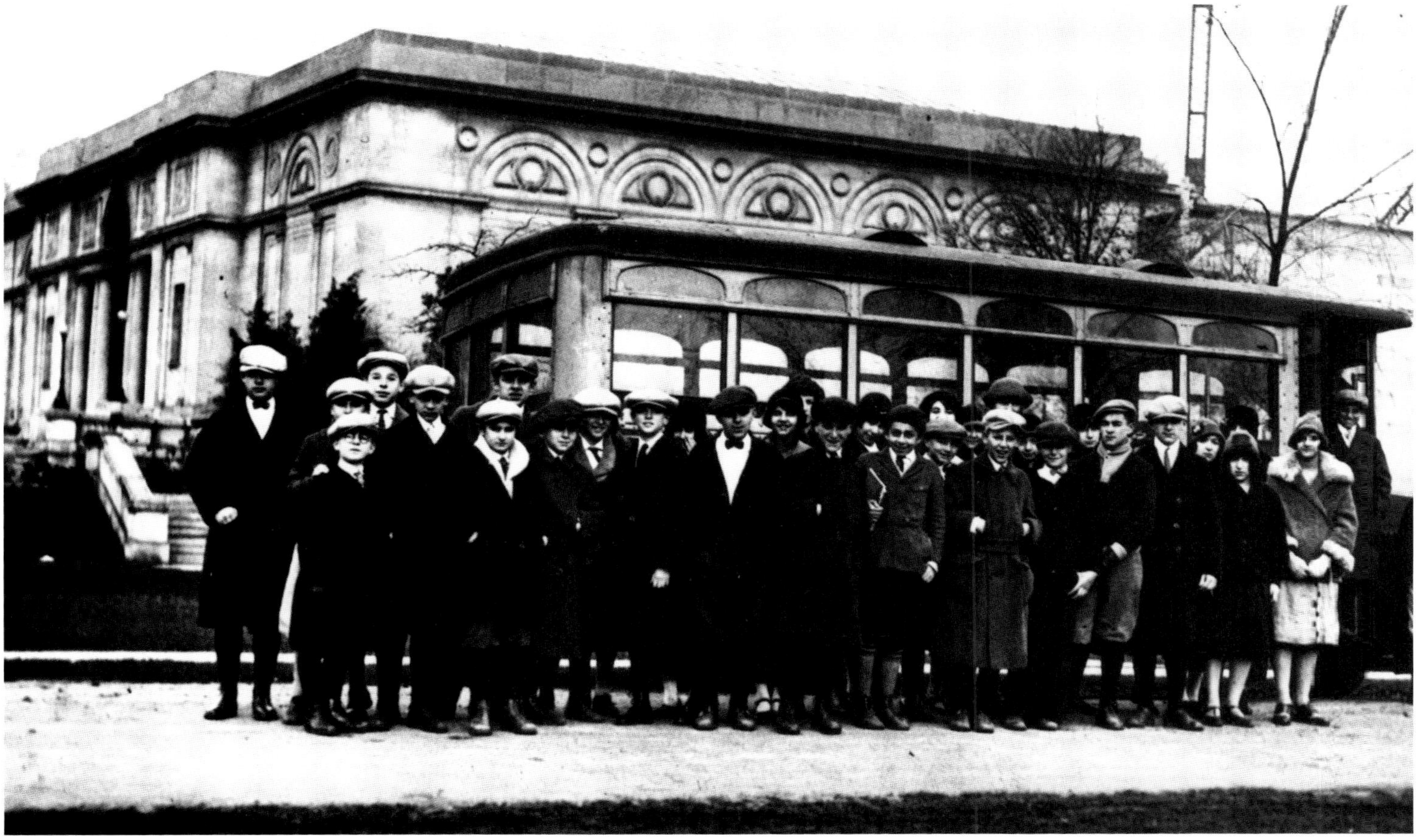

1 *A bus load of school-children arrives at the Gallery for a tour, 1926.*

2

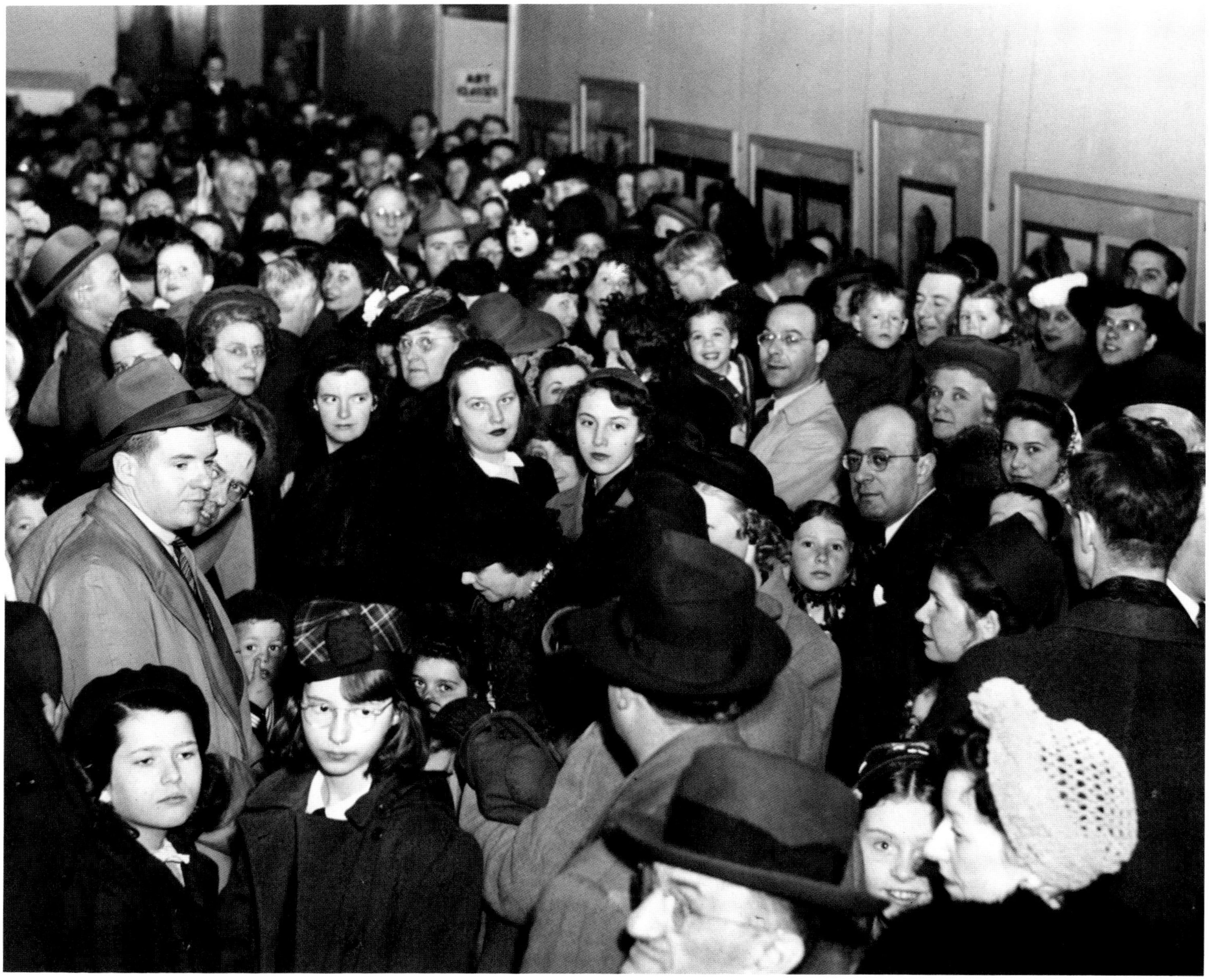

2 *The crush at a Christmas Open House.*

In 1936 James and Emily Watson gave $200,000 anonymously as the first endowment for operating expenses. Previously, the Watsons had made up annual shortfalls out of personal funds, and well into the 1950s their son was still providing anonymous gifts for that purpose.

Tension may be inevitable in this kind of relationship; over the years an ambivalence has developed. As Gallery board member since the 1950s and officer of the university for almost that long, George Angle is a unique liaison between "town" and "gown." He characterizes the ambivalence as "Go away. Come closer." The "come closer" body of opinion asks that "the university take better care of the Gallery, give it more money," Angle says. The "go away" group believes that "the university should let the Gallery manage its own affairs." At least twice the second group has organized sufficiently to suggest that the Gallery be rechartered independently of the university. Even if building and collections were not university property, most Gallery board members over the years and probably all six directors have viewed the relationship as mutually supportive. And during periods of retrenchment such as the depression years when membership dropped and staff, exhibitions, and publications had to be curtailed, the question remained: could the Gallery have survived if it had not been a part of the university?

The relationship "is by no means hostile," Gertrude Moore and Isabel Herdle maintain. "One can and does serve the other. In the continuing growth of the Gallery's kaleidoscopic survey of art, university faculty members have identified and helped to fill gaps. There was continuing consultation about acquisitions, about serving the university's needs as well as ours with objects meaningful to art history," they say. For instance, Carl Hersey, chairman of the Department of Fine Arts, wanted examples of Early Christian or Byzantine mosaics, and as a direct result the *Head of an Angel or Saint* was acquired. Professor Diran Kavork Dohanian, a specialist in Asian art, located a set of three Japanese hand scrolls for the Gallery to acquire through the Gould Fund in 1962. In 1974 Dohanian recommended the purchase of a carved wood Japanese *Bodhisattva Kannon*, of the twelfth century, and in 1979 Dohanian's recommendation was sought concerning the purchase of two rare Japanese Buddhist mandalas. Professor Howard Merritt organized the Thomas Cole exhibition and wrote its catalog. Merritt and medievalist David Walsh (and sometimes Walsh's students) have researched many objects in the collection. Walsh, Dohanian, Remy G. Saisselin, Grace Seiberling, and Bonnie Apgar Bennett, all of the Department of Fine Arts, have written about the collection for *Porticus*. The list could go on and on.

Thus, in the realm of scholarship, collaboration has been particularly beneficial. Gallery directors and staff members have taught at the university, and faculty members have functioned as visiting curators. The earliest such experiment came about when five university students enrolled in a credit course on museum training that Gertrude taught in the 1940s as a member of the fine arts faculty. The students were to plan and execute an exhibition project by originating the theme, locating sources, gathering and installing objects, and carrying it through into interpretation, publication, and publicity. It was soon apparent that the students did not have the requisite background. Some, for example, had never heard of Winslow Homer. The course should have been given on the graduate level, but the university lacked enough courses in art history to offer graduate work.

Later, during the period in the 1960s and 1970s when the university did offer graduate work in fine arts, Harris Prior taught the first graduate course in museum management. Again there was difficulty in attracting enough qualified students.

Under John Mahey's term as director, 1975-1979, members of the university fine arts department served as consulting curators to the Gallery: Dohanian for oriental art, Merritt for nineteenth century American art, Archibald M. Miller for contemporary art, and Saisselin for seventeenth and eighteenth century European art. Saisselin also taught several courses in art history at the university and one course on the history of art criticism at the Gallery—the first such experiment since the department moved in 1955. These courses were open to Gallery docents as well as to university students. Auditing university fine arts classes continues as a privilege for active docents.

From 1913 until 1955 the university art history and studio arts courses had their classroom and faculty headquarters in the Gallery. With the men students removed to the River Campus in 1930 and the women students in 1955, much valuable interaction on a daily drop-in level, as well as minor frictions, were gone forever.

The most difficult repercussion for the Gallery was the removal of two-thirds of its library to the River Campus. "The art library which contains both books purchased by funds from the Gallery and the general art division of the university will be moved to the River Campus when the merger of the men's and the women's campuses takes place this fall," a melancholy *Gallery Notes* reported in 1955. "Only a small reference library of about 2000 books [out of 6000] and small slide collection will remain at the Gallery, a great blow to the Gallery."

Books purchased with the Willard or Hollister funds remained. But great blanks made research in the presence of a work of art difficult. James G. Cutler's architecture volumes, still identifiable in the stacks of Rush Rhees Library by their Claude Bragdon-designed MAG bookplates, were among those moved. Yet the rare *De Architectura* by Vitruvius, given by Bragdon, was kept after a protest was mounted. Almost immediately, Mrs. Adrian Devine started a fund to replace the volumes which were taken. Subsequently the Frederick Hoeing Fund and Susan Schilling Book Fund have admirably filled the gaps with books of more recent vintage. And almost yearly since the Friends of University of Rochester Libraries was founded in 1972, generous donations have come to the Gallery library.

One positive effect of the university leaving the Prince Street Campus was that for $1,200 the Gallery was able to buy the "Brown House," former Prince Street residence turned faculty club, and expand its overflow Creative Workshop classes into that building.

Community programming was burgeoning. Inside and outside of Gallery walls the staff worked with school groups, ethnic groups, worker groups, and the handicapped. The Homelands Exhibitions begun by George Herdle in 1919 were continued into the 1950s, celebrating Rochester's melting pot. An exhibition of church and synagogue art treasures organized in the 1950s from local sources celebrated Rochester's religious heritage.

Classes for the blind were started in the late 1930s. Special neighborhood classes, held at the Genesee, Lewis Street, and Baden Street settlement houses and in inner city schools, led to scholarships to the Creative Workshop.

Original art and reproductions were lent to nursing homes, teacher colleges, and factory cafeterias; framed pictures went to invalids selected by the Visiting Nurses Association and to the State Hospital, the Children's Shelter, and the Children's Convalescent Hospital. "There are some poignant little stories connected with that," Gertrude says. One concerned a child whose prints had to be mounted on the ceiling so he could see them; others concerned the bonds formed between the volunteers who delivered the art and its recipients, or between the invalids and "their" prints.

During World War II exhibits were mounted at military camps, and immensely popular weekly art demonstrations featuring Creative Workshop teachers Ralph Avery and John Menihan were organized by the Gallery to travel to Sampson Air Force base in Geneva. Servicemen were given free entry to evening classes in sculpture, ceramics, and painting. Old clothes were collected from Gallery members for refugees. Car pools were formed to bring people to the Gallery. If gas rationing kept school children from the Gallery, Susan Eisenhart

3

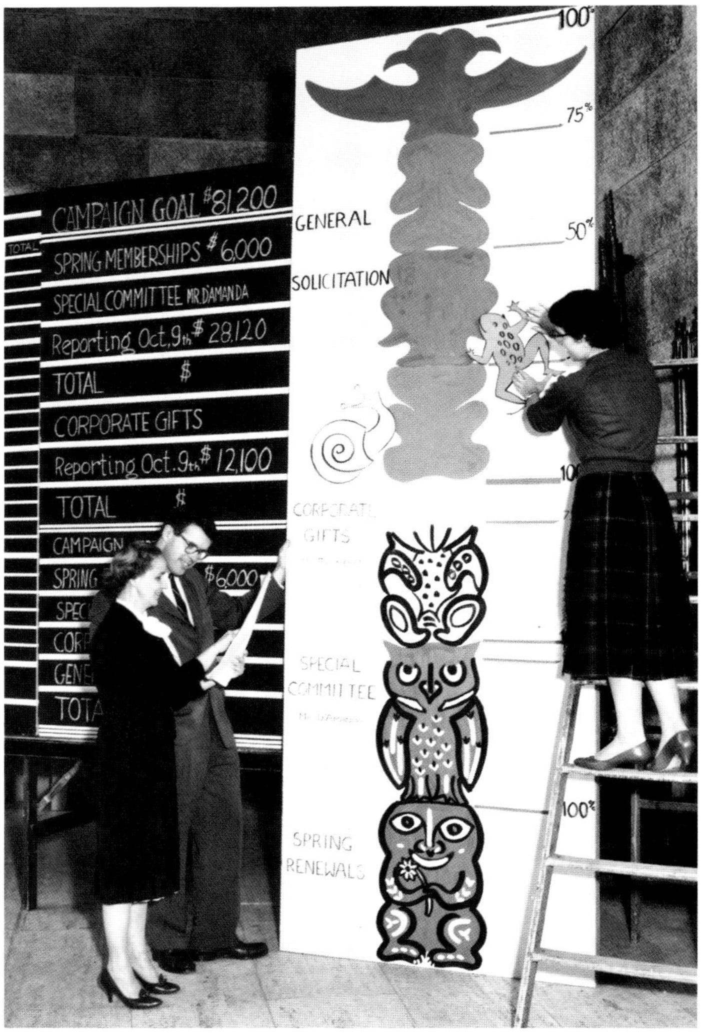

3 *The climax of an annual membership campaign, 1950s. Ruth Van Dusen, membership chairman, and Langdon Clay, director of education, standing. Faith Munson, education assistant, on ladder.*

Schilling brought Gallery programming to the schools.

The economic depression of the 1930s, followed by the outbreak of the second world war, signalled retrenchment for the museum. *Gallery Notes* was reduced to a four-page multigraph folder. Publication of *The Bulletin* was curtailed. Delays were encountered in receiving exhibitions. Attendance was affected—averaging 50,000 per year, down from more than 100,000. In 1940 the exhibition budget was cut from $2,000 to $1,600; the lecture fund and director's travel fund were sliced to $400 each.

Retrenchment did not curtail innovation. In 1941 a Lending Library of original work by local artists was started, with the Gallery taking only a small percentage to cover overhead. A Lending Library fund was started with these nickels and dimes which proved enough to buy about two paintings a year for the collection. Some years later both a Junior Lending Library and a University Prints program were started: about 300 framed colorful prints, some original, some reproductions, were for rent. For fifty cents (per print and per semester) university students and children of members could plaster their walls with art. Some lovely Japanese prints were among the selections.

An Art Patrons Fund was started. Letters were written: Would you like to contribute? Buy something from the Finger Lakes Exhibition for the Gallery? Once a nest egg was in hand, a collection of contemporary regional art was under way, and during Harris Prior's years after the completion of the 1968 addition, it was displayed in the corridor gallery surrounding the new auditorium.

The first Christmas program was held in 1939, featuring music by the Eastman School of Music and medieval dancing. It was also the occasion for Leopold Mannes—co-inventor of Kodachrome film—to meet Evelyn Sabin, his future wife, in the Fountain Court. This event grew into the still-popular Holiday Open House. As for Mannes, he and his colleague C. E. Kenneth Mees returned to the Gallery regularly to lecture on aerial and color photography.

A useful Intermuseum Council composed of delegates from the Gallery, the Rochester Museum of Arts and Sciences, the Landmark Society, the Rochester Historical Society, the Rochester Public Library, and the Rochester Institute of Technology was established in 1942 to define the territory and mandates of each institution.

In 1943 experts in various fields were drawn from the community and named consultants to the Gallery. Among them were Walter Clark of the Eastman Kodak Company, photography expert; Harriet (Mrs. Thomas) Spencer, consultant for lace, period exhibitions, and decorative arts; and Elizabeth Holahan, president of the Landmark Society.

For three years in the early 1950s, the staff conducted "Rubberneck Rochester Bus Tours" with Gertrude, Isabel, and Susan Schilling shouting out the history of local architecture through megaphones while they and their charges were riding down Main Street en route to the Campbell-Whittlesey House to tea. After the third year of lost voices and dispositions this worthy program was discontinued.

At the grand opening of the Community War Memorial in 1952, the Gallery staff curated an exhibition on good design as produced by Rochester area industry. The show featured products from large companies such as Eastman Kodak and Taylor Instrument plus a miscellaneous assortment of doorbells, knives, textiles, and so forth. First prize, which art purists considered shocking, went to a plastic garbage can.

After the war attendance rose once more. Almost 113,000 people came to the Gallery in 1952, 70 percent of whom participated in Gallery events or classes. This figure did not include the 2,000 who attended Gallery events outside of those limestone walls. The Creative Workshop was enrolling some 1,230 students (not including the waiting list) in fifty-five classes in painting, ceramics, wood and stone sculpture, weaving, and jewelry making.

The first postwar reunion of nine Lithuanian printmakers (including Alphonse Dargis) twice exiled (by the Third Reich and the Soviet Union) from their homeland, was held at the Gallery.

In 1954 the Education Department started the Adventurers Club. Sixty children, ages eight to twelve, came once a week to the Gallery and made models of early American houses.

"Object of the Month" spotlighted one single work from the collection with interpretive labels explaining its place in the history of art.

With the arrival of the School for American Craftsmen at the Rochester Institute of Technology in the early 1950s, the Gallery played the role of host to "Designer-Craftsmen USA," the school's first large-scale faculty-student exhibition. Demonstrations and several consultant programs accompanied the show.

Frank Lloyd Wright came to lecture at the Gallery in 1932. Lecturing was his main livelihood then, his architectural commissions having all but dried up. He charged $700—an enormous sum for Depression days—but he had prepared nothing for the talk, not even one lantern slide. Instead he had the audience put questions to him.

He came early and let Gertrude drive him around all day while he caustically sized up Rochester for her.

Colgate Rochester Divinity School: "What a fine site, but

you know that isn't architecture—just picture plates strung together. It doesn't exist in three dimensions."

The new River Campus of the University of Rochester: "Why, if they design buildings that bad, do they multiply it?'

The house on East Boulevard he himself designed in 1905 but forgot existed: "They wrapped conduit pipes around all my plain spaces. What a poor site! That's the last time I'll design for a space I've never seen. I thought it was sited on a hilltop surrounded by a stretching expanse of space."

There are people who swear that Wright not only saw the lot on East Boulevard but actually camped out there during construction with meals delivered to his tent. We may never know the real story. In any case the Rochester connection to Frank Lloyd Wright ended with a note dated 2 December 1932 from Taliesin, Spring Green, Wisconsin:

This is to thank you for your very kind reception in Rochester. The little dinner the good company and to apologize for such pessimism as crept into the talk at the Gallery. Next year if you like... we'll stage a "picture" evening which I am preparing but not *through a lecture bureau.*

To Mrs. Moore my best
Sincerely

FLW

The Fountain Court had been added in 1926, at least in part, to accommodate performing arts groups. Accommodate it did. Period music—especially medieval and Renaissance—on unfamiliar early instruments, was "in" and the Fountain Court was the perfect setting for it. The Rochester Chamber Opera performed operas in the round, accompanied by early instruments. Ars Antiqua presented "An Evening at the Court of Louis XIV." On Sundays hymns and folk tunes were sung by madrigal singers. A dance group under Olive McCue performed regularly.

Famous musicians came to perform. Virgil Thompson played the piano, outlining the libretto of *Four Saints in Three Acts* by Gertrude Stein. The New York Woodwind Quintet presented a program of music by Alec Wilder. Because he was a native son whose patrons were the Sibley Watsons, the painfully shy Wilder sometimes agreed to talk about his work on these occasions. In a related vein, Hildegarde Watson's friend Dr. Emanuel Winternitz, curator of musical instruments at the Metropolitan Museum of Art, spoke each year. His topic in 1958, for example, was "Handel in Italy."

The supreme effort of the year was the membership drive. Each year was a cliff-hanger: no one knew until the last minute if the drive would go over the top or who might win a mysterious little prize for the most pledges. By simple, if time-consuming means, organized for years by staff members Bernice Meyer and Margaret Bennett, an impressive museum membership was built—one of the largest (by percentage of population) in the country. The final night found Langdon Clay up a ladder by a huge blackboard, chalking in the suspenseful results.

"It's a precarious way to live," Gertrude says, "but it has its benefits because it forces the Gallery to stay close to the people and gives the people a proprietary interest in the Gallery—a sense of being at least partially responsible."

The Board of Managers approved an annual membership drive in 1952, but a conflict with the university's development program postponed it until 1953. The era of successful campaigns began under Arthur Hughes, president of the Marine Midland Bank, who came in as a volunteer, ran the campaign for six years, and turned financial matters around. (George Angle was a campaign worker—the beginning of his long association with the Gallery.) In 1958 for the first time the Gallery exceeded its goal ($84,000), raising $20,000 more than it had ever raised before. Goals have risen steadily ever since, and projected membership income for 1988 is $740,000.

At one time the Gallery's only sister institutions were the Museum of Arts and Sciences and the Rochester Historical Society plus some modest community orchestras. The advent of the Rochester Philharmonic, the Landmark Society, the George Eastman House, the Genesee Country Museum, the Public Television Channel WXXI, GeVa Theatre, and the Strong Museum have enriched the community immeasurably but made the competition for the cultural dollar from the same population base ever more keen.

Once too the Gallery had more members than any other cultural organization, but the high point of 9,500 memberships was reached shortly after the opening of the 1968 wing and has not been equalled since. Financial growth continues to increase, however, through the upgrading of memberships into the more committed groups of Associate Patrons, Patrons, and Director's Circle.

Much programming during the 1950s centered on family-oriented occasions. The perks of membership included the Members' Lecture series on Wednesday mornings, which Clay and Schilling conducted. For membership suppers the staff could be pressed into service not just as lecturers but also as entertainers. A guard might play the sax, Clay the guitar. Others would tackle the clarinet and drums.

The annual Holiday Open House had all the excitement of an opening night for a grand theatrical production. Expec-

4

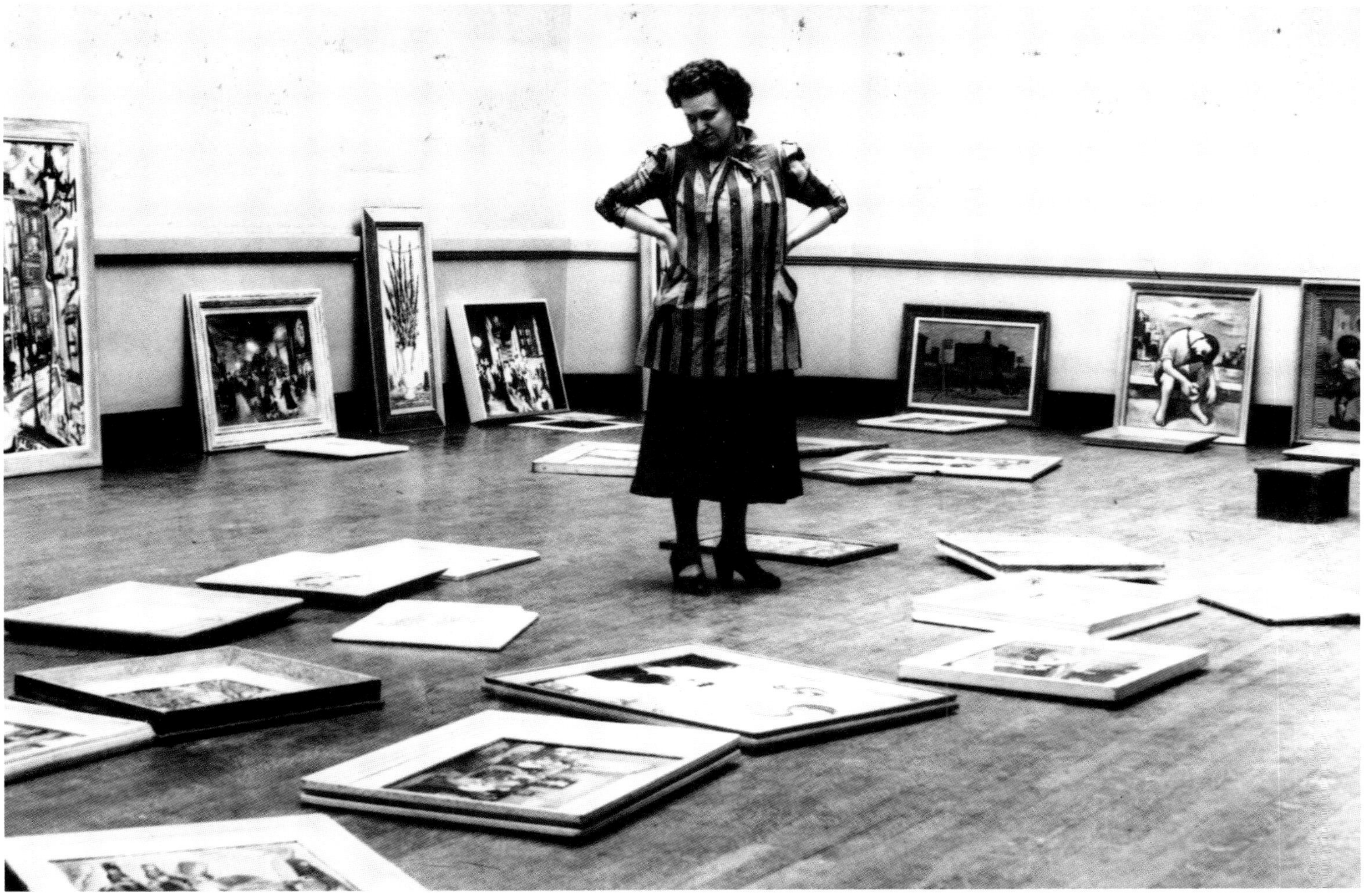

4 *Isabel Herdle contemplates installing a Finger Lakes Exhibition.*

tant crowds massed at the front door waiting to rush in once the doors opened while inside the staff put last-minute touches on the splendid display.

Typical of the informality of the 1950s was the mystery animal who came to Holiday Open House. (After 1968 the creature was confined to the less critical area of the Creative Workshop.) One year two raccoons got loose in the main galleries and had to be traced and recaptured by dusting powder on the marble steps and placing smelly live fish strategically here and there. Another time a monkey escaped while being transferred for return to Lollipop Farm; his skeleton was found months later. A fox who got wet and smelled, some sheep, and a cow were among the menagerie.

This sampling of the wide range of community programming held during Gertrude's directorship, when the Gallery had not yet expanded beyond the Fountain Court, gives a clue to the vitality of those years. Once a poll was taken to determine which activities were most popular. Classes, Lending Library, lectures and programs (Sunday afternoon, Monday afternoon, Wednesday night, and Private Views) were named—in the order listed.

"Slowly by degrees we became more professional," Lang Clay has mused. "Things became more pigeonholed, more boring, not as much fun."

The annual Rochester-Finger Lakes Exhibition, still the most prestigious juried exhibition in the region, grew out of the annual Rochester Art Club shows. In March 1914, five months after the Gallery opened, the club held its thirty-first Annual Exhibition in its new quarters. Largely a members' show, it consisted of 161 paintings and drawings by fifty-six artists, juried by the officers and Board of Control of the club.

Until 1927 the annual juried show continued as a joint project with the Rochester Art Club, with works by guest artists, crafts from Mechanics Institute, and photographs from the Kodak Camera Club. In May 1927 the first out-of-town jury was assembled consisting of an artist, a teacher, and a museum director. (Also debuting at the Gallery in 1927 were the Exhibition of the Rochester Guild of Illustrators, the Salon of Photographic Art, artwork done in public schools, and the annual student exhibition from the School of Applied Art at Mechanics Institute.) The next year "The 15th Annual Exhibition of Work by Rochester Artists and Craftsmen including the 46th Annual Exhibit of the Rochester Art Club" was held. Clearly a catchier name was needed.

The year 1937 marked the last combined show with the Art Club. In 1938 artists from nineteen counties were eligible and the title "Rochester-Finger Lakes Exhibition" was coined.

5

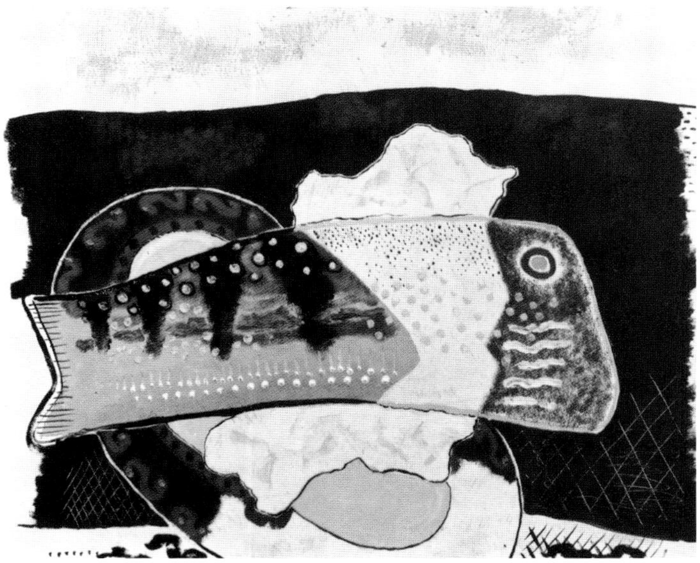

This version attracted 150 artists exhibiting 389 works. Twenty works went on to the Great Lakes Exhibition, which spanned several states, and three received Nelson Eddy Purchase Prizes in oil, watercolor, and sculpture categories. In 1941 five Purchase Prizes for the Gallery collection were given as well as the Jurors' Show Award of a one-person exhibition during the coming year. Painters Frederick Bennett and John Menihan shared the first Jurors' Show award.

The brouhaha of the decade came in 1944 when a cubist rendition of a *Fish* on a plate by one "Zoute," nom de plume for Leon Salter, won the Jurors' Award in the Finger Lakes Exhibition. The public rose in ire, columnists thumped, members resigned, but the Gallery survived and Zoute's little *Fish* looks pretty tame today.

Distinguished Finger Lakes jurors have included artist Charles Burchfield of Buffalo; John Bauer, director of the Whitney Museum of American Art; Thomas Messer, director of the Guggenheim Museum; and Harris Prior, who judged in 1950 when he was director of the Munson-Williams-Proctor Institute and in 1958 when he was director of the American Federation of Arts.

From 1941 until the closing of the Gallery for renovation after the April 1966 show, the Finger Lakes Exhibition continued to grow. In 1966 the jurors (two for paintings, one for crafts, one for awards) worked independently for the first time, with the fourth juror conferring awards on the selections of the other three.

The best configuration of jurors was perennially debated and combinations of from one to four jurors tried without resolution. Artists, especially the 80 percent rejected each year, were vocal in their denigration of all jurors. As director, Harris Prior

6 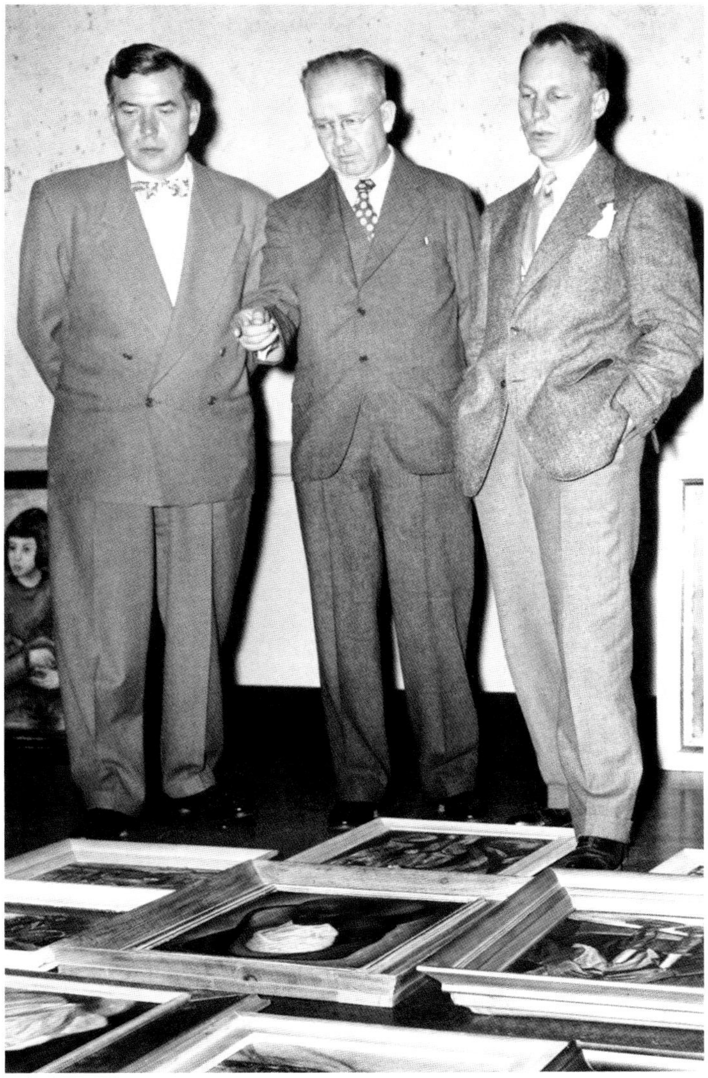

took this dissatisfaction to heart and agonized in print over the rejected artists' feelings. In the forewords to the 1966 and 1969 exhibition catalogs (here combined) he wrote:

This exhibition does not attempt to prove anything, except perhaps that art is alive and well in the Rochester-Finger Lakes region.... The mere mention of jurying works of art evokes violent reactions on the part of artists, and even of non-artists....The qualities jurors look for (expressiveness, intensity, integrity, depth, originality, good technique, etc.) are not scientifically measurable.... The only thing on which all will agree is that there is no perfect system. Yet artists seem to want to pit themselves against their peers from time to time in selective shows of this sort. Therefore, varying the method of selection from year to year is probably the best solution....

"The 'balance' of a show is a matter often discussed," Prior had noted in 1966, "meaning balance among the many currents of art today. Desirable as this might seem on the surface, it is obviously impossible to create a balanced show if the work submitted is not balanced—unless, of course, different standards of quality are applied to the various categories."

The arguments continued. One year the show was criticized as "all abstract," another year as "too conservative," or "too funky." A *Salon des Refusés* was held. A perennial criticism was that artists, once established, no longer submitted. More than twenty years ago, Harris Prior wrote of "the large number of young artists in our area experimenting with new trends." For at least that long the Finger Lakes Exhibition has been weighted toward the young and experimental rather than the established "name" artists. Various "solutions" were proposed but not tried, generally involving a "director's" or "curator's" or "jurors' choice" section for established artists. About the only appraisal most would agree on is Prior's: "This exhibition shows that great vitality is still to be found in our region."

As new art forms became fashionable they were introduced. A photography section proved unsatisfactory and it was decided to leave photography to the Eastman House. Yet in 1988 photography returned as a sizable segment of the show. A video category was added in 1975 but was soon gone. The predominance of the crafts in the region makes it often the strongest segment. As the number of submitting artists increased and Gallery space was pinched, succeeding directors responded. Prior reduced the number of entries from three to two and had them received and judged at a separate location. John Mahey tried splitting the show into "art" one year alternating with "craft" the next, but a popular uprising caused them to be reunited. Bret Waller had artists submit slides of works instead of the works themselves; this did nothing to increase submissions, but instead gave participants something else to complain about.

5 *Zoute (Leon Salter) (American 1903-1976) Fish, 1944. Art Patrons' Fund Purchase Award from the Finger Lakes Exhibition, 44.47*

6 *The 1949 jury, Rochester-Finger Lakes Exhibition. Left to right: Paul Parker, artist, Hamilton College; Charles Burchfield, artist, Buffalo; Robert Tyler Davis, director, Museum of Fine Arts, Montreal.*

7

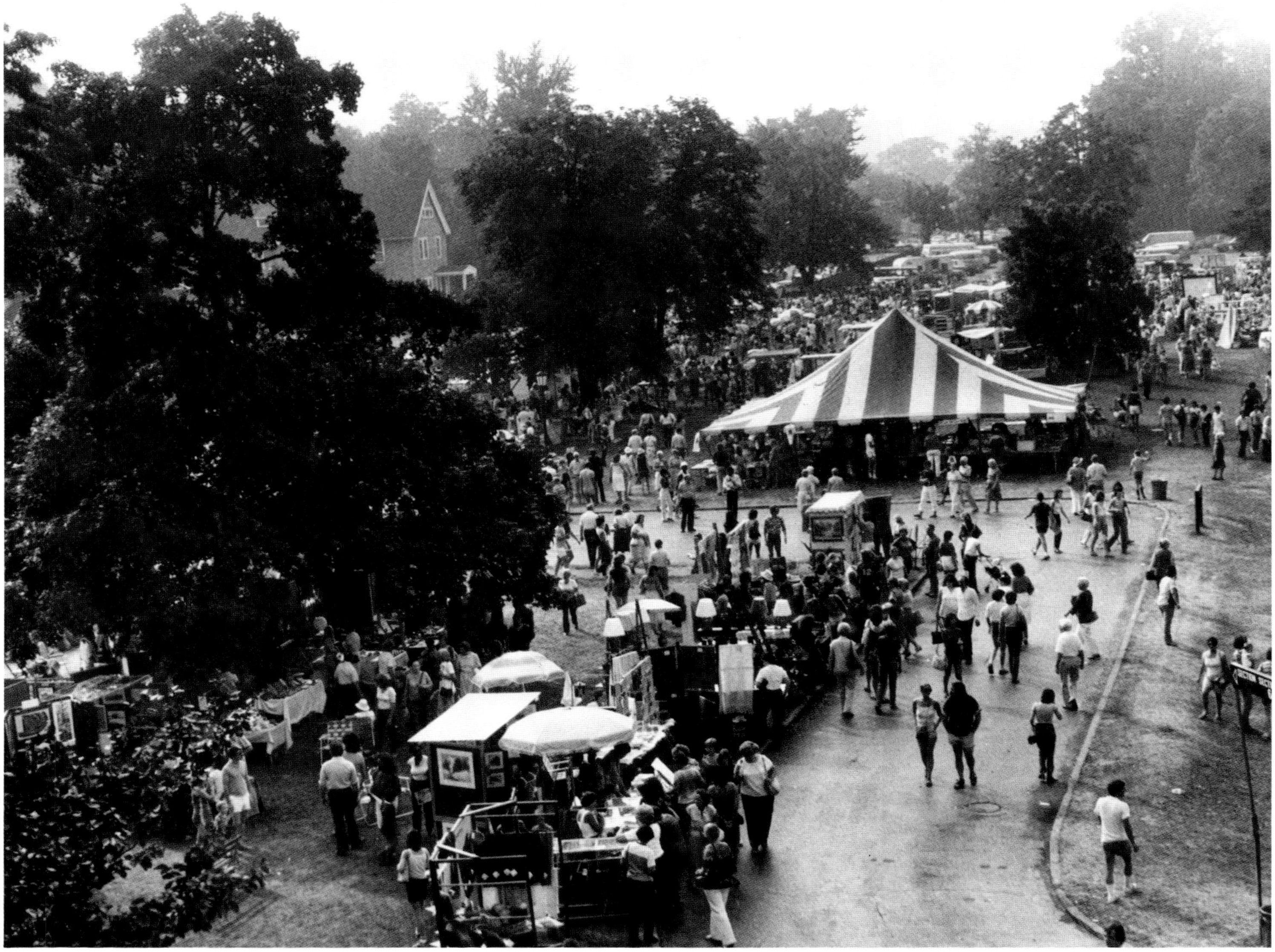

[redacted]

7 *Clothesline Show and Sale.*

Special features over the years have included panel discussions by jurors and artists, slides of winners accompanying the award announcements, slide-tapes or videos of jurors' comments on view (but rarely watched) at the opening, and a WXXI-TV documentary filmed at the opening. The last three were first tried in 1972 and have been repeated occasionally since.

Eliminating the jurors has been suggested too (and some very upset artists might have meant that to be taken literally).

"Whatever its shortcomings, the jury system is still the best one we know of to choose a show like the Rochester-Finger Lakes Exhibition," Prior wrote in 1966. "Over the years, the best area artists will be accepted most of the time. That does not ease the pain suffered by the rejected, even though there is still the Clothesline Show... and many other opportunities to exhibit."

The bleats of the rejected for an unjuried show on Gallery grounds probably played some part in the establishment of the Clothesline Show in 1957, and in its uninterrupted popularity as a community happening ever since.

For some years Clay and Creative Workshop teacher Edna Weeks Smith had privately discussed the possibility of an open-air "clothesline" show on the Gallery grounds. Clay had seen such a show in his years of living in Greenwich Village. Smith took up the cause as her own.

"We tried to shut her up," Isabel says in discussing Smith's persistent call for an unjuried show. "We didn't want an open show; we wanted selectivity. But she was right." In 1957 the Finger Lakes jury was particularly harsh and the need to placate hurt feelings of rejected artists was particularly strong, so the Herdles capitulated. They would not regret that decision as they watched the Clothesline Show grow, year after year, into the major community happening and Gallery fund-raising event it is today. As a bonus, many rising artists got their starts at Clothesline.

"On June 30 and July 1 the Gallery staged its first free-for-all open-air summer art exhibit," *Gallery Notes* said by way of introducing the first annual Clothesline show, "complete with band concert, bagpipe serenades, hot dogs, and pony rides for children. For two days art was supposed to hang peacefully on fences, walls, and tables around the grounds but since little Audrey [a hurricane] tagged along too most of the work was viewed in mid-air as it cruised by. Despite wind and rain, sales amounted to $3,000. Artists and art bargain hunters had a great time."

When the jobs were passed out, Clay got the refreshment detail. He ordered hot dogs and soft drinks, acquired some refrigerators, and made arrangements for suppliers to stay open on Sunday. He lined up three bank presidents and a university professor to man the hot-dog stand, while he, having underestimated the hungry crowd, trudged back to the suppliers again and again. At day's end, Clay locked the proceeds in his office.

Gradually the Clothesline Show gained some sophistication. When the weather is good, and organization clicks, the two-day festival can net as much as $60,000 for the Gallery.

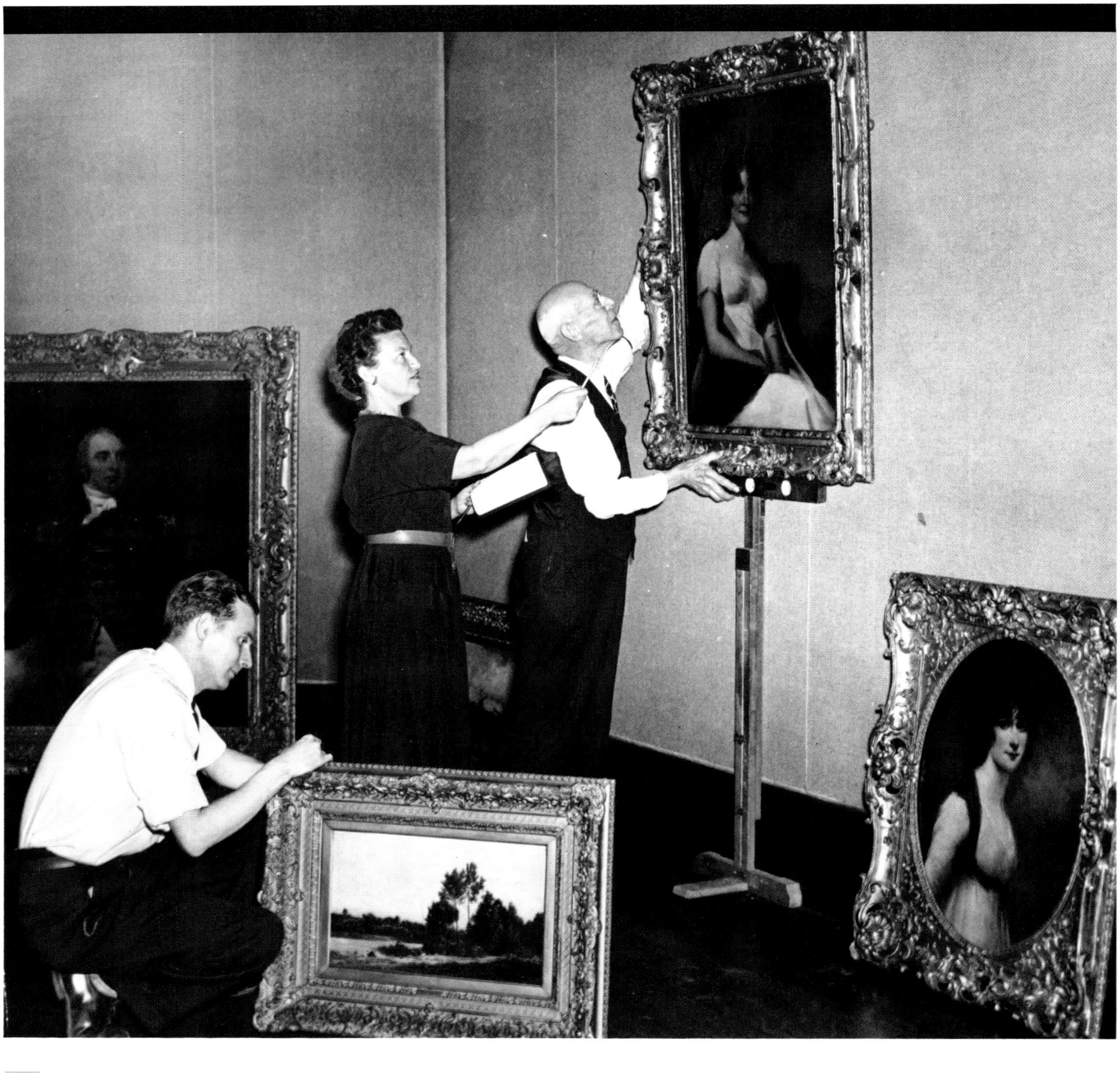

7

Isabel always claimed she wasn't an artist yet her creativity came shining through her exhibition installations which became renowned throughout the museum world.

—Langdon F. Clay

In retrospect it's amazing how many different things the staff learned to do just because there was no one else to do them.

—Susan E. Schilling

Bob Young, Isabel Herdle, and Mr. Pike hang the George Eastman Collection of the University of Rochester when it "boarded" at the Gallery, 1949.

The Herdle sisters determined to serve as many different community groups as possible with their exhibition program, while spending as little of the meager exhibition budget as they could. Over the years exhibition themes evolved that attracted a wide variety of audiences.

A survey show of, say, American art, might appeal to the community at large, while one concentrating on the avant-garde would be aimed at the art community. Regional art and craft shows, such as the Finger Lakes Exhibition and Clothesline Show, served local artists. A whole series of shows which spotlighted ethnic art drew on the collections of the many first-generation immigrant groups in Rochester and brought these people to the Gallery. Special interest shows such as those concentrating on photography or lithography were mounted to demonstrate interest in local industries.

Exhibition sources changed over the years. George Herdle had been able to assemble shows by going directly to his contemporary artists. In his daughters' era, dealers more and more controlled the lending and sale of art. Next came the heyday of traveling exhibitions circulated by the Museum of Modern Art's traveling exhibition service, the American Federation of Arts, the Smithsonian Institution, or individual museums themselves. As the monetary value of art works skyrocketed, problems arose concerning security, dramatically rising insurance rates, extended itineraries, and works deemed too delicate for travel.

Major industries—Johnson Wax, Standard Oil, and the Meade Company—circulated top-notch exhibitions of contemporary arts and crafts with help from curators and scholars. After the 1960s, industry's cultural dollar would go more into public television programming.

Foreign governments assembled exhibitions through their fine arts commissions. Arts and crafts from Norway, Denmark, Poland, and Sweden were all exhibited at the Gallery in the 1940s and 1950s. Indeed the exhibition of Danish crafts opened in Rochester, and an exhibition sponsored by the Intermuseum Cultural Relations of Latin America was opened by the ambassador from Argentina.

Proximity to Canada and the Herdles' sensitivity to trends led the Gallery to be the first museum outside of Canada to show that country's "Group of Seven." Three directors of museums in the Netherlands assembled an exhibition of contemporary Dutch art that came to the Gallery in 1956.

The Gallery's first showing of Eskimo art—from a private collection and the Canadian Handcraft Guild—took place in 1957. Eskimo sculpture was then at the peak of its great period before the slide into commercialism began.

1

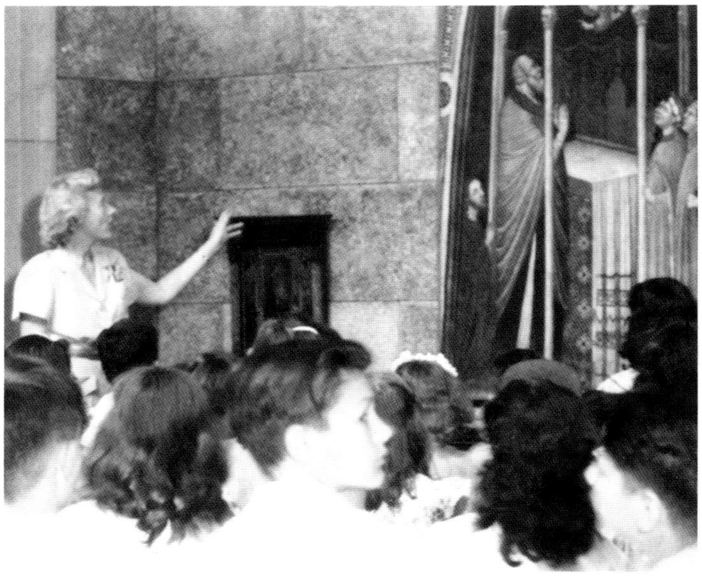

1 *Susan Eisenhart (Schilling) presents medieval art in the Fountain Court, 1947.*

Surprisingly the star exhibition of 1957 was "Everyday Objects Made in Japan." The objects, not handcrafted but mass-produced and for sale, included stunning little bowls and the throw-away teapots found on Japanese trains—"so beautifully balanced and designed for the function," Isabel Herdle explains, "that everybody had to have one. It was just about the most popular exhibit ever held at the Gallery," Isabel continues, warming to the subject. "Franz Wildenhain nearly wrecked it, though, because he came in and bought everything. We had to send Bob Young to New York twice with the truck [to replenish the supply after Herr Wildenhain had been through]." British artists and designers who reconstructed churches and public buildings after the bombings of World War II were the subject of a show sponsored by the Arts Council of Great Britain in April 1959. Henry Moore, Barbara Hepworth, Jacob Epstein, Graham Sutherland, John Piper, and Reginald Butler were featured, particularly their work for the new Coventry Cathedral.

That year too an exhibition of Israeli art—thirty-five paintings in oil and watercolor—was cosponsored by Temple B'rith Kodesh. Although the artists originally hailed from many countries, they now shared the common home of Israel. Contemporary Jewish ritual objects—Torah scrolls, spice boxes, Chanukah candelabra, many of them from Poland—were borrowed from the Jewish Museum in New York, whose director, Dr. Stephen Kaiser, came to lecture.

"**E**thnic" shows could be homegrown. Begun by George Herdle in 1919 and continuing for four decades, the popular Homelands Exhibitions signaled the first local evaluation of the cultural inheritance of various national groups represented in the Rochester population. After World War I attitudes began changing as ethnic groups no longer sought to bury their heritages, but instead to celebrate them.

Through his work with the Chamber of Commerce and at Exposition Park, Herdle paid evening calls to homes in immigrant sections of the city. Soon he was combing these areas in search of exhibition material. Often the most interesting objects were to be found stored away in cellars and attics—indicating the owners were attempting to put their "foreignness" behind them. Yet once an object had appeared in a Gallery exhibition, it was accorded a place of honor in the parlor.

Homelands Exhibitions celebrated the heritages of Italians, Poles, Danes, Dutch, English, Near Easterners, Greeks, Armenians, Lithuanians, and Ukrainians. Sunday afternoon programs of song and dance augmented visual displays. Sometimes a traveling exhibition coincided, as in October 1928 when the paintings, furniture, and decorative arts of seventeenth century-Holland, drawn from both local and outside sources, were displayed. The galleries assumed the aura of Dutch Renaissance interiors in which cupboards of oak and rosewood, Flemish tapestries, tall floor clocks, and hanging wall cabinets provided the setting for seventeenth-century Dutch paintings and local loans of pewter and Delft from the Oothout, Ellwanger, and Herdle collections, and from the Rochester Museum of Arts and Sciences.

After World War II the material brought in for the Homelands Exhibitions was markedly more sophisticated and refined. A spot check of lenders indicated that more than 70 percent were now college graduates. These exhibitions did not continue beyond Gertrude's regime. However, something of the same genre still takes place at the annual outdoor Folk Festival of the Rochester Museum and Science Center but without the careful selection of exhibited material based on aesthetic standards.

Competitive spirits sometimes surfaced at the Homelands Exhibitions. A contingent of Poles watching the Ukrainians perform suddenly marched to the center of the Fountain Court, demanding an apology: "That's a Polish song, not Ukrainian." Howard Hanson, director of the Eastman School of Music, was designated arbiter. Following conferences with all parties, Hanson consulted the Library of Congress. Weeks later the answer arrived: the song came from the Carpathian Alps which separate the Ukraine from Poland and could with justice be claimed by both groups.

"The Dutch in New York" honored the New York State "Year of History" in 1959. Fifty area collectors lent materials, which included paintings, furniture, textiles, silver, and ceramics from the period when New York was "New Amsterdam." Sponsored by the Women's Council, the exhibit featured these objects within two re-created rooms of a step-gabled Hudson River Valley house. The first National Exhibition of American Ceramics was organized by the Gallery—with regional judging points, including one in California—but proved too expensive to continue. Two years later the lists were used by the Syracuse Museum (forerunner of the Everson Museum) with the financial backing of the Syracuse Pottery Company.

The National Jewelry Exhibition, organized by the Gallery and sponsored by the Hickok Company, featured craftsmen such as Hans Christensen and Ronald Pearson, who created excitement with their three-dimensional jewelry—a concept that today appears dated although a revival could come any time. In 1952 a second contemporary jew-

2

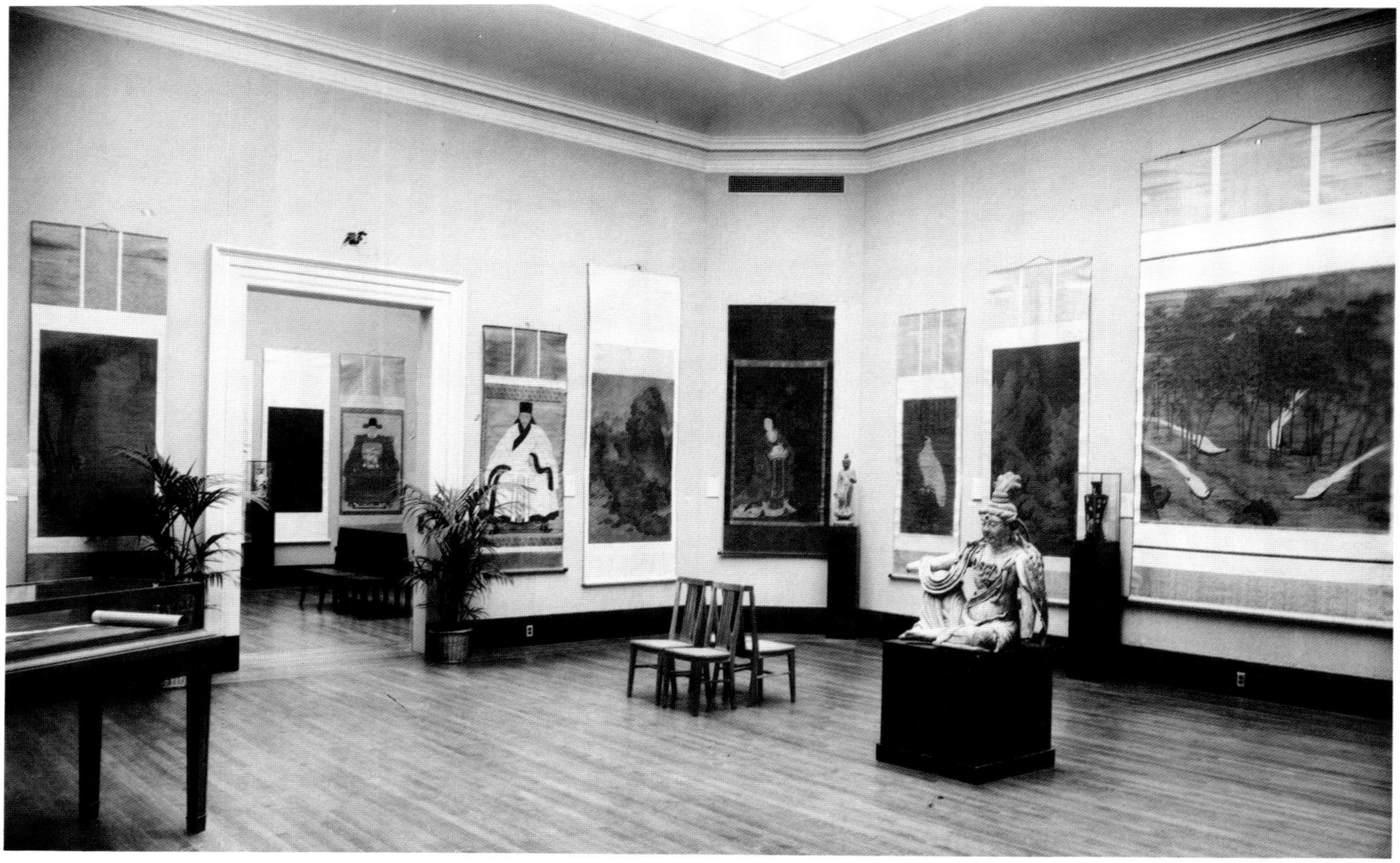

2 *The 1926 Inaugural Exhibition: The Dubois Morris collection of Chinese art was displayed in a gallery with monks cloth wallcovering.*

elry show was organized; again sponsored by Hickok, it circulated to seven museums.

"Designer-Craftsmen USA" in the early 1950s was the first large-scale exhibition of faculty and student work sponsored by the new School for American Craftsmen of the Rochester Institute of Technology, which was pumping tremendous energy into the crafts being produced regionally. Demonstrations and several consultant programs accompanied the exhibits.

Some exhibitions were local manifestations of national trends.

The American Decorative and Industrial Arts exhibition of 1933, for example, inspired the Gallery to feature furniture, textiles, lighting fixtures, and ceramics in the Art Deco style of the period.

"Testing Your Taste" was a light-hearted exhibition of 1944 as Gallery staff combed department stores for machine-made objects to be exhibited as contrasting examples of good and bad design. The most memorable finds were of the "bad design" variety such as square buttons that would not button; a lamp in the form of a skull with light blazing through the eye sockets; and another lamp featuring a ceramic slice of watermelon as base. "Oh look," cried a salesperson as Isabel marched out carrying the watermelon lamp, "Someone actually bought that thing." What she said when the lamp returned after the show is not recorded. Isabel also entered some beautiful but tipsy crystal goblets—given to Gertrude as a wedding present—in the bad design section. The best designs were not always the most expensive. Modest but handsome and functional lamps and ten-cent molded ashtrays so impressed visitors that stores had a run on them—thus reaping some benefit for their sportsmanlike participation in this successful antidote to the drab war years.

In April 1961 the "Art of India" exhibition, the most important loan collection gathered at the Gallery in many years, celebrated the opening of the university's nonwestern civilizations program. (Started by Vera Dean, the program brought Diran Kavork Dohanian, specialist in Asian art, to the university's Department of Fine Arts.) Organized with the help of Mr. and Mrs. Nasli Heeramaneck of New York and drawn from many museums and private collections—including those of Abby Aldrich Rockefeller, John D. Rockefeller III, the Boston Museum, and the William Rockwell Nelson Museum in Kansas City—the exhibition covered eighteen centuries with Indian and Nepalese paintings and stone and bronze sculptures. The one disappointment was that the sculpture the staff hoped to buy from the exhibition went to Toronto. In its stead the ninth century Tara relief sculpture (used on the cover of the 1961 handbook and a fine work in its own right) was purchased through the R.T. Miller Fund and Bequest.

Stimulating loan exhibitions arrived when art museums in Buffalo and Montreal underwent major building construction. In 1961, for example, twenty sculptures and thirty major paintings came and stayed for many months while the Albright-Knox Art Gallery in Buffalo was building its new modern addition.

Exhibiting folk art—at an early date for an art museum—eventually led to including it in the permanent collection of American art. In the mid-1950s an exhibition of "Early American Folk Sculpture, 1760-1860" included tavern signs, ship figureheads, weather vanes, trade signs, and other specialized Americana from the Willard Gallery and Olde Print Shoppe in New York. From this show came the impressive and much-borrowed pair of blue heron decoys that now grace the folk art gallery.

"Rediscovered Painters of Upstate New York" was a first-rate exhibition of little known painters and limners working between 1700 and 1875—a combined effort of the Albany Institute of Art, the Munson-Williams-Proctor Institute in Utica, the Syracuse Museum of Fine Arts, the New York State Historical Association at Cooperstown, and the Gallery. Agnes Jones, art historian, had discovered some exciting but unknown paintings in Albany, which sparked the effort. In preparing for this 1958 exhibition, the Gallery staff rediscovered four forgotten paintings from the Powers collection in the dim recesses of the Piranesi-inspired Powers Building—two original eighteenth century Italian paintings and two large-scale copies of works by Veronese and Gilbert Stuart which had hung in the upper lobby of the Powers Gallery and were too big to take to New York for auction after Powers closed his gallery in 1897.

Occasionally single-artist exhibitions were organized. Forty-five sculptures by David Smith included his "Medals of Dishonor," a series of bitter attacks on the social and political scene of the 1940s and 1950s, and created something of a rumpus in Rochester. In 1956 paintings by Nicholas de Stael were shown, and in 1962 prints, drawings, and a few sculptures by Käthe Kollwitz were exhibited.

Lang Clay and Isabel took particular interest in organizing children's shows—which were then equally enjoyed by

3

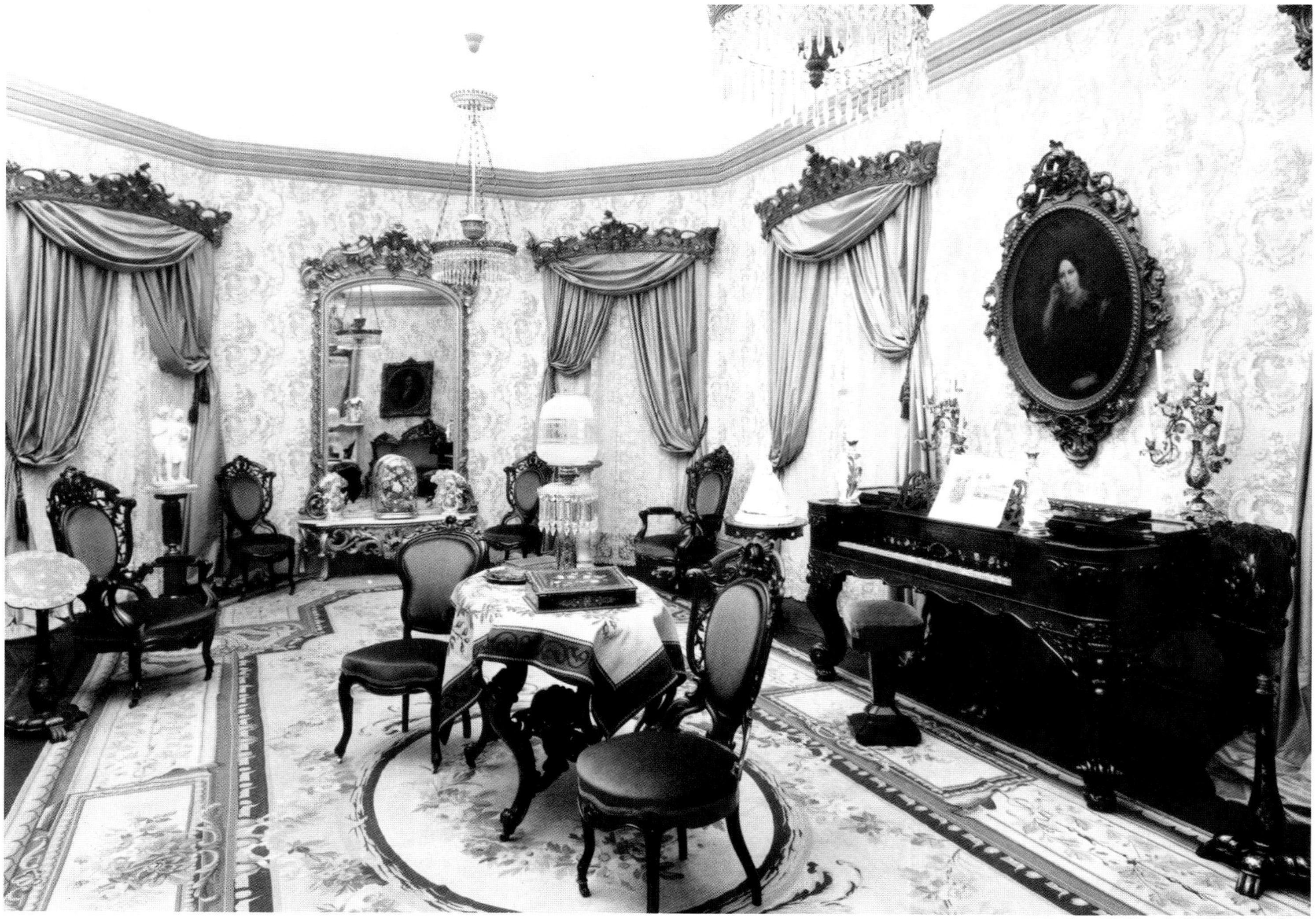

adults. "C is for Cat," "Me and My Shadow," and the "Circus Minimus" were among Isabel's most famous. Clay put together "Art Takes Shape," "Fancy Free," "The Fantastic in Art," and "Sports and Games in Art" during the 1950s.

Prior to the opening of the George Eastman House as a museum of photography in 1949, the Gallery exhibited photography, both motion picture and still. In 1937 a film series consisting of seminal motion pictures, 1893 to 1928, was put together by Iris Barry, director of the Museum of Modern Art's film library and a pioneer of cinema studies in both Britain and America. The series proved highly popular, as people crowded in to see Sarah Bernhardt, Mary Pickford, and *The Great Train Robbery.* James Card, whose "masterly little introductions" accompanied the films, went on to become head of the film department at the George Eastman House. In 1956 an exhibition of the "art" photography of Minor White, creator of the magazine *Image,* was mounted.

Survey and theme exhibitions such as "American Landscape Painting" proved popular favorites.

During the 1930s when American regionalism was a hot topic, joint exhibitions were assembled by a consortium of museums in the Great Lakes area—those in Cleveland, Buffalo, Detroit, Toledo, Toronto, Chicago, and Rochester. Each museum selected its own outstanding local work. The exhibitions proved, the Gallery staff decided, that regionalism in American art, if it ever existed, had been superseded by an international style made possible through art publications and exhibitions such as these.

In 1944 works by "The Eight" were shown. Rapid execution and spontaneity marked the styles of these Americans of the early part of the century who had developed as newspaper illustrators before the adaptation of photography to these purposes.

The pairing of the precursors of modern art—African sculpture, and pre-Columbian works— with their contemporary descendants made for a provocative presentation. The exhibition "Rebels in Art" nominated El Greco and Corot as revolutionaries in their own times.

"Signed in Paint," a significant topical exhibition originated by the Gallery in 1957, was a study of the personal handling of paint and the brush strokes of artists throughout the ages. The way an artist puts paint on canvas reveals who he is, the thesis went: no signature is necessary. The exhibition story was carried from a thirteenth century Tuscan *Virgin and Child* to Jackson Pollock. The seventeen examples, and X-rays thereof to show paint structure, included works by Poussin, Rubens, Hals, Rembrandt, Velázquez, El Greco, Monet, Renoir, Constable, Van Gogh, and Vuillard, on loan from museums and dealers. Since no one would insure one van of such big names, two vans were engaged.

Local history was grist to the mill.

The annual "Picturesque Rochester" competitions, started by Elmer Adler in 1910 and taken over by George Herdle after the Gallery opened, returned briefly in the 1920s. So did exhibits by Rochester architects, renderers, and craftsmen—James Arnold, Herbert Stern, Walter Vars Wiard, Storrs Barrow, John Wenrich, Harwood Dryer, the Pike Stained Glass Studio, and so forth. The architectural works formed part of the Rochester Art Club show of 1924.

A series of exhibitions of American furniture and decorative arts from the seventeenth to early nineteenth century was brought together from sources in the Genesee Valley. This was the series, starting with period rooms and furniture in 1932, that captured the imagination of R. T. Miller Jr. Two years later "The House of 1834" celebrated the centennial of Rochester's incorporation as a city. Designed by architect Walter Vars Wiard with content determined by Harriet Hollister Spencer, the centennial exhibit re-created rooms in each of the eight galleries through the use, when possible, of original architectural parts, textiles, wallpaper, and color schemes.

"Interiors Then and Now, 1850-1950" celebrated the centennial of the University of Rochester. A Victorian parlor and dining room, flocked wallpaper and gold valances, a crystal chandelier from the Genesee Valley Club, and a fireplace from the Brewster-Burke house contrasted with contemporary interiors.

The Erie Canal show of 1953 marked the one hundred thirtieth anniversary of the aqueduct that carried the famed ditch over the Genesee and made Rochester a boomtown of the 1830s. "The canal was the thruway of yesterday," said *Gallery Notes*, "...an artery of culture." Various ports from Syracuse to Buffalo were represented, and 110 school groups

4

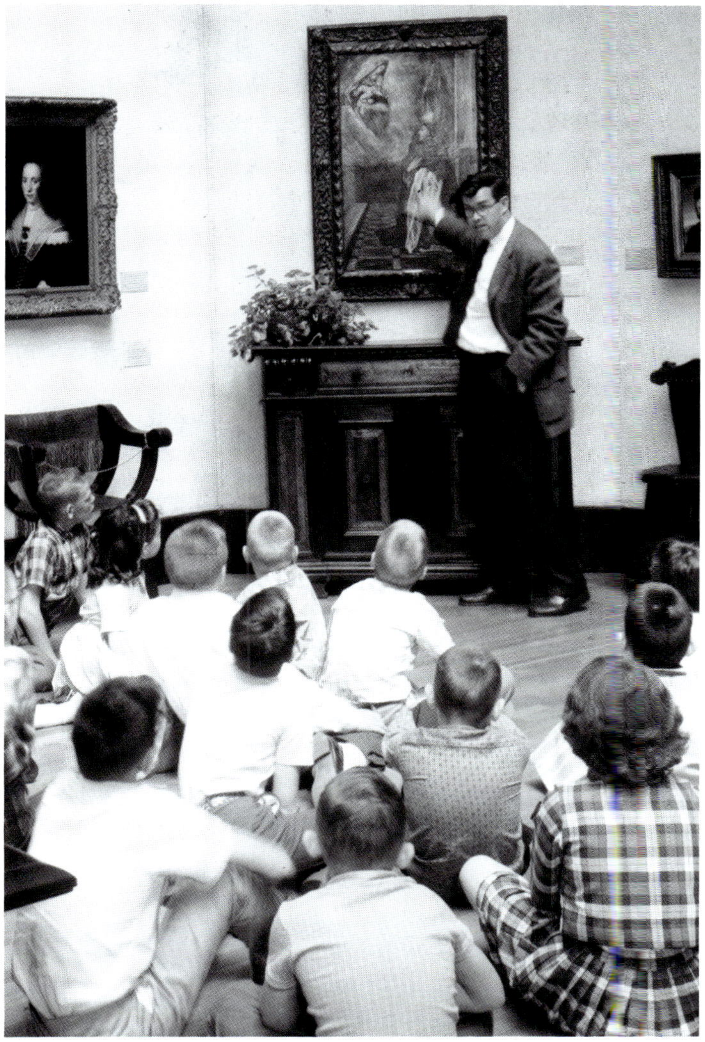

[redacted]

3 *"The House of 1834" exhibition, Victorian period drawing room. This 1934 exhibition was instrumental in interesting R. T. Miller in supporting the Gallery.*

4 *Langdon Clay discusses El Greco painting with school children, 1962.*

5

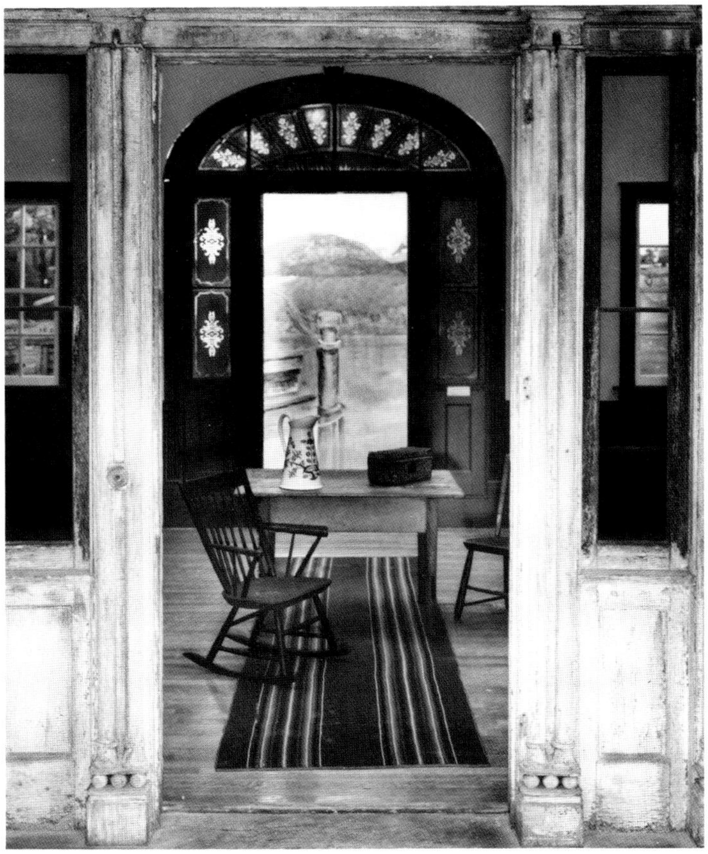

5 *"The Erie Canal: Thruway of Yesterday" exhibition, 1953. The Doorway with Fan Lights of this canalside tavern display would enter the permanent collection.*

6 *Humphrey Bogart contributes two paintings by his mother, Maud Humphrey, to the Rochester Art Club's Seventy-fifth Anniversary Exhibition, 1952.*

from the ports were bussed in. In all, 37,000 visitors came for tours and talks; the canal boat and tavern sections of this reconstruction with background scenery were recorded by Cinevision, a documentary film company out of New York.

When the show was over and lenders had retrieved their material, there remained a pair of red long johns no one would claim waving in the breezes above the deck of the Erie Canal boat. Was this the same tired red underwear later presented to Bob Young when he retired in 1978?

The seventy-fifth Annual Exhibition of the Rochester Art Club in 1952 was celebrated through a nostalgic approximation of Ada Howe Kent's studio, complete with Japanese parasols, peacock feathers, and a Turkish niche (an oriental rug fashioned into a tent). Kent's studio had been in the Powers Art Gallery where many of the founding fathers and mothers had worked. A Thomas Moran painting came from Knoedlers in honor of Daniel Powers's *Moran*, a huge painting which the city lost in the auction of 1897. A round settee, gilt ballroom furniture, and a marble *Mercury* by Guernsey Mitchell completed the period atmosphere. Isabel tracked down Humphrey Bogart in Hollywood, who obligingly sent two of his mother's paintings.

A moth-eaten old stuffed gull, left over from the Erie Canal show, was perched on George Herdle's easel for the art club show. This would not be the gull's final fling: once at a membership dinner when someone had to eat crow, the gull arrived in its stead.

"Illuminations," part spectacular exhibition, part community event, consisted of huge mounted transparencies of fifty-one great works from the thirteenth to twentieth century—all actual size (except for the Sistine Ceiling, which for obvious reasons was one-quarter size). On tour for two years, the show was sponsored by Time-Life, completely filling the whole upper floor of the Gallery. The staff found it a handy way to introduce school children to great works of art and hastily trained fourteen Women's Council members as docents. Since eighteen of the artists represented in the exhibition were also in the Gallery's collection, the Rochester works were exhibited next to the transparency by the same artist. "Illuminations" ran for two months and 40,000 people came.

Many of the transparencies had been prepared at Kodak Park, so night after night special Kodak tours were run. For the first time, however reluctantly, admission was charged to a Gallery exhibition: forty cents for adults, fifteen for children. But the revenue helped to make other

6

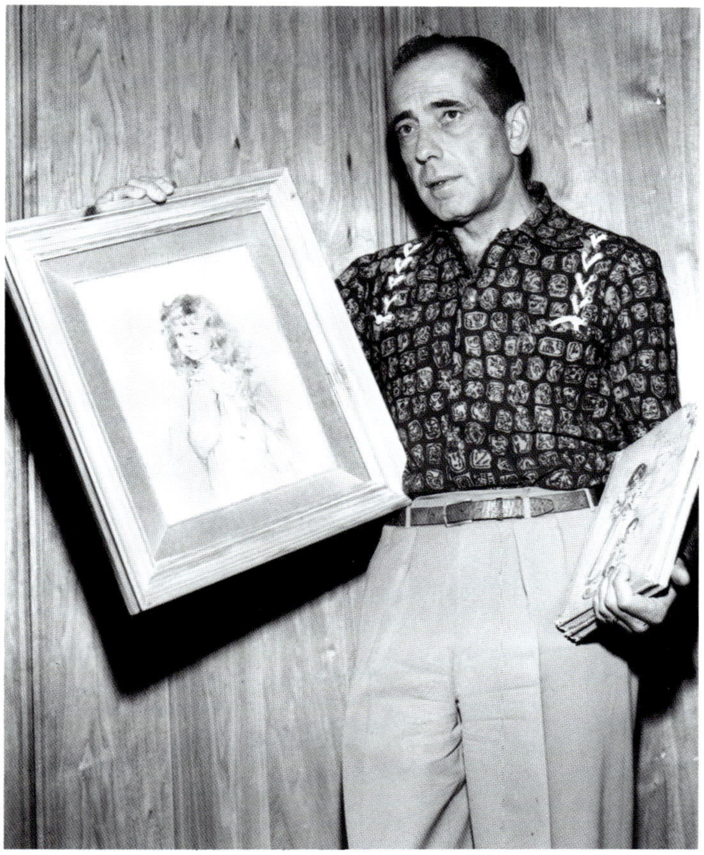

ambitious exhibitions possible.

The Gallery has mounted four exhibitions over the years to inaugurate new space additions. Two of these, in 1913 and 1968, presented contemporary works. In 1913 George Herdle assembled 145 contemporary paintings, and in 1968 a sound-and-light show featured contemporary kinetic sculptures. The two others, in 1926 and 1987, were retrospective exhibitions of historical periods. The inaugural exhibition of 1926 featured Italian paintings, including works by Botticelli, Titian, and Piero della Francesca; ecclesiastical textiles and period furniture from the collection of Carl W. Hamilton, industrialist and financier; and rare Chinese paintings of the Sung and later dynasties belonging to Dr. Debois Morris. In 1987 the inaugural exhibition was "*La Grande Manière, Historical and Religious Paintings in France 1700-1800.*"

Exhibitions from private collections were moderately represented during the first fifty years of the Gallery's existence.

In 1961 Governor and Mrs. Nelson Rockefeller sent three paintings from their own collections on loan to the Albright-Knox Gallery. That prompted a letter to the governor. It was not fair, Isabel said, to lend to only one Upstate museum. Rockefeller soon rectified that, arranging for the sanding of icy roads and police escorts for the huge pieces that arrived in Rochester from Albany, Maine, and Pocantico Hills. Along with works by Gottlieb, Guston, Calder, Giacometti, and Nevelson, he sent the twenty-two-foot tapestry based on *Guernica* (and woven under Picasso's supervision) that ordinarily hung in his dining room.

Flushed with this success in landing loans from a celebrity, the Gallery moved on to a small loan exhibition of paintings and drawings from the private collection of the actress Helen Hayes. She was preparing to tour Europe and the Near East, and so was happy to have the Gallery act as foster parent to her collection while she was away. Bob Young was dispatched to New York to pick it up; Hayes invited him in for tea and he was enraptured. Among the works Young brought back was a painting of the Hayes house in Nyack by Edward Hopper and works by Grandma Moses, Degas, Matisse, Picasso, and Renoir—small domestic choices by big names.

The Arthur and Molly Stern collection was shown in April 1962. This local collection comprised mostly contemporary painting and sculpture, including works by Léger, Appel, Miró, Gottlieb, Baziotes, Frankenthaler, and Reinhardt. There were also selections of pre-Columbian, Asian, and folk art. "The collection's wide range of periods—from Egypt of the Eighteenth Dynasty to the *ateliers* of contemporary Paris—is one of the most marked features of the exhibition," *Gallery Notes* recorded.

The myth that there are no collections of note in Rochester is apparently based on the existence of widely publicized collections elsewhere. It was certainly dispelled by the exhibition of the Stern collection and by four anonymous donors and lenders of the late 1950s and early 1960s. Quiet collectors surface from time to time.

The lenders of October 1957 can now be identified as Dr. and Mrs. Fred Geib, who at the time wished to remain anonymous. It was the first time Rochester had seen the collection. Even as a medical student, Geib had managed to collect some works of art, including Dürer woodcuts and Whistler etchings. Later he acquired silver and porcelains, paintings by Tintoretto, Hubert Robert, a stunning fifteenth century still life, a church interior by Emanuel de Witte, a Rubens sketch of children in a wheat field, and paintings attributed to Rembrandt and Memling.

The Gallery staff may not have always agreed with the attributions assigned by Geib's New York dealer, but that mattered little; the collection was highly interesting even without famous names. Later Dr. and Mrs. Geib gave the Gallery an

7

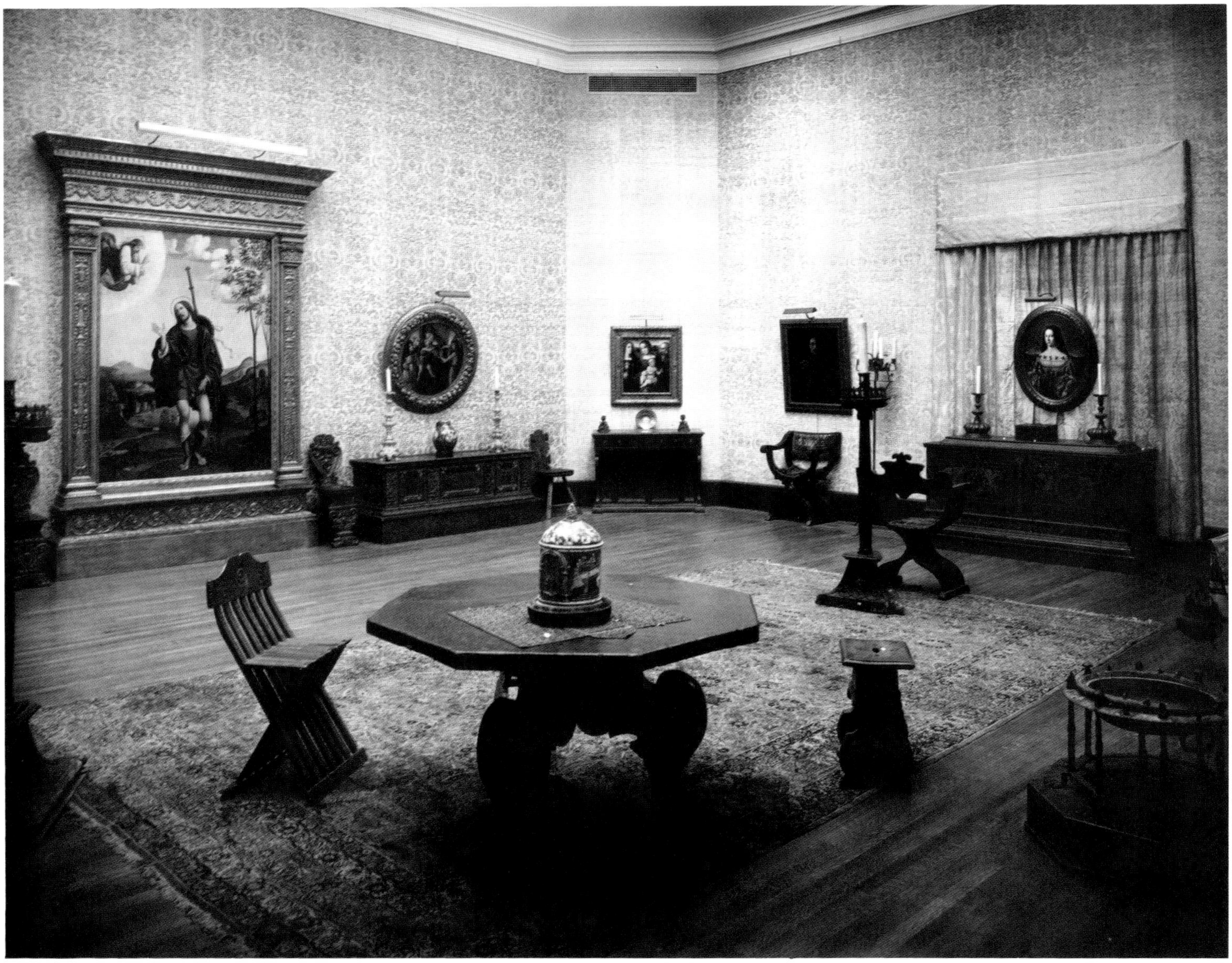

7 *The 1926 Inaugural Exhibition: The Carl W. Hamilton collection of Italian paintings and furniture was displayed in a gallery with Fortuny wallcovering.*

early Constable landscape; *Landing of Ulysses on the Island of the Phaeacians*, from the workshop of Peter Paul Rubens; *Portrait of Elizabeth Jordaens*, by her father Jacob Jordaens, and *Man with Book Seated in a Landscape*, by Thomas Gainsborough.

In 1962 *Gallery Notes* reported that the Gallery's was "the first museum showing of a group of thirty-one important Italian and Northern European paintings from a large and notable collection." The anonymous collector of these late medieval and early Renaissance works had haunted the dealer galleries and auction houses for years; possessing a good eye, he bought panels of tempera, oil, and gold for a song. "The paintings span more than five centuries of development in the north and south and reflect the change from religious themes to the growing interest in landscape, portraiture and genre scenes." Italian masters of the Sienese, Ferrarese, and Florentine schools were joined by examples of early northern painting in Germany, France, Switzerland, and Flanders.

About the same time, Gertrude invited a print collector, who also wished to remain anonymous, to inspect the Gallery's meager print collection. "We never had funds appropriated for this specific purpose," she told him apologetically. "We had to find donors or steal from the painting fund; so the print collection has developed spasmodically." The collector was impressed by the presence of Dürers, Picassos, and Whistlers, however, maintaining that this small collection was worth developing. He agreed to serve on the print committee, and invited the Herdle sisters to see his own collection of drawings and prints. "An unbelievable find in Western New York," they marveled. Selections from this collection were exhibited at the Gallery in November 1959. Some years later the print collector began enriching the Gallery's collections regularly from his own astonishing and apparently bottomless resources.

In 1962 the bronze *Head of a Woman*, by Elie Nadelman, was given anonymously by the familiar "Friend of the Gallery" in honor of Gertrude Herdle Moore, then retiring after forty-four years with the Gallery, forty of them as director. Later the same "friend" also gave Nadelman's marble head of the same subject, which in 1988 creates an arresting counterpoint to the bronze in the sculpture pavilion. Twenty-six years later we know that the "friend" was actually two—Dr. and Mrs. James Sibley Watson Jr.

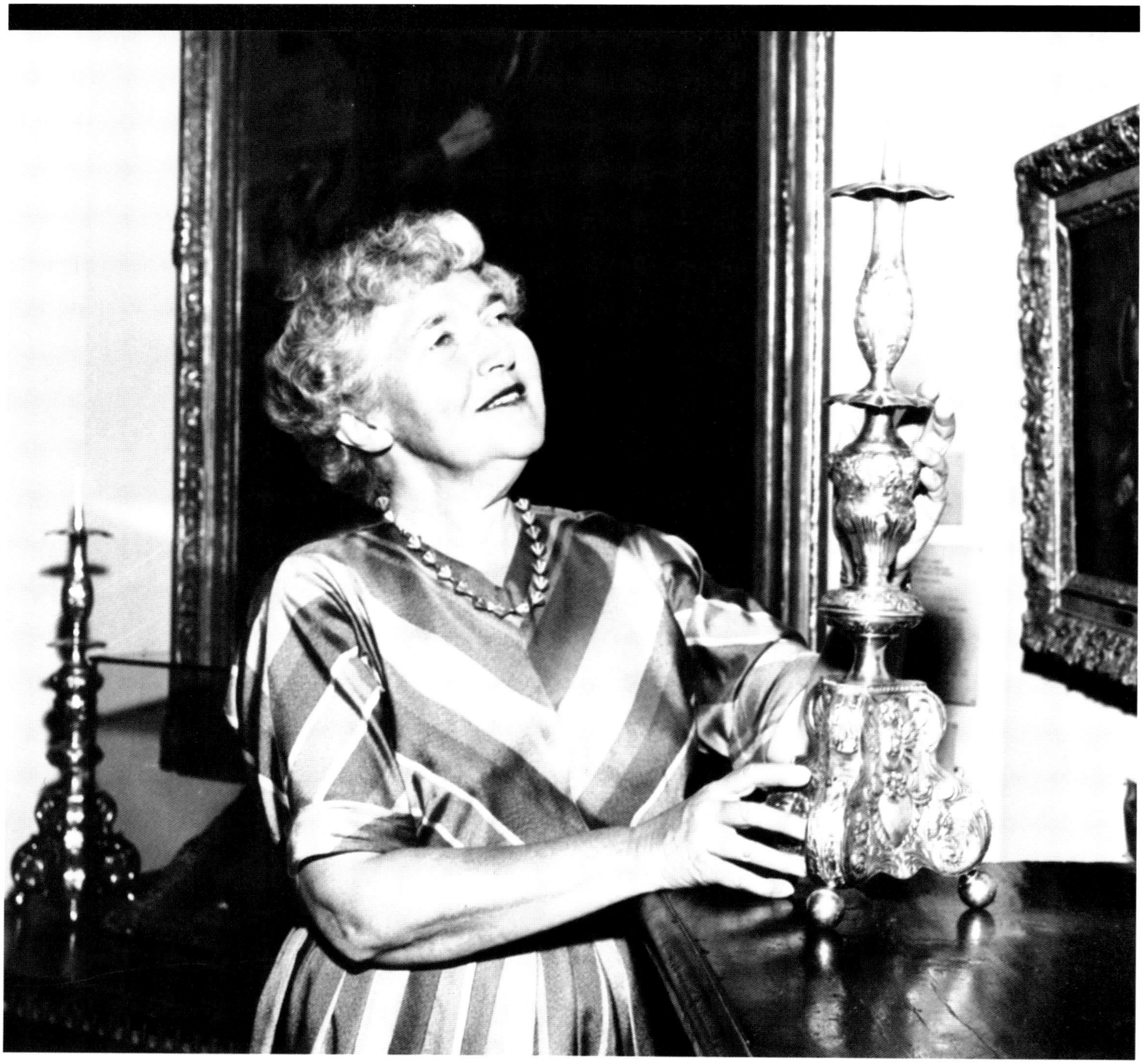

8

In April 1977 some ninety "Treasures from Rochester" traveled to the Wildenstein Galleries in New York City where they were exhibited for six weeks. Included were works from every period of Gallery history. When Director Emeritus Gertrude Herdle Moore and Curator Emeritus Isabel Herdle heard that notable art critics and historians had visited the installation, they were naturally curious.

"What were their reactions?" the Herdle sisters wondered.

The opinions of the intelligentsia were dutifully gathered, and a messenger was dispatched to the Herdle doorstep with the information. Before the bearer of the critical tidings could open his mouth, however, he was halted by Gertrude's upraised hand.

"Before you tell us anything," she said, "I want you to know that Isabel and I have talked it over and we don't care what they say. We know it is a great collection."

The director examines objects from the Buswell-Hochstetter Bequest, 1955, such as these seventeenth century Pricket candlesticks.

The days when George Herdle could obtain art for the Gallery simply by browsing through a studio, making a gentleman's handshake agreement with an artist, tucking a painting under his arm, and waltzing his find down to the Prince Street Campus, had long vanished by the time his daughters took charge of acquisitions. Theirs was an art world already beginning to be dominated by commerce. As art prices rose, so did art dealers, a canny crowd with sharp eyes for undiscovered masterpieces—and for a bargain. While the Gallery's budget was no match for some with deeper pockets, Gertrude Moore and Isabel Herdle were up to the challenge in sagacity. They were shrewd, they were flexible, equally ready to deal with the sharpest, and to "wheel" their prizes homeward by whatever means necessary. "Networking" was an unknown term to them, but that is precisely what they were up to, forming associations with an amazing variety of people who were always willing to put the Herdle sisters onto something good. Windfalls also seemed to be a Herdle specialty. Whether luck is the residue of design or not is debatable, but clearly, under the Herdles, the Gallery had the knack for being in the right place at the right time.

1

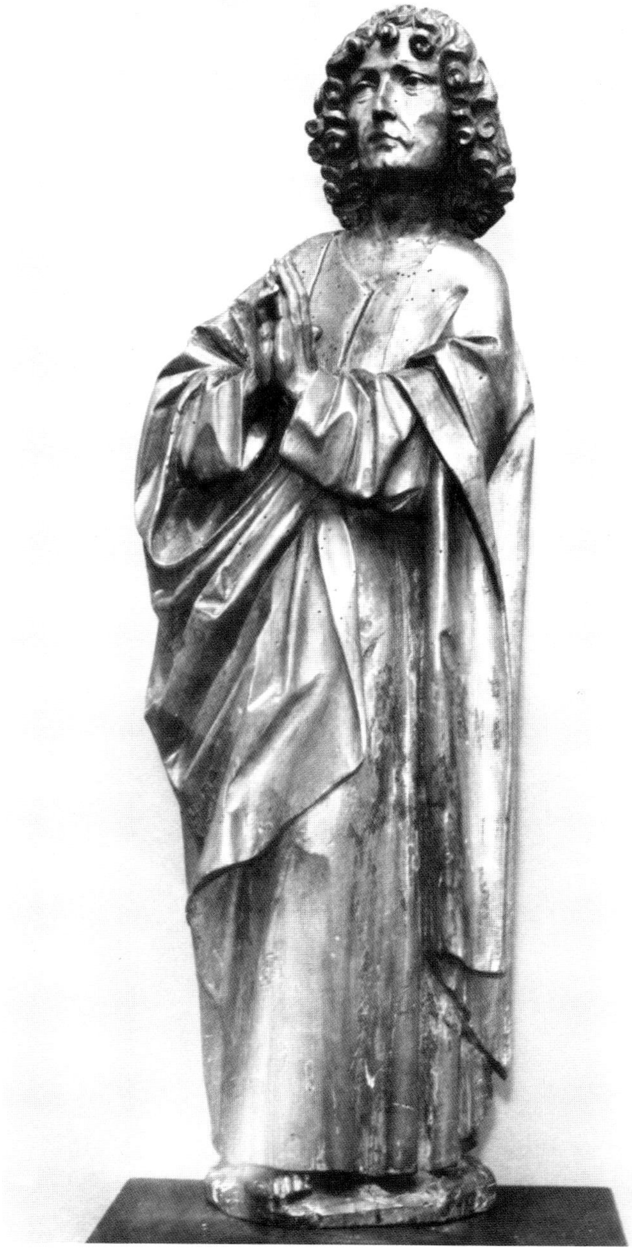

The Buswells of Buffalo traveled widely in Europe in the late 1920s, attending important sales. Dr. Buswell, a Buffalo physician, was treated at the University of Rochester's Strong Memorial Hospital and died there in 1940. In appreciation for the care he had received, Mrs. Buswell, who died the following year, remembered the university in her will, designating life use of her collections to her brother, Ralph Hochstetter. Several objects came immediately to the Gallery and are so labeled: "Bequest of Bertha Buswell." In the last six months of Ralph Hochstetter's life he decided that the University of Buffalo should receive part of his legacy, so at his death in 1955 a codicil to his will was discovered which stipulated that the objects would be shared between the two institutions. In addition the Metropolitan Museum of Art in New York had first choice, opting for a drawing by Van Dyck and a marble head by Houdon.

Carl Hersey, head of the University of Rochester's fine arts department, and Lucea de Kiewiet, wife of the university president, traveled to Buffalo with Gertrude and Isabel to survey the bequest, which included both works of art and household effects. En route the quartet plotted strategies for obtaining the maximum number of their first six choices. We will give them first choice, the plan went, thus virtually guaranteeing second and third choice for the Gallery. The Buffalo representatives were cooperative; indeed, they were

[redacted]

1 *School of Veit Stoss, Franconian (1438/47-1533), St. John the Evangelist, lindenwood, h. 31⅜ in. Bertha Buswell Bequest, 55.111. This sculpture has been variously attributed to the influences of Viet Stoss or Tilman Riemenschneider, the two giants of German Renaissance sculpture.*

overjoyed at the prospect of having the initial bid.

Fortunately for the Gallery, the head of the Buffalo art department was away and his hapless substitute went for the posh household effects, dazzled by the Rolls-Royce, the air conditioner, the elegant dining room suite, the exquisite tea set, the Steinway piano, and the like. Amazed by this stroke of fortune, the Rochester contingent found itself swooping up *all* of the art collection that was high on its list. And so the Gallery received a splendid group of seventeenth century Dutch, Flemish, and French paintings by Cornelis de Vos, Frans van Mieris, Nicolaes Maes, Dirck van Santvoort, Jan Steen, and David Teniers the Younger, plus late medieval, Flemish, and German wood sculpture, including one by Tilman Riemenschneider (currently labeled School of Veit Stoss). On top of all that a few "extras" were tossed in: stained glass, Persian rugs, and some post-Renaissance furniture from Spain, France, and Italy; along with textiles, tapestries, ceramics, majolica, eighteenth and nineteenth century English silver, and early Italian laces.

In November and December of 1955 the Buswell-Hochstetter collection was exhibited as a whole at the Gallery.

One morning in 1948 a beautiful young German woman named Elizabeth Lack appeared on the Gallery doorstep with a roll of lithographs, an odd-looking book, and a sad story to tell. She had been engaged to marry an American G.I., a Rochester man whom her family had befriended while he was with the Army of Occupation. In lieu of a dowry involving cash or property, Elizabeth's war-beset family had given her practically its last possessions of any value: a portfolio of Käthe Kollwitz prints of the *Peasant War* series, and a first edition of George Grosz's *Ecce Homo.* Upon arriving in America, the hopeful bride had found that her intended was already married, with a family. Frantic, mortified, and penniless, she could not find it within herself to return home, since her small village had given her such a glorious send off. Her dowry contained her last assets, and the Gallery was her last hope. Gertrude knew the Kollwitz prints were valuable, but since only $700 remained in the year's acquisition fund, she gave the young woman addresses of dealers in New York who could give her a better price, and wished her well. Yet within a week, the young woman returned, insisting that the Gallery take the prints for whatever money it could give her.

The story had a happy ending. Years later Elizabeth—still stunning, considerably better dressed, and with daughter in tow—dropped in at the Gallery to say hello to Isabel. She had married a New York lawyer she met on a train, and had prospered. Along with its Kollwitz prints, the Gallery has the memory of this poignant story, worthy of a postwar O. Henry.

World War II figured in the provenance of at least two important works. The small oval still life by Braque, painted in 1913, was smuggled out of Germany during the war and recovered by the dealer Kahnweiler from an attic in Switzerland before entering the collection in 1954.

The other piece involved Dr. Paul Drey, learned proprietor of the Drey Gallery in Vienna—a fine old European house that also published books on German art. The Dreys anticipated the anti-Semitic campaign of the late 1930s. One day they quietly abandoned their Vienna gallery full of precious artifacts to the Nazis and fled to Switzerland. From there they went to London where a brother had a gallery, and finally emigrated to New York and established a Drey Gallery there.

After the war, Drey was attached to the American military government in Germany as an expert in the identification and return of art works stolen by the Nazis. Drey was surprised to find one of his own among the works liberated by the allies from the salt mine cache of Himmler and Goering. It was a Florentine (or possibly Pisan) altarpiece, *Madonna and Child with SS. Francis, John the Baptist, Peter, and Dominic*, attributed to Nardo di Cione (ca. 1343-1366). It took years to establish prewar ownership of the Nazi hoard and in the meantime, Drey died. By chance the Herdles were in the Drey Gallery in New York choosing works for the "Signed in Paint" exhibition in 1957 when word was received that legal title to the altarpiece had been established. The work could now be sold by the Dreys, but by a peculiar legal ruling, only at its lower pre-war valuation. That day the tempera altarpiece entered the Gallery collection through the Gould Fund. It stands today as a central attraction of the Renaissance gallery, and for those who know its strange history, a reminder that as a work of art is passed down through the ages, it bears witness to both the best and the worst in human nature.

The three Silbermann brothers were dealers of French-Austrian descent. The head of the firm was Abris Silbermann—intense, austere, and lame, with a beautiful Hungarian wife. His roly-poly brother was full of stories, many of them scandalous, about museum directors. The Silbermanns started many a famous show business figure off as collector—including author Booth Tarkington and Major

2

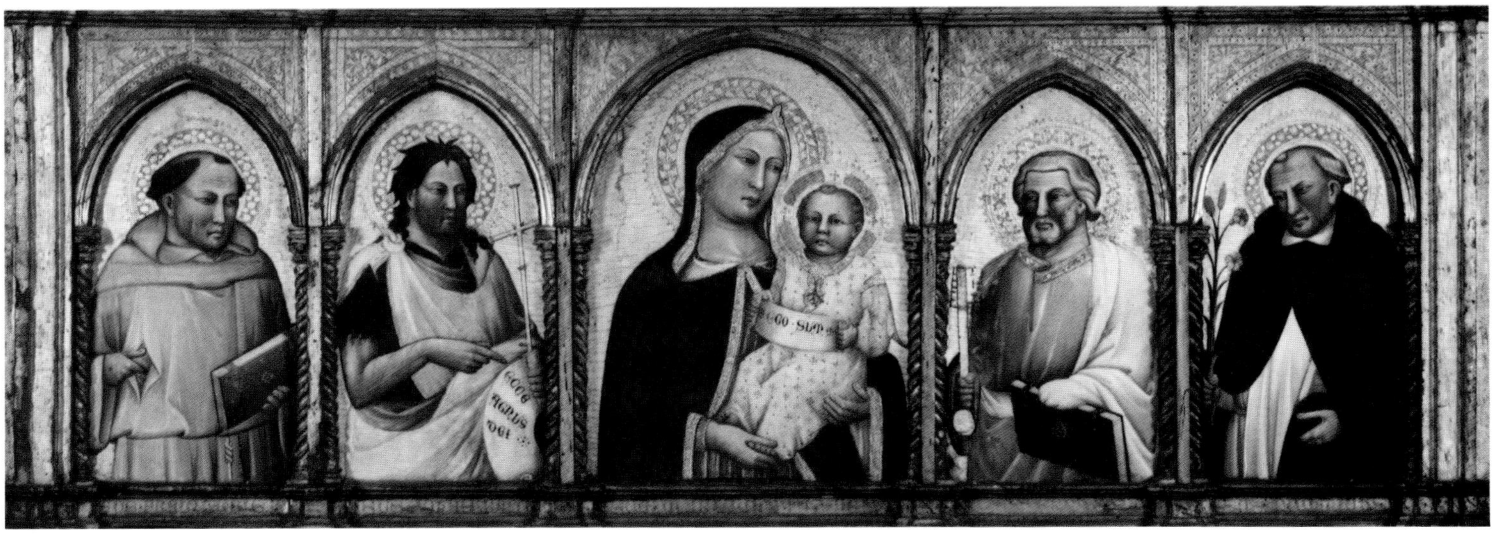

Edward Bowes of radio's "Amateur Hour." The Gallery's Renoir landscape *Environs de Cagnes* went from the Silbermann gallery to Major Bowes, back to Silbermann, and on to the Gallery via the Marion Stratton Gould Fund.

The Gallery's other Renoir, *Woman Leaning on her Elbows*, had a distinguished visitor one day when Gertrude turned a Gallery corner to happen upon the actor Charles Laughton, in Rochester for a series of theater performances. He was standing in admiration before this portrait, for which Renoir's good friend, Gabrielle, had served as model. "I knew her well," Laughton explained to Gertrude. "She was an excellent cook." The actor then treated his audience of one to a vivid mimicry of Gabrielle's gestures and inflections, bowing out with the sweet sounds of "You have a fine little gallery here."

Another casual visitor was ultimately responsible for one of the Gallery treasures entering the collection. George Stevens of Portland, Maine, had accompanied his daughter to Rochester to enroll her in the Eastman School of Music. "Where are your Winslow Homers?" Stevens wondered. "Unfortunately, we don't have any," Isabel ruefully admitted. "Well, our family does," was his dry rejoinder.

He and his sister owned a painting, Stevens told her, that had been given to their father, a carpenter, in payment for enlarging Winslow Homer's studio in Prout's Neck, Maine. With tuition costs for the daughter looming, the Stevens family just might consider parting with the wonderful mood-struck rendition of *Artist's Studio in an Afternoon Fog*. Fortunately, R. T. Miller's fund was waiting in the wings for just such an occasion.

Painted in 1894, *Artist's Studio in an Afternoon Fog* was closely bound to the artist's life. Ten years earlier Homer had retired to Prout's Neck where his father and brothers had bought property. During the long Maine winter, after the relatives had returned to more moderate climes, Winslow stayed on alone painting in the storm-battered, snowbound studio. Freed from the conventional niceties of nineteenth century genre painting that some of Homer's other oils exhibit, *Artist's Studio* radiates a more dramatic yet serene poetry.

Miller's fund was there as well when the opportunity came to add the Frederic Morgan collection of Egyptian, Classical, and Near Eastern objects of art.

Frederic Grinnell Morgan, scion of the Wells-Fargo family of Aurora, New York, had been vice consul and then deputy consul general in Cairo at the turn of the century. With an amateur but nonetheless keen interest in archaeology, Morgan went along on the digs of Maspero and other Egyptian scholars and excavators of the Delta, coming back with a sizable collection of relics. He was present in 1904 when a tomb in Thebes was opened.

When Morgan retired from consular service to return to Aurora to live with his sister, he faced the problem of shipping his vast aggregation of artifacts. In return for favors Morgan rendered in international monetary conversion, the French government offered to transport Morgan's collection in a French man-of-war; flat cars transported the cache on its final lap to the ancestral homestead.

In the mid-1940s, more than twenty years after Morgan's death, Gertrude, along with the president of Wells College, visited the Morgans' old fieldstone house on Cayuga Lake. The callers were met by the sister, Edith Morgan, by then maneuvering as best she could with the aid of two

3

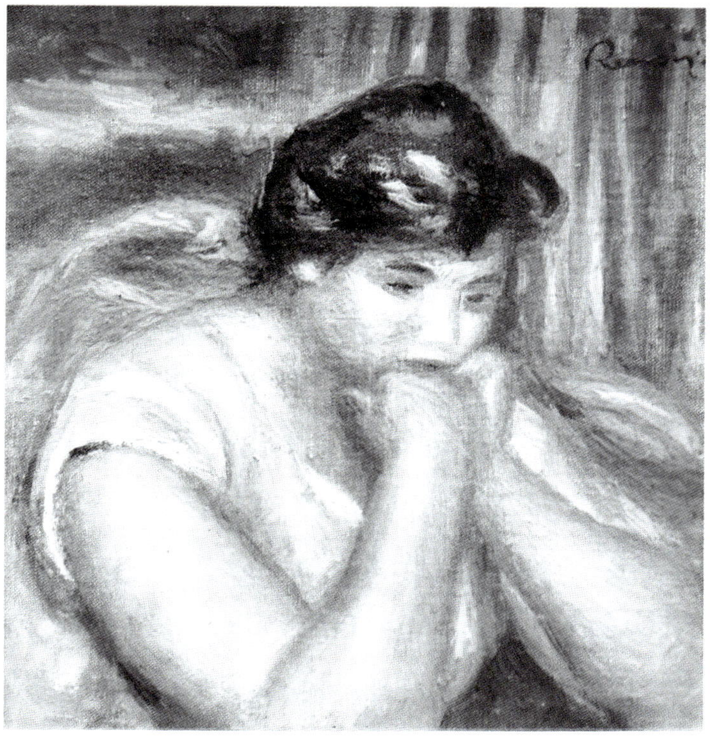

2 *School of Nardo di Cione (Italian, Florentine, active ca. 1345-1365), Altarpiece: The Virgin and Child with SS. Francis of Assisi, John the Baptist, Peter, and Dominic, tempera on wood, 29 x 86½ in. Marion Stratton Gould Fund, 57.4*

3 *Auguste Renoir (French 1841-1919), Woman Leaning on her Elbows, oil on canvas, 8¾ x 8¾ in. Marion Stratton Gould Fund, 45.80*

canes. "I had learned to cast my eye around," Gertrude recalls, "and high on a library shelf was a dusty pair of intriguing vases." When Gertrude inquired, the woman would only say, with an edge to her voice, that her late brother had spent all his money on antiquities, which were now packed away as her unwelcome responsibility. She did explain that she had given his one monumental Egyptian sculpture to the Toledo Museum.

Gertrude could make an educated guess at what might lie within those walls. Then, one hot summer day in 1951, Francis Henry Taylor, the director of New York's Metropolitan Museum, telephoned to ask Gertrude if she would substitute for him in Aurora, as he had an unavoidable conflict. The Morgan estate was being liquidated, Taylor explained, and the heirs needed an appraisal of "some pieces of glass and stone."

"I was immediately interested, greedy even," Gertrude remembers. With Isabel and Bob Young, she set off to meet the heiresses, Eleanor Lovett of New Hampshire and her sister, younger cousins of the late Edith and Frederic Morgan.

"The beautiful old house had been closely shuttered for some time," Isabel recalls, "but as Eleanor raised the shades and opened the cupboard doors in a little room off the main hall, a shaft of light fell on more than one hundred pieces of opalescent Roman glass. The whole room came alive with shimmering color." The women were reduced to oohs and ahs. Way up on a dusty shelf was a pair of rare Mycenaean kraters. In the attic specially constructed drawers held Coptic and Persian textiles. In one corner stood some inlaid Arabic door panels.

"The stone is in the barn," Lovett advised. "Would you like to go sphinxing?" Wading though straw and old dry manure, the two appraisers and their sidekick, Young, discovered row upon row of Coptic and Byzantine capitals, a sarcophagus, and the headless body of a sphinx from the Avenue of Karnak. Young picked up a shovel and dug in the dung looking for the sphinx's head—and actually turned one up! As it eventually turned out, the head was not a true match, but only a modern copy Morgan had commissioned. It is not exhibited in the Gallery.

The 200 objects ranged from the tiniest glass figures, only a quarter of an inch high, to rough unglazed earthen pots; from predynastic totem figures, to terra-cotta figures of the iron age in Cyprus, and enormous column fragments too large to move. Glass from the first to the thirteenth century, unearthed in Egypt and the Middle East, consisted mostly of everyday ware: cups, plates, oil goblets used as lamps, kohl tubes (black cosmetic jars), medicine and storage jars, amulets, and glass coins. Several ancient kinds of glass were included in the collection, the earliest being the core-formed (Phoenician) glass which antedates blown glass.

Three days later, "I rendered my report to Miss Lovett," Gertrude says. She advised the Morgan heiress that there was no local market for such antiquities and that the highest prices would be realized at auction in New York. "We left then, stayed away for three hours, and returned with the absolutely ridiculous offer of $1,500 for the whole collection.

"This is not a realistic price," Gertrude told Lovett emphatically, "but very honestly, it's all that we have." Lovett requested three days to think it over, but only twenty-four hours later called to accept the offer with a definite tone of relief in her voice. She noted that shipping and crating costs would be eliminated if the Gallery would take on the collection, and that the Frederic Morgan Collection could in this way be kept together in Western New York.

Two days later the Frederic Morgan Collection came to the Memorial Art Gallery. Because of the Morgan family's long association with Wells College, a footed bowl was given to the college for its library. Later Lovett would present an Egyptian figure of a man to the Gallery in memory of Edith Morgan.

Wheeling the collection back to the Prince Street Campus showed the Gallery staff at its improvisational best. "You would have been impressed with our cavalcade," Gertrude wrote later to Lovett, "the university truck, four Gallery cars, a rented five-ton juggernaut, and a wreck-hauling windlass.... It required a second trip with the trucks to bring the stone including... several of the broken columns."

Even so, a huge Egyptian column with cartouches had to be left behind. About four columns and many Coptic and Byzantine capitals of the fifth to seventh centuries were transported back. (Much later, one dark night some athletically fit university students managed to cart one of these columns to the belfry of Cutler Union as a prank; the trip back down did sorely tax both the patience and muscles of the Gallery maintenance staff.)

For years the surplus capitals rested under the stairs, and some still remain in storage. Recently David Walsh, associate professor of fine arts at the university and specialist in medieval art, has raised the exciting possibility that two of these capitals, always thought to be late antique in origin, could actually be Romanesque and Merovingian (a rare moment in history, 500-751 A. D., when Frankish kings ruled and from which the Gallery has no examples).

The high spots of the collection are the two rare Mycenaean kraters from 1300 B.C. Dr. Vassos Karageorgas, director of the Cyprus Museum, has identified one of the kraters as having a Linear B marking on its shoulder. Linear B is the only early Minoan system of writing so far deciphered, and the symbol on the Gallery krater (it looks like a weathered Roman numeral *VI*) would make it one of only three such in the world so far identified.

Of course, a "bargain" in the art world often means that someone, at least in his own mind, might feel that he came out on the short end. At an auction at Parke Bernet in New York, Isabel noticed that *Au Tribunal* by Jean Louis Forain, was being ignored by the bidders. Deciding to take a flier, more to test the waters than anything else, Isabel risked a few hundred dollars. To her surprise, she came away with the painting. She discovered later that although the Forain was auctioned under a "front" name, it actually was the property of the famed international *chanteuse* Hildegarde. Wanting some information on the provenance of the painting, she rang up the singer's apartment, only to come away with ears burning. According to Isabel, the singer laid her out in purple, complaining bitterly about the bargain price Isabel had paid. Claiming that she had paid "five times the amount" originally, Hildegarde fulminated for a bit, then hung up.

Other beautiful objects entered the collection with perhaps less drama but no less significance. The Gallery's collection of English and continental silver came primarily from the Woodward and Buswell collections.

In 1896 Orator Woodward, of LeRoy, New York, bought a recipe for a gelatin dessert from a neighbor lady and began producing it commercially. Orator died at an early age and his son Ernest, age twenty-four, took over the business. Although the gelatin recipe was not unique, by producing an inexpensive, quality product and cleverly marketing it, Ernest parlayed his recipe into the famous Jell-o brand. He built the business, the Genesee Pure Foods Company, to the point where it merged with Postum to establish General Foods.

The Ernest Woodwards had a tremendous pride in the region, liberally supporting the university, the Rochester Institute of Technology, and projects for LeRoy such as its library. When Rush Rhees sent out letters in 1913 inviting selected community leaders to become Gallery supporters, the Woodwards joined immediately at the highest level: a $250 patron membership.

In 1952 Edith (Mrs. Ernest) Woodward gave the Gallery seven early nineteenth century American hooked rugs plus

4

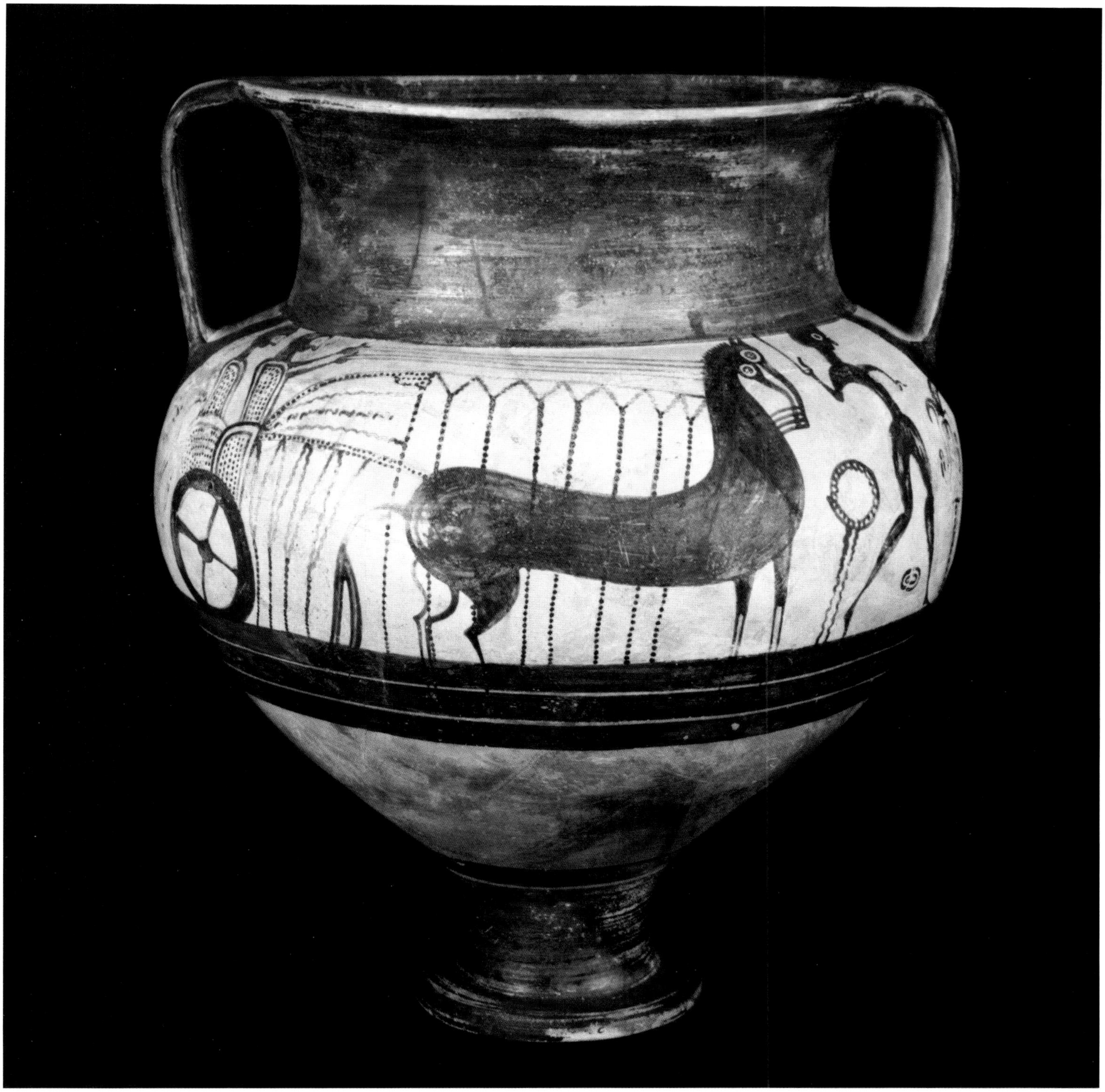

4 *Mycenaean, Late Helladic Period, ca. 1300-1275 B. C.,* <u>*Krater*</u>*, terra cotta, h. 18½ in. Frederic Morgan Collection. R. T. Miller Fund, 51.203*

some silver— "a fine collection," the Herdles say, although "the best silver came later."

Ernest was the real silver collector, getting his start by shopping for silver hunt trophies. With the help of Peter Guille, who sold antique silver and went on to become the first director of the Sterling and Francine Clark Art Institute in Williamstown, Massachusetts, Woodward spent twenty-five years gathering together an impressive collection of English and Continental silver of the seventeenth through nineteenth century. Upon the death of Edith Woodward in 1955 (Ernest having predeceased her in 1948) seventy-two of the finest items in the collection came to the Gallery. Most impressive was the "Saltby Plate" gold caudle cup, fashioned by Benjamin Pyne in 1710 and given by Queen Anne as a trophy in the Saltby races started by the Earl of Rutland in 1685. ("Oh that's where the mate is," a curator from the Victoria and Albert Museum was heard to mutter as he passed the Gallery's silver display. Ernest Woodward had used the Saltby cup for his martinis.)

The accessions of the 1950s from the Gould Fund not only continued to fill the gaps inevitably found in the survey collections of any small museum but also to build on the Gallery's strengths. A large three-piece grouping of a twelfth century Spanish crucifix and a thirteenth century mourning *Virgin and St. John* was added to the medieval collection, creating a dramatic focal point to the main axis of the Fountain Court.

For the Renaissance collection a tempera on panel *Crucifixion* in its original carved and gilded frame by the early Florentine Giovanni del Biondo was acquired. As an example of sixteenth century Mannerist painting, the Gallery purchased the *Conversion of St. Paul* by Francesco Ubertini, called Il Bacchiacca (1494-1557). This artist could cleverly lift details from masters such as Leonardo da Vinci, Raphael, or Dürer, using them for his own purposes. For the Baroque collection one of five versions of *Two Musicians* by the Caravaggiesque Bernardo Strozzi (1581-1644) of Genoa was purchased. To add to the eighteenth century gallery, a storm-tossed, melodramatic seascape called *Exorcism of the Waves* by the Genoese Mannerist painter Alessandro Magnasco (1667-1749) was acquired.

For the early twentieth century collection, *Abandonne* or *Le Miracle*, a typical "oil on paper" with heavy dark contours by Georges Rouault (1871-1958)—later found to have been executed over an intaglio print mounted on board—was purchased from the Gould Fund.

For the Asian collection the Herdles bought a Japanese

5 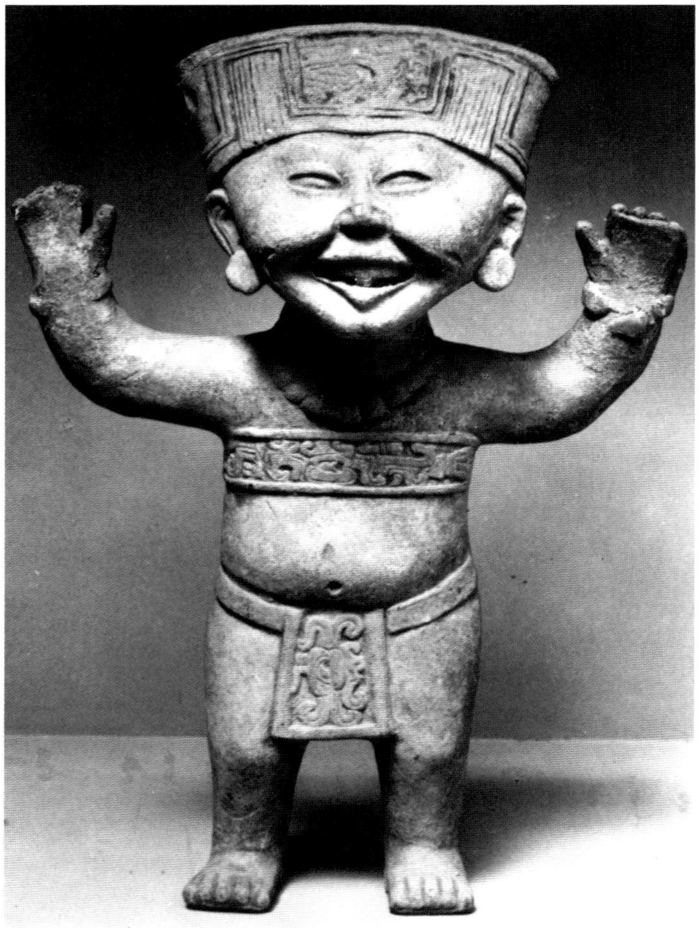

5 *Mexican, Totonac Culture (800-1200), classic Vera Cruz style, Figure of Laughing Man, clay, h. 14 in. R. T. Miller Fund, 54.39*

screen painting. Their first choice (grasses against a gold background) went to Morris Graves, the painter, but they were able to get their second choice—a medieval battle scene in which all the women take on all the men.

The most important acquisition of 1954 was the Ingres *Portrait of Pierre Francois Bernier*, among the earliest surviving works of that great nineteenth century painter. Indeed the cold classicist Ingres looks very romantic in this early portrait. Bernier, later to become one of the top French astronomers, was, along with Ingres, a pupil of Jacques-Louis David.

The Gould Fund was four years in the paying for Mary Cassatt's pastel of *Jeune Mère fillette et fils* from the Oliver H. B. Havemeyer collection (which Cassatt largely had assembled) but it was worth every penny.

For the contemporary collection four nonobjective paintings were acquired, including a "single drip" by Jackson Pollock (so described because it was such a small work and thus affordable), *The Assessor* by Conrad Marca-Relli, and *Ruby Gold* by Hans Hofmann.

Having gone to New York in 1961 with the goal of buying a Hofmann, the Herdles first went through his dealer's stock and found nothing to their liking. But a day with the artist and his wife, which included visits to his Washington Square apartment and studio, a bite of lunch, and acting as rapt audience to a manuscript he was working on, finally allowed them an opportunity to see his personal selection of paintings from each period of his career. In the Hofmann apartment they found one that seemed a summary of his celebrated push-pull principles of composition and his use of strongly colored splotches and free patterns of explosive force. Thinking themselves canny buyers, they began to make arrangements for paying the artist directly, only to find they had to pay the gallery commission anyway.

Among works that would be put off to the next directorship was a painting by Paul Cézanne, crucial figure in the transition from nineteenth-century Impressionism to twentieth-century Cubism. In the 1940s the art committee had turned down a $24,000 Cézanne because of a revolt in staff ranks: "It isn't a typical Cézanne," said Fritz Trautman. "I can't teach from it." Then, in 1955 a special meeting of the Board of Managers was called to consider the purchase of a Cézanne for $58,000 plus the trade of the Paul Klee watercolor, *Fairy Tales*. The final decision not to buy turned out to be right. The Cézanne acquired by anonymous gift in 1969 was much the better one.

Having decided that the Memorial Art Gallery would probably always be a small museum with no room for large-scale sculpture, the staff determined to concentrate on representations of the masters in their smaller work. In 1956 six sculptures by Moore, Lipchitz, Calder, Manzu, Bourdelle, and Lachaise were purchased. "You could always interest a good dealer in a project like this," Isabel says. Works by Edgar Degas, Marino Marini, Gerhard Marcks, Ernst Barlach, and one of Rodin's preliminary studies for his rejected masterpiece of 1893, *Balzac* (the large work is in the Museum of Modern Art, New York), were bought through the R. T. Miller Fund.

In October 1958, R. T. Miller Jr., one of the Gallery's staunchest benefactors since the early 1930s, died at the age of ninety-one. In tribute, all the objects acquired during his lifetime from gifts totalling $125,000 were displayed. Miller had never shown any interest in endowments, so the additional $25,000 from his will was applied to the growing sculpture collection. The first purchase was a large *Torso, Ile de France* by Aristide Maillol (1861-1944) in bronze, cast in 1921, which had been in the artist's own garden and had an unusually beautiful patina.

Next from Miller's bequest came *Calligraphics* by Isamu Noguchi (b. 1904). As it happened, the Museum of Modern Art was competing for the Noguchi, but gallantly relinquished its option because that particular piece was the only one within the Gallery's reach. The work exemplifies Noguchi's belief that good sculpture does not depend on the use of precious materials, that anything can be included. In this case metal calligraphic forms are tied to a metal rod with common rope.

The pre-Columbian department opened in the 1940s with two large terra-cotta figures from western Mexico and Peruvian weavings. Two of the Gallery's all-time favorites were among the pre-Columbian acquisitions of the period: the hammered gold Peruvian *Burial Mask* from the Chimu culture (1100-1470), and the jolly *Figure of a Laughing Man* in the classic Vera Cruz style, the perennial darling of school children.

The African art collection was begun in the 1950s with the purchase of a $50 mask. The folk art collection started about then too with the purchase of a Pennsylvania Dutch stove plate dated 1741 and starring Adam and Eve as subjects. Shortly thereafter, the blue heron decoys, since much borrowed, and a Greek Revival doorway from a house near Lyons along the Erie Canal, were purchased through the R. T. Miller Jr. Fund.

Gifts and bequests to the collection fortunately did not cease. Monet's *Waterloo Bridge, Veiled Sun* (1903) came as the Gift of the Estate of Emily and James Sibley Watson following the latter's death in 1951. (In 1939 Mrs. Watson had given the Gallery the earlier, and stylistically very different, *Les Rochers à Pourville, Marée Bassee*, also by Monet, dated 1882.)

In 1959 a Gandharan head of a Buddha in stucco from the third or fourth century was given by Susan Schilling in memory of her parents, Dr. and Mrs. William S. Eisenhart. Mr. and Mrs. Arthur Stern Jr. gave a painting by Pierre Soulages, and an American Liberty Pole eagle from Brockport was the gift of Mrs. Fred Gordon.

In one of the few recognitions by university graduates that the Gallery is indeed also their university museum, Philip O. Schwarz, UR graduate and friend of Chiang Kai-shek, bequeathed some Chinese objects in 1959. Another university graduate who has been generous to the Gallery is James O. Beldon.

As the Gallery began to accumulate duplicates or acquire a better work by an artist already represented in the collection, funds from deaccessioning became available. Two manuscripts—an Indo-Persian poem of the sixteenth century and a thirteenth century breviary—were both purchased in the 1950s with funds obtained by deaccessioning.

One of the Gallery's favorite art scouts, Charles Carruth, died suddenly during the April-in-Paris festivities of 1958. An antique dealer whose great subject was the Erie Canal and whose pet customer was the Gallery, Carruth could be simultaneously charming and aggravating. He often hadn't a clue as to the historical background of an object, but he had a wonderful eye and almost an innate sense that allowed him to fit objects to customers. Over the years he had developed what amounted to a "milk route," calling on major collectors and fixing his discerning eye on their walls. A memorial exhibit was mounted, from which a committee of friends headed by board member Andrew D. Wolfe purchased in his memory a wooden sternboard carving out of nineteenth century Salem, and an Eagle astride a Serpent, also in wood, ca. 1790. The latter is stylistically related to the one on top of the custom house in Salem, which leads to the interesting thought that Nathaniel Hawthorne must have daily gazed upon a similar Eagle/Serpent when he worked around and about the custom house as Surveyor of the Port of Salem, and was turning over in his mind the events later described in *The Scarlet Letter*.

The noted art scholar and international dealer Joseph Brummer entered Gallery history when Isabel was a member of Paul Sachs's museum training class at Harvard. The class was taken to Brummer's New York gallery and expected to identify unlabeled works and describe how one might research them. This professional and personal association of some thirty years culminated in the acquisition of a "treasure-trove" the Herdles call "unequalled in the history of the Gallery."

A natural teacher, Brummer reveled in the role of mentor. He once escorted Isabel through the medieval collection of the Metropolitan Museum, an area heavy with J. Pierpont Morgan's personal holdings. Describing each object in a husky but penetrating whisper, he pronounced its authenticity or lack thereof. Some works evoked a gleeful, "It's a fake! It's a fake!" Others earned a respectful, "Intact!," his highest praise for works untouched by restoration or repair.

He had been a friend of the Gallery for many years before his sudden death in 1949 catapulted his notable and far-ranging art collection into one of the most significant auctions of art and antiquities witnessed in this century. This was the time, before soaring prices and prohibitions against exporting national treasures cut off a flourishing market, when a knowledgeable dealer could be the best ally an art museum had. Brummer's value to the Gallery lay in several areas. He knew the gaps in the collection (they were legion) and suggested works that were suitable and affordable. In those days before endowment, Brummer cheerfully accepted extended time payments. Most important were his catholic taste as a collector and his universal connoisseurship, as evidenced by the fact that he was once offered the directorship of the Budapest Museum in his native Hungary. Instrumental in forming the collections of Henry Walters, William Randolph Hearst, and the Cloisters, the medieval branch of the Metropolitan Museum in New York, Brummer opened a Paris gallery in 1906 and later a New York branch. On the side he did restoration work on European church sculpture and, as founder to Rodin, cast his bronzes.

Part sleuth himself, Brummer knew how to enlist others to do his leg work, canvassing unlikely spots in the continual quest for art. The rabbit hunters of provincial France were alerted to be on the lookout for anything that smacked of carved stone. It was through tactics like these that Brummer was once able to reconstruct, from a seemingly miscellaneous group of fragments, an almost complete, richly sculptured apse, which he then presented to the French government. Brummer sometimes went on these hunting expeditions himself, and on one occasion invited Gertrude and Isabel to accompany him on a weekend excursion memorable for its marathon stretches of hunting.

6

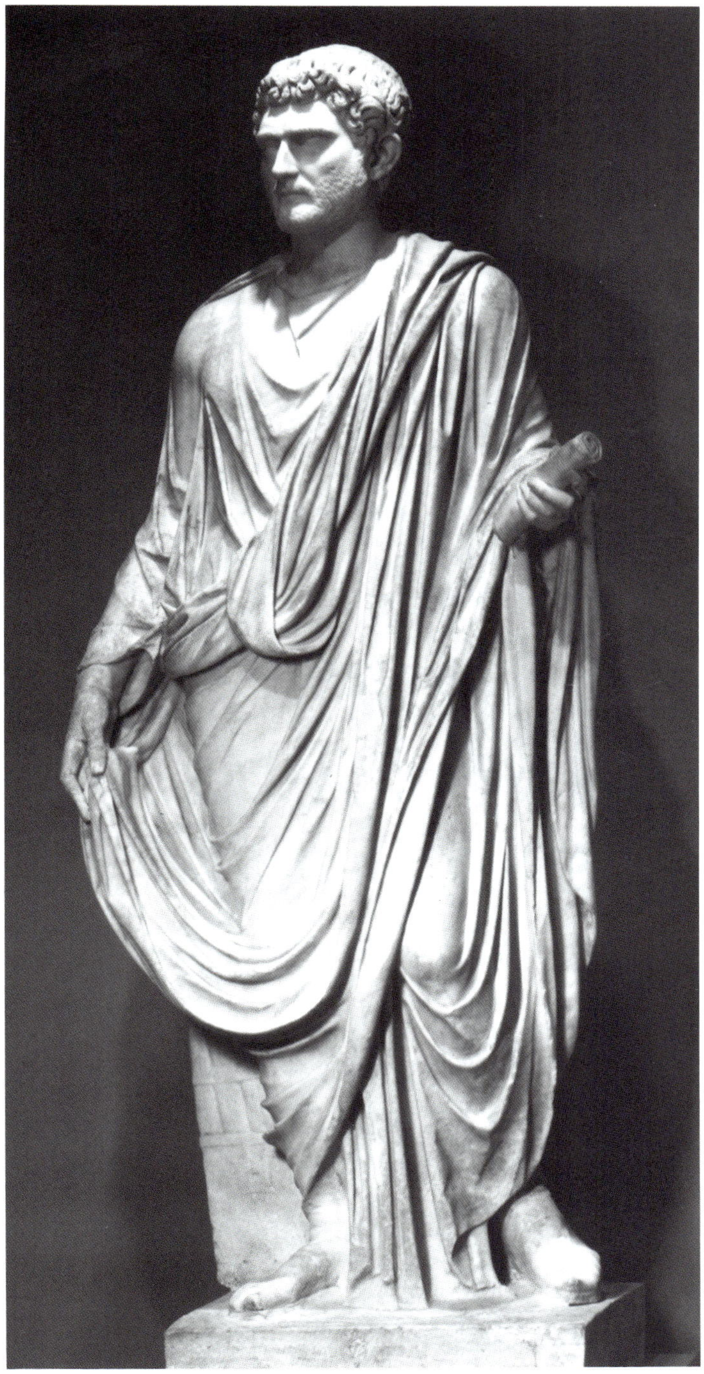

6 *Roman, second century A. D., Togatus, marble. Marion Stratton Gould Fund, 73.146*

The three auctions of Brummer's vast collections, each of which lasted four days, took up virtually all of the spring of 1949. They were attended by representatives of every major museum in the world, as well as by wealthy collectors in search of bibelots for the coffee table. (James Rorimer, later director of the Metropolitan, was buying both for himself and—with Rockefeller money—for his beloved Cloisters, which he then headed.) Although competition was intense, the end of the season was approaching and acquisition budgets were nearly exhausted, creating opportunities of a lifetime at prices never to be seen again. The result was a bonanza of bargains, not just in terms of subsequently inflated prices, but bargains compared with the price tags Brummer himself had placed on the works.

The magnitude of the Gallery's coup may be gleaned from the fact that its representatives headed homeward from the sale with almost every art work they had set their sights on—54 pieces in all—for a total expenditure of $13,865. The book value (a realistic, average appraisal at the time they were purchased) came to more than $180,000. The same objects have been estimated to fetch many millions today, assuming they were available at all. The time span covered by the acquisitions was from the tenth century B.C. to the seventeenth century A.D. with the majority, not surprisingly, since Brummer specialized in medieval sculpture, from the medieval period.

To pay for the acquisitions, the Herdles took some of the R. T. Miller Jr. Fund to New York with them and borrowed the rest from James Sibley Watson. When, months later, Gertrude went to pay back the loan, Watson waved her off with a mumbled "I guess I can give it as well as he [Miller] can."

Typical of the bargains acquired at the first auction was a pair of seventeenth century Portuguese chairs, mates to those in the Victoria and Albert and the Metropolitan museums. When the gavel fell and the chairs were the Gallery's at $120 each, Perry Rathbone, director of the St. Louis Museum (and later of the Boston Museum of Fine Arts), leaned over to murmur to the Herdles, "We paid ten times that for the ones we have."

The importance of certain objects was not always apparent immediately. For example, a small red alabaster pyxis, or toilet jar, was believed to be Babylonian, and was purchased primarily because it was intact and "looked like a good one." Not until 1974, when G. Kenneth Sams, classical archaeologist from the University of North Carolina at Chapel Hill, visited the Gallery and greeted an ambiguously labeled "Babylonian Toilet Jar" with an enigmatic, "Oh, *that's* where that is," did the Gallery wake to its significance. The jar, it turned out, had been well known to specialists in the late 1920s as "the Herzfeld Pyxis," a splendid example of the Neo-Hittite culture of North Syria dating from the tenth to the seventh centuries B.C. Scholars had lost track of the whereabouts of the pyxis, although it was known through drawings, photographs, and articles. Until Sams recognized it—and subsequently published an article in *Porticus*—it was not generally known that the famous Herzfeld Pyxis had been quietly sitting all this time in the extensive collections of Joseph Brummer.

The significance of the 1949 sale to the Gallery collection is reinforced by the *Porticus* publication of eight articles (by David Walsh and Susan Schilling) about objects that came from Brummer either through gift or from the auction. Important works include two Romanesque stone relief sculptures, an Angel and an Apostle, which originally must have formed part of the facade decoration of a church in western France. Among other objects of great merit are: two Limoges champlevé enamels— a pyx and a chasse—plus a small fourteenth century ivory relief, a late medieval red sandstone relief sculpture of the Annunciation, a baptismal font with unusual iconographic nuances, and a Romanesque capital, *Man with Basilisks*. The last, a gift to the Gallery from Brummer in 1930, was originally thought to be a man with birds, but close inspection by David Walsh revealed composite creatures with rooster heads and bodies and serpent tails: the fierce basilisks of medieval Bestiaries.

Part two of the Brummer sale brought much the same results: a set of thirteen Coptic textiles; a marble sculpture of the *Virgin and Child* of the school of the Florentine artist Nino Pisano; a silver chalice and paten; more furniture; and a seventeenth-century French portrait of a lady, once attributed to Mathieu Le Nain.

"It was a matter of being aware of every object as it came on the auction block," Gertrude recalls, "because many times the order of sale was changed and sometimes an item would appear that wasn't listed in the catalogue." After each major piece was auctioned, the specialists would depart, leaving only those who, like the Herdles, never budged when the possibility of a coup still remained.

"Do you need a Roman sarcophagus?" the director of the Walters Art Gallery in Baltimore asked them during one of these lulls when an unheralded specimen went on the block. Gertrude put in a test bid of sixty dollars and the sarcophagus was hers; it cost more than that to transport it back to Rochester.

Among the pieces that almost got away was a coveted marble statue of a Roman senator. As the close of the heady auction neared, a young couple seated next to Gertrude and Isabel asked their advice about bidding on a full-size, toga-clad figure as an ornament for their Long Island estate. The Herdles told the couple the only reason *they* weren't bidding was that they were almost at the end of their funds. The last the sisters saw of the *Togatus* was a glimpse of its head resting on the tailgate of a station wagon jauntily setting off down 53rd Street on its way to Long Island. It appeared that for once an object would be wheeled far from the Herdle grasp. But Isabel couldn't resist a last, "If you ever want to sell, give us first refusal," to the departing owners.

Twenty-five years later, the owner of the *Togatus*, now a widow, suddenly appeared at the Gallery. The sculpture, which had most recently spent a number of years greening in a mossy South Carolina garden, was once again for sale. Restored to its original milky marble, the *Togatus* was reinstalled to greet visitors from its position of honor at the head of the grand staircase sweeping up from the Gallery's lower floor.

Isabel literally stumbled upon the greatest find of the Brummer sale: the so called "Doubting Thomas" capital. This lively sculptured depiction of *The Legend of St. Thomas*, some two feet tall, was among works too heavy to be moved easily to the Parke Bernet auction galleries on Madison Avenue, so interested parties went to Brummer's own gallery on 53rd Street. Originally carved as a console to decorate the end of a vault rib in a medieval French church, the sculpture was hiding, blanched and dusty, on the crowded floor. The tiny chip that resulted when Isabel inadvertently backed into the sculpture indicated that whitewash covered the original brightly colored polychrome of the twelfth century piece. Isabel quietly dropped her raincoat over the capital. To conceal its existence even more, she sat on it.

With less than $3,000 left in their modest purse, the only hope was to try to distract other bidders. "Whenever anyone came by to look at the capital, we'd start talking about something else, most often a silver processional cross nearby," Isabel recalls. "Finally, Charlie Cunningham of the Wadsworth Athenaeum, who'd been watching us very carefully, offered, 'We'll stay off your capital if you stay off our cross.' That narrowed the competition to Wellesley, which also wanted the capital badly, and Honolulu, which would have a shipping problem with the heavy limestone piece—as we were glad to helpfully point out."

The bidding advanced $100 at a time to $1,600, then by $50 increments. Unexpectedly, the attendant taking the bids misconstrued a nod and raised the ante by another hundred. This discouraged Wellesley and the capital was Rochester's for a bargain $1,950.

The staff passed the summer of 1949 painstakingly dabbing and pecking with swabbed orange sticks at the powdery surface of the Doubting Thomas as more evidence of polychrome materialized. The sculpture went on to enjoy a moment of glory in 1970 in the landmark exhibition and film "The Year 1200" at the Metropolitan Museum of Art.

But that moment did not come until after "Thomas" passed a stringent test posed by a twentieth-century doubter who questioned its authenticity. During the winter of 1968, when the Gallery was closed for renovation and construction and "Doubting Thomas" was stored in a huge crate the size of a small room in the center of the Fountain Court, the French art historian Leon Pressouyre, then teaching a term at Yale, came to the Gallery as a result of having seen the "Doubting Thomas" in the Gallery handbook. In the course of investigations at the Bibliothèque Nationale in Paris, Pressouyre had become convinced that the sculpture came from the church of Saint Martin de Candes in southwest France—which now had an identical console in its place. One or the other was surely a fake. The church had been renewed in the 1880s during a wave of overeager restoration, in which "worn out" originals "got away" and were often replaced by spanking new reproductions. The twelfth-century sculpture would be identifiable by characteristic fossils.

Isabel and Susan Schilling held their breath as the maintenance staff opened the big box to allow Pressouyre, flashlight in hand, to crawl inside its darkened interior. After what seemed an eternity, the verdict resounded from within:

"Eureka! You have the original!"

7

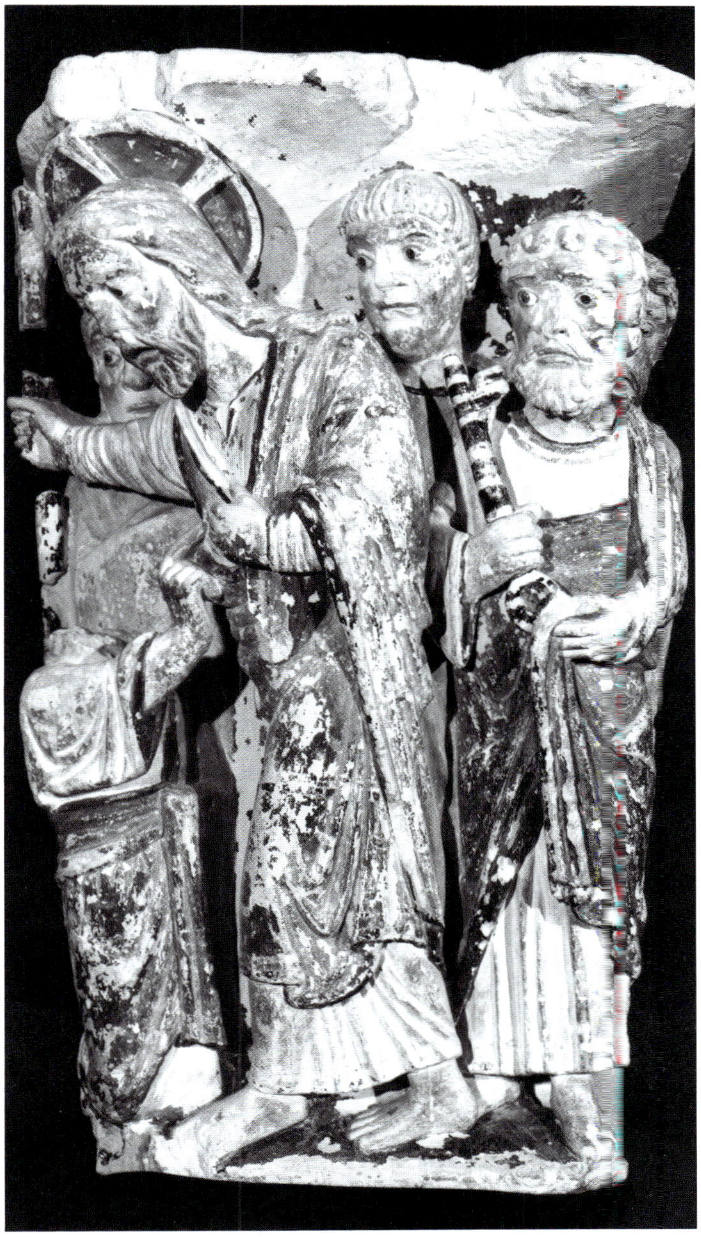

7 *French, late twelfth century, Console: The Legend of St. Thomas (Doubting Thomas), limestone and polychrome, h. 24 in. R. T. Miller Fund, 49.76*

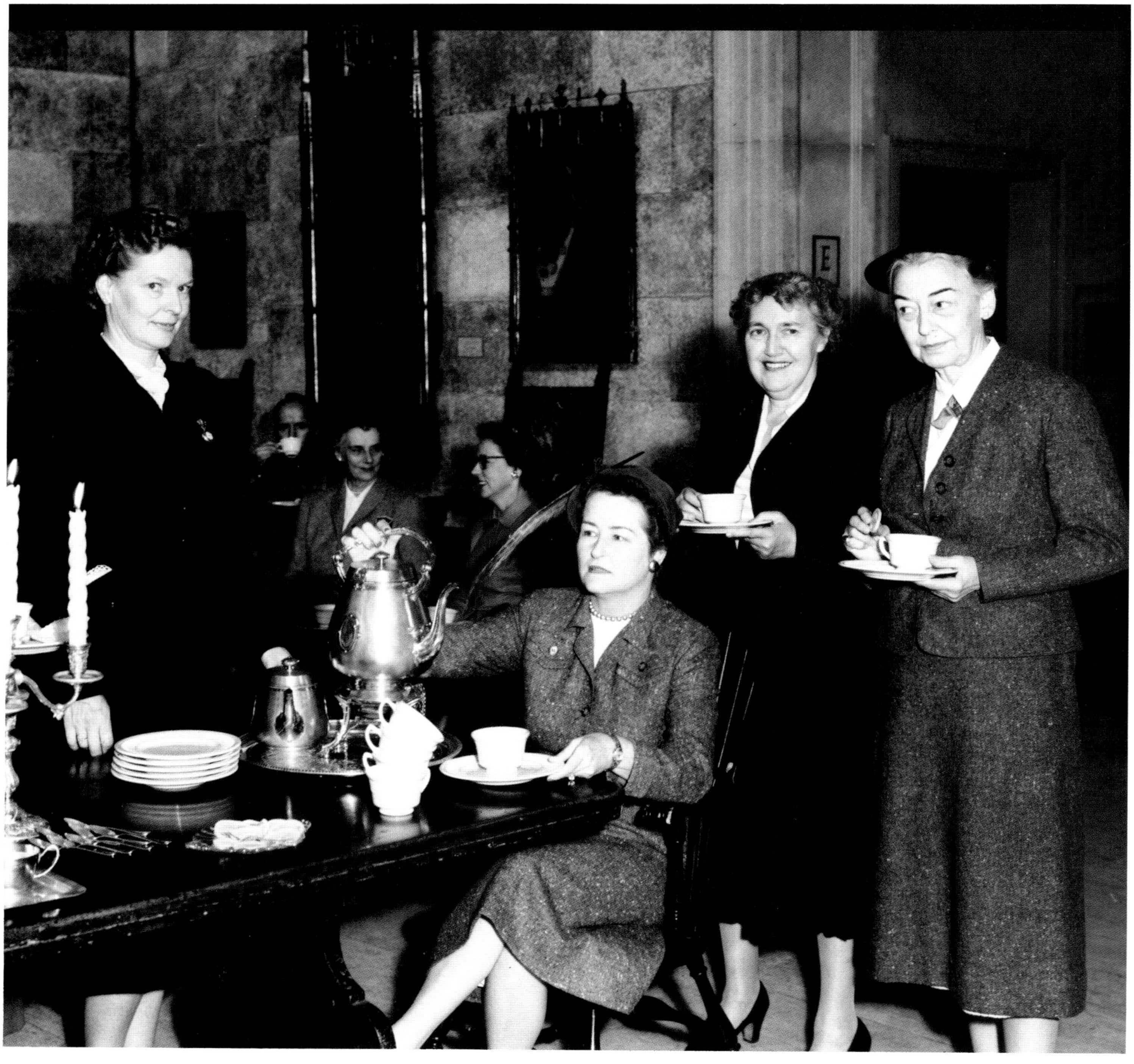
E

9: "A Company of Self-found Friends"

9

> The Gallery is enlisting in its service to the community a group of its members who have shown faith in its work and values through years of interest and active support. Organized as the Women's Council, this service group will assist in developing and promoting those relationships...which a professional staff cannot make...so well as a company of self-found friends.

Gallery Notes | *November 1940*

Tea in the Fountain Court, ca. 1955. Mrs. Balzer, pouring, Miss Osbourn, right, next to Gertrude Moore.

The first Women's Council was founded and immediately proceeded to founder in 1928. Fifty women met on 19 October of that year at the Plymouth Avenue home of Mrs. Charles Babcock, chairman, "as a solution of a long-felt and lately pressing need. With the steady growth of the Gallery's activities and conception of its work...the limited personnel of the Board of Directors [Managers] cannot serve the new range of social, advisory, and membership duties. A now-organized group of Friends who have already proved their interest in the Gallery will undertake such active duties as assisting at the private-view teas, planning of certain exhibitions which will have particular reference to phases of the life of industrial, domestic, or historic Rochester, and cooperating in the work with the children, and certain of the public programs." Despite this auspicious beginning, the council of 1928 was an idea whose time had not yet come.

During the late 1930s Gertrude Moore searched for financial support for free summer classes for children. She also envisioned more public outreach than the staff had time to cultivate. Following informal meetings during the fall of 1939 among Gertrude, Mrs. Herman Bakker, and Mrs. James Craig Potter—who became the council's first two presidents—a new Women's Council was founded on 14 February 1940. Broadening the base of the Gallery's support was on Gertrude's mind when she insisted that mothers of children in the free classes be included in the membership along with the wealthy elite of the city. In essence, creation of the Women's Council placed an organizational structure around a pre-existing group of Gallery enthusiasts.

Raising money became the council's first and continuing assignment. A program of films from the Museum of Modern Art, including *The Birth of a Nation*, netted only $50. But when thirty of the Thorne Miniature Rooms, first seen at the New York World's Fair of 1939, opened on Easter Sunday of 1942, 19,000 people trooped in. After expenses were paid—including the unexpected cost of refinishing Gallery floors worn to bare wood—an amazing $1,500 remained, enough to support summer scholarships for three years.

Collections of Thorne Rooms returned twice more, bringing in as much as a $2,800 profit. A garden fête in the Sibley and Watson gardens in June 1946 featured quick-sketch artists Edna Weeks Smith and Ralph Avery, silhouettes, handwriting analysis, ponies, a fashion show, an art sale, and the Pittsford Players. The intent was to raise $200, but this precursor of the Clothesline Show brought in $1,300.

Collector's Corner, a council innovation headed by Jean McCurdy, brought teapots and trivets, old dolls and old lace, antique firearms and family miniatures into the small case by the Gallery entrance. The first exhibit, in October 1940, featured Mrs. Bakker's Chinese textiles and jewelry collected during her six years of residence in China.

"Rochester is full of privately owned treasures which are not sufficiently seen or enjoyed to their full social and aesthetic desserts," *Gallery Notes* commented. "Too personal, informal, or miniature in scale, they do not lend themselves to staid exhibition treatment. Or too scattered, they mean little out of association with other related objects. To bring them to light, be instructive, playful, or even provocative with them is the plan of the Collector's Corner."

The Corner became a fixture by the front entrance for twenty years and then seemed to have run its course. The best of the city's collections had been shown, went the rationale, and modern servantless households had less space and patience for the practice of the collector's art. Tastes and judgments varied. Fortunately the cessation of the project was just a hiatus. In recent years Collector's Corner has returned, and become more popular than ever.

As early as 1943 council volunteers were delivering and setting up school exhibits. Later the program would be called Art Ambassadors, engaging many volunteers beyond council membership to carry exhibits to thirty city schools.

"Visiting Prints" was an important service although the prints themselves were fragile. Circulated to shut-ins at hospitals, nursing homes, or private residences, the prints got hard usage. In 1963 the project ceased, with institutions that had prints still hanging receiving them as gifts and the Education Department inheriting the remainder. But while Visiting Prints lasted, the scenes were frequently touching: ill and aged persons appreciative of both the prints that brought beauty into their lives and the visits from friendly and interested outsiders. Some individuals became so attached to "their" print that some good soul had to be found to purchase the decoration for them.

In addition to serving tea and cookies (and sometimes sherry), hosting, and providing floral arrangements for exhibition openings, council members were driving blind students to weekly Creative Workshop classes and, by 1970, transporting inner-city children to summer art classes.

So well did members perform their multifaceted roles that in 1952 the Board of Managers decided to adopt its stepchild by making Hilda May, Women's Council president, an ex officio board member. Two delegates, Jean McCurdy and Mrs. Robert Heilbrunn, were sent to the first Conference of American and Canadian Women's Councils of Art Galleries and Museums in Toronto, also in 1952. Eventually this

1

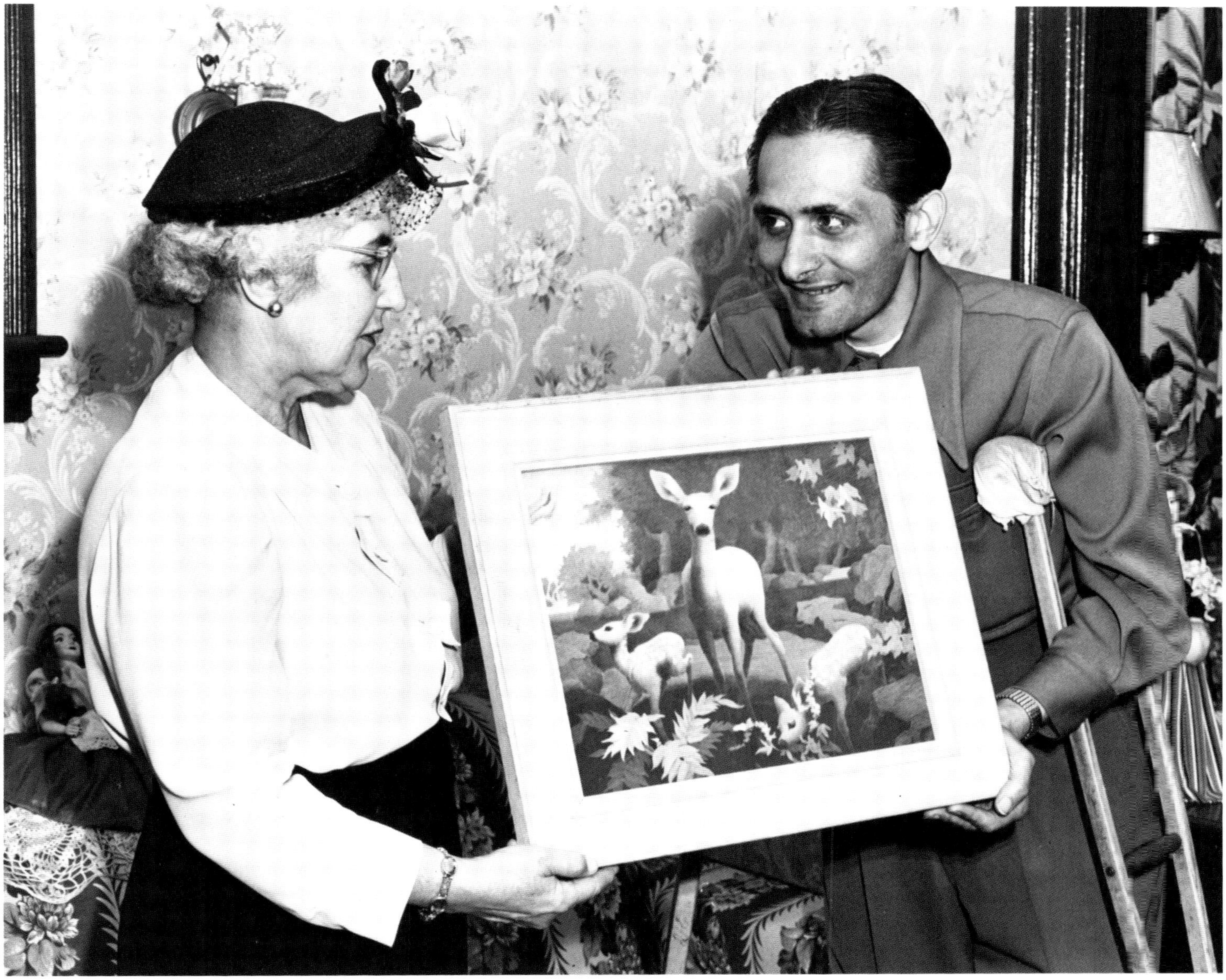

1 *A Gallery volunteer delivers a framed print to a shut-in in 1952 as part of the Visiting Prints program.*

2

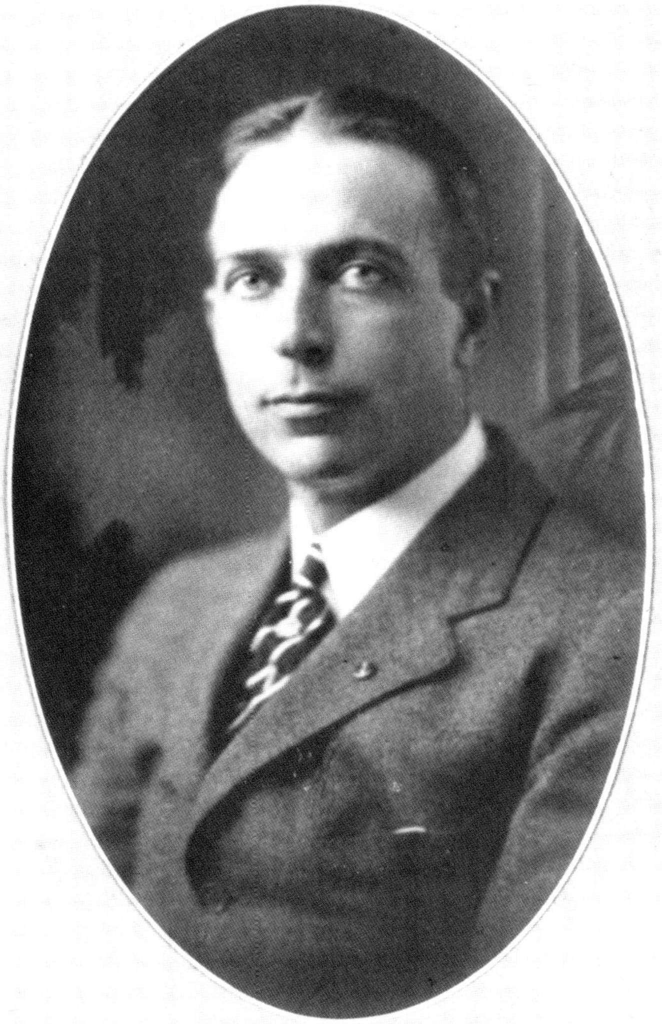

2 *F. Harper Sibley, 1917. Photograph by J. Ernest Mock, courtesy of the University of Rochester.*

mouthful evolved into the Volunteer Committees of Art Museums (VCAM), to which the Women's Council still belongs.

In November 1953 Harper Sibley, president of the board, directed the Executive Committee to organize a Men's Council modeled along the lines of the highly successful women's Council. Except for the Industrial Arts Committee, which put on annual exhibitions of advertising art called "The Art Directors Club," the Men's Council never got off the ground. The Women's Council represented organic growth. The women were used to volunteering; forming a group that organized more efficient use of their time and talents was the natural outcome. The Men's Council was a group in search of work and as such did not last long.

Little did anyone guess what had been set in motion when the council decided to convert the Gallery into a Paris street scene in April 1956. Even though it lasted for only a day, the whole upper floor of the Gallery offered glimpses of well-loved Parisian scenes: boutiques, a flea market, a Latin Quarter, bookstalls, fashion shows, gourmet dining, and so forth. A lot of work for one day but Bob Young's spirit with those thousands of women never flagged. Afternoon and evening performances plus a drawing for a trip to Paris rounded out the day. The net profit from this first gala, named appropriately "April in Paris," was $4,600.

Flushed with success, the council planned an even more elaborate show for 1958, recreating an Alpine village complete with coffee garden, Bavarian band, donkey cart, fashion show, and shops filled with imported Swiss articles. Staged on two nights in 1958, "April in the Alps" was spectacularly successful financially—netting $13,050—and as a feat of organization, although highly disruptive of Gallery routine. A big parade down East Avenue to an "oompah-pah" band and Swiss flags lining the approach to the Gallery door brought the Swiss ambassador into the Gallery to serve a huge wheel of Swiss cheese.

After $5,400 was set aside for the summer classes of 1958-1959 and $600 given for Lending Library prints, a substantial balance remained. At Gertrude's urging the council underwrote an illustrated handbook of the collection. Several years in preparation, the 120-page handbook had nine sections, each devoted to a different period or culture, and 300 illustrations, nine in color. With Susan Schilling and Lang Clay doing the research, writing, and layout; Gertrude and Isabel, the introduction; board member Earl Kage, the color photography; and the Case-Hoyt Corporation, the printing at half-price— the cost was kept to $7,000. Long needed and wanted, the handbook was symbolically presented to Gertrude at the February 1962 meeting of the Women's Council and, with the supplement published in 1968, remained in circulation as the "bible" of the collection for the next twenty-five years. Publication of the handbook brought status to the collection and requests to see it from scholars from around the world.

Although elated over the immense popularity and success of the two "Aprils," the growing enormity of the projects and the labor entailed suggested the concept be reviewed and scaled down. Fatigued, the Women's Council planned "April at Home" for 1960. Using professional decorators to show residential and business interiors, a painting or sculpture from the collection as a focal point, plus lectures, demonstrations, a fashion show, and chamber music, the "downscaled April" raised a creditable $6,450.

When the Clothesline Art Show and Sale made its first hurricane-plagued appearance, the council assisted and by 1962 had accepted responsibility for the food concession. That first council food sale was a do-it-yourself affair, with each member contributing two dozen sandwiches. An army of volunteers manned the food booth. As Clothesline began growing into the mammoth community happening it is today, the council turned to a professional food service in 1967, with members, husbands, and children continuing to serve as sales personnel. Profits were used during the 1960s to underwrite children's scholarships to the Creative Workshop.

"Artists in the Kitchen," a cookbook of favorite recipes, was under way in 1959. Sales lagged after a few years but finally members were assured that the last had been sold. Then the Brown House was demolished in 1970 and another whole carton of cookbooks discovered in its basement.

Along with hosting and flower arranging two new programs were emerging: an art lecture series and docents. The word "docent" kept drifting back from volunteer conferences, but in most museums the trained volunteer who conducts guided tours had preceded the formation of an education department. It was the popular Erie Canal show of 1953 when volunteers were first pressed into service as docents. Then another six years would pass until "Illuminations" proved to be so popular that fourteen Women's Council members were trained to guide the many visitors.

The enthusiasm built up by that experience led to a permanent docent program, with Clay and Schilling conducting training sessions in the spring of 1961. Then the public schools, potentially the greatest users of docents,

3,4

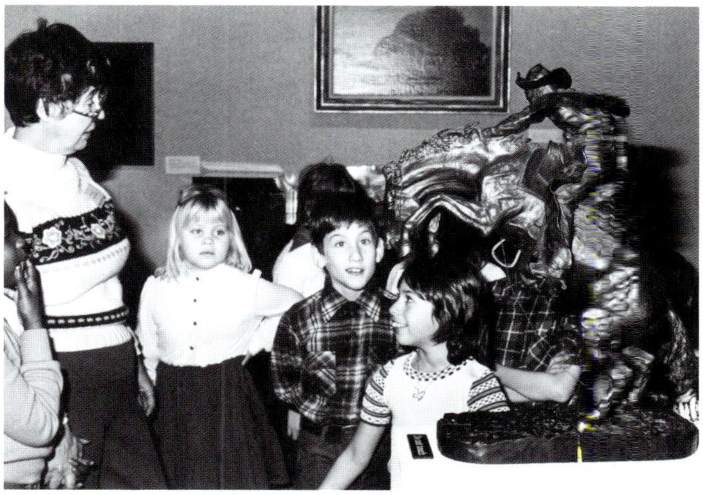

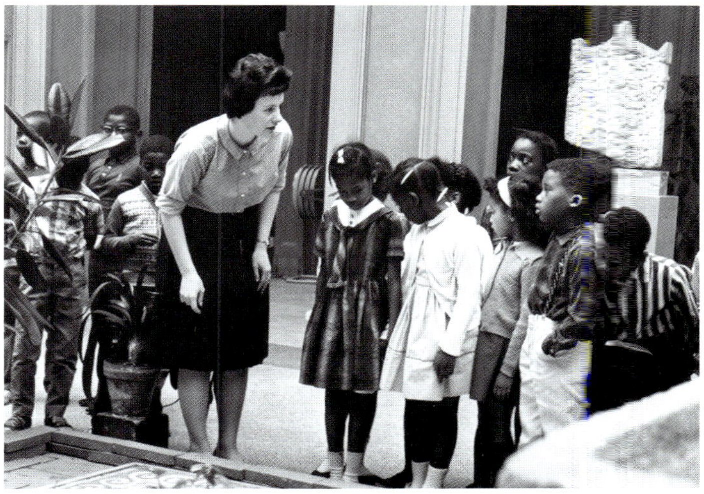

3,4 *Docent and staff tours of the collection.*

found they were financially unable to transport children to the Gallery. For more than a year a carefully trained crew sat idle.

At last, in the fall of 1962, the Rochester School District sent all its sixth graders to the Gallery as part of a new art and history curriculum. The docents guided two to four classes each morning, concentrating on the Renaissance period. Their first experience in guiding adults came during the "Montreal Masterpieces" exhibition in the spring of 1966, which brought 102 paintings on tour from the Montreal Museum of Fine Arts, then closed, as the Memorial Art Gallery would soon be, for renovations.

In anticipation of the opening of a new facility (first discussed in 1954 and finally opened in 1968), which meant that familiar works long in storage would be rehung in spanking new surroundings, the docent program crystallized. Joan Morgan, the energetic first chairman, described the Gallery's new corps in her survey of American museum docent programs at the Volunteer Committees of American Museums (VCAM) conference in Montreal in October 1967. The result was a detailed set of rules and guidelines used throughout North America for well-organized docent programs.

In the fall of 1960 Sylvia Davis, artist and art historian, with assistance from the Education Department, organized the first course of Gallery lectures on the appreciation of modern art. A variety of advanced courses followed, and more sections of the introductory course were added. By 1963 the Gallery staff had taken over the introductory course and even the Gallery's closing for remodeling could not interrupt the series' momentum entirely. While the introductory section was suspended for lack of meeting space, the advanced course moved its 120 students to the George Eastman House and continued on schedule.

When Davis indicated in 1974 that she no longer wished to continue with the contemporary art lecture series, Jean France, architectural historian, proposed a series of architecture lectures featuring national and local authorities to be called "The Art We Live In." That program continued successfully, sponsored by the Women's Council.

The council continued to strengthen its relationship with similar organizations. In 1961 it hosted a regional conference of ten women's councils—seven from Upstate New York and three from Canada—and explored the possibility of cosponsoring a ball with the Civic Music Association to be held at the George Eastman House. While the latter fell through, a more successful collaboration developed in 1964 with the Women's Council of the Museum of Arts and

5

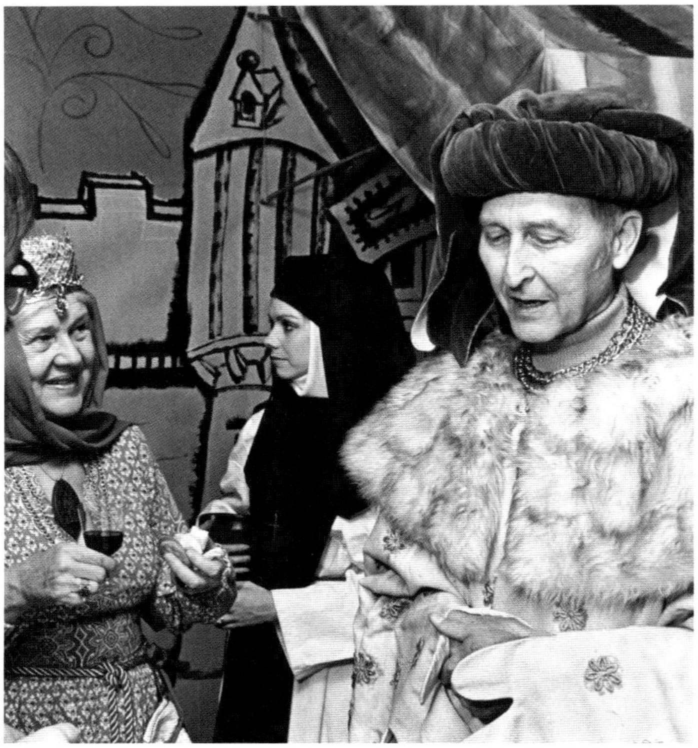

5 *Mr. and Mrs. Harris Prior as "king" and "queen" of the Medieval Faire in 1974 which was co-sponsored by the Gallery, the Women's Council, and the Junior League of Rochester.*

Sciences, when a two-week downtown festival of displays and demonstrations called "Partners in Culture" was organized to coincide with the Gallery membership drive.

Internally the council reorganized over the years: It enlarged its executive committee with standing committee chairman to create a board; it coped with the perennial problem of inactive members by creating membership classifications of active, sustaining, honorary, and nonresident; and it increased its recommended number of active members from 100 in 1955 to 125 in 1967, 150 in 1970, and so on. In 1988 there were about 325 active members. Dues increased modestly over the years from their dollar-a-year beginnings too.

Following the recommendations of the New York consulting firm of Booz, Hamilton & Allen, engaged to study the Gallery and its relationship to the community, the Women's Council was formally adopted by the Gallery through recognition in the bylaws of the Board of Managers. In 1962 the council elected Gertrude an honorary member and renamed its annual Finger Lakes Prize, established in 1957, the Gertrude H. Moore Prize.

With the retirement of godmothers and cheerleaders Gertrude Moore and Isabel Herdle in 1962 and 1972 respectively, council members and the new director, Harris King Prior, eyed each other warily at first. "So you're going to a museum that has a women's council!" Prior's colleagues had said with knowing smirks. But mutual suspicions turned into a love affair, and 1963 minutes record, "Mr. Prior very kindly praised the Women's Council, and called it the 'heart of the Gallery,' which warmed the hearts of the members."

With construction impending, the council turned by necessity to a new fund-raising activity: trips.

The first journey was a relatively simple one—a two-day bus tour in 1963 to Director Prior's earlier haunt, the Munson-Williams-Proctor Museum in Utica, with an overnight stay in Cooperstown. The educational and financial success of the tour prompted a 1964 trip to Winterthur, in Delaware, with increased profits. In 1965 council president Florence Macomber and tour chairman Brenda Rowntree cast their eyes abroad to a tour of Rome and Florence and the hill towns between, reintroducing the "April" theme. "April in Italy" took 144 people to Italy for twelve days, netting almost $10,000. "April in Iberia" in 1967 was similarly successful.

With the "Aprils" a resounding success, the council began looking beyond children's scholarships, which were virtually assured by the Clothesline food sale each year. Continued delays and revisions of Gallery plans postponed a decision until 1967, when the council voted to give up to $15,000 to whatever was most needed: the building fund if absolutely necessary, but preferably a work of art. This represented a significant change of direction in fund-raising aims.

In January 1968, with the Gallery closed, Prior scouted Europe, returning with recommendations of several works that would fill gaps in the collection. A large and spectacular eighteenth-century *Portrait of Monseigneur du Vintimille du Luc, Archbishop of Paris*, by Hyacinthe Rigaud, was purchased in May with funds primarily raised through the two "April" trips. *The Archbishop* continues to reign as one of the most beloved paintings in the Gallery collection.

Trips continued to be important council money-makers. A European trek was planned every other year, alternating with a North American tour. In 1969 President Lyndon Johnson requested that Americans limit their travel abroad to help stabilize the dollar, so "April in the Aegean" was postponed until 1970. During this period, proceeds from trips went directly into the Gallery rather than the council treasury.

Throughout the late 1960s and 1970s the proceeds from council fund raisers—balls both "Grecian" and "Venetian," needlepoint seminars, sales of Christmas miniatures, champagne previews of exhibitions, tours of local private collections—found plenty of uses. The members' lounge was furnished for $6,000; tapestries designed by Calder and Léger were hung on the blank and echoing walls of the conference room for $5,000; and kitchen facilities in the 1926 wing were renovated for $2,000. This last caused grumbles among the contingent that preferred, except in dire circumstances, to avoid purely housekeeping expenditures in favor of more art-related uses for its funds. This would not be the last time a similar difference of opinion occurred.

The first art purchases were made when the Priors accompanied the Women's Council on European trips to Spain, Italy, and Greece. A large and arresting gold leaf and polyvinyl work by the Spanish painter Gustavo Torner was the gift of the council in 1967. From the Greek trip in 1970 came a painting by Jannis Spyropoulos. In 1974 Asher B. Durand's *Genesee Oaks, 1860* was presented by the council in Prior's honor.

Council funds for acquisitions were used to purchase the *Portrait of John Monck* (1763), by Angelica Kauffmann, and to supplement funds donated in memory of Brenda Rowntree to purchase the gorgeous and chilling *Still Life* by Rachael Ruysch. The next purchase from council funds, again for a work by a woman artist but this time a contempo-

6

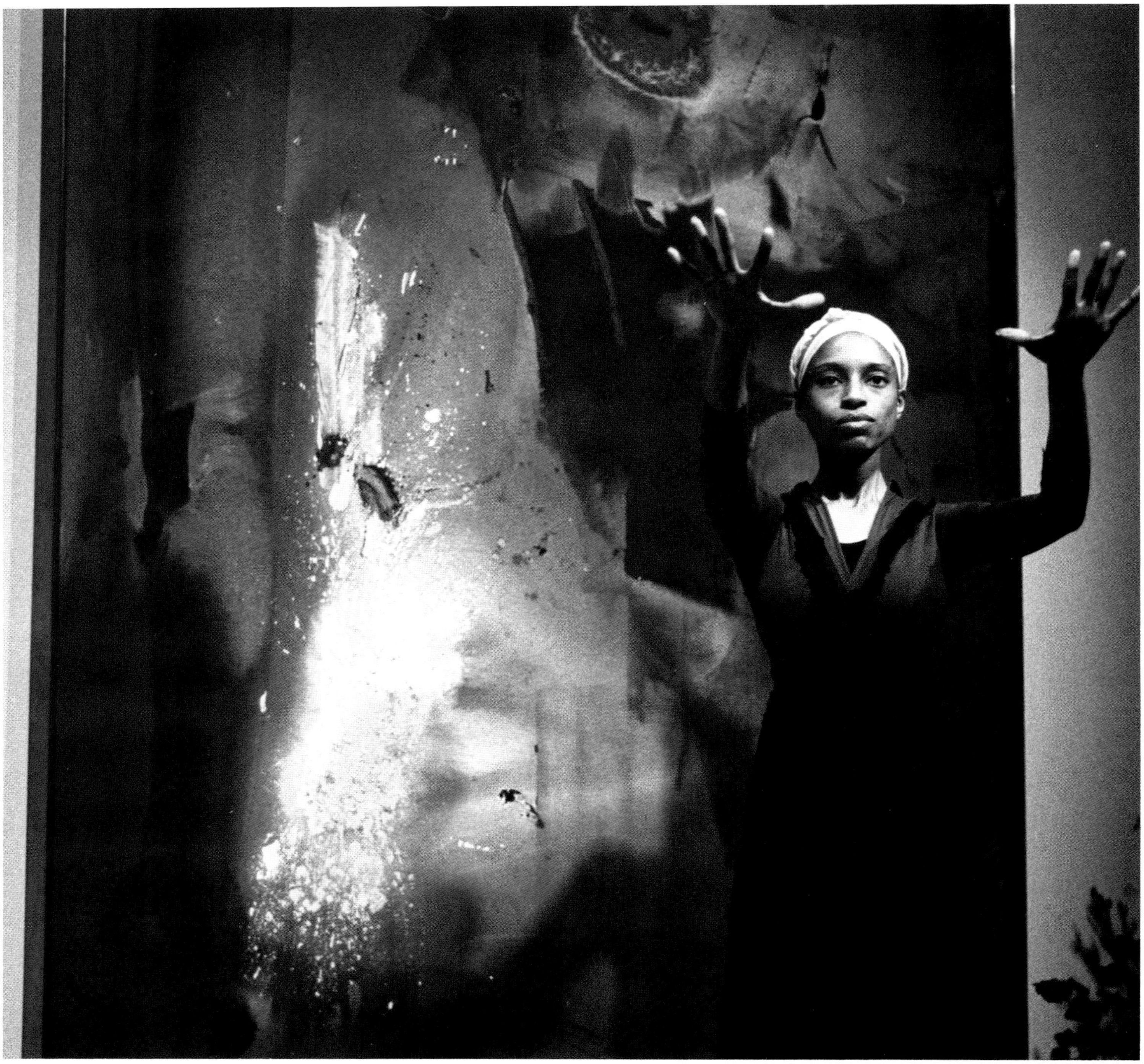

6 *At a patron's event in 1982, Pat Woodlock from the Bucket Dance Theatre dances before Helen Frankenthaler's Seer, gift of the Women's Council.*

rary one, was the stained canvas *Seer* by Abstract Expressionist Helen Frankenthaler. As the Gallery's seventy-fifth birthday approached, the council gave $100,000 and voted to have it go toward a nineteenth century American genre painting, *Peeling Onions* by Lily Martin Spencer.

One project did not materialize in the 1960s, despite years of analysis, hopes, and disappointments: the restaurant. Included in the original Skidmore, Owings and Merrill plans, it was removed as a cost-saving measure. Some council members were outraged and in 1965 the Board of Managers asked the council to further investigate and possibly manage a restaurant or cafeteria if cost problems could be solved. Cutler Union was eliminated as a location as being too remote from the hub of activity. The possibility of using the second story above the conference room as a restaurant site was rejected by the new architects as interfering with the sight lines of the new wing. In 1971 council and board regretfully laid the restaurant idea to rest.

The 1968 wing demanded more volunteer services, beginning with the Grand Opening itself. The council under Nancy Turner performed the hosting role for a patrons' tea, served up a luncheon in Cutler Union for out-of-town guests, presided over the formal viewing of the new space, and organized a dinner for guests, patrons, and contributors. And the council was responsible for the Grand Opening Ball, at which 600 guests danced in the "new" Renaissance Room and sipped champagne at torchlit tables on the terrace. Ninety council members served as greeters during the members' openings as some 16,000 visitors took "their first amazed looks at the 'new' Gallery," council minutes recorded.

The expanded Lending and Sales Gallery and the new Gallery Shop rapidly absorbed volunteers, many of whom were council members. All the old roles continued—docents, Driving for the Blind, Art Ambassadors—and the expanded library and membership office provided new volunteer opportunities.

The expanded facilities gave the Gallery a chance to work with another volunteer group and experiment with a concept Prior had long wanted to try. In 1970 a Junior League committee under Elizabeth Brayer organized an exhibition of participatory art created expressly for children. Twenty artists from western and central New York were commissioned to build works which the children would somehow complete. Kinetic, electronic, musical, build-your-own, and sound-and-light sculpture predominated, augmented by felt boards, balloon sculptures, collages, and assemblages created from everyday scrap materials. League volunteers plus Scouts, teenagers, Women's Council members and Gallery staffers ran 182 tours. In twenty days, more than 7,000 school children, grades four through six, from a ten-county area attended. In all, 21,670 people visited the five-week show. "Mirrors Motors Motion" won an impressive number of local and statewide community-service awards and traveled to the Albright- Knox Gallery under the auspices of the Junior League of Buffalo. The idea of a children's exhibit originated with Marilyn Kayser, League and Gallery board member and Women's Council president, as a means of demonstrating the need for a permanent children's gallery. That need was finally answered by the ChildSpace gallery in the 1987 wing.

"Mirrors Motors Motion" can also be viewed as a precursor to the Hallmark-designed "Kaleidoscope," which has visited the Gallery grounds in more recent summers, again sponsored and staffed by the Junior League of Rochester.

A full-fledged collaboration between Women's Council and Junior League occurred in 1974 with the mounting of a Medieval Faire, an unprecedented community production. A cast of thousands headed by Elizabeth Rennert participated in a sound-and-light show narrated by curator Robert Henning in the Fountain Court, and a medieval village designed by Elizabeth Brayer and Carl Zollo in the Grand Gallery. The village featured shops designed and staffed by the docents under Diane Grosso. Daily demonstrations by area craftsmen were held, along with medieval music, puppetry, and entertainments, plus activity rooms run by Junior League volunteers. Authentic medieval manuscripts were for sale in Lending and Sales. These activities kept the Faire humming for six weeks. All wore costumes designed by Eleanor Jones and her committee. Drawn by the massive publicity the event generated, visitors stood in line for hours in the worst possible weather, patiently waiting a turn to join the crowd inside (whose size was limited by the fire laws) When the Faire was over, some 35,000 people had participated.

On opening night Director Prior in crown and ermine-trimmed cape joined 499 others in medieval costume to attend the sumptuous Medieval Banquet in Cutler Union under the direction of Nancy Buckett. In one of his last appearances on the job, Prior led the grand procession of subjects into the Gallery to the wild applause of the waiting throngs.

A Women's Council goal has been to establish signature events, such as the "April" balls, improve upon them each year until they became institutionalized in the community, and launch major fund-raisers as well. "Art in Bloom" is a case in point. Begun in 1978 with Roberta Ierardi and Helen Berkeley as chairmen, that first program raised $3,743. The next time, 1981, under Pat McBride, it netted $5,652. A quantum leap came in 1983 with a $19,871 return, under cochairmen Heidi Payment and Joan Williams. In 1985 "Art in Bloom," under Ann Ray and Jackie Richie, produced $25,185 for the council treasury.

Clothesline food booths had netted about $2,800 annually from 1962 to 1981. Then Naomi Erdmann and Mildred Boylan suggested to Emille Allen, council president, that a change of vendors might help. (The university food service overhead was very large.) Under Mildred Boylan and Sue Hyde, the food booths brought in $8,758 in 1982 and $15,099 in 1983. The next year Judy McKelvey as president switched vendors once more, and booths chaired by Pat Legge brought in over $28,000 in both 1984 and 1985. "We just keep tinkering until we get it right," Emille Allen says.

The Erté project of April 1980 while Dorothy Centner was president raised $11,743. It consisted of an exhibition of Erté's art and costumes; the Erté Ball, chaired by Alva Angle and Connie Aquavella; an Erté Day, chaired by Esther Germanow and Nancy Lee; and a boutique under Mildred Boylan.

"Artists of *La Revue Blanche*," a 1984 exhibition curated by Director Bret Waller, evoked a cross-cultural series of events involving the George Eastman House and the Rochester Philharmonic Orchestra. Because of an anticipated $200,000 pledge to the capital campaign, the Women's Council quickly came up with three fund-raising projects, which eventually netted over $33,000. They were launched within four days, each requiring large numbers of volunteers, excellent coordination, and much staff support. On 20 January the exhibition previewed to the strains of the "Moulin Rouge Ball," chaired by Nan and Peter Brown. On 24 January "The 1890s in Review" opened, organized by Esther Germanow and Nancy Lee from the costume collection of

7

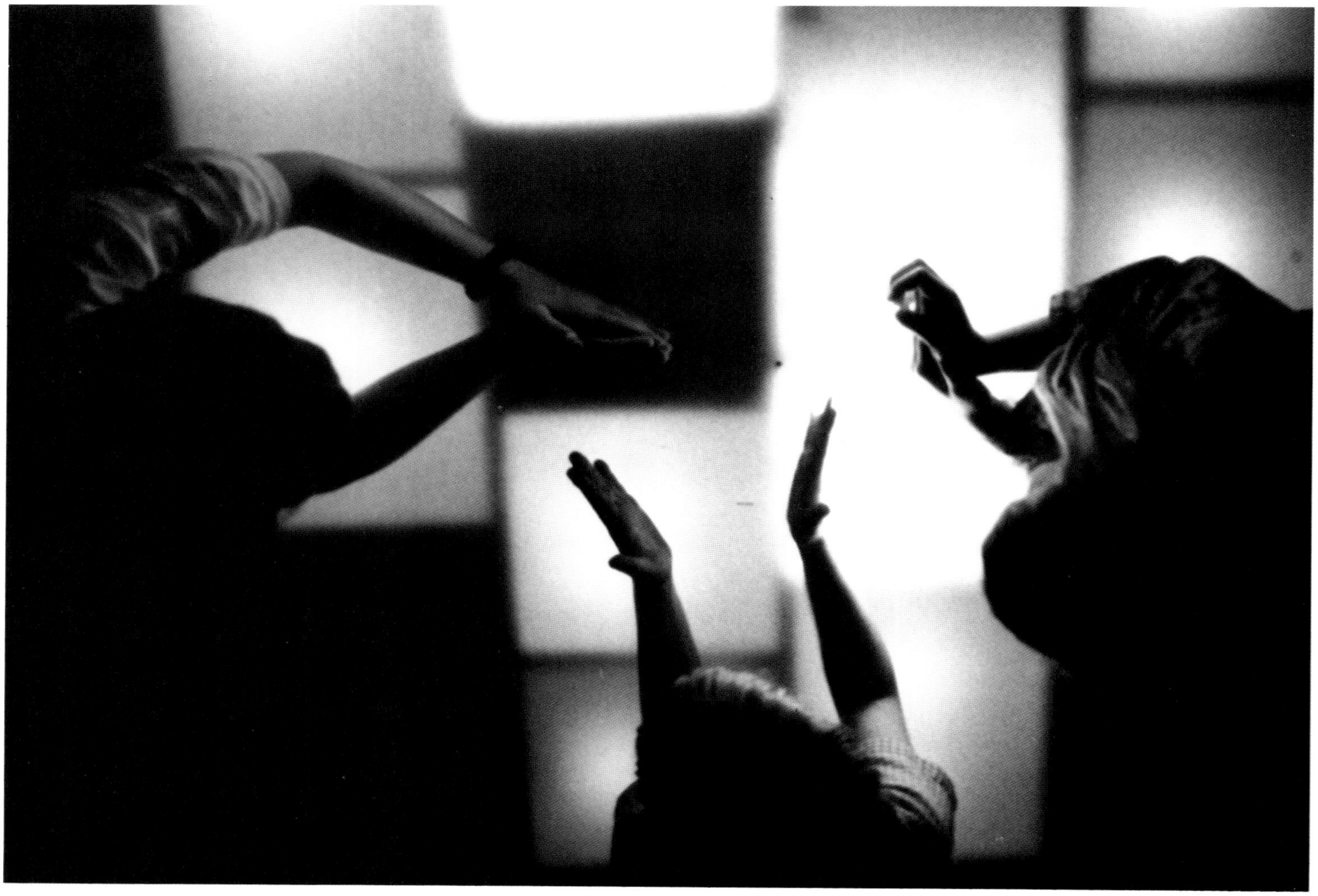

the Metropolitan Museum. From 25 January until 14 April the "Café Française" opened for lunch, Tuesday through Saturday, chaired by Emille Allen (then also president of the council) and cochaired by Dorothy Alexander and Mildred Boylan.

The café had a history of its own, beginning with the doubter who suddenly resigned as chairman in November, and three other prospective chairmen who declined the dubious honor of creating a restaurant in ten weeks during the holiday season. Yet the Allen-Alexander-Boylan trio soon had the conference room partitioned and painted, found a caterer, activated a decorating committee which induced the county parks department to participate, planned menus and purchased equipment, secured sixty volunteers per week for thirteen weeks, devised work plans and dress codes, and managed to get some plastic tableware donated. The quest for a liquor license turned into a circus. One Gallery administrator wanted the entire Board of Managers to stand as licensees, which would have involved numerous trips to the police station, background checks, and the finger printing of all forty-four members. In the end saner heads prevailed, and one hapless staff member was "volunteered" to take on the responsibility.

Turn-away crowds of 100 and more each day netted a nice profit from the café, had a dramatic effect on sales from the Gallery Store, and reinvigorated interest in somehow creating a permanent restaurant for the Gallery. That goal would finally be attained in 1987.

The Cartier Ball in 1986, under president Judy McKelvey and chairman Elizabeth Harvey, and the Oriental Ball in 1988, under president Elizabeth Harvey and chairman Leone Lubin, brought the council to the threshold of the Gallery's seventy-fifth anniversary. The decorations for both were superb, and the accompanying exhibitions—of Cartier jewels and Hoya glass, respectively—excellent. Thousands of people came on both Sundays, the days after the ball, to see the exhibits and decorations. The balls plus the biennial "Art in Bloom" and the ongoing Clothesline food sales, trips, and Holiday Open House, provided the council with sufficient funds not only to purchase *Peeling Onions* for the Gallery collection in 1988, but also to sponsor the Wendell Castle exhibition, scheduled for 1990, in honor of the council's own fiftieth year.

8

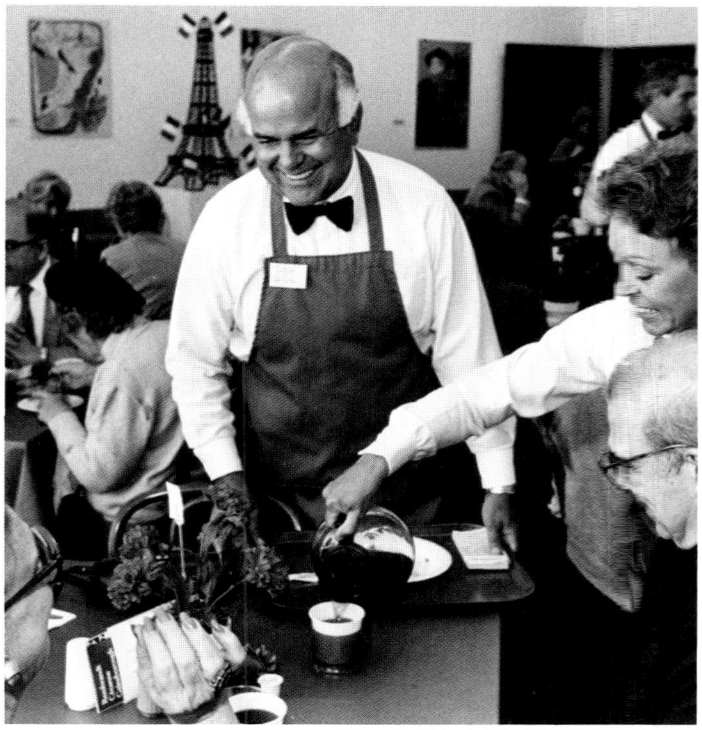

7 *"Mirrors, Motors, Motion" was an exhibition of participatory works of art created by New York State artists in 1970 and cosponsored by the Gallery and the Junior League of Rochester.*

8 *Bausch and Lomb president Daniel Gill was one of the distinguished waiters when husbands of Women's Council members served lunch in Le Café Francais, which operated daily during the Gallery's 1984 exhibition "Artists of La Revue Blanche." The successful operation of the cafe played a large part in the inclusion of a restaurant in the next addition to the Gallery, which opened in 1987.*

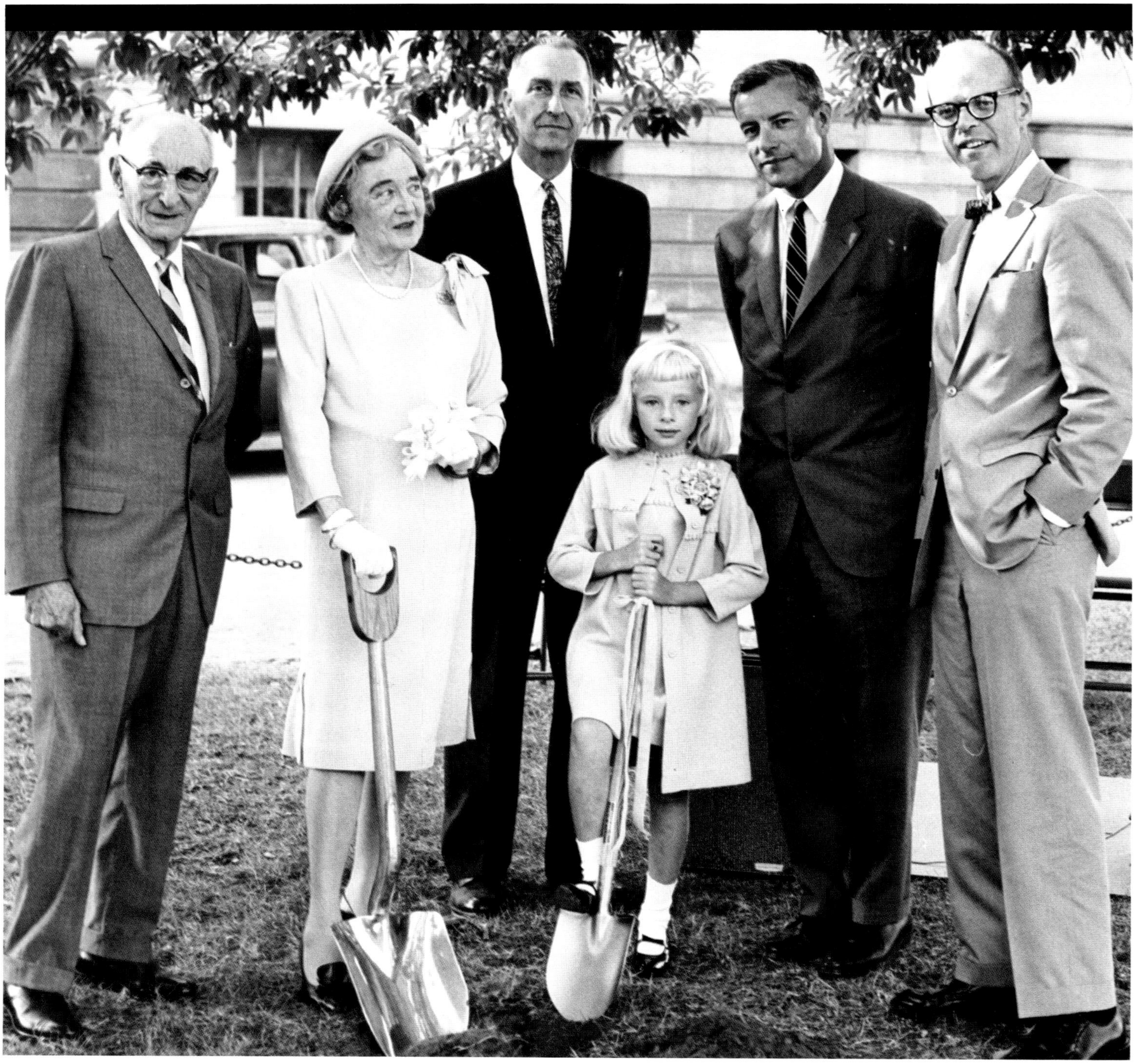

10

There's no logic to the tall skinny corridor. It's just for fun. But it makes the auditorium sit there like a great big egg.

Carl F. W. Kaelber Jr., Architect | 19[illegible] Wing

I wouldn't want to live through it again, that frenzied time when we were all creating a "new" Gallery—but I wouldn't have missed it for the world either.

Margaret Bond, Public Relations Manager | 1962-1978

Groundbreaking for new Gallery wing 12 September 1966. Representing various sections of the Gallery community were Fritz Trautman, artist and Creative Workshop instructor, Mrs. James Sibley Watson Jr., Harris K. Prior, Barbara Wadsworth (daughter of board vice president Dorothy Wadsworth), George M. Angle, board president, and Carl F. W. Kaelber Jr., architect.

Late in December 1966 the strains of "Auld Lang Syne" wafted through the Gallery. Patrons and staff had gathered in fancy dress for a champagne farewell to the old and a foretaste of marvels to come. The next morning the building closed except to construction workers. Public exhibition spaces were stripped of all but the heaviest pieces. Scaffolding was erected to rip down wall coverings, lower ceilings, and tear out all partitions, except for load-bearing walls, for this top-to-bottom renovation. Paintings would wait out "the duration" in other museums. Sculptures that could not be moved were left in place and protected by a series of wooden structures, "that have," *Gallery Notes* reported, "temporarily changed the character of the Fountain Court from a medieval great hall into a hotbed of twentieth century cubism."

Plans for an expanded Gallery had been under way long before Gertrude Moore retired as director in June of 1962. As early as 1954, for instance, the board examined renderings of a projected expansion of the Gallery to the north. Whether these were the ones prepared in 1925 by Lawrence Grant White or new ones is not clear, but they struck out from the rear brick wall of the Fountain Court as planned by White. Shortly thereafter the university moved its women students to the River Campus; transferred Cutler Union to the Eastman School of Music in exchange for its $650,000 endowment; sold the Brown House to the Gallery for $1,200; and sold the Eastman Laboratory building, the Gallery's neighbor to the northwest along Prince Street, to the Taylor Instrument Company. That last sale would influence future expansion plans. It would have been difficult for the Gallery to add to the north where the "temporary" brick wall stood; only wings to the east or west would be practical on the remaining land, regardless of the fact that Sibley Watson had always felt that such wings would destroy the lines of the original building.

Just before this flurry of activity the Gallery acquired a new parking lot of seventy-two spaces to the southwest, designed by architect Allen Macomber and paid for by an anonymous donor (later revealed to be Sibley Watson). Previously the Gallery had had perhaps a dozen spaces on the circle between it and Cutler Union, and many a university program did Gertrude have to interrupt with pleas to move those cars.

The 1950s also saw changes in the interior of the Gallery. The Hall of Casts, which had been renamed the Sculpture Hall (although casts from the Parthenon still lingered), was turned into a gallery of primitive and ancient art: African, Egyptian, early Classical, and pre-Columbian works

1

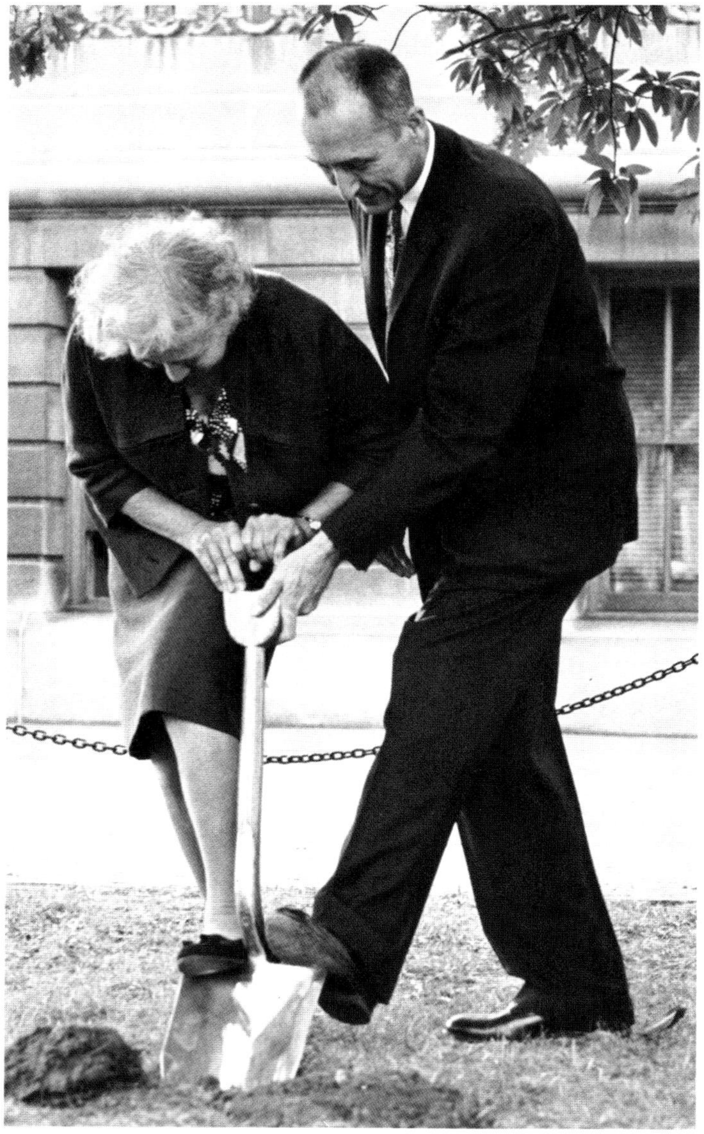

[redacted]

1 Moore and Prior break ground, 1966.

filled cases designed by Tage Frid of the School for American Craftsmen. The cases, each with its own lighting system, encircled the room.

In February 1961 Roger Austin, university architect, and Carl Kaelber of Waasdorp, Northrup and Kaelber, outlined to the Gallery board, then presided over by George Angle, two further options: a $1 million plan using the basement of Cutler Union for the Creative Workshop, or a $2 million plan for an all-new wing.

Meanwhile the Albright Gallery in Buffalo had recently expanded—and been renamed the Albright-Knox Gallery—with a wing designed by Gordon Bunshaft of Skidmore, Owings and Merrill. Arthur Stern Jr., Gallery board member, organized a trip to see the Albright-Knox addition, and on the strength of that impression Bunshaft was hired to prepare plans for a new Gallery wing.

Presented to the board and the Gallery's new director, Harris Prior, in July 1962, the Bunshaft plans showed expansion to the west (toward Prince Street) with a two-story wing for offices, library, restaurant and snack bar, and workshop studios. The auditorium would remain on the ground floor of the 1926 building surrounded by permanent galleries for twentieth century American art. The second floor of the 1913 and 1926 buildings would remain as galleries. Shown too was an on-grade entrance into the glass connection that also served as sculpture court—not unlike the Vanden Brul Pavilion in the 1987 renovation.

But the price came in too high: $25 a square foot! As priced by A. W. Hopeman & Co., the new building and renovation of the old would cost $1.8 million. The Gallery had but $1.2 million. Go back and modify the plans and program, the architects were instructed, but the revised plans still came in at $1.6 million. Moving the wing to the east side and putting Gallery offices in Cutler Union was discussed, but that would have meant buying Cutler Union for $650,000 from the Eastman School. The resulting impasse found the Gallery dismissing Bunshaft's firm, even though it meant having to pay Skidmore, Owings and Merrill $60,000 for its preliminary drawings.

The next two years, 1963-1964, were ones of uncertainty as to whether the Gallery and the Eastman School of Music might follow the College of Arts and Science to the River Campus. 1964 was a year of conflict between university chancellor W. Allen Wallis, who wished to locate all divisions of the university, including the Gallery, on or near the River Campus, and Sibley and Hildegarde Watson, who had remained in the family home on Sibley Place during the flight to the suburbs, and resisted all thought of these changes. In the end economic considerations played a major role in leaving these two divisions of the university exactly where they were.

The Rochester firm of Waasdorp, Northrup and Kaelber (which had done the preliminary work in 1961) was now hired, and new plans began to evolve from sketches Kaelber had hastily scrawled in a "back of an envelope" manner, he recalls. In these plans the new wing was shifted to the east and would reach toward Cutler Union over a narrow driveway. Creative Workshop classes could then be held in basement space rented from the Eastman School. Doors into the Gallery and the Cutler basement were planned and constructed on each side of the driveway to facilitate the flow from one building to the other. Eventually it was realized that the costs of extra guards to patrol these open doors would be overwhelming, just as the cost of an extra guard at the original 1913 entrance defeated the plan to continue to use that access in addition to the new on-grade main entrance (legally required as access for the handicapped).

As it had with previous additions, the Watson family contributed the lion's share toward the capital improvement. In 1962 Sibley Watson had made a challenge gift of $250,000, but with inflation, the change in architects, delays caused by strikes in the construction trades, and the irksome discovery that extensive repairs to the existing building were needed, it was found that the total cost would be $2.6 million. A second campaign had to be mounted and some $400,000 borrowed from the university—in addition to the $280,000 the university had previously given. In 1966 Sibley Watson gave $300,000 more, anonymously, earmarked for a new auditorium. He requested that the new on-grade entrance not steal the thunder from the 1913 facade. Depressed driveways and parking lots along University Avenue were considered, but ultimately it was decided to place the main entrance on the north, or rear, side as the most economical and least obtrusive solution.

At Sibley Watson's request too, Fletcher Steele, renowned landscape architect, was engaged. Steele's initial plan called for trees lining a circular drive in front of the 1913 grand entrance, where, he said to Kaelber, possibly tongue-in-cheek, "carriages could draw up in splendor and discharge their occupants." This impractical if glorious notion was discarded; instead, an *allée*, or double row of low trees with a walk between, was used to integrate the several buildings and to soften the transition in architectural style between the Renaissance jewel box

2

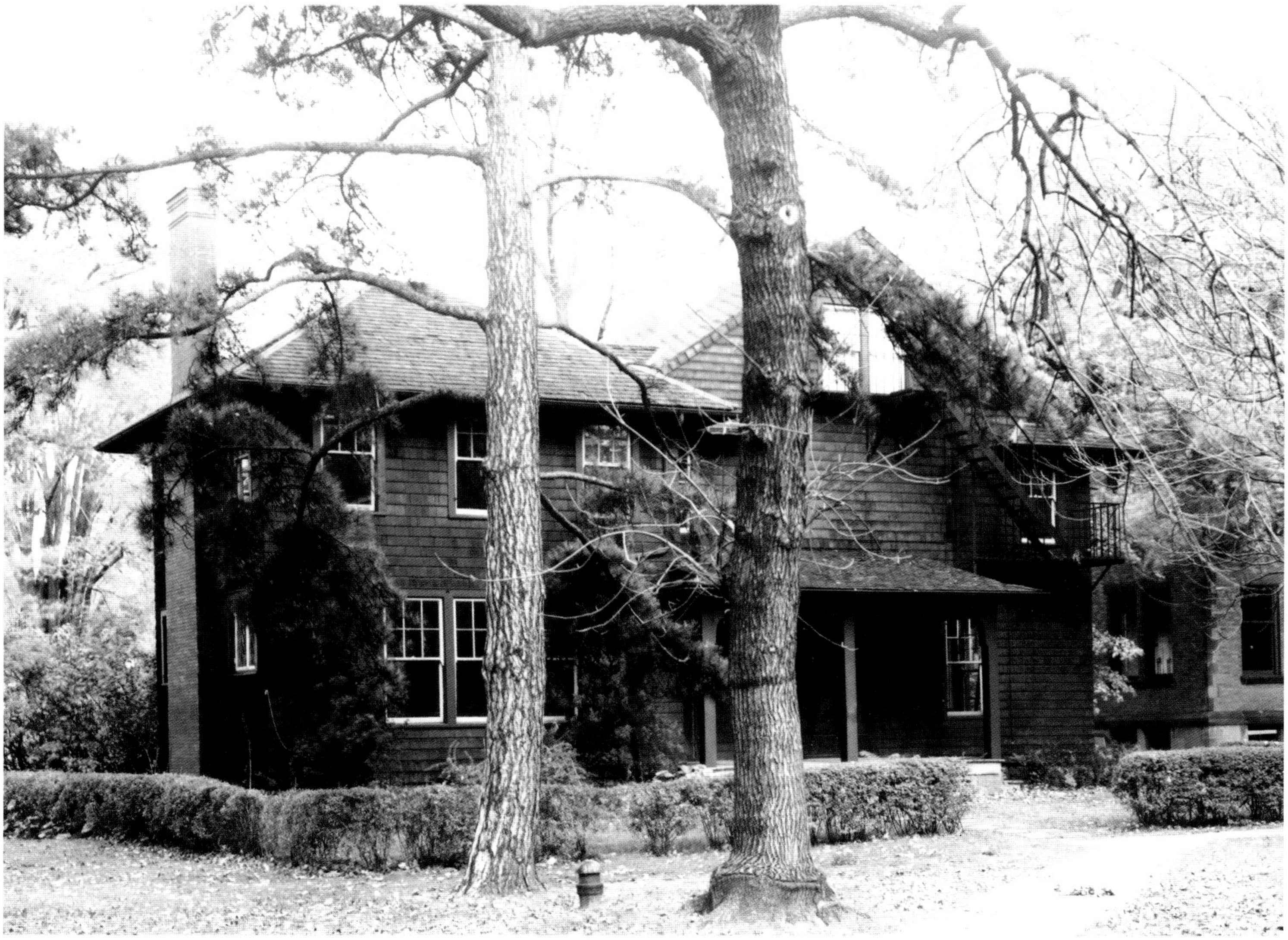

2 *The "Brown House" served first as University of Rochester faculty club, then as Creative Workshop extension, and finally as interim home for the Gallery administration, 1966-1968.*

and that romantic hulk out of a Van Eyck painting, Cutler Union.

At 4:30 in the afternoon on Monday, 22 September 1966 Mrs. James Sibley Watson Jr. attacked the ground with a silver shovel and the new 30,000-square-foot building was under way. It would double the size of the original building and the 1926 addition combined. Along with the architect, board president, and Hildegarde Watson, Fritz Trautman of the Creative Workshop staff was chosen to participate in the symbolic ceremonies. Trautman had contributed $10,000 of his personal funds to the capital campaign— an impressive sum for a working artist, and one that showed the depth of his regard for the Gallery.

A year later the outlines of that one-story addition were plainly visible in a skeleton of steel that was beginning to acquire its limestone and glass skin. The art was on sabbatical and the existing building closed, so that wood and cement dados, terrazzo and wood flooring, monks cloth and Fortuny wall coverings, auditorium seats and library shelves could be removed. New parquet floors were laid, old skylights covered, and a whole new layout began to take shape.

The administrative offices spent the construction period in the Brown House, that former private residence turned faculty club and, later, Creative Workshop. In 1966 Workshop classrooms (but not the campus squirrels) moved out of the Brown House and Gallery basement to their present space in the basement of Cutler Union. The Brown House has since been demolished.

The "Brown House years" were a marvelous exercise in making do. The master bedroom became the board room and director's office, off of which Janet Otis, the director's secretary, kept her files in the bathtub. The Membership Department set up shop in the dining room. Margaret Bond, head of public relations, was installed in the attic, which afforded her privacy, a listening post for sounds that burbled upward in the old building, and a conning tower view of ongoing construction. The overload on the ancient electrical system was such that power failures stilled the typewriters every time a coffee pot was plugged in.

"I wouldn't want to live through it again," Bond says, "but I wouldn't have missed it for the world."

Programs and activities were moved rather than cancelled in a kind of "museum without walls" arrangement. Lectures were held in Cutler Union. A new weekly series of talks over a box lunch was started, called "Art à la Carte." Forty people were expected for the first program and 140 showed up.

The Education Department and library operated out of a Pittsford house borrowed for the duration from Michael Watson, grandson of the donor of the 1913 building, Emily Sibley Watson.

"Here was a peaceful spot for preparing lectures and doing research, with an uncluttered landscape view from my work table," Susan Schilling recalls nostalgically. She was also able to help Sibley Watson find an obscure book on jade from a pile that was still not shelved in the temporary library.

In announcing the move, the Michael Watsons' unlisted telephone number was inadvertently printed in *Gallery Notes* as that for the Education Department. When Harris Prior was informed of this gaffe he turned quite pale, threw back his head, looked heavenward, and howled like a beagle. "It was the only time I ever heard a human ululate," Bond says. "But he immediately made the only sensible proposal." Everyone close at hand was recruited to sit for two days with 8,400 copies of *Gallery Notes* and correct the offending digits.

Strangely enough, Lang Clay remembers the "Brown House Years" as an exciting period for a museum educator, with many things coming together at once. (Ellen Clay remembers those years as a time when Lang was never home.)

Title I funding for programs began during the years 1966-1968. Partly under Clay's auspices, the Artmobile, a forty-foot trailer cosponsored by the city school system under a Title I grant, brought thematic art exhibits to area schools. He also plunged into a series of fifty-two art lectures entitled "The Look of Art" on RAETA (Rochester Area Educational Television, forerunner to WXXI—Channel 21). The docent training was systematized by Schilling and Clay to be given annually—in homes at that point, with lectures and programs in Cutler Union. Clay taught art history courses at the University of Rochester. And the Genesee Valley School Development Association produced generous funding for nine components, one of which was art. Mary Lipscomb of the Education Department, and later education director at the Boston Museum of Fine Arts, took it over.

Finally this period following Rochester's urban riots of 1964 was an idealistic one in which cultural organizations wanted to do anything they could to encourage inner city participation. Following four days of rioting that left four persons dead, hundreds injured, and millions of dollars worth of property destroyed, Rochesterians were forced to face the problems of their changing city. For the Gallery, and other cultural institutions, the challenge of connecting with an alienated group had just begun.

As a start Clay organized cooperative programming with the Haiti Gallery and Puerto Rican Art and Cultural Center. Programs and art reproductions were circulated through schools, churches, and storefronts, but with mixed results. In searching for a role the Gallery could play, Clay and Prior hired a black staff member to help define ways the Gallery could serve the minority population. With funds from the New York State Council on the Arts (NYSCA), in 1970 they offered the new Gallery position of coordinator of neighborhood services to Luvon Sheppard, a black painter and printmaker who had grown up in Rochester and worked as a recreation leader and teacher for the city and in several community and storefront art programs.

Sheppard would be successful in bringing minority audiences to the Gallery for special events. Garth Fagan's "Bottom of the Bucket...But" dance group (later going on to national prominence as The Bucket Dance Theatre) gave some of its earliest performances at the annual "Soul-In," conceived by Sheppard. He also started neighborhood art-lending galleries in three locations. Before coming to the Gallery, he had been the leader of a group of community artists who called themselves "Allofus." Rather than trying to bring new students into the Creative Workshop, which he considered "intimidating" to the black community, Sheppard persuaded the Gallery, the NYSCA, the Rochester Public Library, and the Rochester Recreation Bureau (which provided an old police precinct station) to start a new neighborhood art school. The Allofus Workshop opened its doors in 1972.

Two art schools within one institution was a doomed concept from the start. Creative Workshop enrollment initially fell off (from 1,300 in 1962 to 1,200 in 1973) but eventually rallied. The change of Gallery administration in 1975 was another reason for an eventual parting of the ways between the Gallery and Allofus in the late 1970s.

The new wing was planned to harmonize with the classic lines of the existing Gallery, and to create an unobtrusive connecting link to the Collegiate Gothic Cutler Union. "If the Renaissance building had not been there," Kaelber says, "who knows what the art gallery would have looked like." The architectural style was International Modern. The goal was a nearly invisible "nonbuilding," stressing volume of space rather than either mass, as in the original building, or thrust, as suggested by the Cutler tower. The rear entrance and *allée* of street-side trees further mitigated the contrast in styles between two neighboring prima donnas.

3

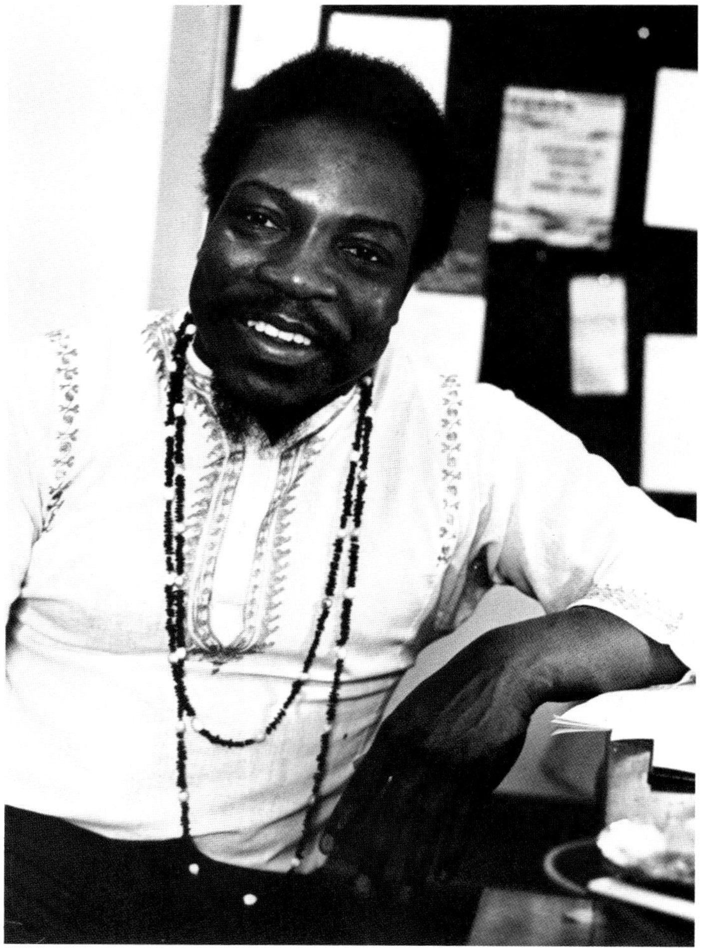

In choice of materials the architects worked from the palette set by the Gallery's original architects, Foster and Gade. Applied ornament was eschewed; the emphasis was on consistency, good proportions, the intrinsic qualities of limestone (enormous, eight-inch-thick slabs) and glass, plus the regular rhythm of horizontal girders evenly distributing the weight of the roof. Fenestration details were clean and crisp.

The arcade facing south toward University Avenue was functional, shading the offices inside from the sun. The arcade facing north, next to the new main entrance, was a deliberate device to create human scale. (The Renaissance facade of the 1913 building features a monumental entrance portico under which a giant could stand. The 1968 entrance and arcades are scaled to human dimensions.)

The basic unit of space was the open-ended cube. Two large cubes—one for exhibition galleries, one for service areas around an auditorium—were to contain smaller cubes grouped in related patterns. The visitor would enter the Main Concourse, a large, high gallery that flowed into the Grand Gallery, a second versatile exhibition area. The glass curtain wall of both would wrap around an outdoor sculpture garden. A procession of nineteenth and twentieth century art was to be mounted on movable panels in flexible space so that upon entering, the visitor would have teasing glimpses of this march of modern art throughout the galleries and sculpture garden.

"People called it an easy space in which to hang a show," Kaelber remembers. "The wall of glass answered the need to impart a sense of natural light somewhere in the building." It was also an easy space in which to move, with few bottlenecks and an uncrowded ambience, even when the Gallery was bursting with people.

The 1968 wing represented a quantum leap into the latter half of the twentieth century. Not only were there air conditioning, temperature, and humidity controls in both old and new buildings, but a more radical change architecturally than in any addition before or since. Suddenly the space of the constrained Renaissance building, with galleries and service areas forced into its classical shell, had been doubled in a building where form truly followed function. The huge L-shaped exhibition area, flooded with natural light from the wall of glass facing the sculpture garden, had only panels as constraints. This allowed, for the first time, many different configurations in exhibit design. (The windows would later cause conservation problems for works of art and have to be screened by a permanent wall.)

Beyond the high-ceilinged exhibition area one could enter the former basement of the original building, where the Lending and Sales Gallery, two temporary exhibition galleries, the Asian Gallery, and the Members' Lounge were located. The transition was so successful and disguised by consistent wall treatment that few were aware of where old met new.

Studies of the original auditorium concluded that the shape was awkward and that acoustics, sight lines, and location with respect to the main entrance were poor. The new auditorium was so located that without having to go through galleries, one could walk up the slight incline—a device to heighten the drama of entering—to the doors of the assembly hall. Designed as centerpiece of the ser-

4

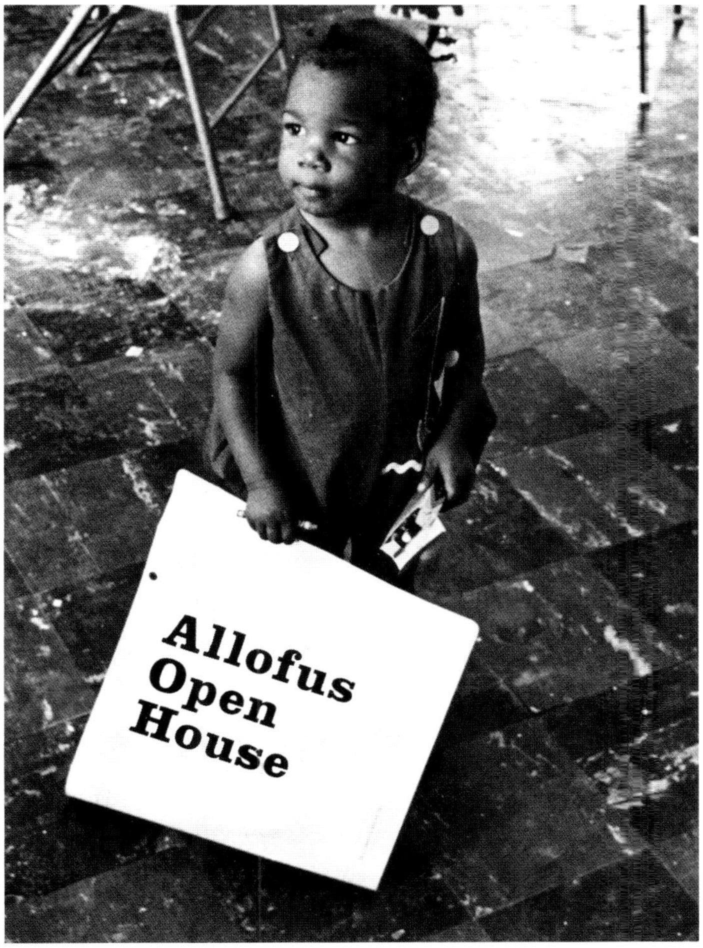

3 Luvon Sheppard, coordinator of Neighborhood Services and director of Allofus Art Workshop.

4 Allofus Art Workshop.

5

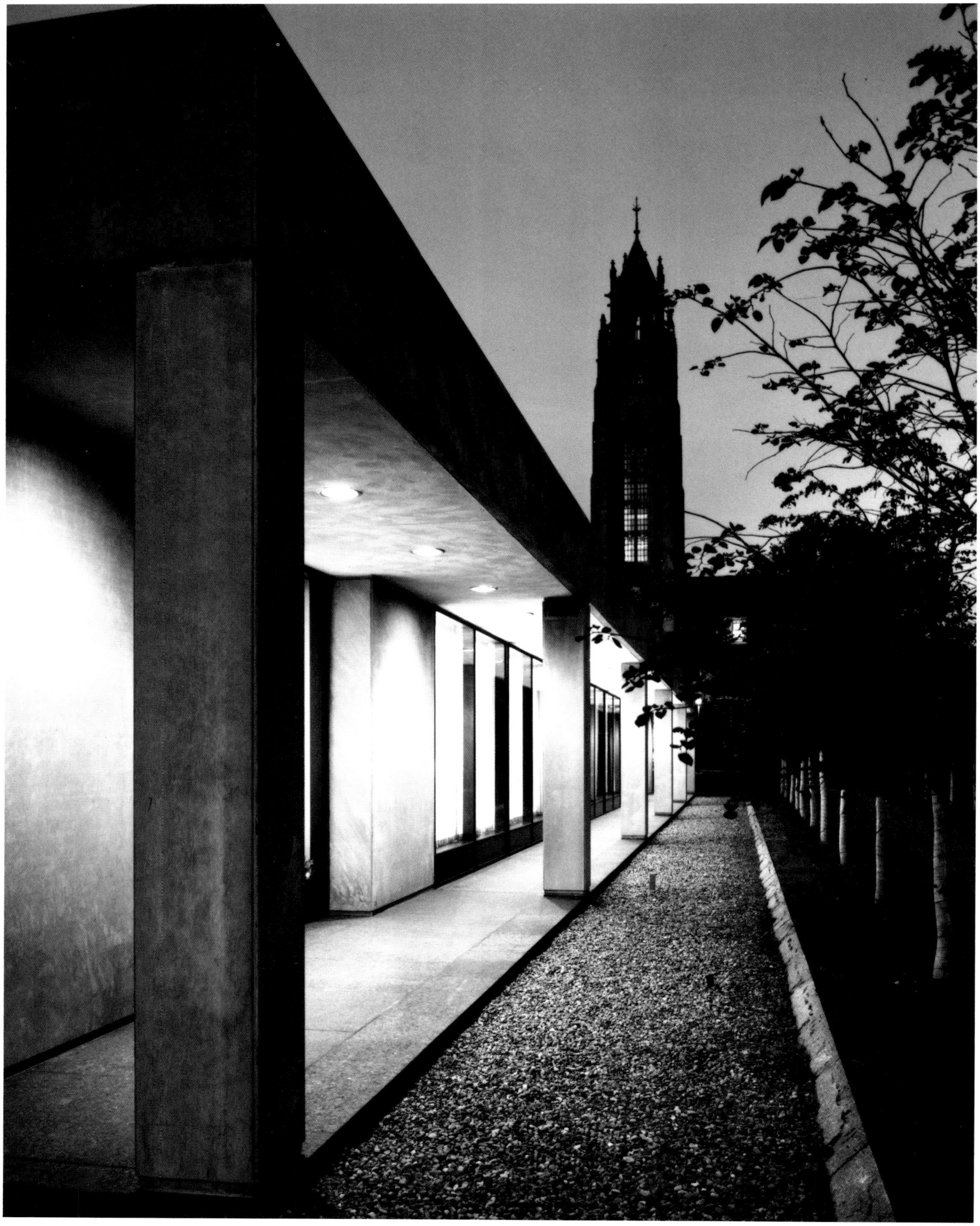

vice wing, the auditorium sat in the middle of an exhibition corridor, offices, conference room, and library. Behind the stage ran an incredibly tall and skinny corridor, loved by school children and docents. "Without it," the architect said, "the space would be clumsy. By virtue of being able to just squeeze through, the auditorium reads as a sculptural shape."

Inside the auditorium, the sight lines would be excellent from each one of the 300 seats. Walls of oak flooring would contribute not only to good acoustics but to a sense of spare elegance as curves turn into reverse curves.

"Once it began, the reconstruction proceeded with astonishing rapidity," *Gallery Notes* remarked, "and Gallery staffers who in theory should have known better, took to returning from exploratory tours with reports of having got completely lost while investigating the new ground floor, where the greatest changes are taking place."

Even before the rest of the project was finished, Cutler Union's basement cafeteria—where so many lunchtime hot fudge sundaes had been consumed and so many "College Suppers" celebrated—had reemerged as ten bright and roomy studio classrooms surrounding a lounge.

The collection had long since gone on loan to the Munson-Williams-Proctor Institute in Utica or the Des Moines Art Center. Pieces needing restoration had gone to the Intermuseum Conservation Laboratory at Oberlin. The rest languished in bank vaults and warehouses. The heaviest objects were stored in a great wooden igloo constructed in the Fountain Court, into which visiting scholars would occasionally make their way, armed with flashlights, to shout out findings to fellow scholars stationed outside.

The grand opening was scheduled for June, but there was a six-week delay when the new front doors failed to arrive as ordered. Minutes before those doors opened on Saturday, 17 August 1968, Prior, the very proper director, was upstairs pushing a broom while his wife was earnestly vacuuming the auditorium. Guests who arrived early were pressed into service polishing brass, even though they were attired in their finery. Others were seen swooping from the floor bits of flotsam left by the departing workers. "Everyone pitched in like grazing sheep," Bond recalls.

Later, as the crowd assembled out-of-doors with dignitaries ensconced under the new entrance portico, board president Walter Strakosh rose to speak of the

6

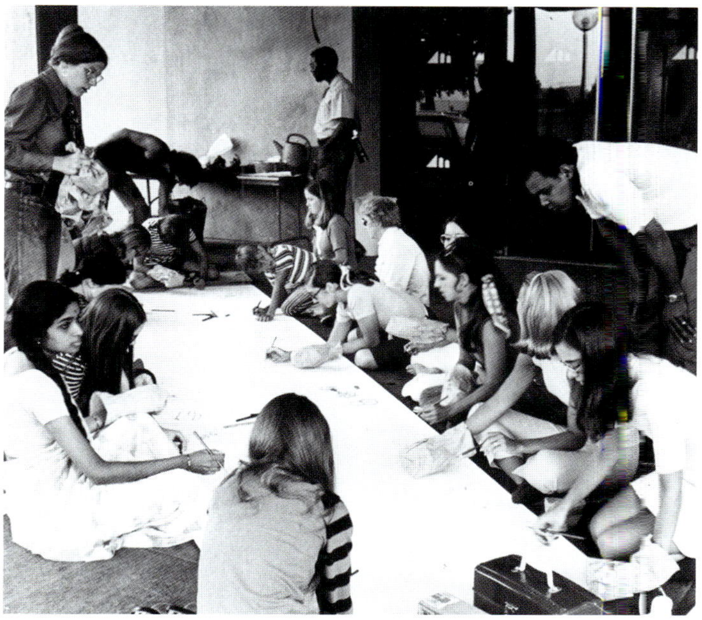

5 *The arcaded 1968 wing with Allée of trees stretched towards the Gallery's nearest neighbor, Cutler Union where Creative Workshop classes and some offices were moved.*

6 *Summer classes were held just outside the Gallery's new main door.*

7

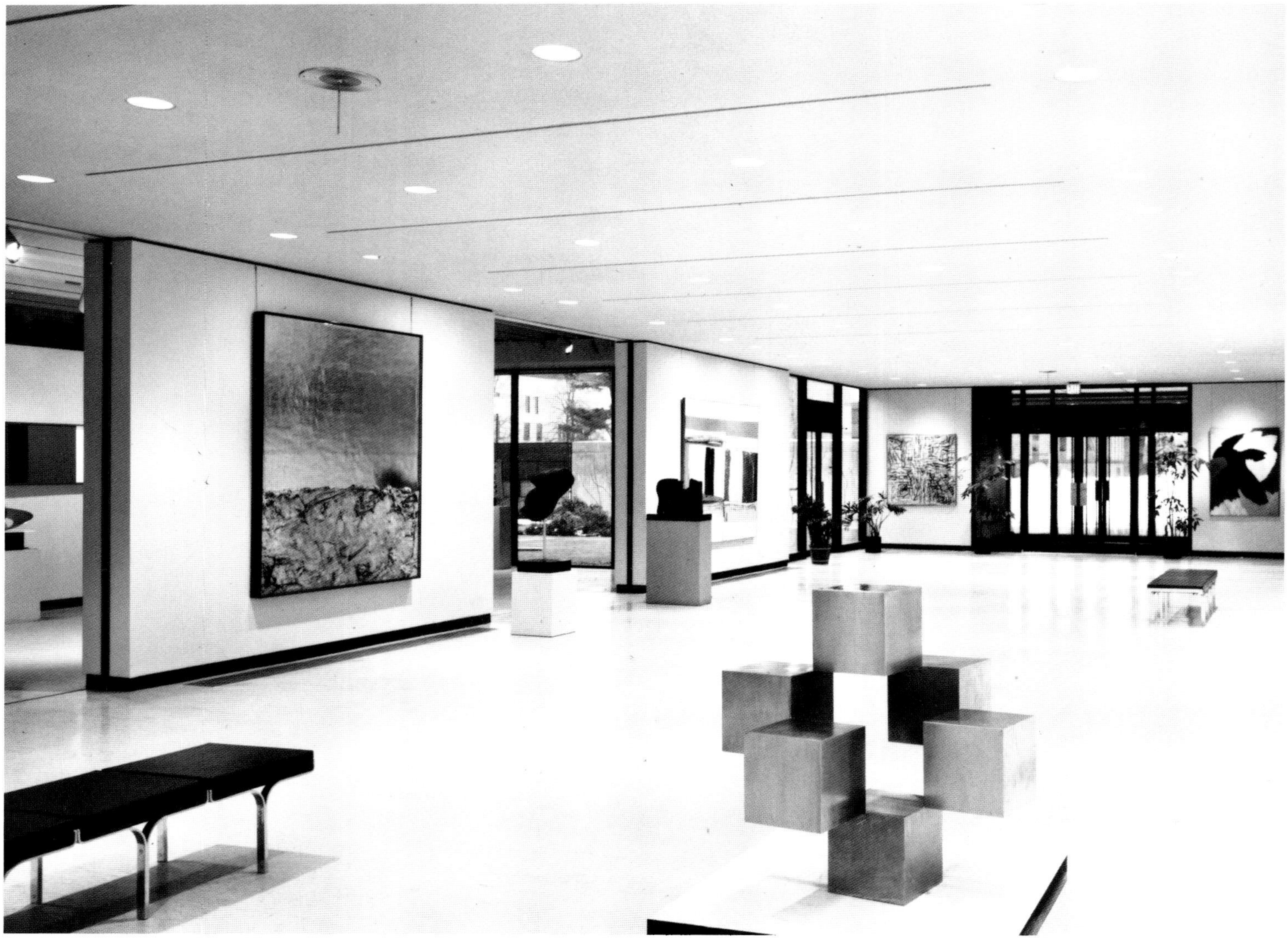

beautiful weather that had blessed this auspicious occasion. Yet even as he spoke, the audience watched in fascination as great black thunderclouds gathered behind him, and as the sudden storm broke, everyone scurried into Cutler Union for the rest of the ceremony. Even so, "the occurrence failed to dampen the festive spirit of the occasion," *Gallery Notes* decided. Programs for members continued for the remainder of that day and the next, with a Gala Opening Ball for 600 held Saturday night, and the completed Gallery open to the public, from 10 to 10, on Tuesday, 20 August.

"The general reaction," *Gallery Notes* concluded, "even among those who have been watching its progress since the expansion and renovation project was nothing more than a sheaf of blueprints, was: 'I had no idea it was going to be so beautiful.'"

8

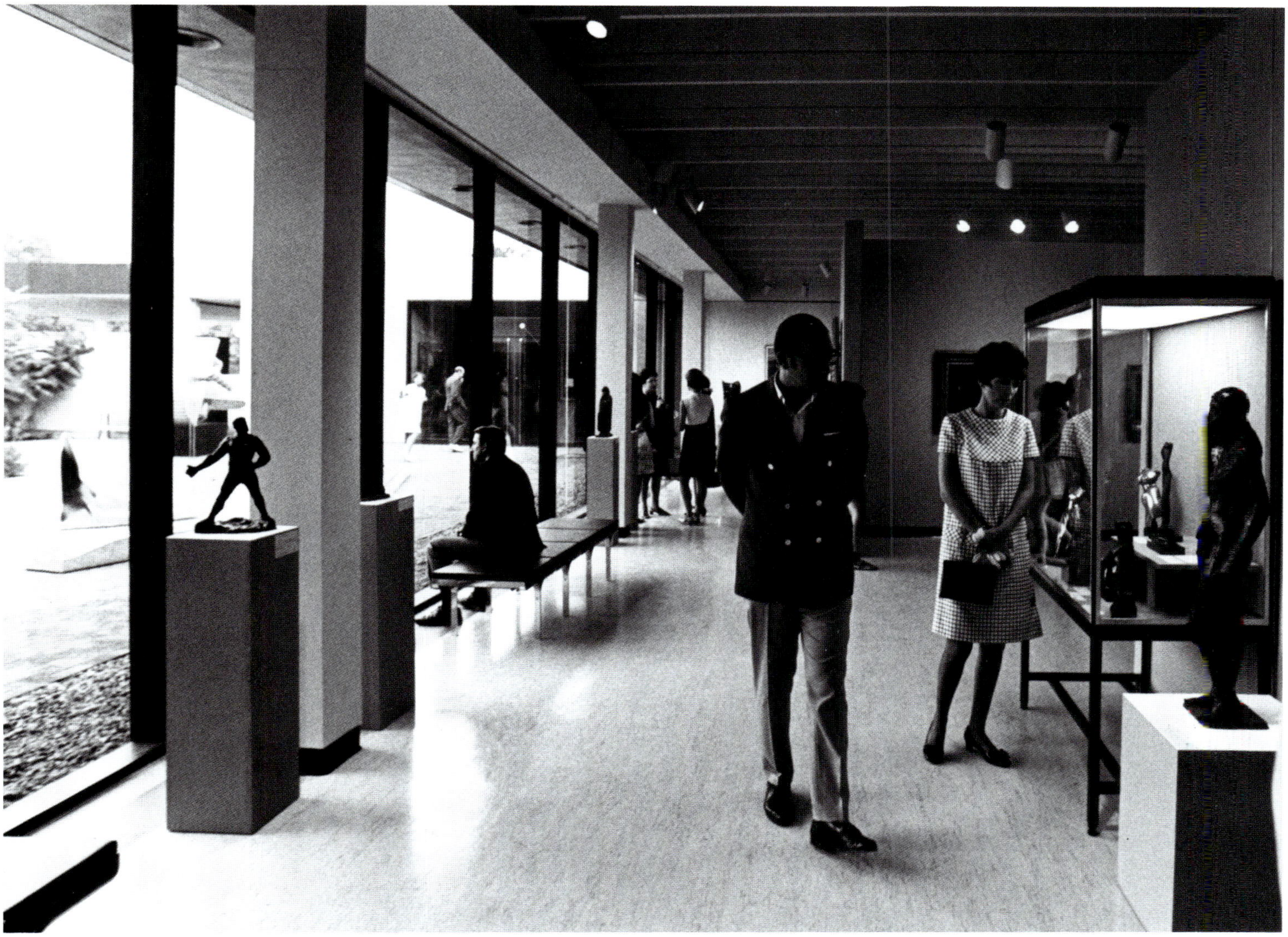

7 *The Main Concourse of the 1968 wing opened into the Grand Gallery. The new exhibition space was initially used for the installation of the twentieth century collection.*

8 *A glass curtain wall separated the Grand Gallery of the 1968 wing from the Gertrude Herdle Moore Sculpture Garden.*

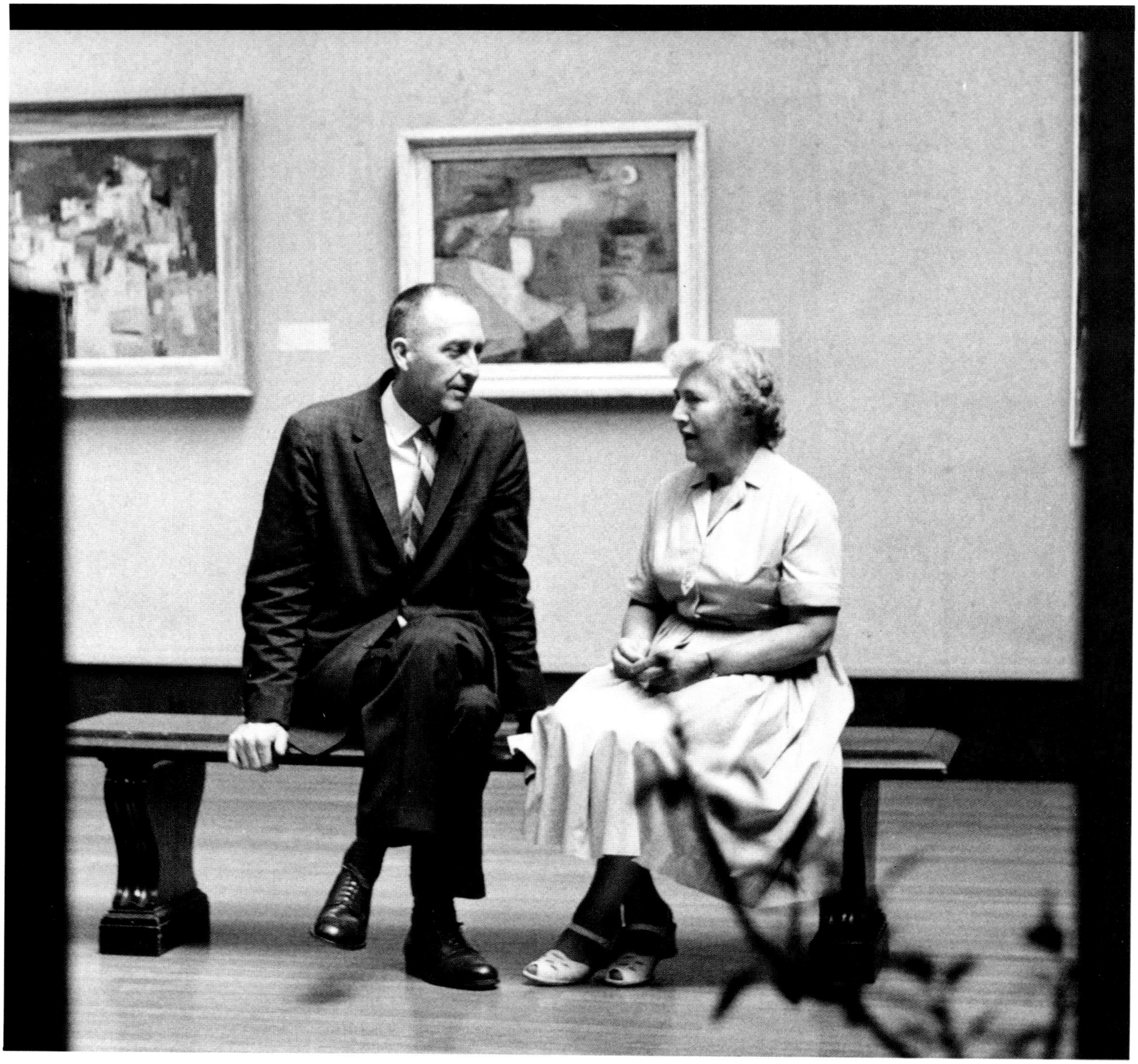

11

Judging works of art is not like judging chickens—according to a published "American Standard of Perfection." It is perhaps a little more like judging tea. At any rate a subjective element is bound to enter in. Because art addresses itself to the emotions, few objective standards exist. The best judges (i.e. jury members) are those who have seen a great deal of art and have had constantly to make critical comparisons and evaluations. In general, the artist-teacher has a broader outlook than the non-teaching artist. The museum curator who has had wide experience also rates high.... Good jurors tend to agree in their choices to a very large extent, even when their personal predilections are at wide variance.

Harris Prior | *Finger Lakes Exhibition Catalogue, 1966*

The Changing of the Guard, 1962.

Harris Prior *was* an accomplished chicken farmer. His distinguished and diverse past also included stints as a professional magician, a college instructor, an engineer, and a catapult expert for the U. S. Navy who served on active duty in World War II and the Korean War. Born in Hazardsville, Connecticut, he grew up on a farm picking strawberries and tending those chickens. "Art came to me as a great revelation in my senior year at [Trinity] college [in Hartford]," he wrote. He later studied architecture at Yale and art at Harvard, the Sorbonne, the University of Brussels, and New York University. After teaching English and fine arts at Trinity from 1932 to 1937, he headed the School of Fine Arts at Olivet College in Michigan from 1937 to 1939.

For ten years before he came to the Gallery Prior had been director of the American Federation of Arts. He was happy to leave that post. "Umbrella organizations do not generate any loyalty," he once told this writer. Loyalty, from both staff and volunteers, was what he would receive in signal measure during his thirteen years as Gallery director.

Before his stint with the AFA he had directed the Community Arts Program at the Munson-Williams-Proctor Institute in Utica. (In essence he was the museum director.) A skilled writer, he was the author of numerous articles for encyclopedias, art journals, and exhibition catalogs. At the time of his death in 1975 he was working on a book about museum practices, one of his several academic specialties.

Since Gertrude Herdle Moore was approaching the mandatory university retirement age of sixty-five, a search committee combed the land for her successor. One of the persons whose suggestions and advice the committee sought was Harris Prior. Prior listened politely and then said, "Why not me?"

Why not indeed?

Although all signs indicated potential trouble—a century's combined service by one family could easily have provoked acrimony over the territorial imperative—the transition was particularly harmonious. Isabel Herdle was asked to stay on as assistant director for curatorial services; Lang Clay became assistant director for educational services. Gertrude Moore was engaged as a consultant to work on the print collection. The folk art gallery, which the Herdle sisters had long wanted, could be situated in the new wing, Prior said. Bob Young was apprehensive about this new director until the ex-Navy captain said, "You operate your department. I'll operate mine. If there are any complaints, you'll hear from me." Young never did.

The new wing was six years in the making. In the meantime exhibitions, acquisitions, and programs continued, hampered by the ongoing need to raise sufficient funds to accomplish all that was wanted in the new building. Harris Prior was particularly sensitive to the tensions involved. Given his way, he would have run a strictly serious, scholarly museum. The way the Gallery was financed, going to the community for funds, using the Gallery for fun and frolic and balls, made him uncomfortable. One always suspected that noisy carnivals such as the "Mirrors Motors Motion" children's show of 1970 or the Medieval Faire of 1974 were not to his personal taste. Yet he recognized their value as a means to reach that large segment of the community who had never visited an art museum. He worried over these things the way he worried over the artists who were rejected in the Finger Lakes exhibitions or about the police investigation of an alleged pornographic work in the Clothesline show. Every detail, no matter how minor, would engage him completely until it was settled. He was thorough, dedicated, often obsessive. Many who observed him, including this writer, thought that he in the end sacrificed his health to his vocation.

People were surprised therefore to find that this intensely serious, almost monkish director had a puckish sense of humor. A sculpture of a female nude destined for a children's show troubled him, but then he declared triumphantly: "This time when the sheriff comes, we'll refer him to the [cosponsoring] Junior League!" Once security feared that a mysterious package, purporting to be a Greek vase, was actually a bomb. It turned out to be a practical joke from a member of the Women's Council. Prior was tickled by the whole episode. In relaxed moments he was a delightful raconteur.

"He was proud of his profession," George Angle says, "knowledgeable and determined to maintain high standards. He was an effective administrator with a sense of order and the ability to lead people and to inspire loyalty and hard work. He recognized without condescension the importance of volunteers to the financially pressed arts and was able to instill the notion that people, be they Women's Council members, docents, campaigners, whatever, were doing something really important. The Gallery family was a happy band under his tutelage. "We loved him," Angle concludes. "He was a decent man."

In March of 1963 a Buffalo art dealer wrote to Prior: *I have a friend and client, Charles Rand Penney, who has a fine collection of American paintings. He is setting up a foundation for the promotion of American art.*

1

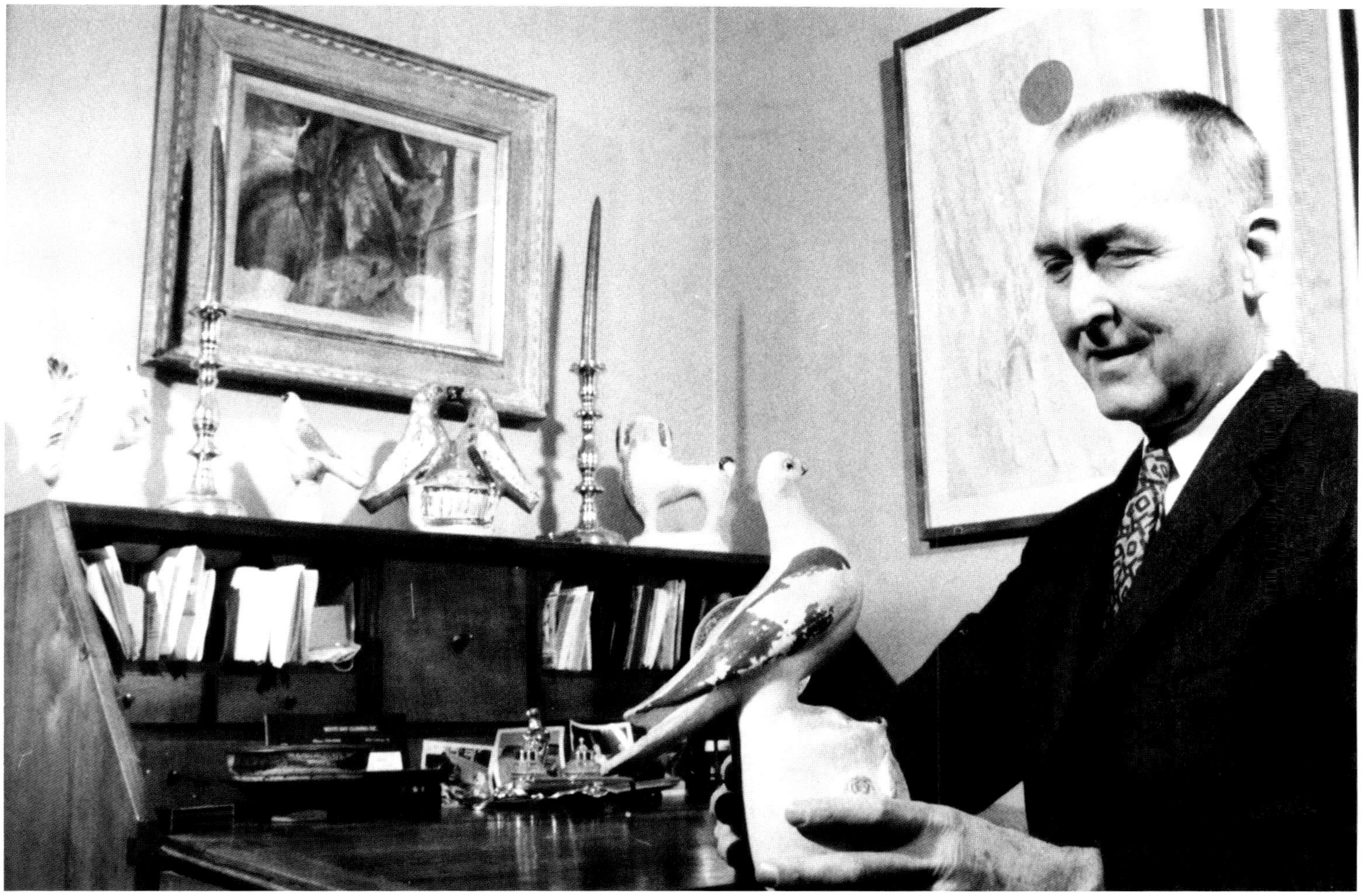

1 *Harris Prior and a favorite fowl.*

2

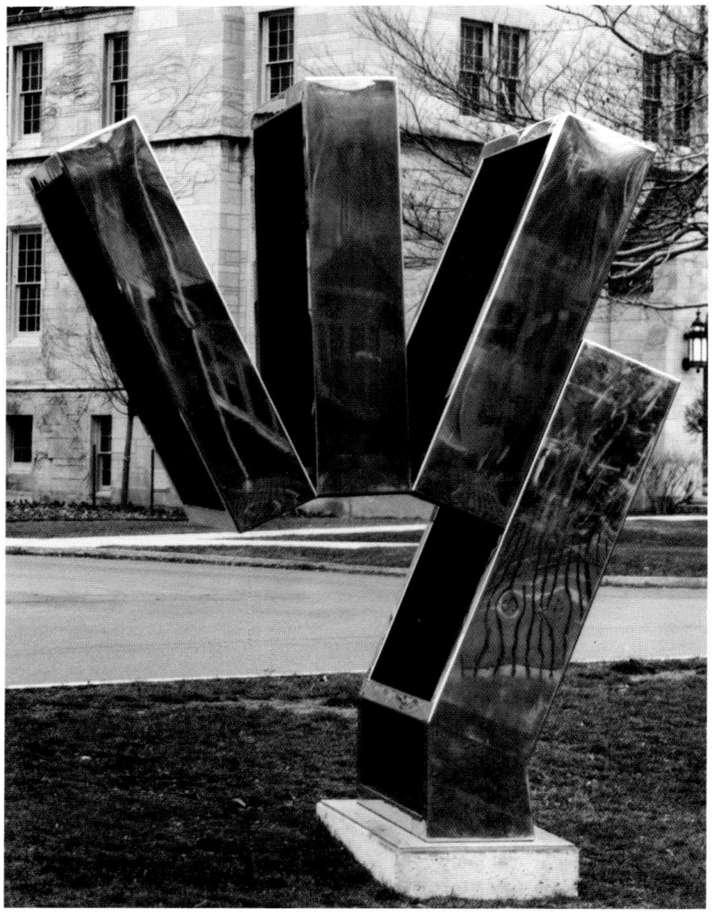

2 *Beverly Pepper (American, 1924-) Vertical Ventaglio, ca. 1967-1969, chrome and painted steel, 114 in. h. x 85 x 43. Gift of Charles Rand Penney, 78.195*

3 *Gallery-goers admire painting: Thomas Cole (American, 1801-1848), Landscape composition: Italian Scenery, 1831-1832, oil on canvas, 40¼ x 61⅞. Marion Stratton Gould Fund and gift of Mr. and Mrs. Thomas H. Hawks, 71.37*

He is a member of the Memorial Art Gallery and... would like to present a painting to your gallery.

Penney's interest in collecting art began in his Sunday School class of 1934. The youngster's teacher was a painter who gave him a small watercolor sketch. A resident of Lockport, New York, Penney went on to a multifaceted career as attorney, collector, world traveler, promoter of the arts, and civic leader. Over the next half-century he amassed more than forty individual collections—quilts and coverlets, hooked rugs, Staffordshire figurines, tribal arts of Africa and Oceania, World's Fair memorabilia, as well as American and European art in the major media. The work he gave to the Gallery in 1963, beginning a happy relationship between museum and collector, was Harriet Greif's canvas *Red Noon*.

Over the years Penney has lent the Gallery five exhibitions from his collections, the first such selection being mounted in the spring of 1973.

A major gift and exhibition of 380 objects came from the Charles Rand Penney Foundation in February 1976, the fruit of negotiations begun by Penney and Prior. The drawings, prints, watercolors, collages, photographs, and sculpture formed one of the largest gifts ever to come to the Gallery. The foundation was a charitable trust formed in 1963 to further contemporary American art; the concentration of the collection is on American prints (including twelve complete portfolios) of the 1960s and 1970s.

Among the late twentieth century artists represented in the Penney gift were Alexander Calder, David Smith, Jackson Pollock, Claes Oldenburg, and Ed Ruscha. Earlier artists included John Marin, Thomas Hart Benton, James Abbott McNeill Whistler, and Charles Burchfield. Before the Penney gift the Gallery's print holdings had been strongest in European and American works of the nineteenth and early twentieth centuries. The Penney collection significantly enriched the holdings of the latter half of the twentieth century.

In 1978 Penney gave *Vertical Ventaglio*, a large, tour-de-force outdoor piece by Beverly Pepper. The reflective chrome surfaces of *Ventaglio* (Italian for fan) spread out, defying gravity.

Charles Burchfield became a close friend of Penney's after the two met in 1963. Penney's own collection of watercolors, oils, drawings, prints, doodles, and wallpapers by Burchfield is the most comprehensive body of that artist's work in private hands. In 1978 an exhibition drawn from the Burchfield collection was organized for the Gallery by curator Bruce Chambers. It toured the nation until 1983 under the auspices of the Smithsonian Institution Traveling Exhibi-

3

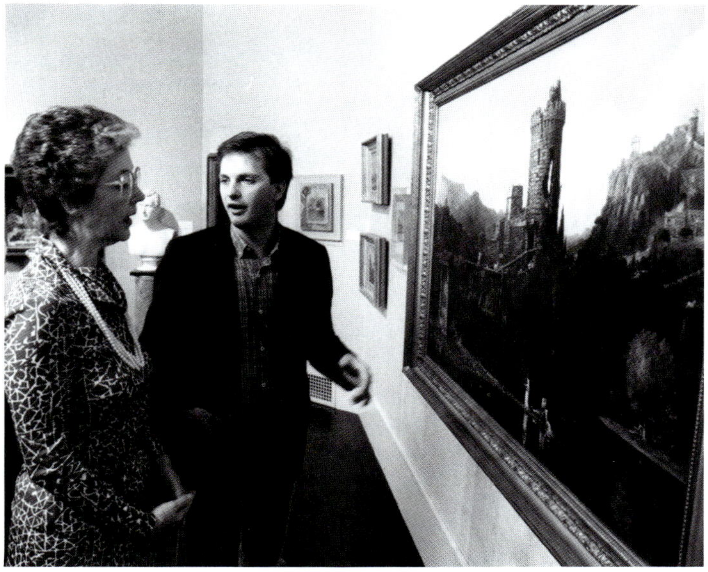

tion Service. A second Burchfield exhibition, this time emphasizing his skills as a master draughtsman as seen in his drawings and watercolors, was mounted at the Gallery from Penney's collection in November and December of 1987.

Earlier, in 1983, "Twentieth Century Art: The Charles Rand Penney Collection" was organized by Patricia Anderson Junker and Bret Waller. Following its Gallery opening, the exhibition traveled to twelve museums in the United States and Canada. Because of its popularity, it was extended into the 1988 season.

In the 1960s Marion and Thomas H. Hawks rekindled a tradition, begun in the 1920s by the Watsons, of celebrating personal milestones with gifts to the Gallery. In 1965, in honor of their wedding anniversary, the Hawks gave the painting *Interlude*, by the American John Koch. In 1971 *Landscape Composition: Italian Scenery* (1832), by Thomas Cole, was in part a gift from the Hawks and in part a Gould Fund purchase. Then in 1974 *Boy with Dice*, by George Luks, was given in honor of Harris Prior, who had often admired the painting when he saw it on a wall of the Hawks home. Most recently *The Clown, No Laughs* by Everett Shinn, a member of The Eight (those eight, mostly "Ash Can," artists who exhibited together at the Macbeth Gallery in 1908), was given by Thomas Hawks in honor of a significant Marion Hawks birthday.

The large Cole work was painted during the one year that the artist, who is credited with fathering the rise of a native American school of landscape art, spent working in Florence. The painting was commissioned by a patron who specified only that it must fit above his parlor mantel. He left the subject up to Cole. (The patron later ordered a companion piece of the same size, which is now at the National Gallery of Art in Washington.) Before the Gallery unveiled its Cole, a cleaning brought out the jewel-like color of the romantic Italian scene of mountains, ruined towers, still and rushing waters, and noble peasants.

Mrs. Hawks also persuaded her father to give *Tobias and the Angel* in memory of her mother. A fine example of a classical landscape in the tradition of Poussin and Claude, this formalized and highly structured Baroque painting by the seventeenth century Dutch painter Jan Glauber came to the Gallery through the Robcliff V. and Irene C. Jones Charitable Trust.

The Käthe Kollwitz prints, which had been sold to the Gallery in 1948 by the jilted immigrant woman, were joined in 1963 by *Woman in a Blue Shawl* (1903), a second-state lithograph in three colors. It was a gift of family and friends in memory of Carl F. W. Kaelber, one of the founders of the Rochester Print Club and father of the architect of the 1958 Gallery addition.

The year 1964 was the last time art works could be given to a museum as a tax deduction while retaining life use. A small windfall resulted. The lithograph of George Bellows' famous painting *Stag at Sharkey's*, Raoul Dufy's *La Fontaine, Vence*, and Alexander Calder's *Mobile* were given by Charlotte Whitney Allen. (The Calder is of particular historical interest in that it was the first outdoor piece by the artist who created the "mobile.") A Corot landscape was received from Dr. and Mrs. Wallace O. Fenn. *Basket of Fruit* by Rubens Peale and *Window Sill in Venice* by Giorgio de Chirico, were gifts from Helen C. Ellwanger. And an English tea caddy and a Tang Dynasty Chinese *Kwanyin*, wood with traces of polychrome, were given by Mrs. Gertrude Herdle Moore and Miss Isabel Herdle. At another time Gertrude gave the Gallery a wooden spoon from the Ivory Coast. With Isabel she presented a Charles Henry Demuth watercolor, *Zinnias*, in memory of their father. Isabel has also given a Chinese horse in grey clay from the Northern Wei Dynasty and a Central African funerary figure.

Prior's professional contacts through his earlier affiliations, plus the coming to the forefront of the New York State Council on the Arts (NYSCA), further gave his regime its flavor. NYSCA sponsored many of the exhibitions and programs during his tenure and through a subsidy allowed the Gallery to stay open Tuesday evenings with no admission charge. It funded specialized staff members such as the neighborhood coordinator, school lecturers, and people to write labels for the collection. It made possible a full-time director of the Creative Workshop. Foreshadowing the 1987 expansion, when staff offices would move to Cutler Union, these earlier staff members also had offices there.

Prior knew Roy Neuberger from his years with the American Federation of Arts. In 1963 Neuberger, "one of the legendary risk-takers of Wall Street," presented the Gallery with *Haircut by the Sea*, by Milton Avery. For years Neuberger had invested in works of living artists and distributed them to various museums of his liking. Later he would build his own museum in Purchase, New York.

Milton Avery (1885-1965) had maintained a confident detachment from the ideological struggles swirling around him in the heyday of Abstract Expressionism. Indeed many nonobjective painters were highly influenced by his seemingly traditional art. *Haircut by the Sea*, an ordinary subject imbued with poetic vision, has the Avery hallmarks: rigorous design; strong sensibility for color; and clear, simple, luminous images of contours and surfaces distilled from copious drawings and watercolors.

The Gallery's first mural-scale work, *The Bathers*, by Childe Hassam (1859-1935), arrived in 1963 during that period of uncertainty as to whether the Gallery would move to the River Campus, and before there was a wall large enough to display it. And so *Bathers* sat for a while in a storage room deep in the bowels of the Gallery (or, as Gallery wag Margaret Bond, who knew her Byron, put it: "Childe Hassam to dark storage came").

A major work by the American Impressionist Hassam filled a long-felt need. Gertrude, who knew the artist personally, had wanted to exhibit about twenty of his works in the 1920s. "Let me see," mused Hassam. "You're asking me to withdraw these from the New York market for a month?" The paintings did not come.

Then in 1940 Mrs. Childe Hassam gave the Gallery thirty of her husband's lithographs.

Bathers, which indicates that Hassam studied Puvis de Chavannes as well as the French Impressionists, was painted in 1904 as a large (48 by 148 inches) mural for a library wall in the Portland, Oregon home of C. E. Wood. Two owners later it was hanging in the Hirschl and Adler Gallery, New York, when Mr. and Mrs. Harris Prior walked in and admired it.

"Would you like it for the Gallery?" Norman Hirschl wondered aloud to Prior.

Would he ever. The owner of the mural, Mrs. Ogden Phipps, was making gifts to selected museums. Up until that

4 *The evolution of the Gallery logo, 1913-1988.*

moment Hirschl had been advocating that Phipps give the Hassam to Smith College, where his daughter was enrolled. Friendship with Prior changed his mind. "It was," Anne Prior Whitcomb says now, "a case of being in the right place at the right time."

That same year, 1963, the Gould Fund was used to purchase *Personnages et Ruines*, by Hubert Robert (1733-1808), and a work of the American Impressionist Maurice Prendergast (1859-1924). In *Woodland Bathers* Prendergast, usually celebrated for his brilliant little watercolors, had taken a typical subject and made an oil mosaic of highly intense colors that diminish the illusion of distance. In 1965 the Gould Fund was used to purchase works by two American masters of trompe l'oeil painting: *Articles Hung on a Door*, by John Frederick Peto, and *Torn in Transit*, by John Haberle (1856-1933). In 1966 *Portrait of a Woman*, by the Dutch painter Kees van Dongen (1877-1968), came as the gift of Mr. and Mrs. Irving S. Norry.

Prior was fascinated by the life and work of Arthur B. Davies (1862-1928), who had been much involved with the two exhibitions which symbolically mark the triumph of progressive tendencies in American art. Works by Davies hung in Prior's office. As the recognized authority of his time on Davies, Prior, at the time of his death, was working on a book about this painter of fantasy.

The first landmark exhibition for Davies was that of "The Eight" at the Macbeth Gallery in 1908, which explored subject matter foreign to old-fashioned ideals of beauty. A reviewer of that show described Davies's idyllic fantasies as somewhere "between genius and insanity." The second, the Armory Show of 1913, introduced to America the new art that rejected traditional form and realization of subject matter. It was Davies who whipped the famous, indeed infamous, Armory Show into shape. But first, he had been transformed, according to Guy Pene du Bois, from a "perfervid dweller in the land of romance...incapable of making contacts of the real world" into a "dictator, severe, arrogant, implacable."

Davies's personal life was at least as wild as his artistic theories seemed to be at the time. For years he led a complex double life as the head of two separate families. During the Prior years at the Gallery his descendants gave two works to the Gallery, joining several already in the collection. In 1963 *The Gates of Morning*, a large tapestry designed by the artist, was given by Mr. and Mrs. Niles Meriweather Davies of Congers, New York. *Child's Portrait* was the gift of the estate of A. David Davies in 1967.

———

So excited was the community about its new Gallery after years of waiting and construction that membership rose by 1,770, soaring to 9,500 in 1969, almost double the numbers of 1965, just before the addition. The inaugural exhibition was a combination "welcome home" for the collection and for the ground-breaking "Light: Object and Image" exhibition from the Whitney Museum.

A new logo, the third in Gallery history, was designed by Douglas Baker. Previous designs, by Claude Bragdon and John Menihan, had both featured the Palladian entrance to the 1913 structure. Baker's asymmetrical design is composed of a right triangle and two diminishing arches. Simple, functional, and flexible—like the 1968 wing—it is still in use today. In 1987 the logo was updated again by Bill Buckett.

The Thomas Cole retrospective exhibition of 1968-1969 was the first major exhibition devoted to Cole in 100 years, beginning a wave of rediscovery. It was also the first exhibition assembled by the Gallery to travel to four museums, including the Whitney. The 120-page catalog, written by Howard Merritt, after he had selected the paintings, was the most elaborate in Gallery history, in such demand by scholars that the supply soon ran out. From this exhibition came the Gallery's Cole, described above.

"Objects USA," sponsored by the Johnson Wax Company, attracted 15,000 people in January 1970. The first American museum exhibition devoted to the German Expressionist group *Die Brücke* brought patrons and connoisseurs from far and near, some of whom complained that their contemplation was interrupted by the clackety-clack of the kinetic sculpture show for children down the hall.

The big outdoor-sculpture acquisition, partly a gift of the artist, was Tony Smith's *Playground*, which sturdily lives up to its name since countless children have crawled all over it with no damage to the sculpture.

The year 1970 also saw the retirement of Carl Hersey as chairman of the Department of Fine Arts at the university; an exhibition of "Shaker Arts and Crafts"; and the "Doubting Thomas" capital starring in a showcase installation at the Metropolitan Museum for the exhibition "The Year 1200." How beautiful that capital is, thought the Herdle sisters when they saw it in New York. There it was, high on a pedestal as if in the nave of a church, and for a moment they did not recognize it as the Gallery's own.

"Another Chance for Cities," sponsored by the Urban Development Corporation, featured Rochester's new Genesee Gateway project in the Southeast Loop. Artists honored by exhibitions during 1971 included Georges Rouault on the centennial of his birth, William Sidney Mount, Ronald Pear-

5

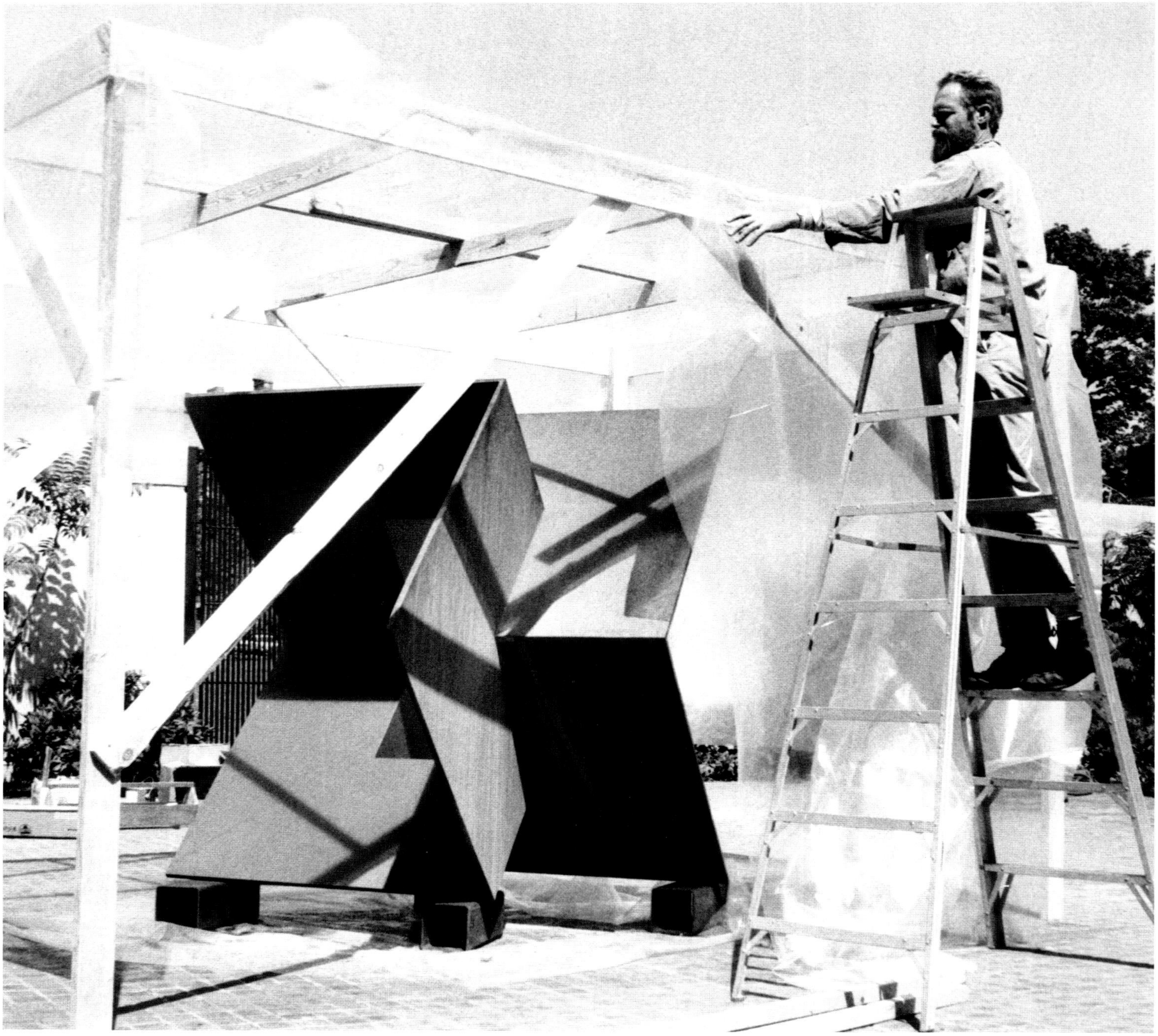

5 *William Sellers installs sculpture in the Gertrude Herdle Moore Sculpture Garden.*

son (a local jeweler who won the Jurors' Award in the Finger Lakes Exhibition and thus was awarded a show of his own), and Albrecht Dürer (marking this artist's five hundredth anniversary). A hologram exhibit signalled the current interest in laser art. "Signs and Symbols: American Folk Sculpture" was a big, comprehensive show. The university faculty exhibition showcased seven artist-teachers, including sculptors Thomas Bang and Archibald Miller; painter Michael Venezia, then "concerned with documenting air-dispersed coatings and spray patterns"; and Lynda Benglis, her pigmented wax constructions.

Prior took a six-month sabbatical in 1971 to research and write about museum management. In his absence Isabel, Clay, and administrator Bernice Meyer managed affairs, assisted by Angle, who came over from the university to meet weekly with the Gallery "troika."

"The Rise of an American Architecture" in 1972, like "Illuminations" twenty years before, featured enormous backlit transparencies, this time mounted on a system of prefab pipes screwed together manually. Bob Young and Stan Brew's installation marched through the Main Concourse, on into the Grand Gallery, to the Lounge and, when finished, resembled an enormous jungle gym. Young and Brew did not quite get it all screwed together by opening night, however, and those who came then found that the show ended abruptly at the first turn. During the rest of the week the show just grew and grew.

When something piqued his fancy, Prior went all out. He was entranced by the work of Norman Daly of Cornell University, who had created a mythological civilization—"half in jest and all in earnest"—which he called "Llhuros." In spoofing archeological exhibits, Daly fashioned handsome artifacts; but what looked like stone and metal turned out to be Styrofoam. Prior gave Daly a show that nearly filled the Gallery.

The year 1972 marked Isabel Herdle's fortieth year on the Gallery staff. And so she retired, but in her own fashion. Returning immediately as curator emeritus, she whipped together one of her typically ambitious shows-on-a-shoestring. Called "In the Footsteps of Marco Polo," the exhibition was complete with photos, artifacts, and enormous maps to illustrate each stop on the route. The next year she curated an exhibition of "Antique Toys" drawn from the collections of the Strong Museum. That was followed by "Touch and Know," a wonderful show for the blind—as well as for the sighted—held in a darkened room with special ramps and railings. It forced visitors to rely on their senses of touch and hearing rather than sight in understanding and appreciating works of art.

Groundbreaking children's shows by Isabel would continue, along with an experiment in babysitting for the mothers who came to the auditorium for a program about toys. As was usual in those days, the whole staff was pressed into service. Playpens lined one entire Gallery. One mother handed her baby to Isabel and left for a pleasant day in the galleries and auditorium; the babe meanwhile had bonded to Isabel, and would not let her out of his sight without raising a ruckus. It would be a one-time-only experiment.

Since 1932 paintings from the George Eastman Collection of the University of Rochester had hung in several university properties: the Gallery, the River Campus, the Eastman School of Music, and the George Eastman House. Many works "boarded" at the Gallery in 1948 and 1949 as "The George Eastman Collection of Paintings" while the Eastman House was being converted from a residence for university presidents to an independently chartered photography museum. They were illustrated in the Gallery *Handbook* of 1961, but when scholars or tourists asked to see them, they had to be directed over to East Avenue.

Until the new wing opened with its sophisticated temperature and humidity controls, the paintings were probably as well conserved in that four-story, concrete and steel bunker that is Eastman House as anyplace else.

Prior was determined to see them placed at the Gallery, however, and the 1968 renovation was his opportunity. His efforts were helped not inconsiderably by a predawn theft of the Rembrandt from its post over the living-room fireplace at the Eastman House. Prior was highly involved, along with Beaumont Newhall, director of the Eastman House, in the negotiations and detective work associated with the bizarre theft and the safe return—this time to the Gallery—of the *Portrait of a Young Man*. The Rembrandt was joined in 1968 by *Portrait of a Venetian Patrician* by Jacopo Tintoretto, *Portrait of a Man* by Franz Hals, *Portrait of an Italian Nobleman* by Anthony Van Dyck, *View off the Dutch Coast* by Jan van de Cappelle, and *Portrait of General Hay MacDowell* by Henry Raeburn. Portraits by Reynolds, Gainsborough, Romney, Hoppner, Lawrence and Raeburn, plus nineteenth century French, American, and Dutch landscapes, were acquired in the 1970s. The collection, parts of which are lent regularly to the Eastman House, was most recently exhibited as a whole in 1980 as the opening event of the Eastman Kodak Company's centennial year.

A major work by Cézanne was long desired, but as the

esteem for this seminal figure of twentieth century art and the prices his paintings commanded rose, the Gallery's hope of acquiring one almost sank. In November 1969, however, an anonymous gift of that wonderful landscape of the 1880s, *L'Estaque*, came the Gallery's way. Given in tribute to Edward Harris, president of the Board of Managers, and in memory of H. L. Stirlin, a Swiss art collector, it arrived as a surprise package one day at the end of a successful annual campaign. Dropped off at the Gallery early one morning by a member of the donor's family on the way to work, the Cézanne was up and hanging in the new Grand Gallery within the hour—to the delight of staff and volunteers who had gathered to stage a little party in its honor.

The pre-Columbian collection received a major boost in 1967 and 1971 with the purchases of a Mayan *Stela no. 9* (859 A. D.) and a Mayan *Tripod Plate* (ca. eighth century A.D.), both through the Gould Fund. Both stela and plate depict the same important deity—Pauahtun, an "aged supernatural with toothless gums and a large, Roman nose... [who] often fondles handsome young...moon goddesses"—according to a *Porticus* article by Michael D. Coe, professor of anthropology at Yale University.

A superb outdoor study for a monumental sculpture by Henry Moore, *Three Piece No. 3: Vertebrae*, and three Moore drawings were given in 1972 in memory of Joseph C. Wilson, Xerox board chairman and honorary chairman of the Gallery Board of Managers, by his family and friends. The final selection was made by his widow, Marie Curran Wilson, when she visited Henry Moore at his home in England.

One of Moore's series of sculptures shaped in the forms of ancient polished bones, *Vertebrae* was installed in the outdoor sculpture garden of the 1968 wing and reinstalled in a fountain setting as the centerpiece of the Vanden Brul Pavilion in 1987.

Vertebrae aptly illustrates Moore's organic imperative—at once gentle, powerful, erotic, and pastoral—which is derived from sources as diverse as the sculpture of Arp and the poetry of Wordsworth. Elements of the human anatomy have been generalized into landscape, a delicate lyricism combined with monumentality. The bronze forms were meant to be seen in natural light, and happily, they still are.

David Smith's *Big Diamond*, from the Penney Collection, forms a splendid counterpoint to the Moore piece. Smith's basic method was direct metal construction derived from Picasso, the Cubists, collage, Abstract Expressionism, and eventually the color abstractionists. Smith conceived his sculptural constructions in fundamentally pictorial terms which constituted an important break with the Moore sculptural ethos.

American paintings of the late nineteenth and early twentieth centuries were among Prior's special interests. Hence the acquisition of the Cole, the Hassam, the Prendergast, and the Asher B. Durand (given by the Women's Council in his honor). So was the contemporary Northwest School of Mark Tobey, Carl and Hilda Morris, and Kenneth Callahan.

A small gestural painting by Tobey, tempera on paper, was acquired through the Gould Fund in 1963. *Sun Remembered*, a painting by Carl Morris, was an anonymous gift through the American Federation of Arts in 1964. *Mountain Piece*, a bronze sculpture by Hilda Morris, was the 1975 gift of Dr. Frank W. Lovejoy in memory of Suzanne Trimble Lovejoy. A preparatory drawing for that piece was given by the artist in memory of Harris Prior in 1976.

Mountain Storm, by Kenneth Callahan, for more than twenty years curator of the Seattle Art Museum, was purchased in 1964. Long a disciple of Tobey until they drifted apart, Callahan became the Gallery's first artist in residence. For several months he worked on charcoal drawings and a set of screens in the upstairs galleries while playing host to Creative Workshop students, whose paintings he discussed.

"Harris felt museums should have contemporary paintings of their time whether or not they turn out to be *the* masterpieces of the age," his widow, Anne Prior Whitcomb, explains. "He believed that in building the collection of a teaching museum you looked for something of everything, from the archaic [period] on up." And so Prior continued the policy of filling the gaps. Under his tutelage the pre-Columbian and African collections as well as the contemporary collection grew.

Prior had a talent for explaining art simply, stripping it of its mystique, without patronizing the observer. "Art is something man-made for contemplation" was his concise definition.

"I think some people take art altogether too seriously," he said. "They think it holds mysteries that only some people have been initiated into. This is nonsense.

"It's simply a matter of tuning one's senses to receive whatever the work of art is giving off. Too many people feel uncomfortable in the presence of a work of art. I say relax and keep looking. If you really want to go into it, do some reading."

When Langdon F. Clay retired in 1986, he was the last member of the staff to bridge several periods of Gallery history. Taking a sentimental journey through his more than

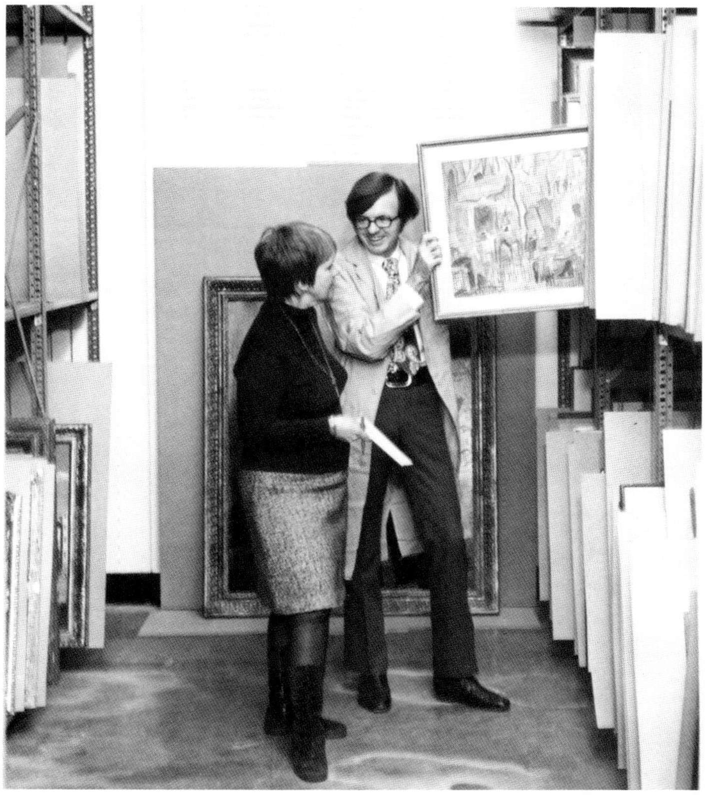

6 *Curator Robert Henning and assistant Joan Rongeras in new storage area.*

three decades of experience, he characterized each period in turn. His first ten years were marked by essentially "a small staff working closely together in a small space." Then the emphasis in art education nationwide was on the "art historical," a lecture approach with a smattering of educational theory. The succeeding periods, beginning with the directorship of Prior, were more expansive and sophisticated as the size of the Gallery building doubled and redoubled—and with it the staff.

When the enlarged building reopened in 1968, programs and funding kept pace. Artist Dorothy Glaser was made the first director of the Creative Workshop. Docent Jacqueline Adams became associate in education, with the mission of training the docents. Her strong leadership for ten years was influential in keeping the group together and providing study materials. The position of associate was later filled by Jim Lavilla-Havelin, a poet Clay describes as having a "wonderful eye and a feeling for art but coming from a literary background," as the Gallery continued its broad interpretation of the arts: "looking at works not simply from the point of view of art history," Clay says, "but also in relation to music, literature, and dance."

During the 1970s a strong Socratic orientation to art education was coming to the fore. The emphasis was on asking questions and encouraging museum visitors to respond directly to works of arts. Telling people what to think or how much you knew was downplayed. A mixed educational approach blending art history with educational theory, of inviting a response from visitors and then focusing on that response, continues today.

Beginning in 1974 volunteers in the Art Ambassadors program visited classrooms and rotated art exhibits in the schools. Other exhibitions organized by the Education Department in the 1970s included "Through the Looking Glass," "The Lines of Time," and "Man the Incomplete God." Circulating school exhibitions were concerned with print-making techniques, symbols in art, and Rochester painters.

Eric Bellmann of the Creative Workshop staff took demonstrations into the schools. Programs for the elderly were organized in conjunction with a city-wide program. A new docent-training program was initiated. National consultants conducted two- and three-week workshops. Part-time people were hired to write labels for the permanent collection.

"**O**ne plus one equals one," read the eye-catching headline.

In 1972 a royal portrait bust of an unknown Egyptian

king which had been in the collection for thirty years suddenly acquired an identity, a write-up in *Time* magazine, and the cast of a bottom two-thirds from which it had separated some 4,400 years ago.

The Gallery's involvement began in 1942 with the purchase of the eleven-inch portrait bust from the estate of Vladimir Gregorievitch Simkhovitch, professor of economic history at Columbia University. The Aswan-granite figure had been broken at the elbow with the right arm bent above the break line and holding a mace. Assumed to be from a larger statue, it had been found by Simkhovitch's expedition to the Temple of Amun at Karnak in 1922.

The scholarly sleuth who put the king back together again was Egyptologist Bernard V. Bothmer, curator of ancient art at the Brooklyn Museum, who had been "on this case," as he put it, for twenty years. While lecturing in Rochester in 1952, Bothmer stopped by the Gallery and "noticed in the small Egyptian collection the head and shoulders from a royal sculpture which appeared to date from the Old Kingdom. "At that time," Bothmer wrote in 1974, "I jotted down a summary description of the piece and, as had long been my habit, noted not only the customary measurements but the dimensions of the break as well." He also photographed the bust from all four sides and then forgot about it for eighteen years.

"As so often happens with one's notes, not much was done with them.... However, the sculpture's...remarkable similarity to the head of a complete statue of Ny-user-ra in Cairo was noted" in those 1952 notes. Several years later Bothmer saw another related royal bust on view in the Musée National at Beirut, and fifteen years after that, in 1970, he had the chance to study and measure it closely. Then a footnote in Vandier's *Manuel* beginning "Le Musée du Caire possède une seconde statue de Nioussere" caught Bothmer's eye, and soon he was rummaging through the vast uncataloged storerooms of the Cairo Museum.

The headless torso "representing the king, standing, in the position of marching" that Vandier and then Bothmer had uncovered languishing in Cairo had originally been found in 1904 by Legrain in the cave of Karnak. The chief historical value of the Cairo torso is a small cartouche on the base identifying Ny-user-ra, an obscure pharaoh who ruled circa 2370-2360 B.C. The Cairo base did not match the Beirut find; but then "a light clicked," and on the basis of the position of the arms Bothmer reasoned that it might fit the Rochester bust. Old notes, measurements, and photographs strengthened his surmise. He made a cast of the Cairo base to be shipped to Brooklyn, borrowed the Rochester original,

7

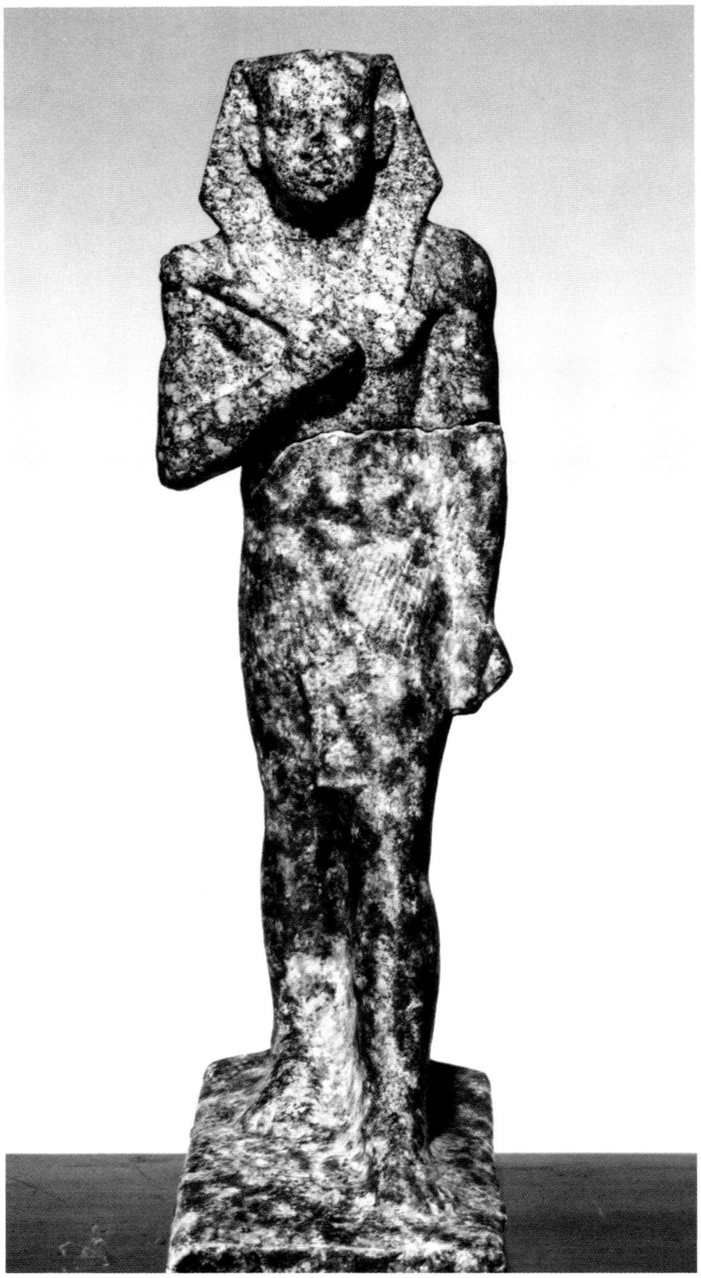

7 *Egyptian, Old Kingdom, Fifth Dynasty, Royal Portrait Bust of King Ny-user-ra, 2370-2360 B.C., granite, h. 11 in. R. T. Miller Fund, 42.54*
The bust is displayed on a plaster cast of the bottom part of the statue which is in the Cairo Museum. In Cairo, a plaster cast of the Gallery's upper section is displayed on the original bottom section.

then got on the phone to Prior and Isabel with the grand news: "It fits!"

The attempt to ship the plaster cast of the bust to Cairo was trickier, running afoul of complex Egyptian import regulations. Taking no chances, Bothmer packed the Ny-user-ra cast as "research material" and flew to Cairo where the two pieces were put together during a ceremony in the office of Dr. Henri Riad, director of the Museum of Egyptian Antiquities. Cairo's two halves remain on view with the label, written in French, English, and Arabic:

. . . Upper part: a copy from an original displayed in the MEMORIAL ART GALLERY, Rochester USA

Ny-user-ra himself may have been obscure, but obscure can mean rare and the sculpture is one of the few existing pieces that can be positively ascribed to the period in Egyptian history known as the Fifth Dynasty of the Old Kingdom. Kings wielding a mace with bulbous head, symbol of royal power, are common in Egyptian painting and relief, but, according to Bothmer, only two sculptures of the king carrying his mace are known, both in repose and both from the Old Kingdom. One is in Boston and the other is "the Rochester-Cairo statue of Ny-user-ra." The empty but clenched left fist is rare and puzzling too, Bothmer says.

Bothmer and Vandier both theorize that the red granite statue was made at Thebes, brought to Karnak, and separated in antiquity, tossed out of the Temple of Amun by priests on a housekeeping binge. Despite the priests' contempt and the unfinished ears, the carving on the face is fine, Bothmer says, with eyebrow and eyelids well-executed. "While the face of the [unbroken] seated statue [of Ny-user-ra] in Cairo has a brooding, almost sullen, expression, the Rochester king appears to be direct, forceful, and somewhat haughty."

"One plus one equals one," said Bothmer.

On 18 March 1975 Harris King Prior died at age sixty-four after a long and cruel illness. "He was a lovely person, a scholar, a diplomat, and a gentleman," said his friends, and they were legion. Six months earlier a special Prior Fund had been started to purchase a work in his honor. A week before his death an Arthur B. Davies exhibition in his honor opened at Knoedlers gallery in New York City. Like George Herdle before him, Prior worked to the limit of his strength to fulfill his unbounded aspirations for the Gallery.

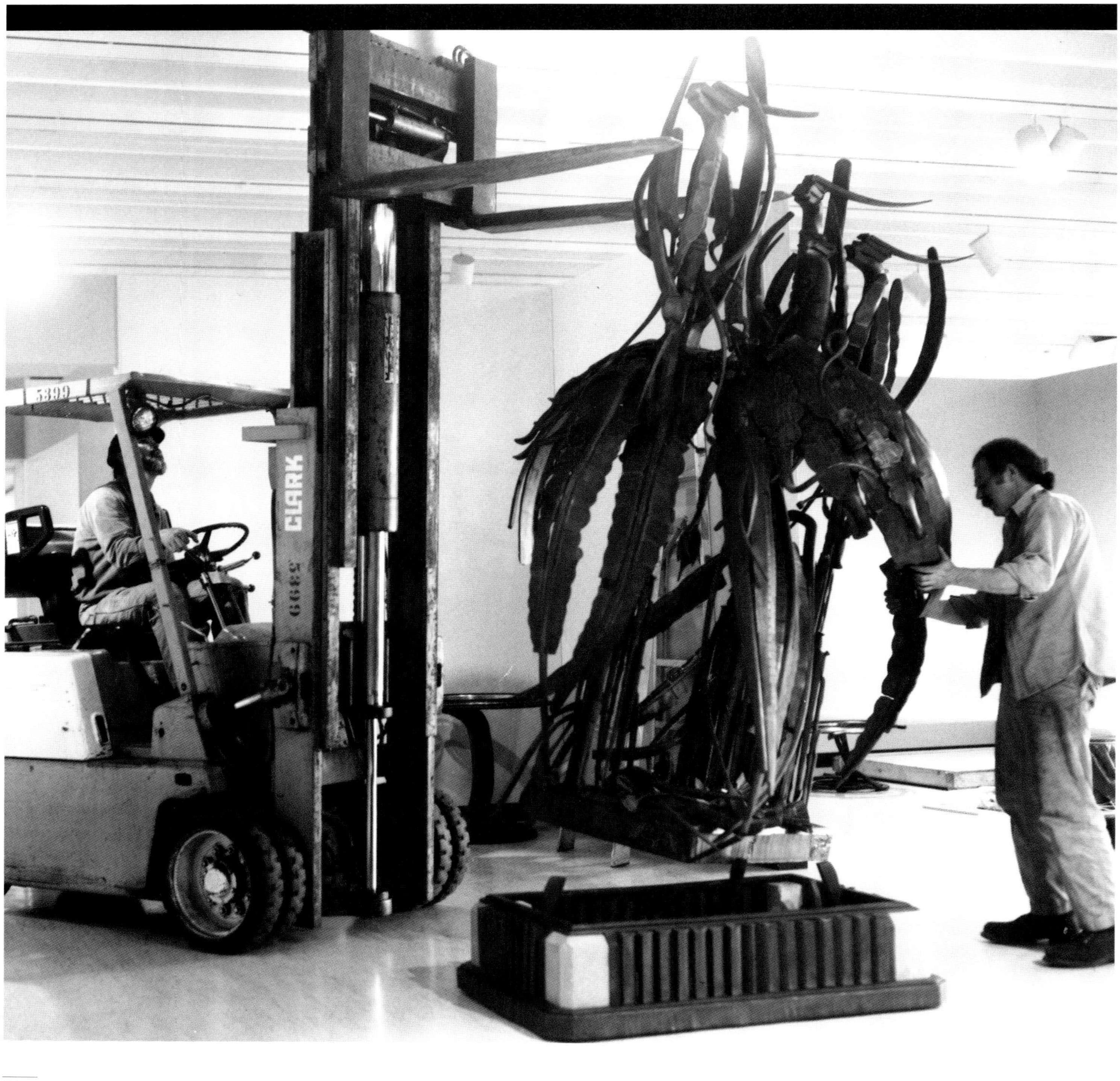
5399
CLARK
5399

12

> Small museums exist in part to give the visitor an index—vivid, if incomplete—to the modalities of feeling and behaving which art has preserved for our instruction; and the Rochester show does very well in this respect.

John Russell, "Three Cheers for Small Museums" *New York Times* | March 1977

Installation by Albert Paley of "Albert Paley: The Art of Metal," 1985.

1

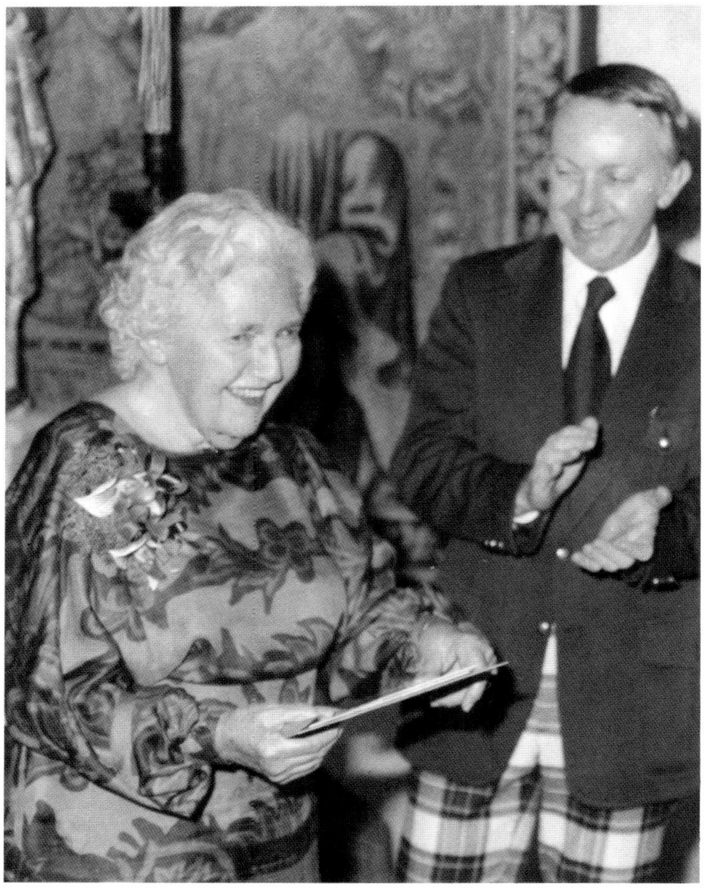

1 *Director John Mahey applauds Gertrude Herdle Moore on her eightieth birthday, 1976.*

2 *Bruce Chambers and Bret Waller at the opening of the "David Gilmore Blythe Exhibition," 1981.*

When Harris Prior was first taken ill, he announced his intention to retire in June 1976. While the Board of Managers searched for a successor, the day-to-day administration of the Gallery was conducted by George Angle, representing the university, and members of the Gallery staff—much like the old "troika" that operated during Prior's sabbatical.

Angle's role was "significantly less than most people realize," he says today. Three board members—Angle, Walter Strakosh, and William Maxion—functioned as inner executive committee; and of the three, Angle was the most available to meet with key staff members: Isabel Herdle, Langdon Clay, Robert Henning, Bernice Meyer, Bob Young, and Margaret Bond. After Prior's death the same procedure was followed.

Meanwhile the board named a Long Range Planning Committee and charged it to "develop plans for the optimum utilization of the resources of the Gallery—in the next five to ten years—for the benefit of the university and the community." From solicited opinions, including a random telephone survey of members, the committee found that, "in general, the Gallery and its programs are highly rated." That comforting appraisal did not keep the committee from recommending a plan for advancement.

Top priority was given to "the maintenance of the art collection, conservation, researching and cataloging the present holdings, and publications, including an up-to-date handbook." This would include "a complete slide and photographic record of the collection, deaccessioning inappropriate material, and investigation of ways to expand present facilities, including the feasibility of using Cutler Union." The committee recommended the use of more "minority docents" and other volunteers as well as "making the collection meaningful to an ever-increasing audience—children as well as adults."

The creation of two new positions was urged: a director of development "with responsibility for public relations, membership, deferred giving, governmental relations, and grant applications," and what was called an "exhibits technician" who would devise various strategies for "improving the interpretation of the collection to the public." So the recommendations went, pointing toward the Gallery of the future and indicating the inevitable physical expansion and capital campaign which would come with implementing them.

Plans for the future, however, would have to be put on hold until the search committee, headed by the university's Dean Kenneth Clark, combed a list of candidates for the directorship. It was not an easy task. Needed was someone who could handle the Gallery's particular situation as both university department and community art museum with a teaching collection spanning 5,000 years.

On 1 October 1975 John A. Mahey, director of the Cummer Gallery in Jacksonville, Florida, became only the fourth director of the Gallery in sixty-two years. Of the candidates interviewed, Mahey had been the most enthusiastic about the permanent collection and its potential. Although his tenure was to be only four and a half years, before increasing differences between board and director precipitated his departure, Mahey's lasting accomplishments grew out of the implementation of the long-range recommendations. Catalog production and conservation efforts were stepped up. An "exhibits technician" was hired. The Development Department and Director's Circle were established, the latter consisting of patrons who gave $1,000 or more each year to the Gallery's annual campaign. Beginning with nine members and chaired by Mr. and Mrs. Thomas Hawks, the Director's Circle continues to grow; 107 members in 1988 make it one of the Gallery's most significant sources of financial support.

The kind of loyalty the Gallery attracts is exemplified by the contribution of Jacqueline Adams, associate in education, who took the accumulation of four years of her part-time salary to purchase for the Gallery Martin Johnson Heade's *Newbury Hayfield at Sunset* in memory of her parents. The luminist painter Heade, who wandered the world in search of unusual effects of light and color, is thus represented in the collection by examples from two phases of his peripatetic career—the minute renderings of exotic floral forms (orchids) and the luminist interpretations of distant objects (haystacks) transfixed in a still, cloudless day.

With the Margaret Woodbury Strong Museum not yet open, the Gallery played host to several elaborate exhibitions drawn from that gargantuan collection. "Oriental Art from Area Collections" and a group of portraits marking the one hundred twenty-fifth anniversary of the University of Rochester were other exhibitions. The university portraits included one of Azariah Boody, whose cows had grazed where the Gallery now stood; Susan B. Anthony, who pledged her life insurance to assure the admission of women to the university in 1900; Martin B. Anderson, as painted by Eastman Johnson; and United States Senator Kenneth B. Keating.

The nation's Bicentennial was observed by "The Genesee Country," an exhibition of nineteenth century landscape paintings of regional subjects, with catalog by Howard Merritt. The major acquisition of 1976 was the formal acceptance and exhibition of the Charles Rand Penney Collection.

2

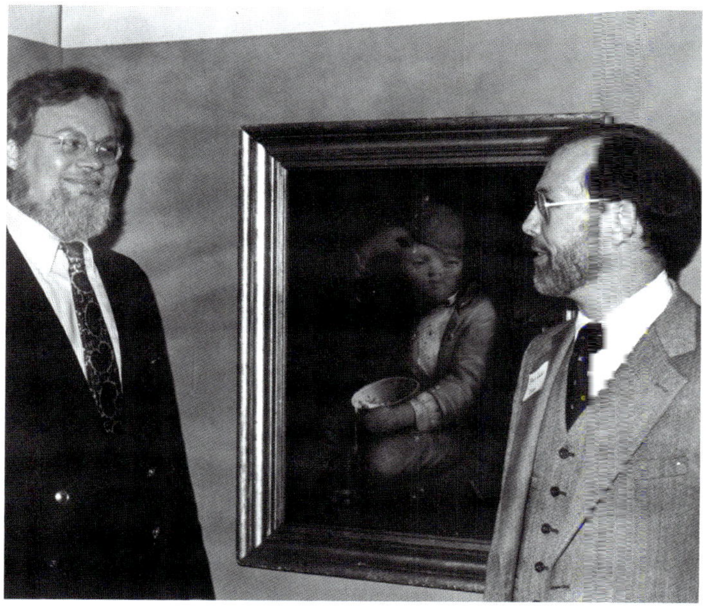

Other acquisitions included Wayne Thiebaud's *River Pond*, purchased through the Wilson Memorial Fund (and since used as the basis of a "walk-in" painting in the 1987 children's room); a decorated Oceanic dugout war canoe; and *Portrait of a Boy of the Bracciforti Family*, by Niccolò dell'Abate. This rare and important sixteenth century Italian painting by the Modenese artist credited with introducing Mannerist landscape painting to France was, in 1976, one of only two dell'Abate paintings in this country, and the only portrait. Martin Johnson Heade's *Hummingbird with Cattleya and Dendrobium Orchids* was acquired by the Prior Memorial Fund; a Harris K. Prior Memorial Exhibition was mounted featuring works acquired during his directorship.

For years the Gallery had drawn only the actual income from its acquisition funds even though the university had long before begun harvesting part of its own appreciation. This was done by taking 5 percent of the five-year moving average of the total value of the endowment. John Mahey proposed that the Gallery adopt the university's policy, thus increasing the funds available annually from the Gould Fund alone from about $35,000 to about $100,000. Coinciding with the art committee's determination to acquire fewer, more important works was Mahey's desire to purchase a Mannerist painting for the collection. Of three paintings considered, the director and committee decided to take the plunge and expend the year's proceeds on the elegant and sensitive dell'Abate portrait, a decision that continues to look good a dozen years later. The painting was included in an

3

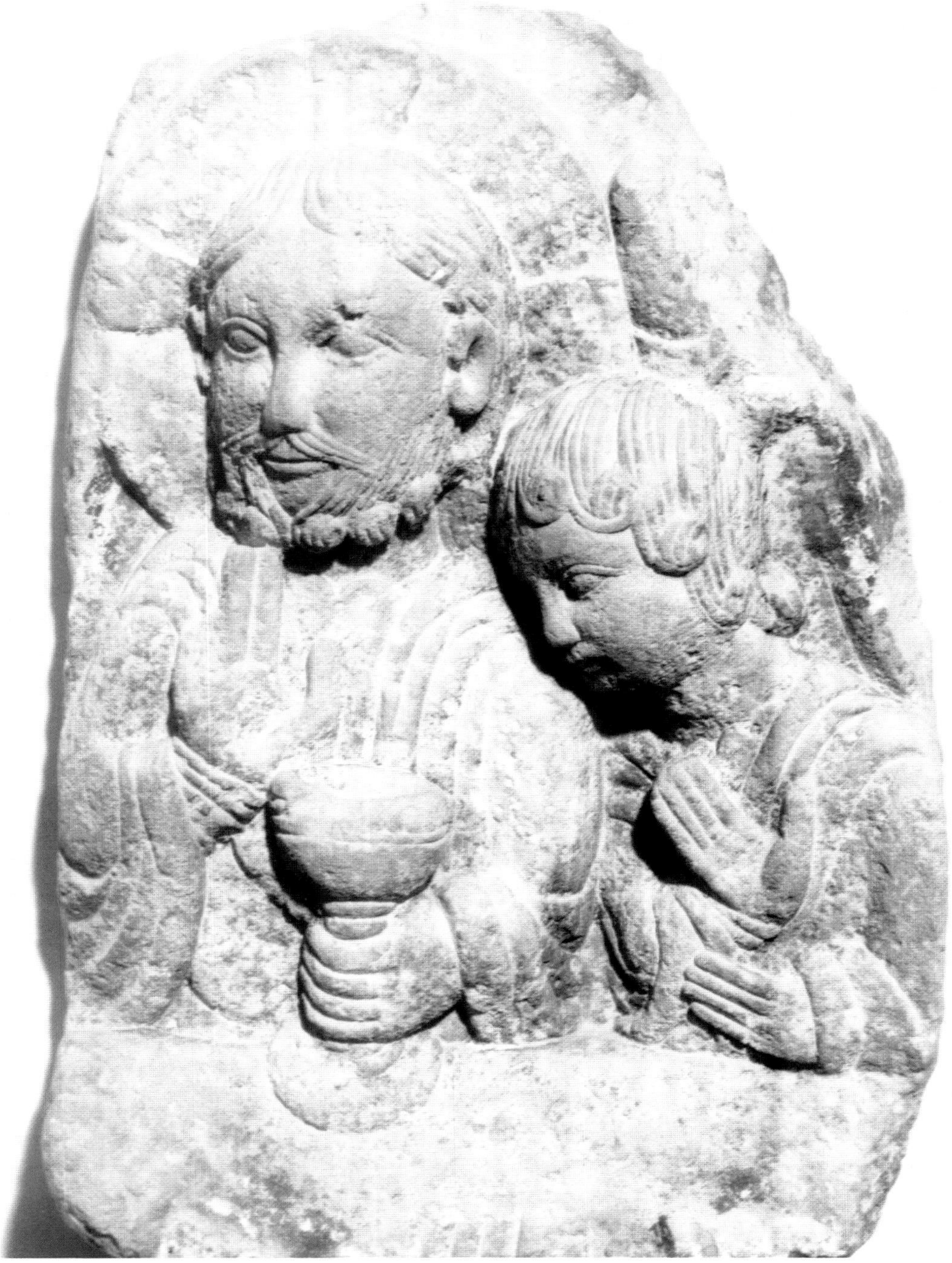

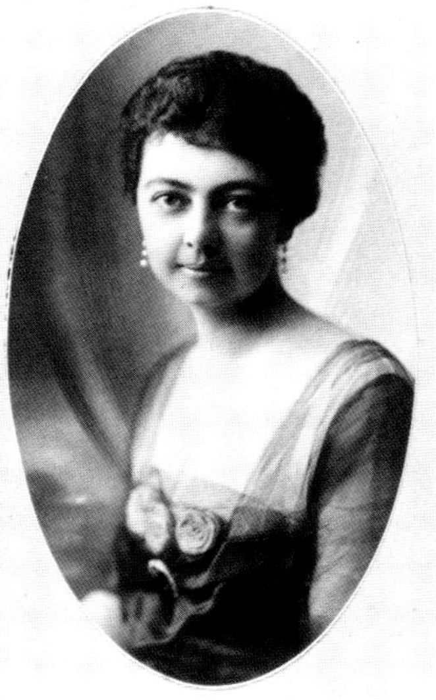

3 *Spanish Catalonia, possibly Cathedral of Vich, ca. 1140-1170, Christ and St. John, limestone fragment, h. 11⅜ in. Marie Adelaide Devine Fund, 84.41*

Marie Adelaide Devine, 1917. Photograph by J. Ernest Mock, courtesy of the University of Rochester Library.

exhibition, "The Age of Carreggio and the Carracci," in 1986-1987, in Bologna and Washington, D. C.

Milestones of 1976 within the Gallery family included an eightieth birthday party for director emeritus Gertrude Herdle Moore. Bruce Chambers was named assistant director for curatorial services in place of the departing Robert Henning. Hildegarde Watson died at age eighty-eight. Her husband, Sibley Watson, presented Gaston Lachaise's small bronze sculpture of *Hildegarde Lasell Watson* to the Gallery in her memory.

Marie Adelaide Devine, once the girlish model for Maud Humphrey's portraits of children in the early part of the century, died too; a bequest of $100,000 for acquisitions in medieval art came from this nonagenarian's estate. The first purchase from the interest, and the first in medieval sculpture in many years, was made in 1984: a limestone relief fragment, a detail from a Last Supper of *Christ and St. John*. The Catalonian sculpture, possibly from the portal of the Cathedral of Vich, was a fine addition to the Gallery's already choice collection of Romanesque sculpture.

The Devine family had long been friends of the Gallery. Charlotte Dodge (Mrs. Adrian) Devine (sister-in-law to Marie Adelaide Devine) gave money to replace subjects needed in the art library when two-thirds of the books were removed to the River Campus. *Madonna and Child Enthroned with Saints and Angels*, an Italian tempera on panel, was the 1927 gift of Mrs. Charles Wright Dodge and her daughter Mrs. Adrian Devine in memory of Miss Bertha Hooker, Mrs. Dodge's sister. Another member of the Hooker family, Elon Huntington Hooker, was a key figure in the negotiations for the presentation of Audubon's *Portrait of Nathaniel Rochester*. Charles Wright Dodge, University of Rochester professor of biology, was an early board member and a close friend of George Herdle.

Since its acquisition in 1927 the early Italian tempera panel given by Mesdames Dodge and Devine was thought to be a minor example of the Florentine School. But, in a *Porticus* article of 1979 Bonnie Apgar Bennett, of the fine arts department at the university, suggested that the panel might be more than that, indeed "one of the relatively rare pieces of Riminese art in American collections."

Thirty-six diverse exhibitions made up the 1977 calendar beginning with Tunisian Mosaics in January. In March of that year "Treasures from Rochester," comprising outstanding works from the collection, traveled to New York City to be on display at the Wildenstein Galleries. There it was reviewed by *New York Times* critic John Russell, who praised the selection in an article "Three Cheers for Small Museums," from which this chapter's epigraph is taken. The show was visited and revisited by John Pope-Hennessy, the famous art scholar, who pronounced Tintoretto's *Portrait of a Venetian Gentleman* and the Van Dyke *Portrait of an Italian Gentleman* "splendid."

Among the year's acquisitions was a watercolor by Vasily Kandinsky and a painting by Francesco Solimena, *Judith with the Head of Holofernes*, the gift of Dr. and Mrs. James V. Aquavella, longtime supporters (and Dr. Aquavella served for many years on the board and is currently an honorary member) of the Gallery. Other works the Aquavellas have given the Gallery include the terra-cotta sculpture *Bacchante and Satyres* by Claude Michel, called Clodion, and the animated painting of Aesop's *Fable of the Fox and the Stork* by Frans Snyders (or his studio) which remains a favorite of docents and schoolchildren.

Attendance for 1977 stood at 188,889; membership hovered around 7,000; and 600 volunteers worked on the membership campaign—typical figures for the late 1970s.

One of the Gallery's "fairy godfathers," as Gallery Notes sometimes called those anonymous donors, lenders, and exhibitors who over many years have provided treasures, opened 1978 by presenting etchings by Rembrandt and Van Gogh, a woodcut by Gauguin, and a drawing by Albert Pinkham Ryder.

Four American folk art paintings of the Lacey family, who lived at what is now 9 Scottsville-Chili Road in the 1830s, were first the loan, in 1976, and then the gift, in 1978, of Mr. and Mrs. Robert Dunn of Pittsford. Three of the paintings are attributed to the remarkable itinerant Noah North (1809-1880), who makes up in charm and forcefulness what he may lack in the mastery of anatomy and perspective. North's poignant *Eliza Pixley Lacey* (she died as a child) joined her festooned but apparently shoulderless mother, *Ann Gennett Pixley Lacey*, and conventional father, *Allen Tobias Lacey*, whose portrait is not by North. The stand out of the family group is *Pierrepont Edward Lacey and His Dog Gun*. Now reproduced as a widely distributed postcard, the massive and unforgettable Gun and his enchanting master Pierrepont adorn sales racks from New York to Florence.

A generous bequest of $300,000 by Clara Strasenburgh established a new fund for acquisitions in 1978. Works came too from the estates of longtime board members Charlotte Whitney Allen and Thomas G. Spencer.

The bequest of Charlotte Whitney Allen, board member since 1916, included twenty-five works of art—

paintings by Dufy and Matisse, drawings by Beerbohm and Maillol, prints by Audubon and Bellows, sculpture by Lachaise and Calder, as well as a cash gift. She had earlier deeded her home to the university but retained lifetime possession of the collection and use of the Oliver Street property. No written stipulation was made as to the disposition of the house, although a tacit understanding existed that it would be used as the director's residence. After several months of deliberation and investigation, the Board of Managers made the difficult decision to sell the house and garden with restrictive covenants. The decision, highly unpopular among some of Allen's many friends, was based upon the perception that the high cost of maintenance would require an annual subsidy from the Gallery's operating budget, a subsidy that could not legally or ethically come from membership, government, or university funds. Emotionally charged and divisive as the atmosphere was then, in retrospect the decision appears to have been the right one for the Gallery. It illustrates too, the perils of museum-running. Even a generous gift can be troublesome in its implications.

Thomas Spencer had also been a life member of the board. His bequest was principally in Early American and European furniture, plus glass and porcelain including a spectacular Dutch marquetry secretary.

Susan Schilling "retired" in 1978 and almost immediately returned as research curator emeritus and editor of the Gallery's new scholarly journal *Porticus*. This first issue was underwritten by Dr. and Mrs. James Sibley Watson Jr.

Funding for a Development Office having been obtained, Christine D. Hyer joined the staff as development officer. The office incorporated both Membership and Public Relations. The Webber Report of a board committee grew out of earlier recommendations to study ways of increasing both space and endowment. It initiated a complete feasibility study of the Gallery's future use of Cutler Union and planning for a capital campaign.

One bizarre incident occurred on 9 April 1978 while Bruce Chambers, assistant director for curatorial services, was delivering a lecture about Charles Burchfield to a packed auditorium. Director John Mahey was in the audience as were several hundred other people. Meanwhile, a few feet away on the other side of the auditorium wall, someone was yanking *Flowers in a Blue Vase* by Pablo Picasso from its place and darting out of a side door. The alarm on that door facing Cutler Union was often tripped accidentally, and on this busy, crowded Sunday afternoon the guard on duty reported it as such; consequently, no one missed the Picasso watercolor until Tuesday when the Gallery reopened. Amazingly, three weeks after the heist, following a bungled ransom attempt and with the aid of television personality Wyoma Best, the Picasso was firmly back on Gallery walls. This strange theft, only the second in Gallery history, produced tons of publicity and a beefing-up of security methods.

Upon being informed that the Picasso watercolor Emily Watson had given the Gallery in 1931 was missing, Sibley Watson, who had seen the work so many years earlier on the walls of Henry Reinhardt & Son, New York, said philosophically and enigmatically: "Ah well, I told Mother she should have bought the Picasso hanging next to it."

The only other art theft involving the Gallery also has an element of comedy. In 1927 an exhibition of Buddhist mandalas from the Rurick Museum in New York resulted in the mysterious disappearance of a locally owned Tibetan banner that had been borrowed by the Gallery to add to the show. Twenty years passed before a Rochester plainclothesman (by the name of "Huzzy"—right out of Agatha Christie) appeared on Gertrude's doorstep to lead her to the lair of a recently arrested local fence. There, hanging in the thief's small bedroom, was the missing mandala. As a boy, he had lifted the banner while leaving one of Gertrude's talks to a vocational school group. He had later pursued a career as a professional criminal, and an apparently successful one at that—he appeared in court wearing a loudly checked but very expensive suit and a pair of natty spats. Through the years his living quarters had been the conduit of many a burgled item, but he had treasured and held on to the mandala.

Following the resignation of John Mahey on 9 March 1979, Bruce Chambers was named Acting Director. Joining the staff that year were Donald Rosenthal, curator; Mark Donovan, exhibits coordinator; and Mary Ann Monley, docent tour coordinator.

Donovan's appointment signalled a response to the Long Range Planning Committee's report of 1975; the arrival of a whole new museum profession of exhibit design; and the recognition of the impact good design, installation, lighting, color, labeling, and traffic flow have on both the viewer's reaction to a single work of art and his comprehension of a didactic exhibition. Almost immediately Donovan began transforming the Gallery. The reinstallation of the Asian and Classical galleries were his designs as are the installations of the 1987 renovation and addition. In 1988 Donovan is associate director for administration and

4

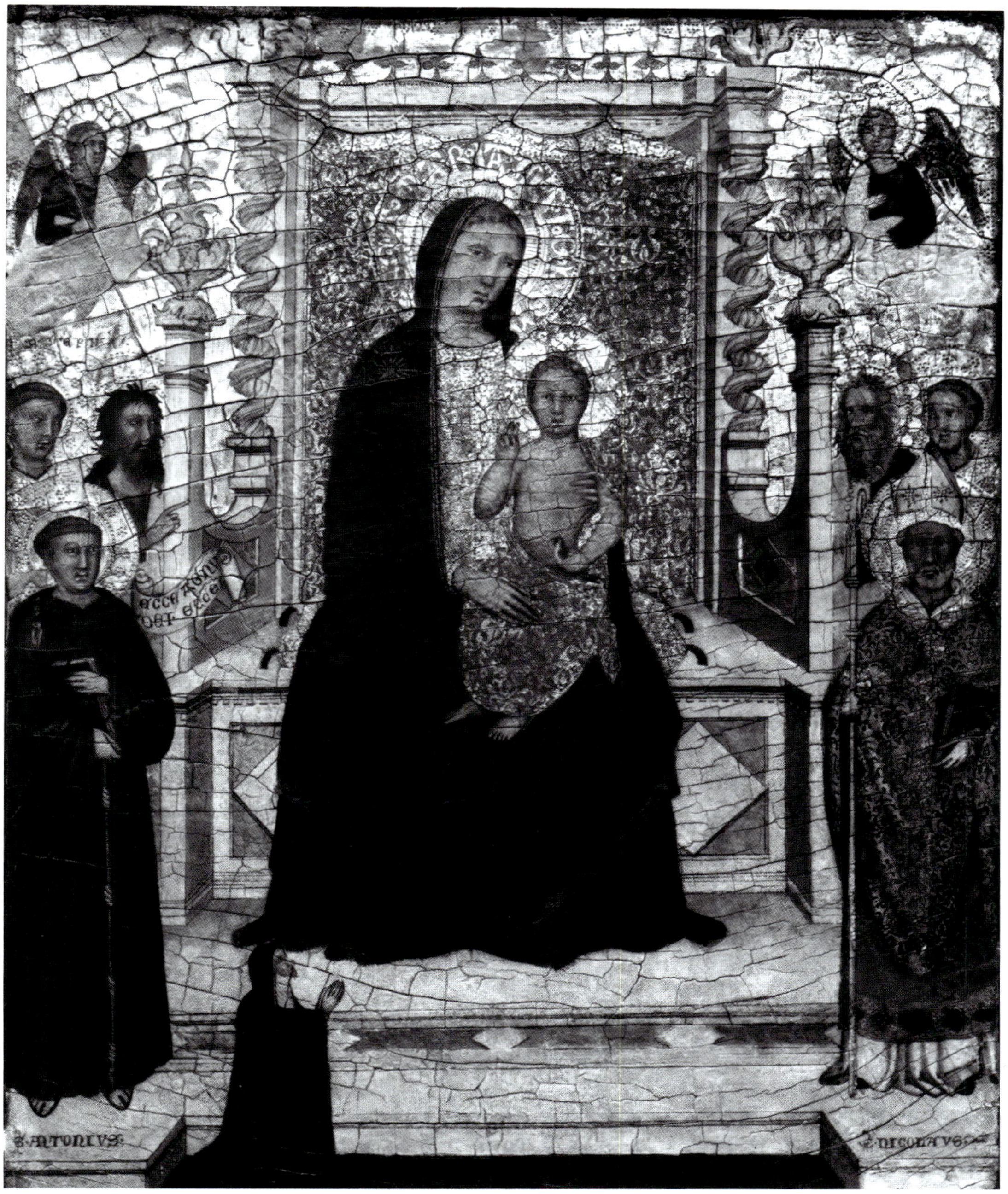

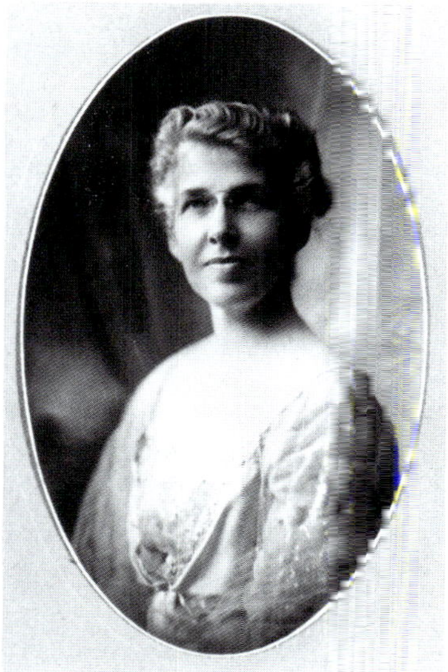

4 *Italian Riminese, fourteenth century, Madonna and Child Enthroned with Saints and Angels, tempera on panel, 18 x 15 in. Gift of Mrs. Charles Wright Dodge and Mrs. Adrian Devine in memory of Bertha Hooker, 27.1*

Mrs. Charles Wright Dodge, 1917. Photograph by J. Ernest Mock, courtesy of the University of Rochester Library.

5

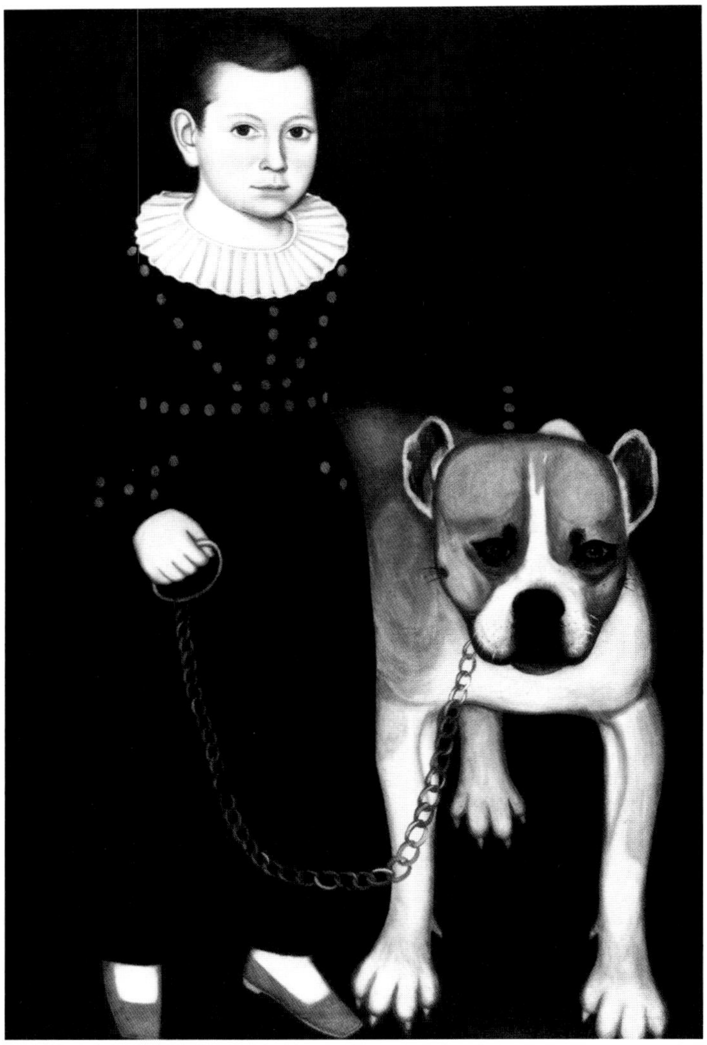

5 *Attributed to Noah North (American, 1809-1880), Pierrepont Edward Lacey and His Dog Gun, Gift of Mr. and Mrs. Robert H. Dunn, 78.189*

6 *Alexander Calder (American, 1898-1976) Untitled Mobile, 1935, iron and steel, painted, 105½ x 72 x 41 in. (irregular), Gift of Charlotte Whitney Allen 64.27*

7 *Charlotte Whitney Allen, 1917. Photograph by J. Ernest Mock, courtesy of the University of Rochester*

art services.

Long before a temporary exhibition arrives, Donovan works up possible floor plans or three-dimensional models of the layout of panels, cases, platforms, and so forth. A soft-sculpture finger pointing the way, careful placement of labels, low walls that beckon the viewers along the correct path without obscuring the art works—all comprise Donovan's low-key approach to directing traffic. "Lighting and color are two of the most significant and least expensive ways to change the appearance and feel of an exhibition," Donovan says. After he had been on staff for two years, he calculated—on the basis that a gallon of paint weighs ten pounds—that the exhibition staff had repainted the Gallery fifteen times, often with two coats, thereby adding 3,000 pounds to the structure.

A Dutch panel painting by the Mannerist Martin van Heemskerk was given in 1979 by James O. Belden of Washington, D.C. and a University of Rochester graduate. Pre-Columbian sculptures came from the collection of the late Harris Prior, the gift of his widow. A Goya drawing arrived from the anonymous donor who had been enriching the collection with old master drawings for twenty years.

An active and varied schedule began with an exhibition of fifty sculptures and drawings by Gaston Lachaise, pioneer American modernist, centering on works in Rochester collections (including, of course, the Gallery's). The Grand Gallery was cleared of its movable walls, thus affording unimpeded views of the sculpture and demonstrating the versatility of exhibit design in this space. A later show, "Uncommon Visions," featured thirty contemporary artists working with representational yet unconventional images; guest curator was Jacqueline Schuman, Gallery board member, working with Chambers. "Arshile Gorky's Aviation Murals for the Newark Airport," lost from view some forty years and then recovered from beneath fourteen layers of paint, spent the summer in Rochester.

"Paley/Castle/Wildenhain" was a major exhibition of the creative innovations of three distinguished, internationally known, and Rochester-based artists: the sculptural metal of Albert Paley, wood and plastics by Wendell Castle, and the ceramics of former Bauhaus instructor Frans Wildenhain.

Three Collector's Corner exhibitions (the revival of an old Women's Council favorite) showcased Art Nouveau, Art Deco objects, and old silver from local private collections. "The Lines of Time" was a joint production of the Education and Curatorial Departments. New events included a young people's art tour and an evening devoted to comic strip art.

Two means of recognizing a longtime benefactor were initiated. The Charlotte Whitney Allen Lecture Series features internationally known scholars, while the Charlotte Whitney Allen Library was designated to honor, as *Gallery Notes* put it, "a wealthy woman who ran a bookstore in the basement of the Rochester Historical Society, chaired the Library Committee of the Board of Managers for many years, and was instrumental in the purchase of books, a lifelong love, for that library."

As 1979 ended, the Eastman Kodak Company kicked off its one hundredth anniversary year by sponsoring an exhibition of "The George Eastman Collection": fifty-five paintings, drawings, and prints from the former board member's personal collection, the bulk of which became the property of the university in 1932. The exhibition represented the first time Eastman's collection had been shown together since it had hung in his mansion; the catalog contained essays by Elizabeth Brayer and Donald Rosenthal. The Eastman exhibition opening and Holiday Open House were complemented by seventy-eight créches found and treasured by board member Earl Kage on his travels throughout the western world.

6

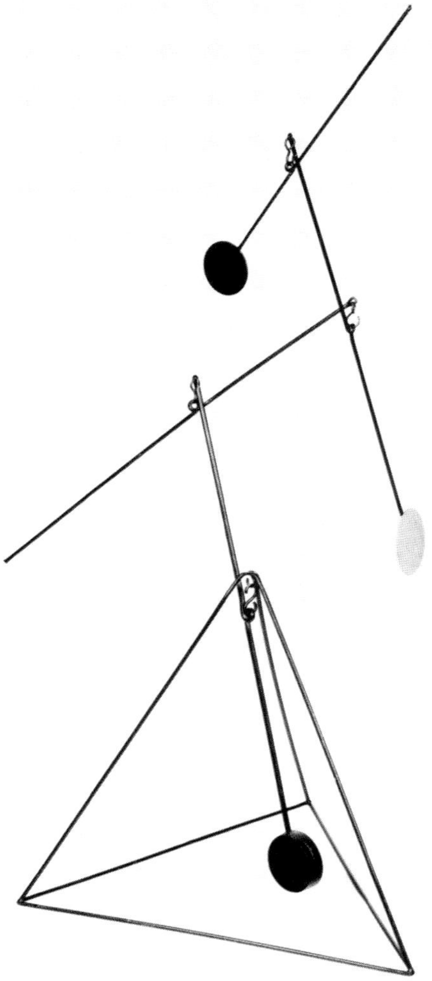

On 31 January 1980 the Board of Managers confirmed the appointment of A. Bret Waller, director of the Michigan Museum of Art, as director of the Memorial Art Gallery. Waller assumed the position on 1 July.

The fall season opened with "African Furniture," the first major show of everyday sub-Saharan household objects—traps, games, headrests, farm and cooking implements. Programming took the form of family craft workshops and demonstrations, films, African dance performances, poetry readings, jazz concerts, and the Charlotte Whitney Allen Lecture Series.

7

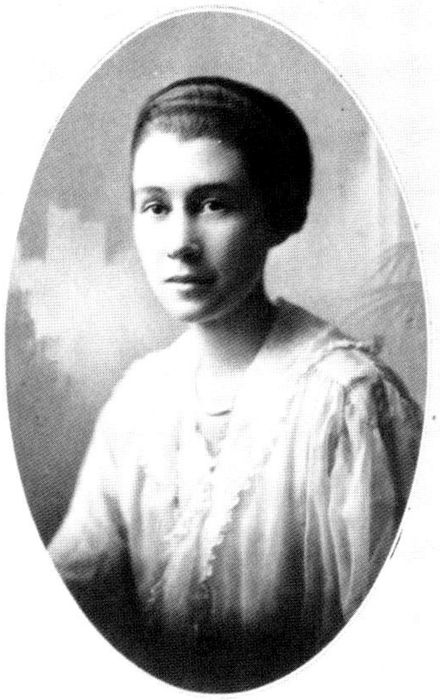

"Through the Looking Glass," an exhibition of selected works from the permanent collection assembled by the Education Department in a conceptual rather than chronological manner, led to a collaborative effort between the Gallery and GeVa Theatre called "Looking Glass Fantasy." This multi-arts production was billed as "a smorgasbord of visual and verbal delights."

Alice Zissler retired in 1980 after twelve years as manager of the Gallery Shop, and Nancy Kelly assumed the management of the combined shop and Lending and Sales Gallery, now known as the Gallery Store. Ninety-four objects were added to the permanent collection—seventy-three through gifts and bequests, twenty-one by purchase—making 1980 an average year. Paintings by Eilshiemus,

Raphael Soyer, and Robert Vickrey (the last the gift of Earl Kage) led the list. There were 1,044 patron members of the Gallery, and 266 corporate members, both all-time highs. The Holiday Open House brought out 1,100 Gallery members.

September 1981 marked the twenty-fifth anniversary of the Clothesline Show, which had grown from 101 exhibitors and sales of $3,000 in 1957 to 600 exhibitors, 45,000 visitors, and $160,000 in sales in 1981. The Board of Managers approved in principle the use of Cutler Union for an expansion of office, work, and storage space. Handler/Grosso P.C., an architectural and engineering firm, whose specialty was the adaptive reuse of existing buildings, was hired to make detailed studies of the proposed changes.

"The World of David Gilmour Blythe," curated by former staff member Bruce Chambers, opened the 1981 exhibition calendar. In April the Print Club of Rochester, whose formation and growth had been nurtured and fostered by the Gallery, celebrated its fiftieth year with a show. "Venetian Drawings from the Robert Lehman Collection of the Metropolitan Museum" occasioned a "Family Celebration of Italian Art and Culture," organized by the Education Department. The summer show was entitled "Modern Art in Rochester" and was drawn from the Gallery's collection of 600-plus works from 1945 to the present, augmented by loans from private collections. More than 65 percent of the Gallery's contemporary collection, excluding prints, had been acquired as gifts.

"Summer '81" consisted of eight large metal sculptures—sprawled, suspended, or stretched every which way across Gallery grounds. They were from the Interpace Corporation collection.

A major exhibition, "The Fine Art of Furniture Making," showed selections of furniture from the past, culled from the storerooms of the Metropolitan Museum by Wendell Castle, who originated the idea and curated the show. The catalog was written by Penelope Hunter Striebel, associate curator of twentieth century art at the Metropolitan.

Staff changes included the retirement of Bernice Meyer, administrative officer, after seventeen years with the Gallery. She was succeeded by Edmund Pease of New York. Stanley G. Brew died. He had been superintendent since 1978 and assistant to Bob Young since 1966.

New acquisitions included *The Trinity*, by the eighteenth century painter Corrado Giaquinto, and an untitled David Smith drawing of the Gallery sculpture *Big Diamond*.

8

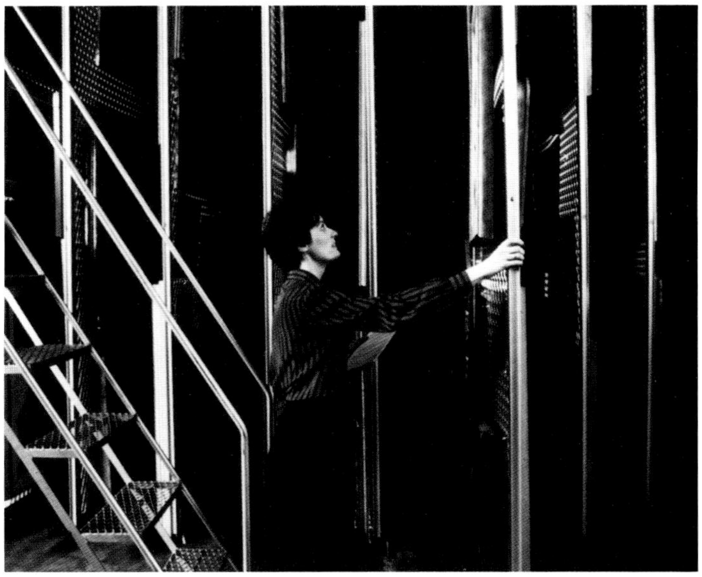

9

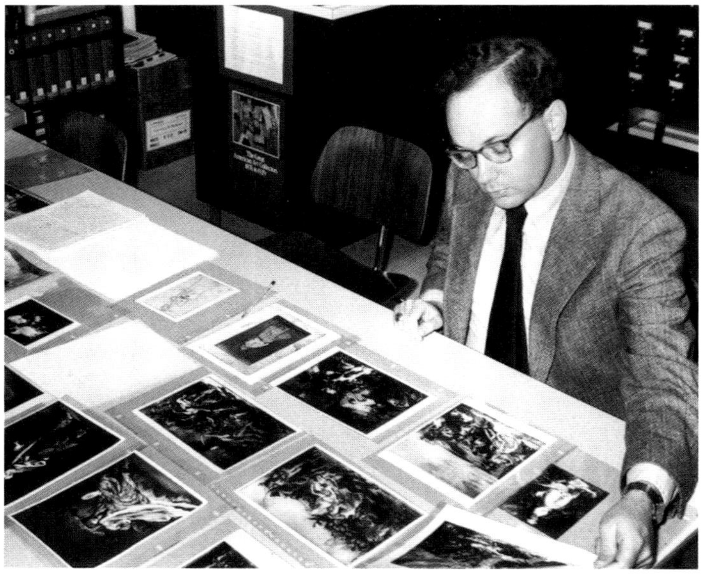

"Traditional Crafts of Saudi Arabia," the first such comprehensive exhibition in the United States, was organized by the Gallery and featured 200 examples drawn from the holdings of area resident John M. Topham. It toured under the auspices of the Smithsonian Institute Traveling Exhibition Service (SITES). "Golden Day, Silver Night: Perceptions of Nature in American Art, 1850-1910" was the third in the continuing series of collaborative exhibitions sponsored by six upstate museums.

The major exhibition of 1982 was "Orientalism: The Near East in French Painting 1800-1880." As the most comprehensive exhibition of its type ever mounted in this country, it included seventy-five works from American and Canadian collections and several French museums, among them the Louvre. Donald Rosenthal, chief curator, organized the show and wrote the 184-page catalog which included 143 black-and-white photographs and six in color, the most ambitious catalog in Gallery history. The Allen Lecture Series explored the subject further.

Among the year's statistics, the annual campaign exceeded its $550,000 goal, 1,535 adults and children were enrolled in the Creative Workshop, 66 objects from the collection were on loan to other museums or exhibitions, nearly 1,000 volunteers participated in the 265 special events during the year, and 155 works of art were acquired, 137 as gifts, 18 by purchase. Among major acquisitions was Francesco Guardi's *San Georgio Maggiore, Venice*, the first purchase through the Clara and Edwin Strasenburgh Fund. 1982 also saw Patricia Anderson (Junker) joining the curatorial staff.

The year was also marked by the death of Dr. James Sibley Watson Jr. at the age of eighty-eight. His credit line, "Gift of a Friend of the Gallery," may still be seen on the more than 150 works of art he gave over a period of sixty years. His affectionate support of the docent corps was well established. Director Waller noted that while Sibley Watson "did not always agree with the actions of the Board of Managers of which he was an honorary life member, his loyalty, visits, and contributions never wavered."

With the capital campaign under way under the chairmanship of William B. Webber, architects Handler/Grosso designed an attractive new link, which allowed the Gallery to expand its offices into Cutler Union and put the entrance once again on University Avenue. The addition, plus renovation of existing space, "will allow the Gallery to exhibit the twentieth century painting and sculpture collection once again, to unify the location of the Gallery Store, to provide limited food services, and put an exciting new face toward the community," said Peter Brown, president of the Board of Managers.

A rare early Russian icon from the fourteenth century School of Novgorod, acquired from the estate of Fletcher Steele, was given to the Gallery in 1983 by university professor of English George Ford and his wife Patricia.

The Women's Council established a Creative Workshop scholarship in honor of its retiring director, Dorothy Glaser. Janet Otis, secretary to the directors, and then archivist, retired after twenty-nine years with the Gallery. Margaret Bennett, membership manager, retired after eighteen years. For the Gallery's seventieth anniversary in 1983, the Fountain Court was rededicated in honor of the Herdle family.

In January 1984 "Artists of *La Revue Blanche*" opened,

10

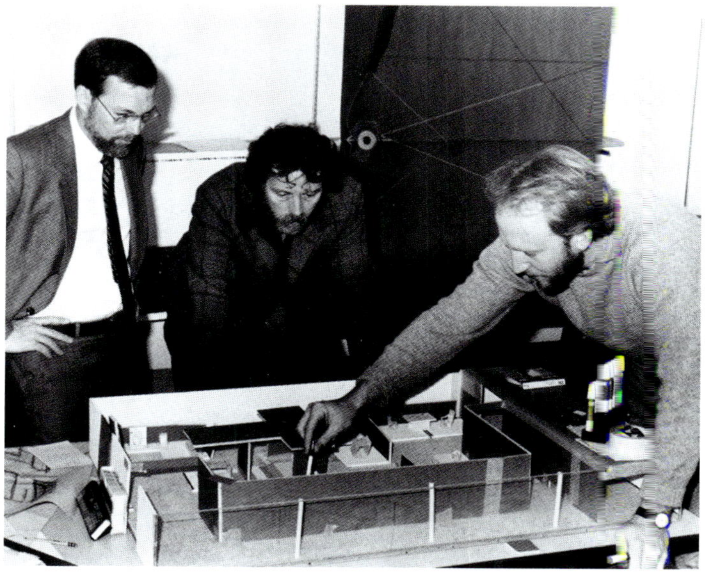

8 *Curator Patricia Anderson Junker examines works in storage.*

9 *Curator Donald Rosenthal prepares the Gallery's 1982 exhibition, "Orientalism, The Near East in French Painting 1800-1880."*

10 *Bret Waller, director, Wendell Castle, artist and guest curator, and Mark Donovan, exhibits coordinator, study a model layout of the "Art of Furniture" exhibition, 1981.*

organized by director Waller. Shown were more than 100 works created by Bonnard, Toulouse-Lautrec, Vallotton, and Vuillard during their involvement with the journal *La Revue Blanche* in the 1890s. Waller and Grace Seiberling, associate professor of fine arts at the university, wrote the catalog. Accompanying this major exhibition were samplings of the era's fashions from the Metropolitan Museum's Costume Institute, sponsored, along with an in-house café, by the Women's Council.

"The Course of Empire: The Erie Canal and the New York Landscape, 1825-1875," honored Rochester's sesquicentennial. Catalog and exhibition by Patricia Anderson (Junker) surveyed depictions of the upstate landscape "from the time the canal first traversed what was considered the savage, sublime wilderness until it imposed itself upon and consumed that wilderness, producing canal towns that seemingly cropped up overnight."

That season too an exhibition of drawings, architectural artifacts, and furniture by "Claude Bragdon: A Pre-Modern Architect" was organized by Jean France. A retrospective of the work of the late Frans Wildenhain was also shown.

William B. Webber, chairman of the Capital Gifts Committee, announced that a quiet effort to raise initial leadership gifts had resulted in pledges of $3.5 million. Negotiations among the leaders of the Gallery, the university, and the Eastman School resulted in the university's offer to make the second and third floors of Cutler Union available to the Gallery for offices and library without charge. In addition the university pledged $450,000 toward the capital campaign.

In December 1984, director Bret Waller accepted a position at the J. Paul Getty Museum in Malibu, California.

Also in December of that year the Gallery's ever-generous anonymous donor presented a Winslow Homer watercolor. *Paddling at Dusk*, painted in 1892 during one of Homer's thirty years of summers in the Adirondacks, further developed the Gallery's small but splendid Homer collection.

Economy of form and material is the Homer signature in both Gallery works. In *Paddling at Dusk* the major masses of water and landscape at twilight are indicated by broad brush strokes. The horizon is summarily scratched through the paint to the white paper, and above that, a single puddle of green suggests that the canoer is paddling across a lake into a distant woods rather than across an ocean. Waves and wake are negative forms left as white paper, and the crisp flashing paddle is intensified by a halo of opaque white pigment. When Homer had finished his painting from the banks of Mink Pond, he signed it (29 August 1892), and presented it to the man in the canoe—this time out of friendship (not barter, as with *Artist's Studio*).

Except for a 1959 exhibit in the Adirondack Museum in Blue Mountain Lake, New York, *Paddling at Dusk* has not been widely exhibited or published. It passed quietly from J. Ernest G. Yalden (the man in the canoe) to the Gallery's anonymous collector in the late 1930s.

Artist's Studio in an Afternoon Fog, painted in 1894, two years after the watercolor, and acquired in 1957, is also closely bound by subject matter to Homer's life. In 1884 at age forty-eight, Homer retired to Prout's Neck; in 1910 he died in his "Artist's Studio." Both of the Gallery's Homer works are impressionistic—gray, tonal works in which suppression of detail causes landscape features to merge into broad, extended planes. In addition to these outstanding watercolor and oil paintings, the Gallery owns three rare etchings by Homer—*Mending the Nets* (1888), *Perils of the Sea* (1888), and *Eight Bells* (1887)—each after paintings of the same titles.

As 1985 dawned, the Gallery stood poised for the future. The search for a new director was proceeding, as were the architectural plans for expansion into Cutler Union by means of a connecting link that would also turn the Gallery's face once more toward the community.

11

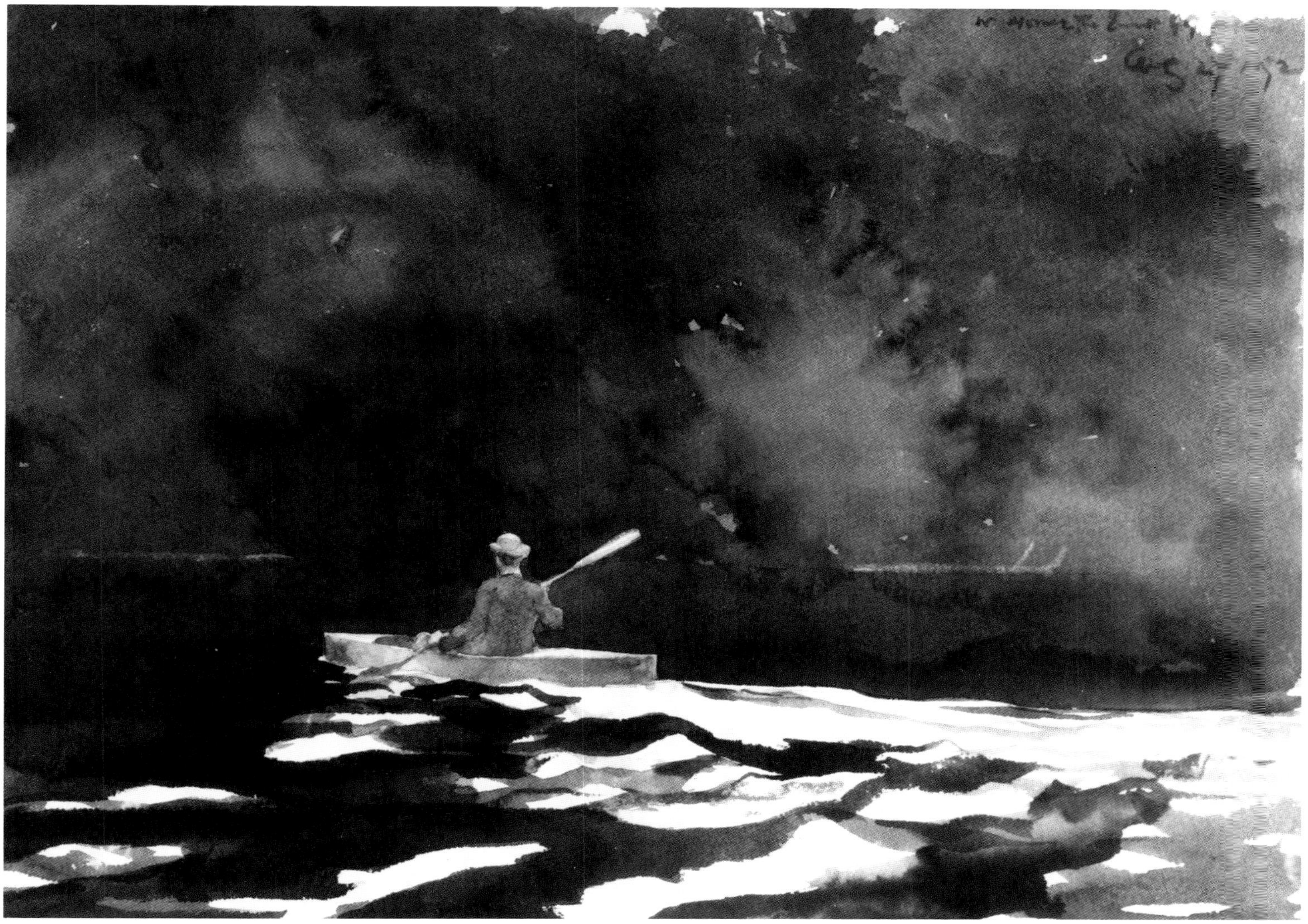

11 *Winslow Homer (American, 1836-1910), Paddling at Dusk, 1892, watercolor, 15⅛ x 21⅜ Anonymous gift, 84.51*

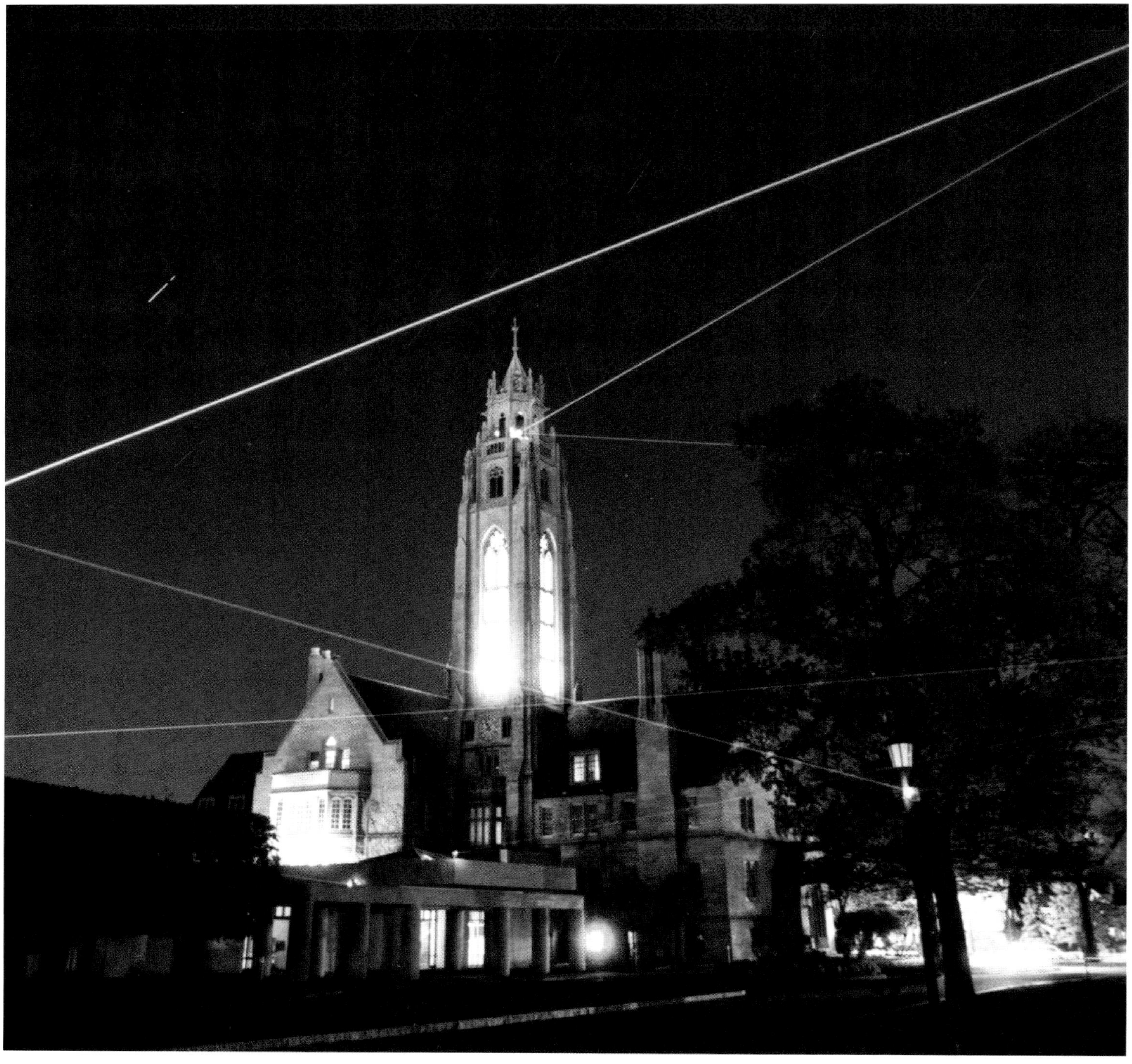

13

The Memorial Art Gallery opened in 1913 with two paintings, four plaster casts, and a lappet of lace.

Gertrude Herdle Moore 1961

May the lasers shine forth and let the ribbon be cut!

Grant Holcomb III 1987

Celebrating the opening of the expanded Gallery, Rockne Kreb's laser sculpture lights up the sky above the Vanden Brul Pavilion linking the Gallery with Cutler Union. Photograph by Jeff Goldberg.

1

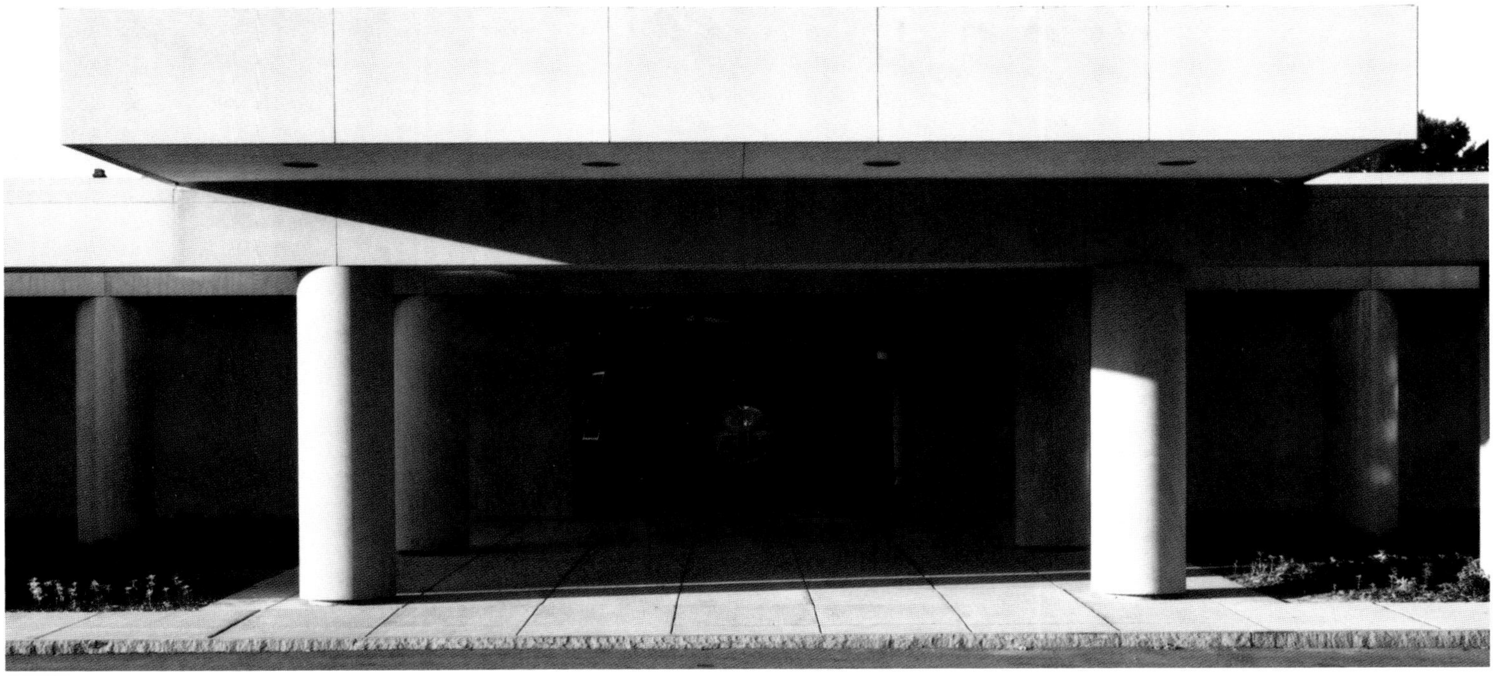

A lappet of lace in 1913 and laser beams slicing the night sky in 1987—no better emblems could be imagined for the changes the Memorial Art Gallery has seen in its three-quarters of a century's existence on University Avenue. Director Grant Holcomb's exclamation was the signal for a riveting and symbolic laser sculpture that linked, by beams of brilliant light, the Gallery, the university's River Campus, and the heart of downtown Rochester. That triangular display illuminated a unique partnership and recalled the words of Emily Sibley Watson, pronounced at the Gallery's creation: "The City of Rochester is finally to have an art museum...vested in the University of Rochester."

Its city has experienced both the woes and wonders of urban change. Its university has grown into one of the leading teaching and research institutions in the land. The Gallery itself has been renewed, expanded, and rededicated to its mission three times, but never so dramatically as on that balmy, spring evening in May when Holcomb's words and technology's special effects revealed the Gallery in its latest manifestation.

The vision of a "new Gallery" had begun to be imagined only ten years after the completion of the 1968 wing, when the collection had already outgrown available display areas and even taxed the seams of MAG's storage space. Ambitious temporary exhibitions had displaced the twentieth century collection. The Gallery Store was scattered in three alcoves. Sentiment was strong to return the main entrance to University Avenue and to finally add the restaurant cut out of budgets of the 1960s.

The plans of the Board of Managers, drawn up under then- director Bret Waller, resulted in a capital campaign headed by William B. Webber to raise construction and endowment funds of at least $6.7 million. Pledges received by September 1986 covered a $5.2 million building and renovation project with another million-plus toward an operating endowment. The $375,000 NEA Challenge Grant for endowment, offered on a three-to-one matching basis, was thus secured.

Waller wished to build a new connection between the Gallery and Cutler Union, where administrative and library space would be located, and convert the existing library, conference room, lounge, sculpture garden, plus curatorial and education offices, to exhibition areas. The Lending and Sales gallery could be a print gallery; increased work and storage areas could be gained by commandeering the Asian and folk art galleries. This plan was given a boost by university president Robert Sproull, who preferred to see the empty second and third floors of Cutler Union used by a university division, rather than by an outside concern. The need to purchase Cutler Union for $650,000 was removed as the university came up with a plan to share the building between the Gallery and the Eastman School of Music. The enlarged connecting link, it was thought, could house the Gallery

Store, a restaurant, and more exhibition areas—particularly for the sculpture displaced by enclosing the existing sculpture garden. The architectural firm of Handler/Grosso was retained, and began to draw up plans.

Grant Holcomb, associate director of the Timken Gallery in San Diego and a scholar with a curatorial and professorial background, joined the Gallery in May 1985 as director—just in time to break ground at 4 p.m. on 17 July. He saw the project through to completion.

For two years staff and visitors gamely put up with much inconvenience until they had a "brand new" arts center of 106,326 square feet. Today one enters once again from University Avenue through a colonnaded portico leading into the new 12,000-square-foot Vanden Brul Pavilion, which connects the earlier Gallery facility to Cutler Union by means of an enclosed, skylit sculpture garden. Combined shop and lending facilities—replete in elegant mauve, dove grey, and glass, with shop windows displaying wares—are located near the entrance. Behind the sculpture court is an exhibition gallery, and to the east the restaurant welcomes its patrons into its two terraced levels. Open for lunch and light meals during museum hours, the Gallery Café is also available for dinner engagements.

"I felt the pavilion should be a bit of magic, a beautiful room, a strong architectural statement," says Frank Grosso, "and still relate well to existing structures." On the exterior the double columns continue Fletcher Steele's *allée* of trees, while the roofline and black aluminum framing continue that of the 1968 building in a current idiom. Even the profile of the skylights echoes the profile of the now-hidden skylights of the 1913 building. To create a sense of grandeur while maintaining the roof line of the 1968 wing, Grosso dropped the floor of the court and raised the ceiling with skylights.

"Suddenly you have the impact of all these buildings coming together, reading as one structure made up of four parts," Grosso says. "At night this is reinforced by new lighting: on the original facade, under the trees, a high-intensity light at the entrance, the Cutler tower all aglow."

Grosso conceived of the new entrance as a kind of a pergola with powerful columns. "Think about any classical building, from the Supreme Court to the Eastman House," he says, "It's the columns that give it stature."

Inside the major axis leads across the sunken court to Henry Moore's bronze *Vertebrae,* resplendent in its fountain setting, and ends in a stepped niche sheltering a Lachaise sculpture of *Standing Woman, 1928,* given by Peter Iselin and Emilie I. Wiggin, grandnephew and grandniece of Emily

2 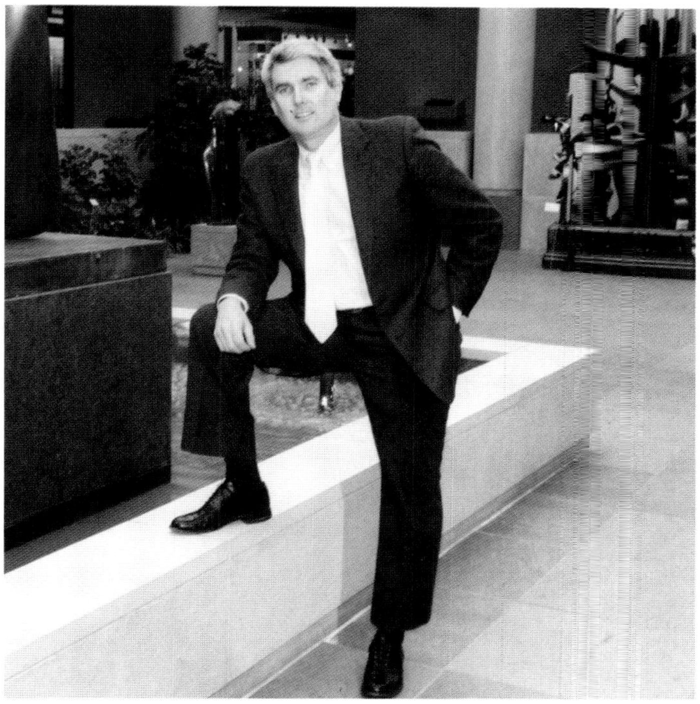

1 *The 1987 entrance joins renovated Cutler Union to the Gallery's 1968 wing and faces University Avenue. Photograph by Jamie Stillings.*

2 *Grant Holcomb, Gallery director since 1985.*

Watson. In the nearby American galleries, four generations of the Sibley-Watson connection with the Gallery are represented by a Lachaise *Portrait Head of Urling Sibley Iselin, 1927*, mother of Peter and Emilie; a Lachaise *Portrait Head of James Sibley Watson Jr.*, Urling's cousin; and Jonas Lie's *Morning on the River*, given by Urling's sister, Ruth Sibley Gade.

Because Grosso felt the ideal place to view sculpture was in a garden setting, the many plants and Vermont slate throughout create a sense of perpetual spring and summer. This indoor "hothouse" garden, bathed in the light that pours through 240 panes of glass, is juxtaposed to a tiny outdoor garden, which is planted to follow the real seasons, given in memory of Richard L. Turner, its former chairman, by the Schlegel Corporation. The viewer who glances up will see the Cutler tower soaring above.

The minor axis also points to the Moore sculpture, but first the visitor must go down steps and through an arch serving as architectural "folly," and around an Albert Paley sculpture that acts as architectural baffle, thus savoring the step-by-step sequence of entering the court.

The same axis leads out of the pavilion into renovated ground floor areas housing American painting and sculpture from 1800 to the present, American folk art, ethnographic collections, prints and drawings, and twentieth century European art. The European and Asian art collections remain in the galleries surrounding the Fountain Court. By enclosing the former sculpture garden, temporary exhibition space has been nearly doubled to 5,500 square feet.

The children's discovery room (where the director's office and a small children's gallery once stood) is designed to help families explore the world of art together through participatory displays. The vestibule to the 1968 entrance, now used as a group entrance, has become a kind of "kiddie cage," complete with cubbies for coats nearby, where docents can greet and contain their charges. The expansive new docent rooms are located near that entrance, an indication of the importance these trained volunteers have today as a vital link between the Gallery and its public.

The spaces in Cutler Union—where partitions are of immovable terra-cotta with no place to introduce or hide new ducts—remain much as they were except for use. The exception is the new Charlotte Whitney Allen Library on the third floor, in which the former attic was opened up to make a two-story, two-level space with pointed ceiling and appropriate Gothic feeling. Stack space doubles that of the former library. Since December 1981 the Allen Library has been directed and supervised by the university's fine arts librarian on a part-time basis.

In May 1987 more than 28,000 people flocked to the week-long festivities surrounding the opening, and watched the lasers flash nightly. More than 900 became new members of what board president Herbert M. Vanden Brul called "this magnificent new showcase for the arts."

"The overwhelming attention from the public and the media was far beyond our dreams and hopes," Vanden Brul noted. And that response was effusive. "It's exciting, world class, and best of all, it's ours!" said Rochester's B. Forman Company in a large, congratulatory display advertisement in the *Democrat and Chronicle*. That sentiment was underscored by the newspaper's editorial page: "The Art Gallery is bigger, better, beautiful... in a word, a joy."

Another kind of light show went off in 1910 when Halley's Comet blazed across the sky, and five-year-old Isabel Herdle was awakened to watch the phenomenon of a lifetime seated on her father's shoulders. In order that she not cry at the sight of this "blare of light with a nice tail," George Herdle presented Isabel with a Pennsylvania Dutch chalkware bird. It marked the beginning of a personal collection for the Herdle sisters, an interest that would later be carried forward through the exhibition, study, and preservation of American provincial arts and crafts at the Gallery.

Because the Herdles began collecting before the craze set in—when prices were low, forgers not yet active, and museums did not have such departments—the Gallery's folk art collection is a particularly fine one. It predates the celebrated collection at Cooperstown. The Gallery's first important exhibition of folk art took place way back in 1931. As part of its larger survey of American art from 1800 to 1940, the folk art collection includes six major portraits attributed to Noah North (or possibly Manuel Hopkins, since both were active in Scottsville), a rare and charming double portrait by M. M. Manchester, a portrait of Josephine Dixon attributed to J. Grant, two fine landscapes by Thomas Chambers, and six important pastel portraits by Micah Williams. In addition to paintings, the collection includes a mammoth cigar store Indian from the old United States Hotel on West Main Street, first home of the University of Rochester; two beautiful and rare heron decoys; and a bullet-ridden weather vane of the Angel Gabriel from a South Bristol church. The *Tramp Art Shrine* (ca. 1865-1900), possibly from western Pennsylvania, was a 1987 addition purchased through the Lillian Utz Fund, the Florence Berg Fund, and the Tribute Fund.

Earlier, in 1985, luck, timing, generosity, and savvy all combined to allow the Gallery to add a portrait by the sud-

3

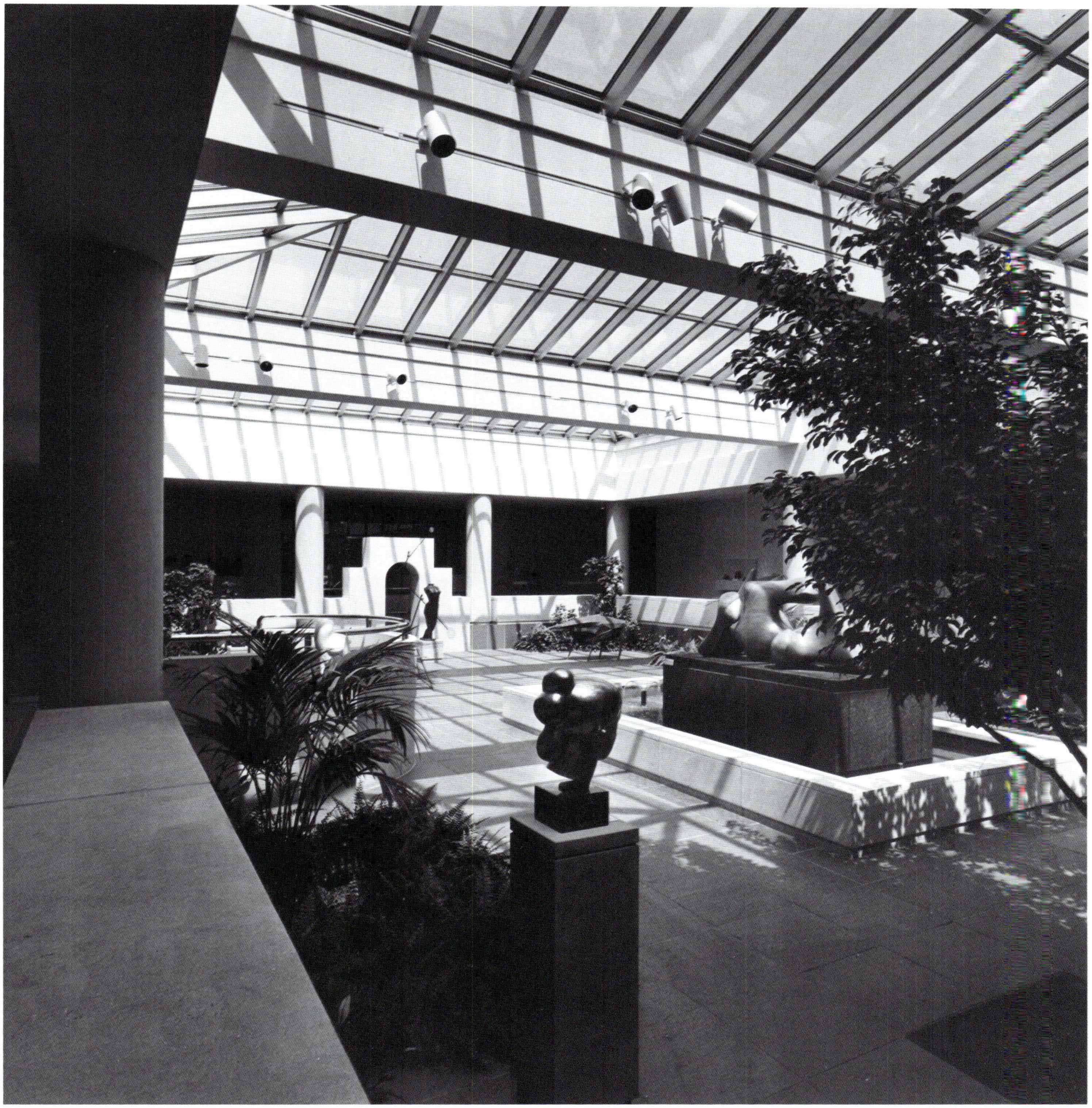

3 *The Vanden Brul Pavilion, 1987.*

4

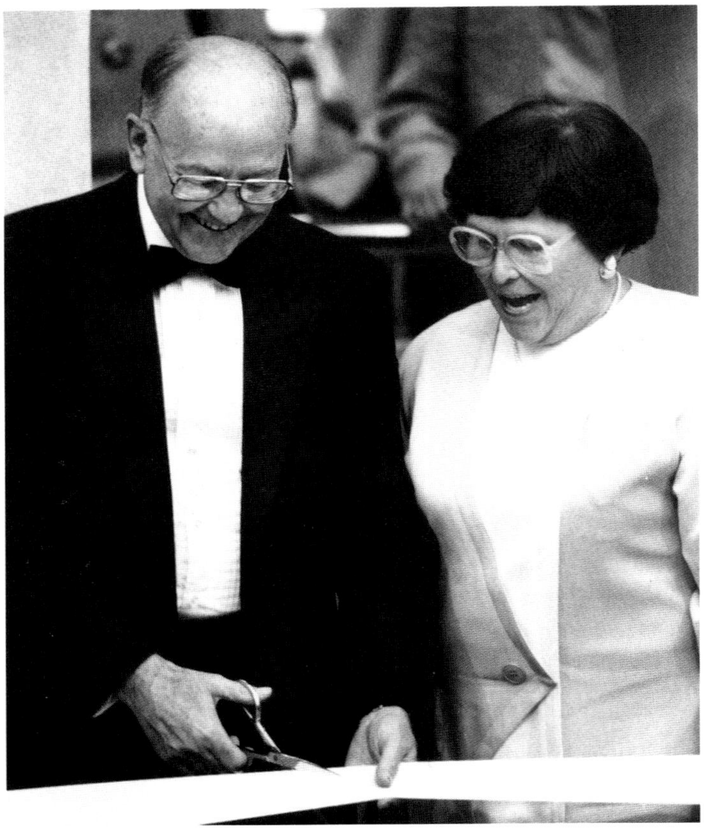

4 *Herbert and Joan Vanden Brul cut the ribbon at the Grand Opening, May 1987.*

5 *The MAGBubble Festival at the Grand Opening, May 1987.*

denly fashionable Ammi Phillips to its already exceptional survey of American folk art. Stories were just breaking in the *New York Times* that portraits by this nineteenth century limner were fetching prices of $682,000 and $1 million, shattering previous records for folk art paintings. Miraculously *Old Woman with a Bible* would be acquired for less than 2 percent of the larger New York tag.

The trail leading to acquisition began when an anonymous antiques dealer in Caledonia, New York, sent photographs of a painting in his possession to collectors and experts from Buffalo to New York including Howard Merritt, professor emeritus of fine arts at the university.

"This looks like an Ammi Phillips," Merritt said in showing the photo to Patricia Junker. By the time Junker contacted the Caledonia dealer, an interested New York City party had offered to buy the folk portrait sight unseen, doubling the asking price.

The Gallery immediately called upon Vanden Brul, then vice president of the Board of Managers, who had previously offered to advance funds to facilitate the cash flow for acquisitions when exceptional works appeared.

Thus *Old Woman with a Bible* rode to the Gallery in the back seat of Junker's car before the prospective New York buyer could act. Permanent funds for the painting's purchase came later through the art committee from the Beatrice M. Padelford Trust, established in memory of a Gallery member, Rochester artist, and Creative Workshop student. "This is a painting Mrs. Padelford would have loved," Isabel agreed.

The portrait was in excellent condition—no overpainting, no unfortunate homemade restorations—and the canvas was attached to its strainers just as the artist had tacked it. Nor did it need to be tightened or relined when sent to Oberlin for analysis and cleaning. Strainers, in contrast to stretchers, are rigid structures for mounting canvas. Phillips's exclusive use of strainers, and his unique method of securing them with wooden dowels set diagonally, helped the art sleuths in attributing the work.

Further tests such as X-radiography and infrared radiation at Oberlin revealed the self-taught limner as a self-assured and capable artist. Phillips painted rapidly without preliminary sketching, immediately achieving a likeness which he altered very little. Phillips, one of the most abstract of the folk masters, was among the first to be "rediscovered." Yet with his popularity and high prices, as Junker notes, a systematic search for a Phillips might have yielded only disappointment. But then came the lucky find.

5

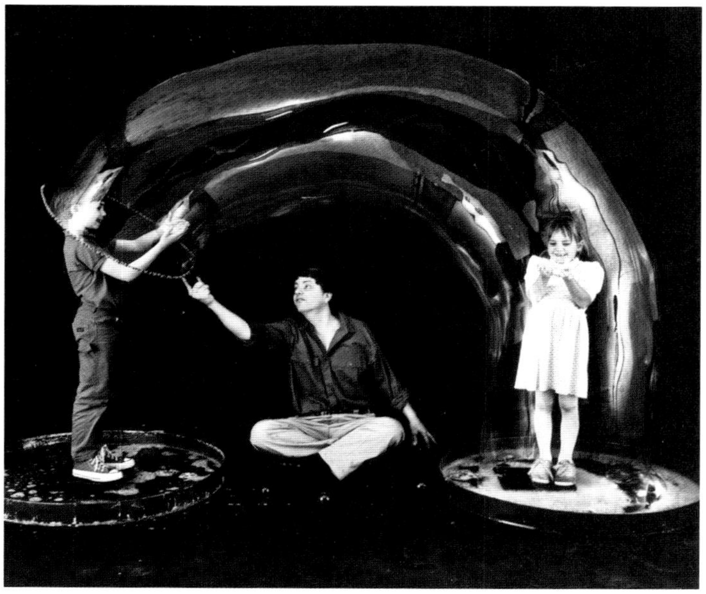

"In order to fill this new grand space, and fulfill the promise inherent in the capital campaign, the challenge continues," director Holcomb says. "Having successfully completed one phase, the ante for quality in all areas of Gallery endeavor has simply been raised." At the Grand Opening of the "new Gallery," Holcomb targeted four areas—art history, contemporary art, the permanent collection, and local arts—to highlight during the coming days. It is worth noting that opening with the expanded Gallery and the laser sculpture was an exhibition of eighteenth century French historical and religious paintings called *"La Grande Manière."* Organized for the Gallery by Donald Rosenthal, formerly chief curator at MAG and now holding the same post at the High Museum, this exhibition pointedly demonstrated that although its enthusiasm for the future of the arts is clear, the Gallery has certainly not forgotten its obligations to the past.

"A Survey of American Printmaking, 1850 to the Present" inaugurated the new Lockhart Gallery for prints and drawings. Seventy works on paper drawn from the Gallery's 4,500-work collection were included, most of which had not been seen for years. Holcomb saw the exhibition as reflecting the Gallery's commitment to print collecting, exhibition, and interpretation.

The commitment continues, as evidenced by the following titles of exhibitions of works on paper held since the Grand Opening: "American Drawings and Watercolor, 1800-1945: Selections from the Permanent Collection," "The Night Before Christmas: Illustrations by Douglas Gorsline," "Charles Burchfield, Master Draughtsman: Drawings and Watercolors from the Collection of Charles Rand Penney," "The Graphic Art of Harold Faye," "The Making of a Print: Intaglio," "Whistler and His British Contemporaries," and "The Delighted Eye: Gifts from an Anonymous Connoisseur."

That last exhibition honored one of the Gallery's most generous, though still anonymous benefactors—the one who, introduced to art by a college friend, began collecting prints and drawings in the 1930s, became involved with the Gallery's print collection in the 1950s, and began to make annual gifts to the Gallery from his collection in 1975. Since then important works by Dürer, Rembrandt, Blake, Ingres, Delacroix, Degas, Picasso, and many others are being shared with a wider public.

During the summer of 1988 "John Menihan: Prints from the 1930s and 1940s" provided a retrospective look at the work of this Rochester artist during the period when he was also an instructor in the Creative Workshop.

The new Lucy Burne Gallery in the Creative Workshop gives the community a chance to see works of contemporary regional artists. Inaugurating the opening of this gallery, a small exhibition featured the work of Syracuse artist Jerome Witkin, a narrative painter whose national reputation is growing and whose monumental figurative canvas *Breaking the Pose (The Art Class)* had just been acquired for the collection. Witkin's lecture and "master class" workshop for Rochester artists were wildly oversubscribed.

Another Holcomb priority is enhanced programming, particularly in the area of contemporary art, paralleling the Charlotte Whitney Allen series of art history lectures and symposia. The curatorial staff has already grown since Holcomb's arrival, and he looks forward to an era of cooperation with the new university president and new chairman of fine arts, perhaps taking the form of a shared curatorial position in some area (such as prints and drawings or ethnographic art) where the Gallery lacks an expert.

To better interpret the permanent collection to its growing and varied visitors, the Gallery began in 1988 to offer "Acoustiguide," a 45-minute recorded tour. Narrated by Holcomb, the audiotour highlights twenty masterpieces of the collection. In honor of the Gallery's seventy-fifth year, the exhibition "Looking Back: A Perspective on the 1913 Inaugural Exhibition" is planned for October 1988.

Scheduled for 1989 is an exhibition devoted to the landscape architecture of Fletcher Steele, landscape architect of the Gallery's 1968 wing and the Charlotte Whitney Allen house, whose fame spread far beyond those commissions. Steele was also the donor of the small oil of Parisian actor *Lugne Poe*, the Gallery's only painting by Edouard Vuillard.

Planned for the spring of 1990 is a major exhibition of Winslow Homer's marine paintings—"Winslow Homer in the 1890s: Prout's Neck Observed." It will be curated by the Gallery's curator Patricia Junker, along with David Tatham and Philip Beam, Homer scholars from Syracuse University and Bowdoin College respectively, and with Lois Homer Graham, grandniece of the artist. For the fall of 1990 the Detroit Institute of Arts is organizing the first retrospective of the sculptures of Wendell Castle. This exhibition will come to the Gallery sponsored by the Women's Council (as the council's gift in observance of its fiftieth birthday).

Staff changes and additions continue. In 1985 Lang Clay retired after thirty-three years as assistant director for education. In recognition of his achievements the university awarded Clay its Distinguished Service Award. The expanded education center in Cutler Union bears the name of Langdon F. Clay. "It's been said that there are two kinds of intelligence—one of the mind and one of the heart," Grant Holcomb said at the champagne reception honoring Clay. "Lang possesses both in full measure."

Penny Knowles joined the staff as associate director, first for curatorial and educational affairs and then for special projects. Gallery programming for adults received a boost when Knowles initiated the immensely popular and educational "Tuesdays at 5:30" programs of twenty-minute lectures featuring works on exhibition in the Gallery. She also started and coordinated art appreciation and art history courses, both open to the adult public and part of a new docent training program. The fall term was devoted to "Developing an Aesthetic Eye" and the winter term to "Art in Context," a survey of Eastern and Western art from 3000 B. C. to the end of the nineteenth century with emphasis on works in the Gallery collection. Through these courses plus extra training classes, fifty-plus new docents joined the sixty active docents and twenty-five honorary docents currently giving adult, family, and school tours. About 1,800 tours are given annually to 15,000 school children. Since the opening of the expanded facilities, adult tours, formerly conducted once or twice a week, are now more frequent.

Susan Dodge Peters became associated with the Gallery as editor of the new handbook of the collection. She then served as acting curator of European art and editor of the 1986 issue of *Porticus*; as of 1988 she is assistant director for education. Marjorie Searl, a specialist in school and family programming who had been associated with the Gallery since 1979 as a curriculum consultant, was appointed curator of education. Her projects include publishing of *ARTWALK*, a family guide to the Gallery, and Artspeak, a pilot program designed to encourage wider participation in Gallery programs by minority students. Selected high school students complete an intensive summer training course, then make presentations to elementary students and, as a follow-up, lead these classes on tours of the Gallery. In 1988 the Gallery was awarded a NYSCA grant to expand Artspeak.

6

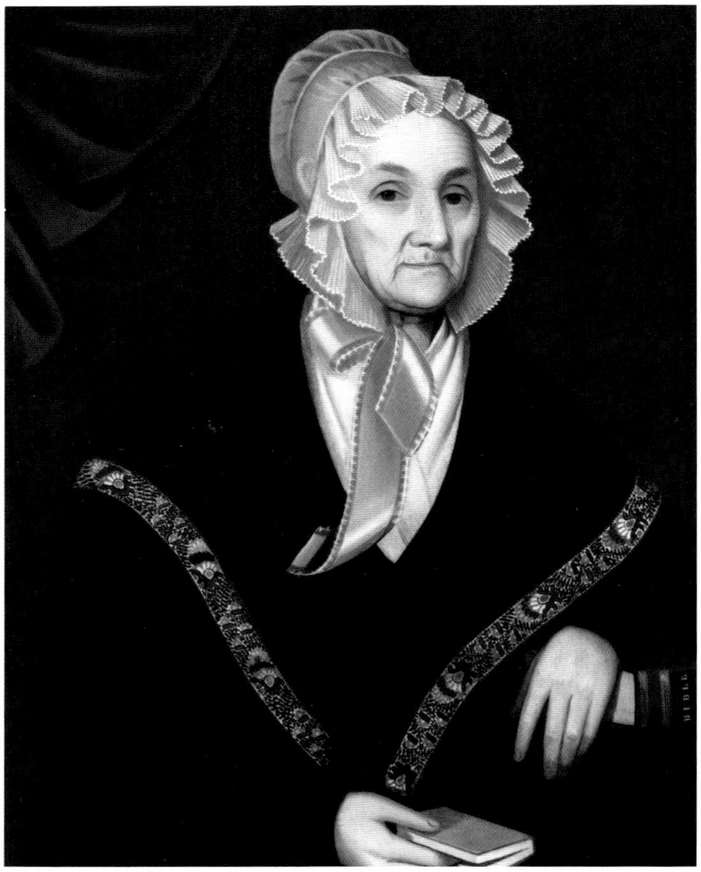

Kim Hallatt joined the Gallery as manager of financial and support services, replacing Edmund Pease, who accepted a position at the Montclair Art Museum. Margaret S. Hubbard served a year as consultant on development before assuming her duties as director of development. Christine Garland, acting director of development for a year, became assistant director of development and grants coordinator. Deborah Rothman joined the staff as public relations manager in 1985. Marie Via has been a member of the curatorial department since 1983. Lawrence Merrill became administrator of the Creative Workshop in August 1986.

And in 1987 Susan Eisenhart Schilling, research curator emeritus, marked her fiftieth year of service to the Gallery.

With a strong staff in place, the second seventy-five years begins.

One of Holcomb's priorities for the collection is increasing the representation of figurative works from the latter half of the twentieth century. Figurative works from the early twentieth century were well represented when he came, he notes, as were abstract works from the midcentury period, whereas latter-day figurative works were not.

The acquisition of *The Beginning of the Fields* (1973) by Fairfield Porter (1907-1975), one of the foremost realist painters of his time and the main influence on a generation of "painterly realists," marked a step toward that goal. This airy, light-filled landscape is typical of Porter's style in its loose, broad handling of paint, its subtle color transitions, and its bordering on abstraction.

Works by contemporary realists Joyce Treiman and Jerome Witkin were further acquisitions enhancing this part of the contemporary collection. Roy De Forest's *The Dipolar Girls Take a Voyage on the St. Lawrence, 1970,* the gift of Charles and Setta Odoroff in honor of Maurice and Minnie Odoroff, represented a foray into funk, fantasy, and the new expressionism inspired by graffiti and comic books.

Evening Glow, a 1982 oil by Wolf Kahn, was a gift of the Mr. and Mrs. Julius G. Kayser and a major acquisition of 1985. A student of Hans Hofmann, whose *Ruby Gold* hangs in the same gallery, Kahn also describes himself as a child of Abstract Expressionism. "He is a powerful gestural painter," Grant Holcomb wrote, "who primarily thinks in terms of resolving formal problems while insisting on the object in his painting." Holcomb continued:

> Evening Glow *reflects the artist's interest in the dynamic interchange of natural forces—the contrasting compositional elements of land, pond, and sky and their meeting place at the horizon. The painting's luminous and sumptuous color establishes the emotional potential and weight of the composition. Kahn's admiration of Titian, Bonnard, Monet, and Rothko is evident in* Evening Glow. *In this aspect, the artist stated that he wanted "to do Rothko over from nature." Certainly the hovering effect of radiant color and glowing layers of veiled light denote the influence of the twentieth century master.*

In 1988 a small oil by Edwin Dickinson was given by Nancy R. Turner in memory of her husband, Richard L. Turner. Dickinson, an American independent who came from nearby Seneca Falls, produced realistic paintings with a mystical or surreal quality—layered fantasies with superimposed images and meanings. The Gallery's *Snow on Quai* is one of a series of *alla prima* oil sketches (each done in one

7

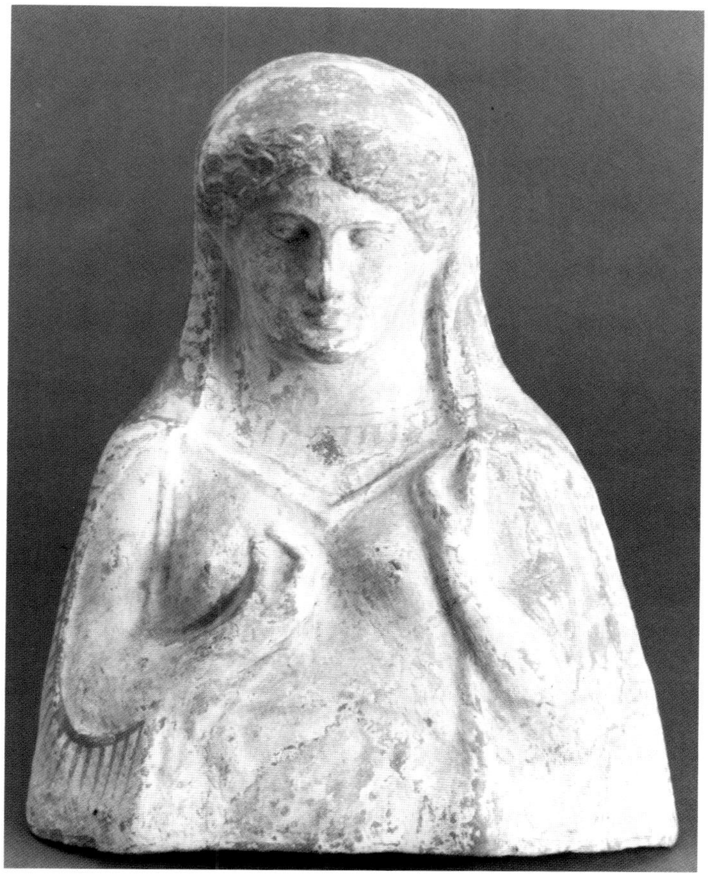

6 *Ammi Phillips (American, 1788-1865) Old Woman with a Bible, ca. 1834, oil on linen, 33¾ x 27⅞ in. The Beatrice M. Padelford Trust, 84.22*

7 *Greek (ca. 450 B.C.) Protome, Terracotta, 14½ x 11⅝ x 3⅞ in. June Alexander Memorial Fund and Tribute Fund, 88.5*

8

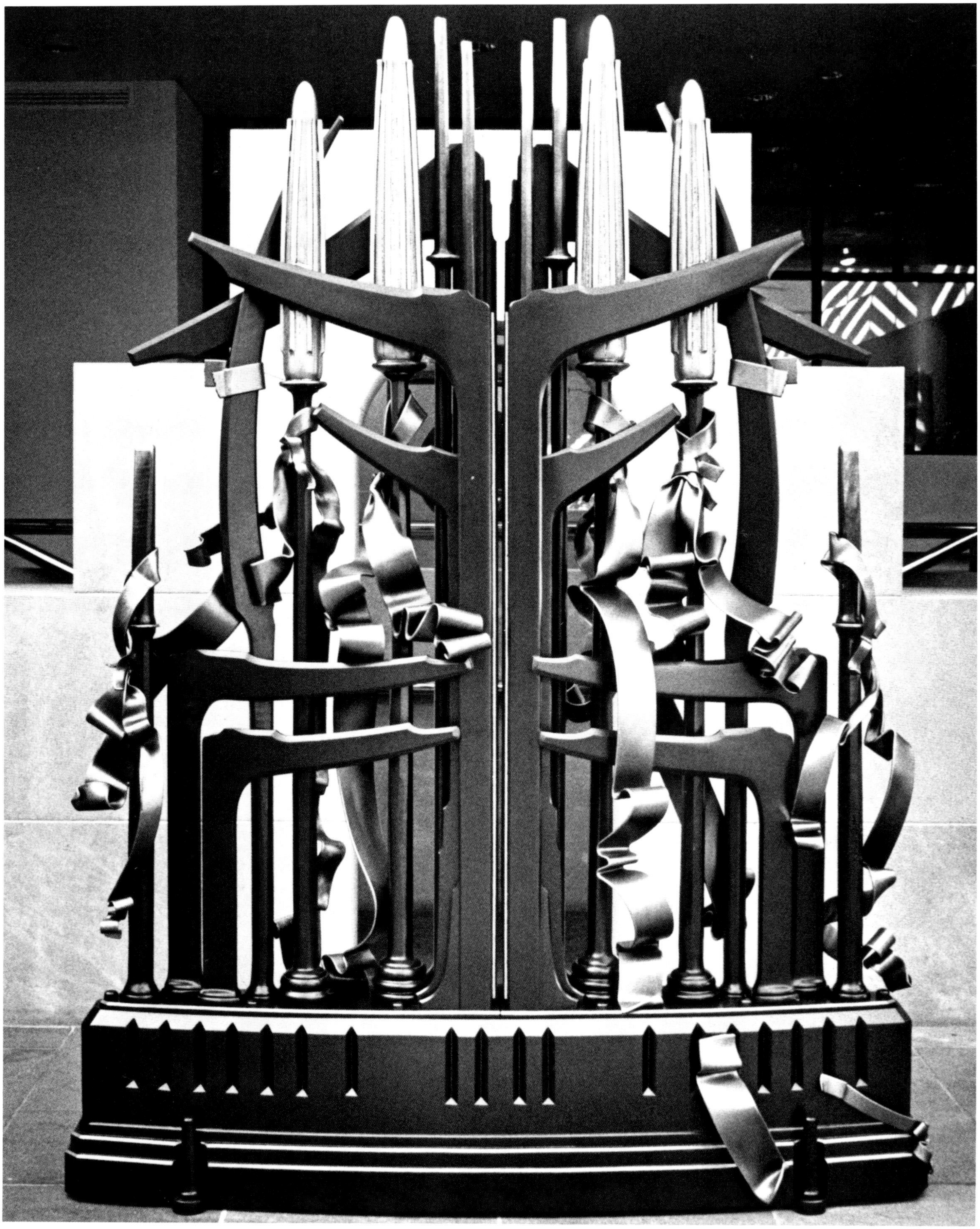

sitting) painted while the artist was looking through a window toward the banks of the Seine.

Nineteenth century American sculpture, which did not approach nineteenth century American painting in breadth of representation, is another area Holcomb has targeted. The Frederick MacMonnies bronze of *Nathan Hale, 1890* and the marble head of *Abraham Lincoln* (ca. 1918) by Gregory Grey Barnard (1863-1938) were the initial purchases in this direction. Holcomb successfully negotiated an extended loan from the Metropolitan Museum of Art of nineteenth century American sculpture and painting to complement the purchase program.

In European art the collection gained a large eighteenth century history painting, the Gallery's first of its genre, with Francis Wheatley's *Death of Richard II.* Commissioned about 1792 for a specific English "History Gallery," where paintings were intended to illustrate the history of England and "to rouse the passions, to fire the mind with emulation of heroic deeds, or to inspire it with detestation of criminal actions," the painting's massive presence, narrative clarity, and histrionic style accomplishes these goals succinctly. Of the several versions of Richard II's mysterious death in 1400 available to the artist—eighteenth century historian David Hume thought that the king was starved to death in prison—Wheatley opted for the most dramatic. His success in creating a melodrama, seen now as a forerunner to today's gory tales on screen and television, is reinforced by the hordes of schoolboys who find this their favorite Gallery picture.

The classical collection received an overdue boost in 1988 with the purchase from the June Alexander Memorial Fund of a remarkable Greek terra-cotta *Protome* (ca. sixth century B.C.). A protome is the representation of the head and neck of an animal or a person—in this case a lovely young woman—as an architectural part. The *Protome* was a fitting tribute to Alexander, a longtime docent, classical scholar, and collector, who also served for many years as the Gallery's excellent (and volunteer) photographer.

What attracts people to the Memorial Art Gallery is different for everyone. Surprise gifts or bequests are not uncommon from former Creative Workshop students who acknowledge that this early experience started them on a lifetime of collecting.

In 1942 a Spanish language teacher took his East High School class to see a painting by Diego Rivera. Among the students who found themselves in the Gallery for the first time was a young Herbert W. Vanden Brul. This field trip

9

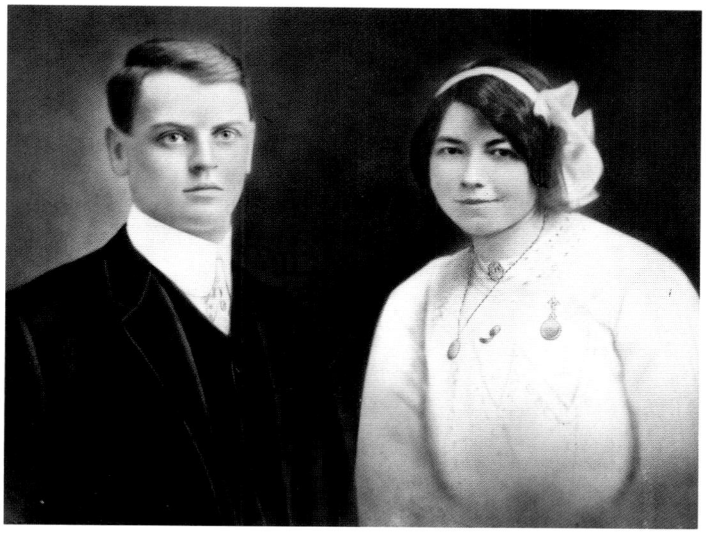

8 *Albert Paley (American, b. 1944), Convergence, 1987, forged steel, polychromed. Gift in honor of Herbert W. Vanden Brul made possible by Harris Corporation R. F. Communications Division, Vanden Brul family members and friends, and the artist, 87.61*

9 *John J. Vanden Brul and Celina de Coninck Vanden Brul in whose honor the 1987 pavillion was named. Their wedding picture of 30 August 1914 was taken nearby during the Gallery's formative period.*

was to begin a long and extraordinary relationship.

In the 1950s Vanden Brul, by then a practicing Rochester attorney, returned with his wife, Joan, this time taking out a family membership. A few years later their young son was pictured in a newspaper photograph of a Creative Workshop class. Gradually the bond was strengthened. In 1972 a friend encouraged Vanden Brul to take the docent training course. He did, becoming the first male docent at the Gallery.

In the 1970s William Maxion, president of the Board of Managers, was soliciting contributions from friends of Harris Prior and of the Gallery to purchase a work in honor of Prior, then desperately ill. Vanden Brul agreed to make a substantial contribution provided the choice was something that interested him. Maxion named Vanden Brul to work with curator Robert Henning in selecting the work. On a trip to New York Vanden Brul found *Orchid and Hummingbird* by Martin Johnson Heade at a price within the limits of the fund. Later he learned to his delight that Prior had admired the work, and still later he saw the painting appreciate in market value, as most of the Gallery's collection has, far beyond what could be afforded in today's market.

Vanden Brul was now fully committed to the Gallery. In 1977 he was elected to the Board of Managers. In 1983 he and his wife Joan made the cornerstone pledge to the capital campaign, which culminated in the May 1987 opening of the renovated and enlarged Gallery, the keystone of which was the Vanden Brul Pavilion. It was named for Herbert's parents, John J. Vanden Brul and Celina de Coninck Vanden Brul, immigrants from Holland and Belgium who probably never dreamed their names would adorn part of an art museum.

In November 1987 a monumental steel sculpture, *Convergence*, by Albert Paley, which also serves as architectural screen in the Vanden Brul Pavilion, was dedicated in honor of Herbert Vanden Brul.

Paley, the Rochester metalsmith who became a nationally acclaimed artist with his *Portal Gates* for the Renwick Gallery of the Smithsonian Institution in 1972, describes *Convergence* as "theatrical in nature, in that it is a presentation to the human spirit. *Convergence* is all about perception and paradox. What the viewer sees and experiences is color, light, and movement, even knowing that it's really hard steel."

As architectural screen, the viewer confronts *Convergence* the moment he walks down the steps and through the stone arch. Although teasing glimpses may be had through the steel bars and colored "ribbons," the viewer must move around the screen to achieve the final "graceful easing into the space" that Paley compares to the sensation of "coming through a grove of trees into an open area." While interacting with the architecture, *Convergence* was also designed "to create focus and accent in what is essentially a monochromatic environment." Positioned squarely on the pavilion's east-west axis, it counterbalances the Moore sculpture in its fountain setting and maintains the symmetry of the sculpture garden.

Wendell Castle is another Rochester artist-craftsman who has achieved a national reputation. He is represented in the collection by a major work given in 1988 in honor of Joan Vanden Brul's birthday by her family. *Dr. Caligari* is one of Castle's series of clocks that was exhibited as "Masterpieces of Time" at the Renwick Gallery, Washington, D. C., in 1986, with a selection coming to the Gallery later that year. Each of the thirteen clocks has a theme of its own.

Castle became interested in tall-case clocks because of their sculptural qualities. "The possibilities for form are virtually endless," he says. "Unlike furniture, you do not use a clock, all you have to do is look at it.... The difference between furniture and sculpture can be great or it can be small. In my work, the two are almost the same. I would prefer to be called a sculptor."

Castle calls *Dr. Caligari*— made of curly cherry stained blue, with ebony trim, a painted interior, a gold-plated brass base, and white-gold hinges—"an abstraction of a grandfather clock." It was inspired by the German Expressionist film, *The Cabinet of Dr. Caligari*, not for its story line, Castle says, but for its visuals. The movie sets are cubistic and asymmetrical, yet with broad brush strokes anticipating a Franz Kline painting. The photography is black-and-white. Castle thinks of black-and- white films as "slightly blue," and blue, he says, "is the furthest from a wood color." Hence, the cherry wood is bleached and stained blue. The interior painting of the clock is done with those broad expressionist strokes.

"If these clocks 'function,'" writes Edward Lucie-Smith, art critic and historian, "the way they do so is indistinguishable from the functioning of fine art. Their real purpose is not to tell time, but to make statements about the nature of time."

In its several incarnations over seventy-five years, the Memorial Art Gallery makes its own statement about time. Linked by stones and mortar, steel and glass, from the balustraded terrace of the original jewel box on University Avenue to Cutler's tower soaring above the Vanden Brul Pavilion, the Gallery is likewise joined to its past by a spiritual bond. It is

10

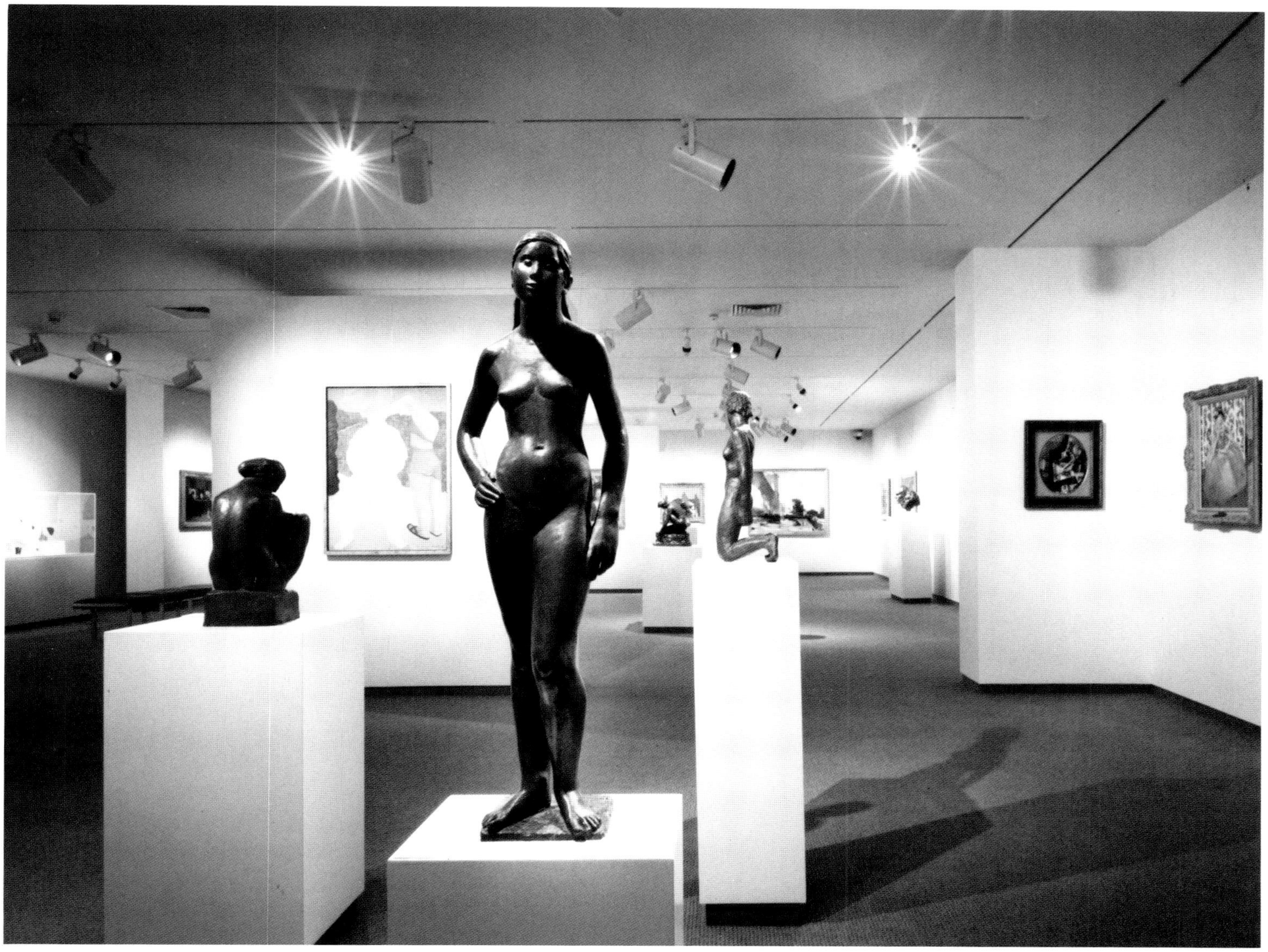

10 *Gerhard Marcks's 1938 Nana stands at the entrance to new galleries which replaced the library and conference room of the 1968 wing. Behind is Milton Avery's Haircut by the Sea and on the wall at the right are works by Braque and Matisee.*

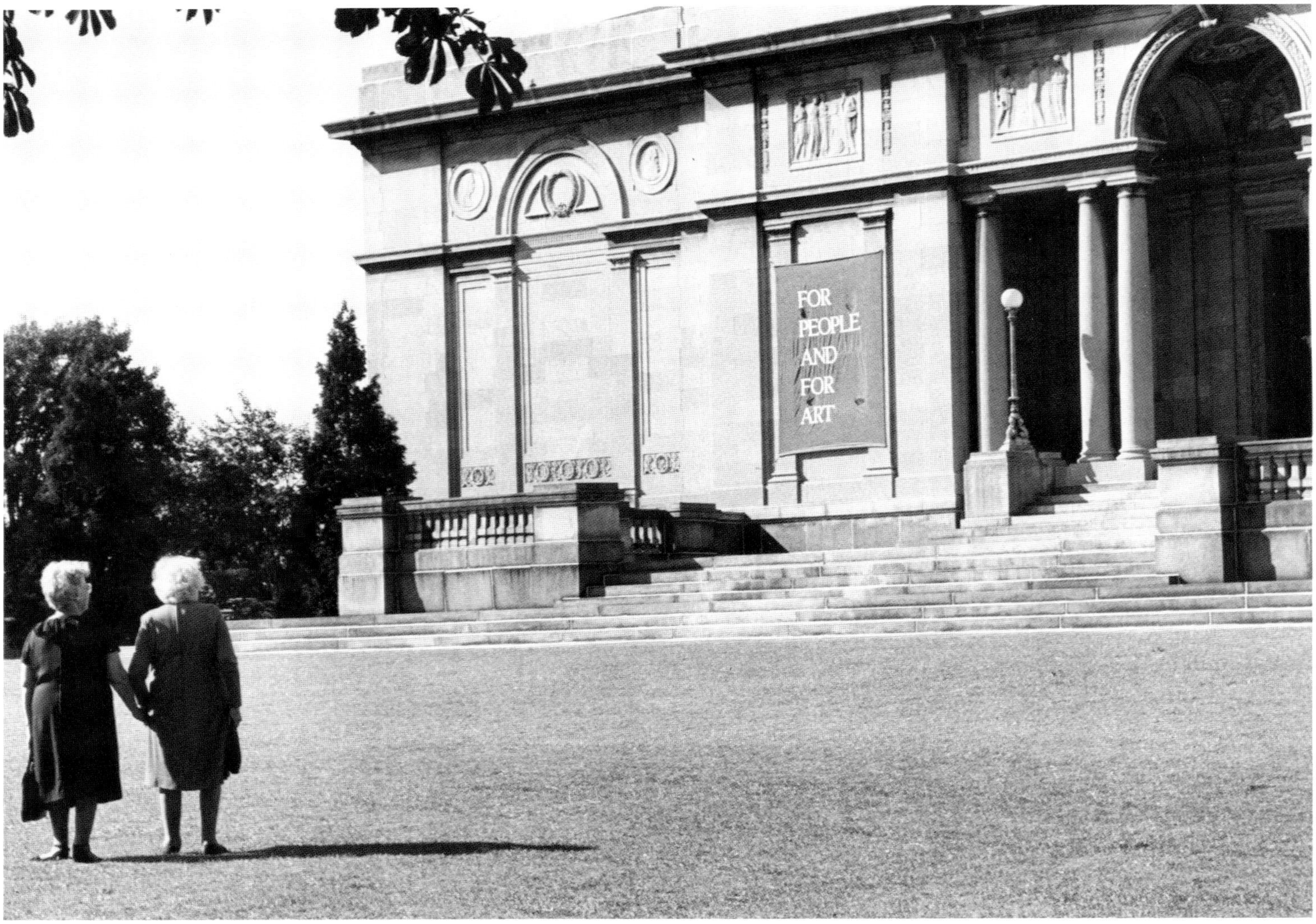

the spirit of giving that has animated the Gallery over time and space. Many of those "givers" were able to be present in May 1987, and the reader will by now be familiar with their names: Gertrude Herdle Moore and Isabel Herdle, Langdon Clay and Susan Schilling, Marion and Tom Hawks, the Angles and the Aquavellas, Joan and Herb Vanden Brul, Jackie Adams and Lyn Kayser, Nancy Kelly and Emily Cassebeer, Dr. Geib and Peter Iselin, Carl Zollo and Earl Kage, Bill Webber and Charles Rand Penney, Maurice Forman and Bret Waller, to name just a few of the Gallery's dozens of staff members, and its legion of volunteers and friends.

Many were not.

But if F. Scott Fitzgerald was able to evoke an entire era by having Nick Carraway write down on the empty spaces of a railway timetable "the names of those who came to Gatsby's house that summer," something of the same sort might be possible with names jotted on the back of a May 1987 Gallery program. Write down Emily Sibley Watson, and she is here, not so much interested in the laser show as she is in gazing wistfully at the initials "JGA," still inscribed on the arcades. Write "Uncle Jim" Watson—and he is in the Fountain Court, admiring the installation of his brilliant stained glass quatrefoil medallions, glad to have seen the Chou ceremonial vessels and T'ang horses in the nearby Asian gallery but wondering if different wall coverings might not enhance them.

Add the name of Rush Rhees— and he is beaming at the

celebrants who are launching helium-filled balloons carrying artworks and messages aloft, some to float down to the River Campus of the university he built. Sibley Watson is smiling at the many labels that carry the tag, "A Gift of a Friend of the Gallery." R.T. Miller, for once the weather matching his white suit and Panama hat, watches the antics of a performance artist encasing laughing kids in giant bubbles, and we hope Miller finds these goings-on "educational in nature." Little Marion Stratton Gould is amazed to see her name on so many labels. Clara Strasenburgh is quietly pleased to see works beginning to be purchased through her bequest. Edith Babcock is standing and for once speechless (a shadowy figure named "Sam" appears to be juggling some of her plates). Herbert Ocumpaugh is pleased to see his *Steatopagus* figure on display, but somewhat confused to learn that the new pavilion containing the sculpture garden is familiarly called "Herb's Place." "Teacher" Bill Erich is heartened but not surprised to see the Creative Workshop doing so well. Edna Weeks Smith makes sure everyone knows whose Idea "Clothesline" was. Fritz Trautman has a host of new theories sparked by his walk through the new *Galaxy*. Charlotte Whitney Allen decides that a bustling library in an attic beats a bookstore in a basement. George Herdle is rummaging around for his old easel, having finally found the time to paint. And the gentle Harris Prior? No doubt Grant Holcomb has his predecessor's undivided attention and silent nods of agreement as the new director sums up both the glory and the purpose of the Memorial Art Gallery:

I believe deeply in the significance of great art [and in the] contagious spirit of Rochester's commitment to the arts.... [The works of great artists] have been entrusted to our care—from the stone carvers of ancient Greece to the woodcarvers of Africa; the resplendent names of Rembrandt, Monet, and Renoir; Homer, Eakins, and St. Gaudens; Picasso, Braque, and Moore. They are, in Keats's words, our "infinite glories... that must be with us or we die."

12

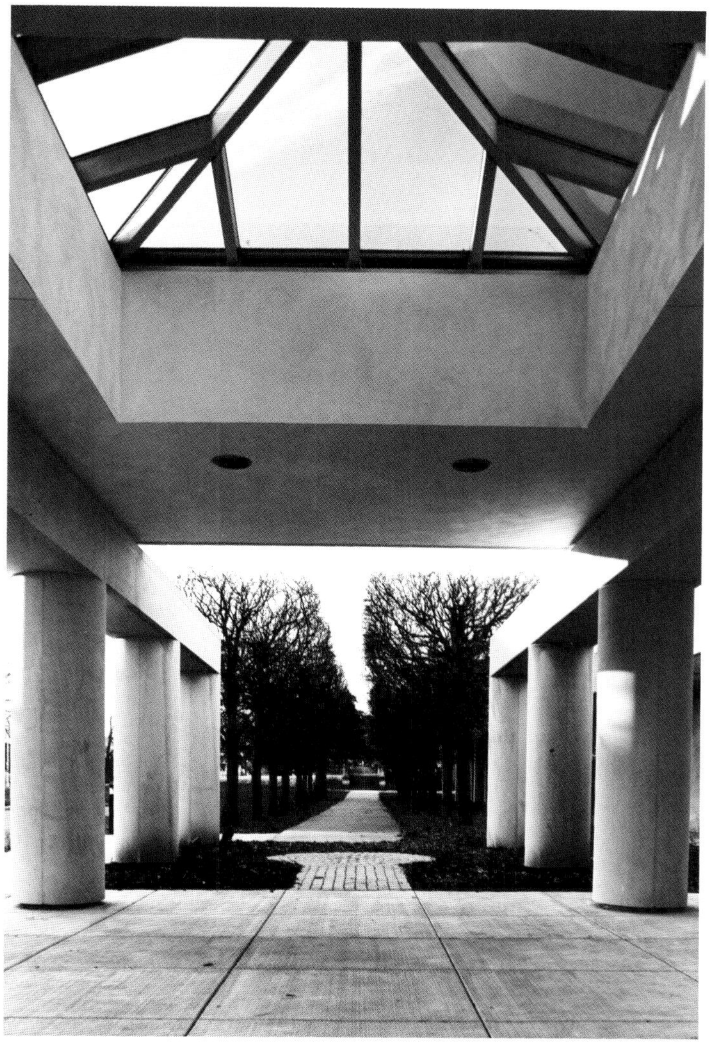

11, 12 *Seventy-five years of "For People and for Art."*

MEMORIAL ART GALLERY BOARD OF MANAGERS, 1912–1988

Term Beginning	*Member*	*Term Ending*
1912	Joseph T. Alling	1931
	Elizabeth Averell Rogerson	1937
	Mrs. George D. B. Bonbright	*d.* 1943
	Claude Bragdon	1922
	Grace Curtice Lindsay	
	Edwina Danforth	1947
	Elizabeth Denio	*d.* 1922
	William A. E. Drescher	
	George Eastman	*d.* 1932
	George L. Herdle*	*d.* 1922 *(D)*
	Elizabeth Watson Hollister	*d.* 1938
	Guernsey Mitchell	*d.* 1920
	Rush Rhees	*d.* 1938
	Charles Mulford Robinson	*d.* 1918
	Hiram Watson Sibley	*d.* 1932
	Mrs. William R. Taylor	
	Frank Von Der Lanckent†	1920
	Emily Sibley Watson	*d.* 1945
	James Sibley Watson	*d.* 1952
	Julius M. Wile	*d.* 1937
	Marie Atkinson Willard	*d.* 1941
1916	Charlotte Whitney Allen	*d.* 1978
1920	Elmer Adler	*d.* 1960
	Royal B. Farnum	1924
1922	Charles Wright Dodge	*d.* 1933
1923	John J. Inglis*	1934
	Gertrude Herdle Moore	1962 *(D)* 1985— *(H)*
1924	Walter H. Cassebeer	*d.* 1964
	Helen C. Ellwanger	*d.* 1981
	Hannah Durand Gould	*d.* 1930
	Clifford Ulp†	
1926	Mrs. L. Corrin Strong	1927
1927	James B. Arnold	1932
	Kathleen McEnery Cunningham	*d.* 1971
1929	Edith Holden Babcock	*d.* 1947
	Raymond N. Ball	1951
1930	Leroy E. Snyder	*d.* 1943
1931	Mrs. Joseph T. Alling	1936
	Thomas G. Spencer	*d.* 1979
1933	F. Harper Sibley	*d.* 1959
	James Sibley Watson Jr.	*d.* 1981
1934	Raymond L. Thompson	*d.* 1962
	Fritz Trautman*	1935
1935	Ralph H. Avery*	1938
	James M. Spinning	1954
	Alan Valentine‡	1950
1936	Mrs. Charles Wright Dodge	1949
1937	Mrs. Ranlet Miner	1941, 1962-1970
1938	Ardery DeFonds*	1945
1939	Carl K. Hersey‡	1969
	Mrs. Abram J. Katz	1946
	Rev. James E. Kearney	*d.* 1976 *(H)*
1941	Mrs. John Christie*	1943
1943	Spencer G. Easton	1944
	L. Dudley Field	*d.* 1981 *(H)*
	Robert Tait	1946
1944	Harwood Dryer	1948
1946	Edward S. Farrow	1948
	James W. Gray	1964
	Joseph C. Wilson	*d.* 1971
1948	Mr. Charles McCartney*	1950
	Jean C. McCurdy	*d.* 1973 *(H)*
1950	E. Willard Dennis	1951
	Howard Schumacher	1956
1951	Cornelis deKiewiet‡	1961
1952	Mrs. Herman Cohn	1961
	Mrs. Richard Delafield	1954
	Mrs. Robert Heilbrunn‡	1954
	Hilda J. May	*d.* 1984 *(H)*
	William E. Sloan	1962
1953	Brenda Rowntree	1972
1955	Mrs. Herman Bakker	1957
	Peter Barry	1961
	Albert K. Chapman	*d.* 1984 *(H)*
	Maurice R. Forman	— *(H)*
	Robert Ginna	1965
	Marion J. Hawks	— *(H)*
	Margaret B. Hayes	1968
	Charles P. Lambiase	1965
	Beatrice Padelford	1963
	Howard C. Seymour	1961
	Clifford VanDerbogart	1963
	Harry H. Wisner	1963
1956	Mrs. Howard Schumacher‡	1958
1957	J. Donald Fewster	1962
	Charles L. Rumrill	1972

1958	Francis D'Amanda	1968
	Arthur M. Hughes	1964
	Ramsay C. Lawless	— *(H)*
	Mrs. Roy Marks	1959
	R. Dewitt Pike	1963
	Barbara W. Reichart	1967
1959	George M. Angle	— *(H)*
	Georgianna Farr Sibley	*d.* 1979 *(H)*
	Arthur J. Stern Jr.	1968
	LaRoy B. Thompson	*d.* 1985
1961	Edward Harris	— *(H)*
	Donald McMaster	1967
	Dorothy B. Wadsworth	1972
	Franklin Weber	1972
1962	Mrs. Edward K. Brown	1968
	Edward P. Curtis Jr.	1964
	James C. Duffus	1969
	McCrea Hazlett	1971
	F. Bradley Lynch	1965
	Mrs. Ranlet Miner	1970
	Carl V. Nitze	1969
	Harris K. Prior	*d.* 1975 *(D)*
	Arnold W. Ravin	1963
	Richard M. Samuels	1967
	W. Allen Wallis‡	1970
	John L. Wehle	1968
1963	Joseph C. Briggs	1968
	Kenneth E. Clark‡	1981
	Vincent S. Jones	1969
	Walter Strakosh	— *(H)*
1964	Morton J. Baum	*d.* 1966
	Willard C. Case	1966
	Florence Macomber	1970
	Eleanor McQuilkin	1970
1965	C. Peter McColough	1969
	Michael L. Watson	1974
	Andrew D. Wolfe	1971
1966	Margaret S. Post	— *(H)*
1967	Edward L. Belcher	1983
	Catherine M. Broderick	1968
	George R. Darcy	1973
	Milton J. Lee	1970
	John C. Menihan	1973
	Lyndon H. Wells	— *(H)*
1968	Mercer Brugler	1970
	Randolph E. Carlson	1975
	Robert V. Gianniny	—
	Elmer Louis	1975
	Roderick M. MacDougall	1973
	Mrs. Peter M. Tolliver	1978
	Nancy R. Turner‡	1970, 1976–1980
1969	Angelo J. Chiarella	1975
	Felix G. Evangelist	1969
	Henry W. Williams Jr.	1973
1970	Earl W. Kage	— *(H)*
	Willard H. Duetting	1972
	Donald A. Gaudion‡	1976
	Rosalind Goldman	1976
	Stephen R. Hardis	1974
	Marjorie M. Ingersoll‡	1972
	Carl F. W. Kaelber Jr.	1980
	Robert W. Miller	1974
	Robert L. Sproull‡	1984
	William B. Webber	— *(H)*
	William C. Young	1970
1971	Wyoma Best	1974
	Rev. Marvin Chandler	1974
	Howard S. Merritt‡	1974
	Arthur L. Stern III	1974
1972	R. Thomas Dalbey	1975
	Janet Forbes‡	1974
	William F. Glavin	1974
	O. Cedric Rowntree	— *(H)*
	Jaquelyne M. Schuman	1981
	Burt A. Towne	1983
1973	Lester B. Frankenstein	1978
	Marilyn W. Kayser	—
	John T. Myers III	1978
	Robert B. Wolf	1976
1974	Peter O. Brown	—
	Kendall M. Cole	1976
	Eugene C. Dorsey	—
	Robert F. Gedger	1976
	Leo Kaplan	1976
	Archibald M. Miller‡	1980, 1984–1986
	Elizabeth L. Rennert	—
	Marie Curran Wilson	— *(H)*
1975	Kenneth W. Abbott	1976
	Dr. James Aquavella	— *(H)*
	Alan L. Cameros	—
	Udai Hoffberg	1983
	John A. Mahey	1979 *(D)*
	Arthur Richardson	1982
1976	Esther Germanow	1986
	John A. Leermakers	1982
	Charles Rand Penney	— *(H)*
	Floyd A. Tekampe	—
1977	W. Rufus Jones	1979
	Herbert W. Vanden Brul	—
1978	Elizabeth B. Brayer	—
	William B. Burks	1987
	Dorothy G. Centner‡	1980
	Douglass C. Harvey	1983
	David T. Kearns	1985
1979	Robert D. Firth	1981
	Richard D. O'Brien‡	1983
	Alan J. Underberg	—
	William T. Ward	1981
	Elaine P. Wilson	—
1980	G. C. Beldon Jr.	1986

	Mildred Boylan‡	1982
	Terry W. Dillman	1984
	Diran K. Dohanian‡	1983
	Sr. Magdalen LaRow	1986
	Albert Paley	1986
	A. Bret Waller	1985 (*D*)
1981	J. Paul Hunter‡	1986
	Neil J. Norry	1986
	Ernest I. Reveal Jr.‡	—
1982	Bruce R. Connolly	—
	Heidi F. Payment	—
	David M. Strasenburgh	—
1983	Jacqueline K. Adams	—
	Emille G. Allen	—
	Colby H. Chandler	1985
	Jack C. Corey	1988
	VanBuren N. Hansford, Jr.	—
	Jay T. Holmes	—
	H. Scott Norris, Jr.	—
	Paul K. Richey	1986
	Margaret D. Stolze	—
	Donald D. Welt	1988
1984	Judith L. McKelvey‡	1986, 1987–
	G. Dennis O'Brien‡	—
	Brian J. Thompson‡	—
1985	Donald T. Berens	1987
	R. Carlos Carballada	1987
	Edwin I. Colodny‡	1988
	Evelyn Damon	—
	Isabel C. Herdle	— (*H*)
	Grant Holcomb III	— (*D*)
	William L. Sutton	1988
1986	Wendell Castle	—
	Carl Chiarenza	1987
	Ann Clark Fehn‡	1987
	Richard W. Greene‡	—
	Elizabeth K. Harvey‡	1988
	Steven G. Herbert	—
	Samuel T. Hubbard Jr.	1987
	Robert D. Hursh	—
	Jack Kampmeier‡	—
	James H. Lockhart Jr.	— (*H*)
	Susan M. McLaughlin	—
1987	Richard F. Brush	—
	William Buckett	—
	Michael Ann Holly‡	—
	Donald D. Lennox	—
	Patrick D. Martin	—
	Richard Niemi‡	1988
1988	Virginia A. Dwyer‡	—
	Patricia Legge‡	—
	Joan Morgan	—
	Cecil D. Quillen Jr.	—
	Deborah K. Smith	—
	James T. Sorenson	—

**Rochester Art Club representative.*
†Representative from the Rochester Athenaeum and Mechanics Institute.

‡Ex-officio.
D: Memorial Art Gallery director.
H: Honorary board member for part of the term listed.

Sources and Notes

Prologue: A Gift for the City of Rochester

The correspondence of Rush Rhees pertaining to Memorial Art Gallery matters, cited here and in following chapters, may be found in the Rush Rhees Library of the University of Rochester. The quotations from Rochester newspapers, whose contemporary descriptions of the early years of the Gallery are quoted here and in following chapters, may be found in the archives and scrapbooks of the Gallery's Charlotte Whitney Allen Library. The praise of the Gallery's aims is from Christian Brinton's article in *The International Studio*, which may be found in the Allen Library.

The Board: The Gallery's board was called "The Board of Managers" when it first convened on 1 November 1912. By October of the following year it had become "The Board of Directors...to conform with the terms of Mrs. Watson's gift," that is, the contract with the University. The confusion in terminology between the "director" of the Gallery (George Herdle) and all the other "directors" led to the return to "Board of Managers" in 1931—the term used here and throughout for the sake of clarity.

Memory: For the dedication, only a plaster cast was on display.

Invitations: Emily Sibley Watson paid Mary Stone Bush $22.44 to address 748 invitations. Earlier, George Herdle had asked Rush Rhees to order between 1,500 and 1,700 invitations, probably for the public opening.

Art director: The use of the term *art* to modify *director* was most likely an attempt to distinguish Herdle from the twenty-two others on the Board of Directors. Rhees's 1913 correspondence refers to Herdle as "Acting Director for the time being." Later, in 1914, Rhees was referring to him as "our Art Director."

Chapter One: The Unlikely Director

Henry O'Reilly's remarks from *Sketches of Rochester* (1838) are quoted by Clifford M. Ulp in "Art and Artists in Rochester," *The Rochester Historical Society Publication Fund Series,* vol. 14, 1936, pp. 29–53. Also consulted for this chapter were Blake McKelvey's *Rochester History* pamphlets: "The First Century of Art in Rochester—to 1925," vol. 17, no. 2 (April 1955); "The Historic Origins of Rochester's Museums," vol. 18, no. 4 (October 1956); "The Visual Arts in Metropolitan Rochester," vol. 32, no. 1 (January 1970).

The remarks on Grove Gilbert are from the *Catalogue of the Sixth Annual Exhibition of the Rochester Art Club* (1885), which were reproduced in the Ulp study cited above.

Contemporary descriptions of the Powers Building are from *Notes on the Powers Building and Art Gallery of Rochester, N.Y.* (1884), and from James Delafield's introduction to *A Descriptive Catalogue of the Powers Art Gallery, Rochester, N.Y.* (1897).

Also cited in this chapter are the Gallery's exhibition catalog *A Rochester Retrospective (1880–1950)* and *The Architect's Eye: American Architectural Drawings from 1799–1978.*

Claude Bragdon's estimation of Harvey Ellis is quoted in *The Architect's Eye.*

The Life of Emily Sibley Watson's musical protégé is described in Grace N. Kraut's *An Unfinished Symphony: The Story of David Hochstein* (Rochester, 1980).

The quotations from Dr. James Sibley Watson Jr., found here and in following chapters, are from an interview I conducted with him in 1980.

Sibley Hall: It stood on Prince Street where the Red Cross Headquarters is now located.

Charles A. Green: He took umbrage when Rhees approached him for a membership contribution, stating that his $250 would "go to George Herdle with whom I am intimate." Green added: "You have in Mr. Herdle as Acting Director a reliable and competent man. I know him well as an artist, executive, and as a Judge of art. He is thoroughly competent. I have been with him through the numerous art studios of New York City where I have observed that he was known and well received."

Bogart: Belmont DeForest Bogart was a cousin of Robert de Forest, the president of the Metropolitan Museum of Art who spoke at the dedication of the Memorial Art Gallery (see the prologue).

Harvey Ellis: His "progress from place to place," Claude Bragdon wrote, "could be traced by the altered character of the work produced by the architects who employed him." (*The Architect's Eye*). Ellis's innovative and visionary ovoid steel tent project for the 1893 World's Columbian Exposition could have held 120,000 people. It was encircled by an electric railroad, and was an early model for the use of cables in a large-scale public building. The design was subsequently "stolen" by LeRoy Buffington, one of Ellis's employers, who submitted it as his own proposal for the 1933 Century of Progress in Chicago.

Art Club: From 1914 to 1938 the Rochester Art Club would exhibit at the Memorial Art Gallery. It then moved to the new Rundel Memorial Building, which was constructed according to the specifications of Mortimer Rundel's bequest to house a library and an art gallery. Art Club shows returned to the Gallery in 1959.

Watson's sister: James Sibley Watson had two sisters, who in succession married Granger A. Hollister. The elder sister, Isabel Watson Hollister, had one of the earliest organs to be installed in a Rochester home. The younger sister, Elizabeth Watson Hollister, was a board member of and generous donor to the Gallery. She died in 1938.

Jesse Lindsay: Thomas Wilmer Dewing's *Portrait in a Brown Dress* was given by Mr. and Mrs. Alexander Millar Lindsay III in memory of Jesse Williams and Grace Curtice Lindsay and their daughter Caroline Lindsay White.

Chapter Two: Treasures from Denuded Walls

George Herdle's correspondence can be found in the Allen Library and in the Rush Rhees collection cited above.

George Eastman's correspondence can be found in the archives of the Eastman Kodak Company.

Gertrude Herdle Moore's recollections of Gallery history, used in this and following chapters, are from a series of interviews I conducted with her from 1980–1988.

The Gallery's collection of rugs was described by John Mahey and Charles Szabo in an article in the *Rochester Times-Union,* 13 July 1978, headined "Museum's Oriental Rugs Have Fiscal/ Historical Value."

"We do not contemplate…": Rhees made the remark in a letter to Margaret Talbot Jackson when she applied for the position of assistant to the director, which Dorothy Carson and later Gertrude Herdle would fill.

Macbeth: The William Macbeth Gallery first exhibited these artists under the catch phrase of "The Eight" in 1908. Macbeth sold George Eastman five of the American and Barbizon Paintings that eventually came to the Gallery.

Pratt: F. B. Pratt of Brooklyn was the brother-in-law of Frank Babbott. The Pratt Institute, where many Rochester artists trained, was begun by his family.

Pioneer woman director: Cornelia Bentley Sage (later Quinton), of the Albright Gallery in Buffalo, and Juliana Force, of the Whitney, were the only women directors of art museums in this period. Sage struck terror into many hearts. George Herdle removed her letters from his file, believing that the unwary would not understand. George Bellows turned ashen when he saw her across a crowded room: "Spare me from that woman. She made me sell my painting [his masterpiece, *Elinor, Jean and Anna*] at half price!"

Morning on the River: This painting by Jonas Lie has held up to the scrutiny of the modern eye. Alone of the works in the original collection, it hangs once more in the 1988 Gallery, and a reproduction is used for school tours. Lie has enjoyed a revival in recent years.

Managing Director: George Eastman employed managing directors through his far-flung photographic materials empire, from Kodak Ltd. in Great Britain to Kodak Australasia in Australia, and so it was natural—and a bit proprietary—that he would use the term in describing Herdle.

Two-color process: In the early Kodachrome process, negatives were taken through two filters, red and green, and transformed directly into positives. A mirror in the camera reversed one of the negatives so that the two color positives could be superimposed face-to-face as a completed picture. The picture had to be viewed by transmitted light as a lantern slide or in an ingeniously constructed illuminator—a shadow box with electric light inside—which made wall mounting and tabletop viewing possible. Later Claude Bragdon exhibited Lumière plates (an earlier process of color photography, marketed in 1907) of his "projected Ornament" in the Rochester Art Club show of 1916.

Any other medium: The disagreement among museum directors over the place of photography in the art museum was prophetic. Years later Gertrude Herdle Moore would accompany Leopold Mannes to an American Museum Directors Association meeting. Mannes—along with Leopold Godowsky, the inventor of Kodachrome film—was there as a guest, reluctantly demonstrating the new process, which he believed was not yet ready for formal presentation. His slides featured objects from the Gallery's collection. The museum directors, particularly Edward Forbes and Paul Sachs of the Fogg Museum, entered purist objections centered on this attempt to duplicate the opaque medium of paint with the transparency of light, an objection that led the Fogg and many other museums to continue to record their collections with black and white film. "*You* invited me to speak," Mannes complained, as the discussion grew heated.

Josephine Haskins Dickman: She was responsible for taking George Eastman to see the Frick collection in New York and the Widener collection in Philadelphia, both important private collections in their day. The painting that Dickman gave, Douglas Volk's *Self Portrait*, was included in the seventy-fifth anniversary exhibition in 1988.

Ellwanger: The Ellwanger collection, the finest in the city, was later sold in New York. Because there was little literature on carpets, the Ellwangers and other collectors relied heavily on Peter White, an expert who worked as a Rochester newspaper illustrator but also was consulted on the subject of carpets by museums across the country.

Architectural drawings: Among the works exhibited by the Rochester Architectural League were Foster and Gade's perspective drawings and watercolors of the Gallery, and sketches and perspectives for the new Church of Christ, Scientist by Gordon and Madden, Architects, and William G. Kaelber, Architect—the firm that would go on to design Cutler Union and the Gallery's 1968 wing. Arnold & Stern, Claude Bragdon, Walter Cassebeer, and Alling De Forest, the last a landscape architect, were also represented in the 1915 show.

"Modern German Posters": The events of World War II have tended to obscure the degree of anti-German feeling aroused during the First World War by depictions of the fiercely mustachioed Kaiser as an even more diabolical figure than Hitler would later become. In 1914 Rochester's largest ethnic group was of German origin. Much of American culture—art, music, architecture, philosophy, theology, medicine, and folklore—sprang from German sources, but overnight it was deemed prudent to ignore these German contributions.

Chapter Three: Making 'People' Critics

I relied, in this chapter as well as throughout this book, on the Gallery's own publications: *The Bulletin, Gallery Notes,* and *Porticus.* Bound volumes of these can be found in the Allen Library.

Thurston V. Darling's review of the Beardsley drawings appeared in the *Rochester Times-Union* in December 1924.

Seminary: The Rochester Theological Seminary was incorporated into Colgate-Rochester Divinity School in the 1920s.

Fairchild: The Lillian Fairchild Memorial Award, administered by the University of Rochester, is awarded annually for a meritorious work of art. The first winner was the painter Carl Peters in 1924. Peters also won first prize from the Rochester Art Club in both 1927 and 1928 and the Hallgarten Prize from the National Academy of Design in 1928, and he was awarded several Public Works of Art Project commissions for murals in the Rochester area from 1940 to 1943.

Chapter Four: The Jewel Box Expands

The correspondence of Lawrence Grant White is from the McKim, Mead & White collection at the New York Historical Society. For the material on Samuel Yellin, I consulted Larry Furnival's article, "Gates and Grills, Locks and Keys: The Art of Samuel Yellin," *Yale Alumni Magazine and Journal* (October 1979), pp. 32–37.

McKim, Mead & White: In addition to the Morgan Library, the Gallery also has architectural roots in three other McKim, Mead & White buildings: the Walker Art Museum of Bowdoin College in Brunswick, Maine (1895); the Wittemore Memorial Library in Naugatuck, Connecticut (1894); and the Orange Free Library in New Jersey (begun in 1900). The Palladian motif, the emphasis on proportions, the triple bays, and the flat pilasters of the facades of the above buildings (including the Gallery's) ultimately derive from such sources as Italian Renaissance garden casinos, the garden loggia at the Villa Giulia, and the entrance at the Villa Medici in Rome. The Tuscan order for pilasters and entrance columns—the "fluteless" Doric of later Roman architecture—became popular again in the late Victorian and Edwardian era for its less rigid proportions, which make it an easy participant when columns are only incidental or background components. One day too, the smoothed and rounded Tuscan columns would complement the poured concrete columns of the Gallery's 1987 entrance.

rushed to finish: The colorful newspaper publicity was prepared by A. J. Warner II, architect turned critic and a neighbor of Emily Sibley Watson. Rush Rhees was less than overjoyed with the results. A typescript in the Rhees files calls into question the story of Rossack's carving of the panels in situ. Whether the fresco was actually the first in this country seems suspect as well.

Foster and Gade: Sibley Watson told this writer in 1980 that, in the firm, the business head was on John Gade's shoulders.

Heins and Lafarge: This firm also designed St. Paul's Episcopal Church on East Avenue in 1899, and the second stage of the

Cathedral of St. John the Divine in New York City.

"match the original": The architect did not consider the arcades of the addition to be temporary: "The drawing showing the next stage of development shows clearly the point brought out by Mr. White in regard to the repetition of the arcades...being relieved by the rectangular panels designed for the present addition," wrote White (speaking, as usual, of himself in the third person) to James Sibley Watson. Instead, the blank arcades of the second section were to function as foil to the decorated arcades of the first and third sections.

Zenitherm: The acoustics remained poor and the Zenitherm has the unhappy characteristic of soaking up moisture. A system of moisture control, including liners behind the tapestries, was introduced in 1968, but the problem continued. Control of ultraviolet light, which over the years has faded the tapestries and damaged other works of art in the Fountain Court, was not addressed (anywhere) in 1926, either.

Circulation corridors: White did not give up gracefully. "We regret extremely that you have been annoyed by the delay," he wrote Watson, "and assure you we have been making every effort to complete these drawings and specifications. The primary cause of the delay was the decision to omit the corridors which required a great deal of rubbing out and changes in the mechanical lines. There are more drawings connected with this operation than you may believe...."

Philip Merz: He had come to Rochester with McKim, Mead & White to work on the detailing of the Eastman Theatre and School of Music in the early 1920s. He stayed on in the employ of Gordon and Kaelber, University architects. So knowledgeable was he about historical styles that it was said he could be taken blindfolded through Florence and still be able to identify all the buildings and name their architects.

Cutler Union: As with the 1926 Gallery addition, the George Eastman House, and the Eastman Theatre, the general contractor for Cutler Union was A. W. Hopeman, while interior appointments and furnishings were designed by the Boston architect Francis Bacon and lighting consultant J. G. Caldwell of New York.

Samuel Yellin: Bruce Gelser, contractor, who worked with the Hopeman Company while Cutler Union was under construction, positively attributes the gates and ironwork to Yellin.

Chapter Five: Collecting with a Purpose

Details of R. T. Miller's life and donations to Oberlin's museum can be found in Laurine M. Bongiorno's article, "Benefactors of the Allen Memorial Art Musem," *Allen Memorial Art Museum Bulletin"* (1976).

number 13.1: Acquisition numbers indicate first the year and then the sequence within that year that a given object entered the collection. Hence, the Fletcher lace was the first object acquired in 1913.

motion pictures: The January 1929 issue of *Movie Makers* remarked that Sibley Watson's "new Cinema technique...does not attempt to tell a story in detail, rather to invoke in its audiences the aesthetic impressions and moods which the tale creates in its readers. This revolutionary approach to the cinema opens a fascinating field for further pioneering...a forecast of amazing possibilities."

Mrs. Charles H. Babcock: Her husband was the owner of the H. H. Babcock Coal Company and the president of Lincoln National Bank. He died in 1919.

The Landmark Society: Miller required the Landmark Society to raise $5,000 to add to his $10,000. The Society's contribution amply covered the cost of the twenty-three pieces of furniture acquired for the Campbell-Whittlesey House.

rejected some gems: Babbott urged Eastman to buy the Homer, to no avail. The dealer Reńe Gimpel recorded in his diary that he had sold a Vermeer to Eastman. The Turner was exhibited at the Gallery in 1915. Gertrude Herdle often encouraged Eastman to buy a work by Goya for the Gallery.

Rembrandt: Earlier, without knowing what Eastman had paid for *A Young Man*, Bode valued it at £35,000, or $175,000 on the 1911 market. Although the painting's attribution has occasionally been questioned in the intervening years, there was no doubt in Bode's mind that the artist was Rembrandt.

Chapter Six: Town and Gown

four members first named: Emily Sibley Watson, Rush Rhees, George Herdle, Frank von der Lancken.

four of the sixty-two: Ellen Dryden died in 1950, her husband in 1959, at which time the four paintings were returned by bequest to the George Eastman House of Photography rather than to the University.

in any year: Except "for good cause," as so voted by two-thirds of the board and the trustees.

Rechartered independently: The first recommendation that the Gallery be so rechartered came from a group organized in the late 1950s and early 1960s by Charles Rumrill. Twenty years later, on 5 October 1979, a petition stated that "since the presidency of Alan Valentine, the University has been treating the Art Gallery like a poor relation," the Gallery needed both "more generous financial support" and independence. The petition was circulated by Sibley and Nancy Watson.

objects meaningful to art history: Over the years *Head of an Angel or Saint* has been variously attributed. Is it Byzantine, style of Ravenna, from the sixth century? Or is it from *The Last Judgment*, Cathedral of Torcello, twelfth century? Or a nineteenth century copy or restoration of a Torcello mosaic?

The carved wood with gesso and overpainting *Bodhisattva Kannon* from the late Heian Period was purchased jointly by Sibley Watson and the Gould Fund. The *Genzu Mandaras: Kongō-kai and Taizō-kai*, ink and colors on paper mounted on silk hangings, were purchased through the Gould Fund.

"Zoute": Leon Salter (1903–1976) was born in North Rose, New York, educated at Dartmouth College, and self-taught as a painter and printmaker. He had a long association with Grandma Moses and owned an extensive collection of pre-Columbian art and modern sculpture and prints. The controversial *Fish* was an Art Patrons' Purchase Award from the Rochester–Finger Lakes Exhibition of 1944.

Chapter Seven: Changing Times and Exhibitions

Eskimo sculpture: The Canadian government tried hard, by controlling the market, to prevent the commercialization of Eskimo art. Canadian museums had first choice, next Canadian dealers, then American museums and dealers. Fortunately, the Gallery bought some of the earlier pieces.

Albright-Knox: While working out this exhibition, the Buffalo staff was handicapped by not knowing which paintings belonged to Seymour Knox, and might be suddenly removed to one of his homes, and which belonged to the Albright-Knox Gallery.

George Herdle's easel: Years later, the easel was inadvertently given to the Strong Museum. When its history was discovered, it was hastily retrieved.

Chapter Eight: "Wheeling" and Dealing

Denys Sutton wrote of the Riemenschneider-Veit Stoss attribution controversy in *Treasures from Rochester*, the Gallery catalog of 1977.

Gertrude Herdle Moore's letter to Eleanor H. Lovett may be found in the Allen Library.

G. Kenneth Sams wrote of "The Herzfeld Pyxis: North Syrian Sculpture," in *Porticus*, vol. 3, 1980, p. 1.

The school of Veit Stoss: Attribution of this German sculpture of the Late Gothic style changes as various visiting scholars pass through. Wilhelm Bode attributed it to Riemenschneider. Julius Held and Justus Bier have suggested that it is influenced by Veit Stoss, although not from his workshop. But Phillippe de Montebello, director of the Metropolitan Museum, on a recent visit to the Gallery said, "That *reeks* of Riemenschneider."

Antedates blown glass: The core of Phoenician glass was made of claylike "sand" on a metal rod, dipped in molten glass. The later Roman glass was blown into a mold. Roman glass is so fragile (the beautiful colors signify chemical decay), pieces cannot even be dusted for fear of destroying them.

The art committee: A less felicitous rejection by The Committee occurred in the 1930s when a Picasso study for *Demoiselles d'Avignon* was turned down.

Sternboard: It was first used on a frigate owned by the Derby family, whose coat of arms appears on the shield. The sternboard then graced the good ship *Angela*, which burned in 1871. The Carruth memorial objects were purchased through the Penrose Gallery in New York.

Brummer: His vaunted ability to tell "real" from "fake" was, of course, limited by the technology available to him during his career. Two works that the Gallery obtained through Brummer, both medieval frescoes, have recently been found to contain modern pigments. Based on the chemical analysis of paint samples, the Apse Chapel fresco of *Seraph, Prophets, and Apostles* (purchased in 1939) is now generally thought to be either a twentieth century reconstruction or overrestoration. Nonetheless, its overarching fresco fragment is still considered to be from the twelfth century. The Gallery now takes the position that no part of the fresco can be positively determined as originating in medieval times. A second fresco, *Madonna and Child*, purchased at the Brummer auction of 1949, has also been scrutinized and its authenticity has been questioned.

Chapter Nine: A Company of Self-found Friends

The November-December 1928 issue of *The Bulletin* details the first attempt to establish the Women's Council.

Material in this chapter is based in part on an unpublished history of the Women's Council written in 1972 by Jean Bub and on notes made available to me by Emille Allen.

Gallery enthusiasts: Despite the desire that Gallery membership and Women's Council membership represent all the area's economic and ethnic groups, both organizations have been largely composed of people who have the time to devote to aesthetic and volunteer pursuits.

Museum of Arts and Sciences: Now the Rochester Museum and Science Center.

Medieval Faire: This was not a fund raiser for the Women's Council, because it was cosponsored by the Junior League. Gallery policy does not permit the raising of monies for outside groups on Gallery premises.

Chapter Ten: MAG Takes Wing

Many details of this architectural history are from interviews I conducted with Carl F. W. Kaelber Jr. in 1977 and 1982. For this chapter I also consulted "Memorial Art Gallery, University of Rochester: 'An Instrument of Art Education,'" *Museums as Educational Institutions*, and other information supplied to me by Langdon Clay.

Previously given: For the 1968 wing the University of Rochester contributed $280,000. Also used was $100,000 from the Joseph Wilson Fund.

Bursting with people: Later the Main Concourse and Grand Gallery were used for temporary exhibitions, an information desk, and an expanding Gallery Store.

Two temporary exhibition galleries: Temporary galleries A and B were later used for the American Folk Art collection and print storage.

Chapter Eleven: The Gentle Art Scholar

I interviewed Harris Prior many times before his death in 1975.

Milton Brown tells *The Story of the Armory Show* (New York: Joseph H. Hirschorn Foundation, 1963).

See again Sutton's *Treasures from Rochester*.

Bernard K. Bothmer quotes Vandier and details the saga of "The Karnak Statue of Ny-user-ra," in *Mitteilungen des Deutschen Archäologischen Instituts Abteilung Kairo* (1974).

Neuberger: From a description in the *New York Times*. The newspaper went on to describe him as "a lion in winter on Wall St."

Vertebrae: Preceding the gift of that Moore work, a small, twenty-inch bronze sculpture by Moore, *Knife Edge* (1962), was purchased from the Gould Fund in 1963.

Chapter Twelve: Images and Enterprises:

Mark Donovan told *Gallery Notes* about the profession of exhibition design in the February issue of 1982.

Long Range Planning Committee: Members were: Chairman Ramsay Lawless, George Angle, Peter O. Brown, Marilyn Kayser, Florence Macomber, William Maxion, Margaret Post, O. Cedric Rowntree, Jacqueline Schuman, Walter Strakosh, and William B. Webber.

Winslow Homer: Rochester almost had another of his paintings. In 1906 George Eastman (who in certain aspects resembled Homer—both were ramrod straight, slim, small, quiet, and hard-nosed) took *Gulf Stream* on approval from William Macbeth. The painting's subject is a young black man awaiting certain death in shark-filled waters while lashed to the deck of his rudderless boat. Macbeth had Homer send this melodramatic work from his Maine studio to New York City so that Eastman and his friend Frank Babbott could see it. *Gulf Stream* had longed failed to find a customer because of its grim subject. Homer told Macbeth to fudge the issue and tell prospective buyers that "the unfortunate Negro who now is so dazed and parboiled will be rescued and returned to his friends and home, and ever after live happily." But Eastman, who paid for the round-trip shipment of the work just to have a look, maintained his sales resistance. He refused that painting, along with another, *Kissing the Moon*. *Gulf Stream* eventually found its way into the American wing of the Metropolitan Museum of Art.

Chapter Thirteen: MAGnificent!

In *Gallery Notes* of January 1986, Grant Holcomb writes about the reference by Kahn of wanting "to do Rothko over from nature." This relates to Paul Cézanne's desire "to do Poussin over after nature."

Bernard Barryte discusses Wheatley's *Death of Richard II* in *Gallery Notes* of July-August 1987.

Quotations from Wendell Castle are from the catalogue essay for "Masterpieces of Time" of 1985, from an article in *Gallery Notes* of July-August 1986, and from an interview I conducted with him in March 1988.

The material on Albert Paley is from a *Gallery Notes* article in the March-April issue of 1988.

The quotations from Grant Holcomb are from *Gallery Notes*, July-August 1987.

Ammi Phillips: In addition to establishing new highs for works by Phillips, the New York sales also made certain that folk art, as Patricia Junker says, "will never again be relegated to a minor-arts position but recognized for its major contribution to the history of American art."

Clay: Under his administration, the docent force numbered almost 100. Extension and loan programs, including portable exhibits called "Art-Go-Round," reached some 40,000 elementary school children each year. Special programs funded through the area's boards of education included teacher in-service training courses focusing on the Gallery's collection.

Convergence: Funding for the project came from the Harris Corporation, RF Communications Division, and from Vanden Brul family and friends. Paley donated his time and effort.

Gallery Staff 1987-1988

Administration

Grant Holcomb III, Director
Mark Donovan, Associate Director for Administration & Art Services
Kim Hallatt, Manager, Financial & Support Services
Marcia Vogel, Assistant to the Financial Manager
Paula Zahniser, Events Coordinator
Mary Ann Monley, Volunteer Coordinator
Donna DeFord, Facilities Staffing Coordinator
Patricia Trivino, Secretary to the Director
Rhonda Olson, Assistant for Computing and Support Services
Karin Harriman, Secretary
Basil Megna, Receptionist

Gallery Store

Nancy Kelly, Manager
Mary Dolan, Assistant Manager
Jeanne Maloney, Store Assistant
Sandra Neal, Store Assistant

Exhibitions and Facilities

Reggie Dyche, Manager of Facilities
Jim Smith, Assistant Manager of Facilities
Stanley Kawczynski, General Services
Glenn Knudsen, General Services
David Kwasigroh, General Services
Nicolas Ricketts, General Services
Rafaela Torres, General Services
Judi Vannais, General Services
Joel Roemer, Building Mechanic

Curatorial Services

Patricia Junker, Chief Curator
Bernard Barryte, Curator of European Art
Marie Via, Assistant for Curatorial Affairs
Isabel Herdle, Curator Emeritus
Susan Schilling, Research Curator Emeritus
Sandra Markham, Registrar

Development

Margaret Hubbard, Director of Development
Christine Garland, Assistant Director of Development
Sue Cook, Administrative Assistant—Corporate Membership Campaign
Patricia Eldridge, Membership Manager
Charlene Hedger, Membership Secretary
Deborah Rothman, Public Relations Manager
Shirley Wersinger, Public Relations Associate
Cynthia E. Mindell, Development Assistant

EDUCATION

Susan Dodge Peters, Assistant Director for Education
Marjorie Searl, Curator of Education
Grace Lyu, Artspeak Coordinator
Pat Marcus, Secretary
Stephanie Frontz, Librarian
Leni Rayburn, Library Assistant

CREATIVE WORKSHOP

Lawrence Merrill, Creative Workshop Administrator
Emily Cassebeer, Creative Workshop Registrar
Joanne Barr
Eric Bellmann
Peter Berg
Jappie King Black
Susan Blumendale
Maureen Brilla
Susan Carter
Nancy Chalker-Tennant
Sherry Clark
Yvonne Cupolo
Arturo DeVitalis
Marge DiSalvio
Elizabeth Durand
Lynne Feldman
Lisa Forster
Sari Gaby
Kathryn Gaspar
Jacquie Germanow
Alice Gold
Alec Hazlett
Wendy Gwirtzman
Hollie Heller
John Kastner
Jeanne Lindsay
Fred Lipp
Sharon Locke
Vincent Massaro
Caroline Maw
Martha Moore
Deborah Pratt
Ruth Rosen
G. A. Sheller
Rose Sherwood
Paul Taylor
Bing Thayer
Mollie Wolf

BOARD OF MANAGERS 1987-88

Mr. Herbert W. Vanden Brul, President
Mr. Floyd A. Tekampe, Chairman
Mr. Robert V. Gianniny, First Vice President
Mrs. Kenneth A. Payment, Secretary
Mr. Richard W. Greene*, Treasurer
Dr. Grant Holcomb III, Director

Mrs. James T. Adams
Mrs. Frank W. Allen
Mrs. G. Sheldon Brayer
Mr. Peter O. Brown
Mr. Richard F. Brush
Mr. William Buckett
Mr. Alan L. Cameros
Mr. Wendell Castle
Mr. Edwin I. Colodny
Mr. Bruce R. Connolly*
Mr. Jack C. Corey, Jr.
Mrs. E. Kent Damon
Mr. Eugene C. Dorsey
Mr. VanBuren N. Hansford, Jr.
Mrs. Douglass C. Harvey*
Dr. Steven G. Herbert
Dr. Michael Ann Holly*
Mr. Jay T. Holmes
Mr. Robert D. Hursh
Dr. Jack Kampmeier
Mrs. Julius G. Kayser
Mr. Donald D. Lennox
Mr. Patrick D. Martin
Mrs. David E. McKelvey
Ms. Susan M. McLaughlin
Mrs. William L. Morgan
Mr. H. Scott Norris, Jr.
Dr. Dennis O'Brien*
Mrs. Eric W. Rennert
Mrs. William J. Stolze
Mr. David M. Strasenburgh
Dr. William L. Sutton
Dr. Brian J. Thompson*
Mr. Alan J. Underberg
Mr. William B. Webber
Mr. Donald D. Welt
Mrs. Richard U. Wilson

HONORARY MEMBERS, 1987-88

Mr. George M. Angle
Dr. James V. Aquavella
Mr. Maurice R. Forman
Mr. Edward Harris
Mrs. Thomas H. Hawks
Miss Isabel C. Herdle
Mr. Earl W. Kage
Mrs. John L. Lawless
Dr. James H. Lockhart, Jr.
Mrs. Gertrude Herdle Moore
Mr. Charles Rand Penney
Mrs. Frederick W. Post
Mr. Ernest I. Reveal, Jr.
Mr. O. Cedric Rowntree
Mr. Walter C. Strakosh
Mr. Lyndon H. Wells, Jr.
Mrs. Joseph C. Wilson

*ex-officio

Index